# Strategies for Minimizing Risk Under the Foreign Corrupt Practices Act and Related Laws

## Elgar Compliance Guides

**Series Editor:** James Fanto, *Brooklyn Law School, USA*

Titles in the series include:

Determann's Field Guide to Data Privacy Law
International Corporate Compliance, Third Edition
*Lothar Determann*

Strategies for Minimizing Risk Under the Foreign Corrupt Practices Act and Related Laws
*Mike Koehler*

# Strategies for Minimizing Risk Under the Foreign Corrupt Practices Act and Related Laws

MIKE KOEHLER

*Founder and Editor of* FCPA Professor *and Law Professor, Southern Illinois University, School of Law, USA*

**Elgar Compliance Guides**

Edward Elgar PUBLISHING

Cheltenham, UK • Northampton, MA, USA

Published by
Edward Elgar Publishing Limited
The Lypiatts
15 Lansdown Road
Cheltenham
Glos GL50 2JA
UK

Edward Elgar Publishing, Inc.
William Pratt House
9 Dewey Court
Northampton
Massachusetts 01060
USA

A catalogue record for this book
is available from the British Library

Library of Congress Control Number: 2018945851

This book is available electronically in the **Elgar**online
Law subject collection
DOI 10.4337/9781788114936

Printed on 30% PCR Stock
ISBN 978 1 78811 492 9 (cased)
ISBN 978 1 78897 357 1 (paperback)
ISBN 978 1 78811 493 6 (eBook)
Printed and bound by Thomson-Shore, Inc.
Typeset by Servis Filmsetting Ltd, Stockport, Cheshire

In the minds of some, complying with the U.S. Foreign Corrupt Practices Act and related laws is easy: "you just don't bribe." The reality, as sophisticated professionals should know, is not so simple and this book is for professionals across various disciplines who can assist in risk management and want to learn strategies for minimizing risk under aggressively enforced bribery laws. This book elevates knowledge and skills by: (i) highlighting legal authority and other sources of information relevant to bribery laws; (ii) guiding readers through various components of compliance best practices from the fundamentals of conducting a risk assessment, to effectively communicating compliance expectations, to implementing and overseeing compliance strategies; and (iii) allowing readers to assess their acquired knowledge through various issue-spotting scenarios and skills exercises.

# Contents

# About the author

Professor Mike Koehler is a leading expert on the Foreign Corrupt Practices Act and related laws. For nearly a decade, Professor Koehler was an attorney in private practice and conducted investigations around the world, negotiated resolutions to enforcement actions with government enforcement agencies, and advised clients on risk assessment and compliance strategies. Professor Koehler's insights are further informed by having read and analyzed the FCPA's entire legislative history, every FCPA enforcement action, and every FCPA judicial decision.

Since 2009, Professor Koehler has run the award-winning FCPA Professor website (www.fcpaprofessor.com). Described as the "*Wall Street Journal* concerning all things FCPA-related," and "the most authoritative source for those seeking to understand and apply the FCPA," FCPA Professor has been named a Top Law Blog for in-house counsel by Corporate Counsel, a Top 25 Business Law Blog by LexisNexis, and a top 100 Legal Blog by the American Bar Association. FCPA Professor readers include a worldwide audience of attorneys, business and compliance professionals, government agencies, scholars and students, journalists, and other interested persons.

Professor Koehler is also the founder and manager of FCPA Professor LLC, an expert consulting company devoted to elevating the FCPA knowledge and practical skills of professionals through a range of services. For instance, the FCPA Institute is a unique two-day active learning experience ideal for a diverse group of professionals seeking to elevate their FCPA knowledge and practical skills. FCPA Professor also conducts uniquely tailored live FCPA training sessions for companies in a variety of industries.

Professor Koehler has testified before Congress on the FCPA and is also a frequent speaker before business and academic audiences. Leading law reviews and journals have published Professor Koehler's scholarship; his work has been cited in legal briefs, judicial decisions, policy papers, and Congressional testimony; and he is a frequent featured source on the FCPA and related topics in various national and international media. Professor Koehler is a tenured law professor at Southern Illinois University School of Law and was previously a law professor in the College of Business at Butler University.

# Introduction and overview

From the start, it is important to understand what this book *is* about and what this book is *not* about.

This book is *not* about the legitimacy or validity of many enforcement theories that impact compliance. For instance, you will learn that Congress intended the FCPA's "foreign official" element to mean bona fide, traditional foreign government officials such as presidents, prime ministers and other heads of state. However, many enforcement actions concern things of value provided or offered to materially different types of individuals such as employees of various business organizations (albeit with some state ownership or alleged control) as well as employees of certain foreign healthcare systems (such as physicians, laboratory personnel and even a mid-wife). These enforcement theories, like many others which impact compliance, have not been subjected to any meaningful judicial scrutiny because of the typical resolution vehicles used to resolve corporate enforcement actions. Moreover, the things of value often provided to alleged "foreign officials" bear little resemblance to classic notions of bribery such as suitcases full of cash, but rather consist of corporate hospitality, charitable donations or internships and jobs for family members. In other words, the underlying conduct may be legal and morally acceptable in most instances, yet, when directed to a certain type of individual, might be deemed bribery by government enforcement agencies.

Likewise, you will learn that Congress qualified the books and records and internal controls provisions, among other ways, through a reasonableness standard. However, many enforcement actions involve business organizations with pre-existing compliance policies and procedures and involve circumstances where it is difficult to reconcile existing legal authority, as well as even enforcement agency guidance, with the theories of enforcement advanced. Yet it is these enforcement theories which impact compliance in meaningful ways by causing risk-averse business organizations to calibrate compliance policies and procedures to existing enforcement theories.

In short, two distinct questions can be asked in connection with many instances of scrutiny and enforcement. The first question is whether Congress, in passing the FCPA, intended to capture the alleged conduct and whether a court would find the alleged conduct in violation of the FCPA? The second question is whether, given the government's prevailing enforcement theories, the alleged conduct can expose a company to scrutiny and enforcement. The first question is obviously important in a legal system based on the rule of law; however, the answer is often unclear given actual legal authority and because the typical resolution vehicles used to resolve corporate enforcement actions bypass judicial scrutiny. The second question is obviously important to compliance professionals tasked with minimizing risk based on prevailing enforcement theories and the answer is often yes. Please remember these two distinct questions when reading Chapters 2–5 in which several references are made to "legal authority" (statutory text, legislative history and judicial authority) vs. "non-legal authority" (enforcement agency guidance and resolved enforcement actions – what some have called "prosecutorial common law"[1]). Visually, think of this dynamic as follows:

**What Does the FCPA Mean?**

Legal authority of course has a firm foundation, but the problem is that, aside from the statute and legislative history, there are few judicial decisions construing the FCPA. When put in the rare position of deciding an FCPA issue, a judge remarked there are "surprisingly few decisions throughout the country on the FCPA".[2] Similarly, in its review of FCPA enforcement, the Organisation for Economic Co-operation and Development (OECD) observed: "although enforcement under the FCPA is strong and increasing, there is relatively little jurisprudence that has developed since the FCPA was enacted."[3] Even the Securities and Exchange Commission's (SEC's)

Director of Enforcement has stated that "FCPA law . . . is not well developed."[4]

Compared with legal authority, there are more non-legal sources of FCPA information. However, the problem with non-legal sources of information is that they rest on an unstable foundation and are subject to change. This shifting landscape has long been lamented and one of the best things ever written about the FCPA was penned in the early years of the statute when it was noted that:

> The government has the option of deciding whether or not to prosecute. For practitioners, however, the situation is intolerable. We must be able to advise our clients as to whether their conduct violates the law, not whether this year's crop of administrators is likely to enforce a particular alleged violation. That would produce, in effect, a government of men and women rather than a government of law.[5]

Yet even as the FCPA has matured, this dynamic remains. A dean of the FCPA bar observed:

> One reality is the enforcement agencies' [FCPA] views on issues and enforcement policies, positions on which they are rarely challenged in court. The other is what knowledgeable counsel believe the government could sustain in court, should their interpretations or positions be challenged. The two may not be the same. The operative rules of the game are the agencies' views unless a company is prepared to go to court or to mount a serious challenge within the agencies.

Regarding this dynamic, compliance professionals simply need to accept the old adage "it is what it is" and recognize that in certain enforcement actions the enforcement theory advanced represents little more than *ipse dixit* (Latin for "he himself said it" – an unsupported statement that rests solely on the authority of the individual who makes it). As highlighted in Chapter 5, this dynamic is particularly relevant to certain of the SEC's internal controls enforcement theories in which a business organization's alleged failure to do *x*, *y* or *z* is an internal controls violation merely because the SEC says it is. Compliance professionals need to be cognizant of this dynamic, yet this book accepts prevailing enforcement theories, related government guidance and policy positions and seeks to provide the necessary skills to minimize risk given the current enforcement landscape.[6] Nevertheless, this book will occasionally encourage you to think for yourself and ask certain critical questions relevant to the FCPA's modern era.

This book is also *not* about *eliminating* risk under the FCPA and related laws. FCPA liability is a form of legal liability similar to tort liability, contract liability, antitrust liability and environmental liability. Compliance professionals rarely encounter literature suggesting that business organizations can eliminate these forms of legal liability, but there are some who market FCPA compliance products and services as a way to *eliminate* risk. Such charlatans are selling "snake oil" for the simple reason that FCPA and related risk, while it can minimized through the strategies highlighted in this book, can't be *eliminated.* This is particularly true given the general U.S. legal principle of *respondeat superior* which generally holds that business organizations can face legal liability based on the conduct of any employee or agent (regardless of rank, title, or position) to the extent the employee or agent: (i) acted within the scope of employment/agency; and (ii) the conduct, at least in part, benefited the organization.

While rogue actors are often portrayed as a figment of the corporate apologist's imagination,[7] they do exist, as even the enforcement agencies acknowledge. For instance, the Department of Justice's (DOJ's) Assistant Attorney General for the Criminal Division stated:

> We recognize that any big company can't control all of its employees all of the time, we recognize that. If you are a company operating in certain geographies you are going to be paying possibly small, but you will be paying some kind of inappropriate payment, we recognize that. We recognize that companies have rogue employees who don't follow company policy so even when there is a strong company policy it may still be the case that somebody in the company does something that is off the reservation, that happens all the time . . . it's impossible for a big global company to make sure that all of its employees are following the law all of the time.[8]

Indeed, certain enforcement actions are based on the conduct of single actors who knowingly circumvent a company's existing internal controls.[9] In other words, a business organization can act consistently with all of the risk management strategies highlighted in this book, yet still face liability under the FCPA and related laws. As noted by a former DOJ FCPA enforcement attorney, this aspect of enforcement is controversial:

> I think that companies' main frustration is that even with an outstanding compliance program and 99% of the employees maintaining strict adherence to the laws, you can still have violations which expose the entire company to extraordinarily serious penalties. I think the government has, at times, lost track of the main motivations for this statute and has become focused on the amounts of penalties, the imposition of compliance monitors, and exercising government control over what are basically private businesses. The vast majority of companies are absolutely committed to following the spirit and the letter of the FCPA, but when a company gets into trouble, the whole enterprise can be put at risk because of the conduct of a few people, and that doesn't seem right.[10]

From a comparative standpoint, it is worth noting that U.S. *respondeat superior* principles are unique because in most other peer nations (i.e. other signatory countries to the OECD Convention on Combating Bribery of Foreign Public Officials in International Business Transactions),[11] criminal liability can only be imputed to a business organization (if at all) based on the conduct of so-called "controlling minds" such as board of director members or executive officers.[12]

Related to this issue, this book is *not* about whether the FCPA as written or whether the FCPA as enforced pursuant to government enforcement agency policy adequately recognizes a business organization's good faith compliance efforts. Although the FCPA does not have a compliance defense, it is important to recognize that the FCPA-like laws of several peer countries have a compliance defense or similar concepts embedded in law.[13]

Amending the FCPA to include a compliance defense (i.e. to legally recognize pro-active compliance policies and procedures and provide business organizations with the best return on its compliance investment) is not a new or novel idea. For instance, an FCPA reform bill that included a compliance defense previously passed the U.S. House of Representatives and the relevant House Report stated: "If a corporation has set up internal controls to avoid illicit payments or has otherwise acted to keep within the law, its due diligence can be used as a defense against both civil and criminal liability in cases where its employees have nonetheless engaged in bribery."[14] Amending the FCPA to include a compliance defense is not a novel idea either. The FCPA is part of the Securities Exchange Act and other Exchange Act provisions excuse legal liability based on good faith compliance efforts.

Last but certainly not least in terms of an FCPA compliance defense is that numerous former FCPA enforcement attorneys support a compliance defense. In the words of a former chief of the DOJ's FCPA Unit, an FCPA compliance defense is "manifestly reasonable" for the following reasons:

> Companies that seek only to be good corporate citizens would have an opportunity to demonstrate not only to DOJ, but also to a federal district court, that they had in fact done everything reasonably required, and that despite that fact an errant employee avoided company policy and violated the law. Affording this type of defense to corporate liability would recognize and reward strong compliance programs; provide a powerful incentive for companies to develop and enforce such programs; may encourage more companies to come forward with voluntary disclosures; and yet still enable prosecution of the culpable individuals. It is time to stop punishing our good corporate citizens and start going after the guilty – both corrupt corporate employees and corrupt foreign officials.[15]

It is true that government enforcement agencies have stated that preexisting compliance policies and procedures such as those highlighted in this book are relevant to how they exercise charging discretion as well as the ultimate fine and penalty amounts in an actual enforcement action. However, given the lack of transparency surrounding enforcement, it is nearly impossible to assess whether the enforcement agencies are acting consistent with their own enforcement policies and the salient point regarding the risk management strategies highlighted in this book is that, under current U.S. practices, they may merely lessen the *impact* of legal exposure, but not *reduce* legal exposure like in several peer countries that have a compliance defense or similar concepts embedded in their FCPA-like laws. Nevertheless, adhering to the risk management strategies highlighted in this book will allow a business organization to tell the best story possible to government enforcement agencies should scrutiny arise.

If this book is *not* about the legitimacy or validity of certain FCPA enforcement theories, *not* about *eliminating* risk under the FCPA and related laws, and *not* about the policy issue of whether the FCPA or enforcement agency practice adequately recognize compliance efforts, then what *is* this book about?

Simply stated, this book is about providing a diverse group of professionals who can assist in risk management (such as lawyers; finance, accounting and auditing professionals; business executives and board of director members; human resources professionals; and others) with the best available tools to minimize risk under the FCPA and related laws given the current enforcement landscape. Towards this goal, this book uses plain English to: (i) highlight legal authority and other sources of information relevant to bribery laws; (ii) guide you through various components of compliance best practices from the fundamentals of conducting a risk assessment, to effectively communicating compliance expectations, to implementing and overseeing compliance strategies; and (iii) allow you to assess your acquired knowledge through various issue-spotting scenarios and skills exercises.

Prior to providing a general overview of the eight chapters of this book, a brief explanation about how the book is organized. As demonstrated by the below visual, the primary goal of this book is to provide you with a pair of "FCPA goggles" and teach you to spot risk so that you can confidently implement and execute specific compliance strategies unique to your business organization.

The teaching goal of this book is advanced through various visual learning devices to best convey relevant information. For instance, Chapters 2–5 go in-depth into the FCPA's anti-bribery provisions and books and records and internal controls provisions and include several real-world issue-spotting scenarios that allow you to assess your acquired knowledge and skills by putting on your "FCPA goggles" to spot risk. To get the most out of this book, do not breeze through these issue-spotting scenarios but rather pause to access your acquired knowledge and skills before reviewing the model answers.

As you learn the specific elements of the anti-bribery and books and records and internal controls provisions, various risk management strategies specific to these elements are introduced through the below visual.

The umbrella visual is a useful reminder of one of the essential take-away points of this book. As discussed earlier, risk under the FCPA and related laws can be minimized, but it can't be entirely eliminated. Similarly, an umbrella is going to shield you from most rain drops and keep you relatively dry. However, using an umbrella is not a guarantee that no rain drop will hit you.

Regarding the risk management strategies highlighted in this book, it is important to recognize as alluded to above (i.e. the difference between "legal authority" vs. "non-legal sources of information") that few of the risk management strategies are technically legally required or found in the FCPA statute. Rather, business organizations have a legal obligation under the anti-bribery provisions not to offer or provide money or things of value, with a corrupt intent, to a foreign official, to assist in obtaining or retaining business. Under the books and records and internal controls provisions, certain business organizations (so-called issuers under the FCPA) have a legal obligation to: (i) "make and keep books, records, and accounts, which, in reasonable detail, accurately and fairly reflect the transactions and dispositions of the assets of the issuer;" and (ii) "devise and maintain a system of internal accounting controls sufficient to provide reasonable assurances that" certain financial objectives are met.

While some of the risk management strategies highlighted in this book may seem fairly obvious (things often do with the benefit of hindsight), sometimes it takes learning of a real company, involved in a real enforcement action, with a real failure to best drive home basic compliance points. Indeed, a skill this book aims to develop is teaching you to read actual enforcement actions and "flip" the allegations or findings in the enforcement action into risk management strategies. Accordingly, this book highlights various compliance failures from actual enforcement actions through the below visual.

In addition to various real-world issue-spotting scenarios, you will also have an opportunity to practice your acquired knowledge in a comprehensive skill exercise at the end of Chapter 6. This exercise, which is introduced with the below visual, requires you to conduct a risk assessment of a real company based on generic corporate information and once again to get the most out of this book do not breeze through the skills exercise, but rather pause to access your acquired knowledge and skills before reviewing the model answers.

One final point to keep in mind is that for the sake of brevity this book frequently refers to the U.S. FCPA. However, this book and the risk management strategies highlighted are relevant to more laws than just the FCPA. While lawyers seeking your business may try to convince you otherwise, the fact is that other FCPA-like laws such as the U.K.'s Bribery Act, Canada's Corruption of Foreign Public Officials Act, Brazil's Clean Companies Act and many others, have elements very similar to the FCPA and thus very similar risk management strategies. In other words, this book is not just for compliance professionals wanting to minimize risk under the FCPA but many other laws as well and it is intended for a global compliance audience.

### Chapter 1

This book begins by highlighting why a diverse group of professionals need skills to spot risk under the FCPA and related laws. The short answer is because risk is omnipresent for business organizations competing in the global marketplace. While all seem to acknowledge this, in the minds of some, compliance should be easy: "just don't bribe." However, this simplistic narrative is a fallacy because the overwhelming majority of business organizations subject to the FCPA and related laws compete in the global marketplace with a commitment to compliance, yet subject to unrealistic legal standards and/or difficult and complex business conditions that often serve as the root cause of scrutiny and enforcement. An examination of these root causes is not meant to excuse the conduct giving rise to an enforcement action, but rather to understand how and why the conduct occurred in the first place. Understanding the root causes of scrutiny and enforcement also serves an important compliance objective in that a key component of best practices is conducting a risk assessment (i.e. understanding unique points of contact with "foreign officials") and prioritizing compliance to specific risks.

Chapter 1 next highlights that a diverse group of professionals also need skills to spot risk because scrutiny and enforcement can result in wide-ranging, negative financial consequences for business organizations. Obviously one reason to comply with the FCPA and related laws is because non-compliance can expose an organization to an actual enforcement action brought by law enforcement. However, settlement amounts in an actual enforcement action are often only a relatively minor component of the overall financial consequences that can result from scrutiny and enforcement. Discussion of these many other "ripples" is intended to shift the compliance conversation away from a purely legal issue to its more proper designation as a general business issue that needs to be on the radar screen of many professionals who can assist in risk management and who should view the importance of compliance more holistically and not merely through the narrow lens of actual enforcement actions.

## Chapter 2

With a clear understanding of why skills to spot risk are important, Chapter 2 begins to construct your "FCPA goggles" by analyzing the core elements of the FCPA's anti-bribery provisions. To competently conduct the risk assessment skills exercise in Chapter 6, you must first be familiar with the myriad ways in which scrutiny and enforcement arise. This requires you to have a comprehensive understanding of legal authority and non-legal sources of information relevant to the core elements: anything of value, corrupt intent, foreign official, and obtain or retain business.

You will quickly learn that while a suitcase full of cash to a traditional foreign government official to obtain a foreign government contract most certainly meets these elements, few modern enforcement actions concern this type of conduct. Rather, and the reason why the "just don't bribe" narrative is often simplistic and naïve, the things of value often provided to alleged "foreign officials" consist of corporate hospitality, charitable donations and internships or jobs for family members. In other words, the underlying conduct is often legal and morally acceptable in most instances, yet when directed to a specific type of individual might be deemed bribery by government enforcement agencies.

Throughout Chapter 2 you will learn risk management strategies specific to certain core elements of the FCPA's anti-bribery provisions that present the greatest compliance challenges and you will also have a chance to assess your acquired knowledge through several real-world issue-spotting scenarios.

## Chapter 3

The FCPA and related laws contain third-party payment provisions which prohibit the above core conduct from being accomplished indirectly through third parties. The upside of utilizing third parties – in connection not just with sales activities but with other aspects of business as well – is that they are efficient, understand the local business environment and have relationships with key business actors. However, these attributes also represent a downside and third parties are often the single greatest risk to a compliance program. Accordingly, an important component of having "FCPA goggles" is understanding the FCPA's third-party payment provisions and Chapter 3 develops this knowledge by highlighting legal authority and non-legal sources of information relevant to these expansive provisions and how they capture so-called willful blindness or conscious disregard of third party conduct.

To minimize the risk of engaging and maintaining relationships with third parties, Chapter 3 also highlights various compliance best practices spanning all three phases of a third-party relationship: pre-engagement best practices; engagement best practices; and post-engagement best practices. In addition, various template compliance documents are provided and you will also have a chance to assess your acquired knowledge of the third-party payments provisions through a real-world issue spotting scenario.

## Chapter 4

Even if all of the substantive elements of the FCPA's anti-bribery provisions are met and there is jurisdiction over the actor, the final step in analyzing the anti-bribery provisions is determining whether the facilitating payment exception or the so-called local law or reasonable and bona fide expenditures affirmative defenses apply. Chapter 4 highlights legal authority and non-legal sources of information regarding these provisions, yet relevant to the two distinct questions highlighted above in connection with many instances of scrutiny and enforcement, you will learn that while the FCPA expressly exempts facilitating payments it is an open question whether this statutory exception has any real meaning or whether the enforcement agencies have, through their enforcement theories, essentially repealed this exception. Regardless, prevailing best practices seem to be prohibiting facilitating payments except in cases of health and safety, and consistent with this approach, training best practices will be highlighted.

Along with third parties, corporate hospitality and related expenditures also present challenges to a compliance program given that business organizations routinely promote their products and services and execute contracts. Because of this, an additional component of having "FCPA goggles" is understanding the contours of the reasonable and bona fide expenditures affirmative defense and you will learn of compliance practices to minimize risk in this area.

Relevant to the facilitating payment exception and reasonable and bona fide expenditures affirmative defense, you will once again have a chance to assess your acquired knowledge through real-world issue spotting scenarios.

## Chapter 5

The FCPA has always been a law much broader than its name suggests. The anti-bribery provisions that were the focus of Chapters 2–4 are just one prong of the FCPA. The other prong, applicable to "issuers" (FCPA-speak for publicly traded companies or those subject to SEC regulation), is the books and records and internal controls provisions. These provisions operate independently of the anti-bribery provisions and are among the most generic and flexible legal provisions one can possibly find. Because of this and how these provisions are currently enforced, the books and records and internal controls provisions are a potent supplement to the more glamorous anti-bribery provisions.

Chapter 5 highlights legal authority and non-legal sources of information relevant to the books and records and internal controls provisions and demonstrates through actual enforcement actions the wide range of circumstances in which the enforcement agencies use these flexible provisions to also address allegations of foreign bribery or similar conduct. Like in previous chapters, you will also have a chance to assess your acquired knowledge through a real-world issue-spotting scenario.

## Chapter 6

Having an element specific understanding of the FCPA's provisions and how they are enforced is a critical first step toward minimizing risk. However, you also need to be knowledgeable about the wide body of so-called compliance "best practices" and Chapter 6 begins by highlighting various potentially relevant sources. At first blush these various sources may seem a bit overwhelming, but Chapter 6 breaks these best practices into bite-size pieces that are easier for you to digest.

A common thread in all sources of best practices is conducting a risk assessment. After all, rarely does a compliance professional receive questions tied to specific legal elements such as "is this customer an instrumentality of a foreign government such that its employees may be deemed a 'foreign official' under the FCPA" or "does this planned corporate hospitality event represent a 'reasonable' and 'bona fide' expenditure 'directly related' to a business purpose." Rather, in the real world compliance professionals listen to stories or receive information and from these real-world stories and information are expected to spot risk.

Chapter 6 graduates you to the next level of compliance proficiency by highlighting the fundamentals of conducting a risk assessment. From there, and with your "FCPA goggles" on, you will complete a skills exercise by reviewing generic business information of a real company and categorizing the company's unique risk points. Perhaps the company's customer base presents risk; perhaps the company's unique product or service presents risk; or perhaps the company's go-to-market strategy presents risk? It will be up to you and your "FCPA goggles" to spot the risk and devise strategies for minimizing the risk.

## Chapter 7

There is more to FCPA and related compliance than just spotting risk in a business organization. Think of this in terms of a sports analogy where a coach devotes hours studying an opponent to learn of its deficiencies and vulnerabilities. This is a great start, but the success of a sports team will largely depend on the ability of the coaching staff to implement a game strategy and effectively communicate it to the players who will be facing the opponent. The success of a business organization in minimizing risk under the FCPA and related laws likewise largely depends on implementing a compliance strategy and effectively communicating it to employees and agents in the global marketplace.

Accordingly, Chapter 7 discusses how to implement written compliance policies and procedures throughout a business organization and effectively communicate the compliance strategy in a way that resonates with the intended audience. Next, training best practices will be highlighted (in terms of both who to include in training and how best to convey important concepts) as well as the importance of holistic compliance in which various corporate actors can play a meaningful role in minimizing risk.

## Chapter 8

Prior to Chapter 8 you will have: (i) learned why spotting risk under the FCPA and related laws is an important skill for a diverse group of professionals; (ii) constructed your own "FCPA goggles" through an element-by-element review of the FCPA's provisions; (iii) practiced wearing your "FCPA goggles" through issue-spotting scenarios; (iv) learned of various sources of compliance best practices and the common elements found in these sources; (v) conducted a risk assessment of a real company based on generic information; and (vi) learned of various best practices to implement a compliance program and effectively communicate compliance expectations within a business organization. These are all critical tasks to minimizing risk within a business organization.

However, a compliance professional's job is not yet finished as Chapter 8 highlights various risk management strategies relevant to oversight responsibility and resources for a compliance program; having a system for internal reporting of compliance concerns and proper investigation protocols; and finally the important step of periodically assessing a compliance program and continuous improvement.

NOTES

1 FCPA Professor, "Prosecutorial Common Law," (Mar. 16, 2011).
2 U.S. v. Kozeny, 493 F.Supp.2d 693, 697 (S.D.N.Y. 2007).
3 OECD, "Phase 3 Report On Implementing The OECD Anti-Bribery Convention in the United States" (Oct. 2010).
4 FCPA Professor, "SEC Official – "FCPA Law .. Is Not Well Developed," (Dec. 5, 2013).
5 FCPA Professor, "FCPA Readings," (Mar. 12, 2014).
6 To the extent readers are interested in learning more about the legitimacy and validity of certain FCPA enforcement theories see Mike Koehler, "*The Façade of FCPA Enforcement,*" 41 Georgetown Journal of International Law 907 (2010); Mike Koehler Supreme Court Amicus Curiae Brief in Support of Petitioners in Joel Esquenazi and Carlos Rodriguez vs. U.S., No. 14-0189 (September 17, 2014); Mike Koehler, "*JPMorgan: A Trifecta of Off-the-Rails FCPA Enforcement,*" 12 Bloomberg BNA White Collar Crime Report 201 (Mar. 3, 2017).
7 Corruption, Crime & Compliance, "The Myth of the Rogue Employee," (Mar. 29, 2016).
8 FCPA Professor, "Must See Video Clips From Assistant AG Caldwell's Recent FCPA Speech," (Nov. 7, 2016).
9 See e.g., In the Matter of Nordion (Canada) Inc., SEC Release No. 77290/March 3, 2016; In the Matter of SAP SE, SEC Release No. 77005/February 1, 2016.
10 FCPA Professor, "Q&A with Martin Weinstein" (May 18, 2010).
11 OECD Convention on Combating Bribery of Foreign Public Officials in International Business Transactions.
12 FCPA Professor, "The Significant Differences Among OECD Convention Countries On Legal Person Criminal Liability," (Sept. 22, 2016).
13 Mike Koehler, "Revisiting a Foreign Corrupt Practices Act Compliance Defense," 2012 Wisconsin Law Review 609.
14 H.R. REP. No. 99-580 (1986).
15 FCPA Professor, "Former DOJ FCPA Chief Supports FCPA Compliance Defense," (Oct. 4, 2011).

# 1 A diverse group of professionals need skills to spot risk under the FCPA and related laws

Spotting risk under the FCPA and related laws is a fundamental skill set for a diverse group of professionals because business organizations face omnipresent risk when competing in the global marketplace. While all seem to acknowledge this, in the minds of some, complying with such laws should be easy: "just don't bribe." Unfortunately, a few companies engaged in international business do so with an intent to bribe as a business strategy and without a commitment to compliance. However, this chapter demonstrates that the simplistic narrative of "just don't bribe" is a fallacy because the overwhelming majority of business organizations subject to the FCPA and related laws are engaged in business with a commitment to compliance, yet subject to unrealistic legal standards and/or difficult and complex business conditions that often serve as the root cause of scrutiny and enforcement. An examination of these root causes is not meant to excuse the conduct giving rise to an enforcement action, but rather to understand how and why the conduct occurred in the first place. Understanding the root causes of scrutiny and enforcement also serves an important compliance objective in that a key component of best practices is conducting a risk assessment (i.e. understanding unique points of contact with "foreign officials") and prioritizing compliance to specific risks.

This chapter next highlights that a diverse group of professionals also need skills to spot risk because scrutiny and enforcement have wide-ranging negative financial consequences for business organizations. Obviously one reason to comply with the FCPA and related laws is because non-compliance can expose an organization to an actual enforcement action brought by law enforcement. However, settlement amounts in an actual enforcement action are often only a relatively minor component of the overall financial consequences that can result from scrutiny and enforcement. Discussion of these many other "ripples" is intended to shift the compliance conversation away from a purely legal issue to its more proper designation as a general business issue that needs to be on the radar screen of various professionals who can assist in risk management and who should view the importance of compliance holistically and not merely through the narrow lens of actual enforcement actions.

## Omnipresent risk

The FCPA and related laws are most logically implicated when engaged in international business and business organizations (large and small and across a variety of industry sectors) are doing just that to achieve business goals. According to a recent analysis, many U.S. companies conduct nearly as much business overseas as they do in the U.S.[1] and financial information from companies across a variety of industry sectors highlights the prominence of international business. For instance, consumer products company Procter & Gamble derives approximately 60% of its sales from outside of North America, its products are sold in approximately 180 countries and it has facilities in approximately 40 countries. Likewise, footwear and apparel company Nike derives approximately 60% of its revenue from outside the U.S. and has approximately 400 stores outside the U.S. as well as 16 distribution centers. For many companies, doing business in high-risk bribery jurisdictions such as China, India and Brazil is necessary to sustain growth and satisfy shareholder demand for profits. As the CEO of a large multinational company rhetorically asked, "Where do you think the growth in the world is going to come from? Would you bet on the U.S.? Would you bet on Western Europe? It's going to come from emerging markets."[2]

More business in international markets means more engagement of foreign third parties, more points of contact with alleged "foreign officials," and more exposure to difficult and challenging business requirements and trade barriers that often create the conditions in which bribery can flourish. Against this backdrop, it is not surprising that there has generally been more enforcement of the FCPA and related laws during the past decade for the same reason that more cars on the road result in more accidents, traffic violations and speeding tickets.

In short, the FCPA is a top legal and compliance concern for business organizations (both public and private and across a variety of industry

*Table 1.1 Representative enforcement actions*

| Business organization | Industry |
|---|---|
| Allianz | Insurance |
| Avon | Beauty products |
| BHP Billiton | Mining |
| Biomet | Medical devices |
| Bristol Myers Squibb | Pharmaceutical |
| Embraer | Air transportation |
| Goodyear | Tires |
| Halliburton | Oil and gas |
| JPMorgan | Financial services |
| Las Vegas Sands | Hotel and gaming |
| Mondelez International | Food products |
| Oracle | Software |
| Qualcomm | Technology |
| Ralph Lauren | Apparel |
| SQM | Chemical |
| VimpelCom | Telecommunications |

sectors) doing business in the global marketplace. Reflective of the omnipresent nature of scrutiny and enforcement, Table 1.1 highlights the variety of business organizations that have recently resolved enforcement actions.

While many of the business organizations represented in Table 1.1 are large, publicly traded companies, smaller companies, privately held companies, and other forms of business organization such as limited liability companies (collectively referred to as small-to-medium-size enterprises – SMEs) have also recently resolved enforcement actions as highlighted in Table 1.2.

Indeed, in connection with an enforcement action against Smith & Wesson the SEC stated:

> This is a wake-up call for small and medium-size businesses that want to enter into high-risk markets and expand their international sales. When a company makes the strategic decision to sell its products overseas, it must ensure that the right internal controls are in place and operating.[3]

The omnipresent nature of scrutiny and enforcement is not just reflected by the variety of business organizations in a variety of

*Table 1.2 SMEs that have recently resolved FCPA enforcement actions*

| | | | |
|---|---|---|---|
| Louis Berger | IAP Worldwide | FLIR Systems | PBSJ Corp. |
| Dallas Airmotive | Bruker Corp. | Layne Christensen | Smith & Wesson |
| Bio-Rad | NORDAM Group | Data Systems | BizJet International |
| Watts Water Tech. | Comverse Tech. | Maxwell Tech. | Akamai Tech. |
| Analogic | CDM Smith | Alliance One | Armor Holdings |
| Lindsey Manuf. | RAE Systems | Veraz Networks | NATCO Group |
| Cinergy Telecom | Latin Node | UTStarcom | Helmerich & Payne |
| Nature's Sunshine | Control Components | Nexus Tech. | AGA Medical |
| Delta & Pine Land | Nortek | Nu Skin Enterprises | NCH Corp. |

industry sectors that have resolved enforcement actions, but also by the below map which pinpoints the locations generating corporate FCPA enforcement actions *in just one recent year.*

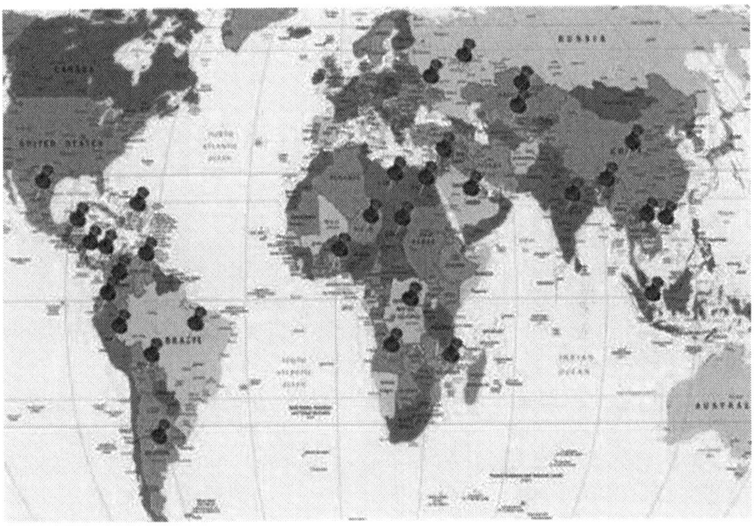

While certain countries may have a higher risk profile than others, enforcement actions have involved conduct in approximately 80 countries, including perceived low-risk countries such as Canada, the U.K., the Netherlands, France, and Germany. All seem to acknowledge that risk under the FCPA and related laws is omnipresent when doing business in the global marketplace. However, in the minds of some, compliance should be easy: "just don't bribe." However, as next discussed, this simplistic narrative is a fallacy.

## The fallacy of "just don't bribe"

In the minds of some, you wasted your money purchasing a book titled *Strategies for Minimizing Risk Under the Foreign Corrupt Practices Act and Related Laws,* because compliance should be easy: "just don't bribe." "Good Companies Don't Bribe. Period" was actually the title of a business column in a major U.S. newspaper which assailed those who have criticized various aspects of FCPA enforcement. In support of the position that "good companies don't bribe – period," the column stated:

> The [FCPA] has established America's reputation as a strong proponent of ethical business practices abroad. As Microsoft recognizes in its anti-corruption policy: 'corruption promotes poverty, hunger, disease and crime, and keeps societies and individuals from reaching their full potential. Corruption is one of the leading obstacles to economic and social development. Microsoft is committed to observing the standards of conduct set forth in the [FCPA] and the anti-corruption and anti-money-laundering laws of the countries in which it operates.'[4]

The absolutist position that "good companies don't bribe – period" was undermined a few months later when it was reported that both the DOJ and SEC "opened preliminary investigations into bribery accusations involving Microsoft in China, Italy and Romania."[5] A Microsoft executive acknowledged the investigation and stated:

> Like other large companies with operations around the world, we sometimes receive allegations about potential misconduct by employees or business partners, and we investigate them fully regardless of the source. We also invest heavily in proactive training, monitoring and audits to ensure our business operations around the world meet the highest legal and ethical standards. [. . .] We are a global company with operations in 112 countries, nearly 98,000 employees and 640,000 business partners. [. . .] We have more than 50 people whose primary role is investigating potential breaches of company policy, and an additional 120 people whose primary role is compliance. In addition, we sometimes retain outside law firms to conduct or assist with investigations. This is a reflection of the size

> and complexity of our business and the seriousness with which we take meeting our obligations. We also invest in proactive measures including annual training programs for every employee, regular internal audits and multiple levels of approval for contracting and expenditure. In a company of our size, allegations of this nature will be made from time to time. It is also possible there will sometimes be individual employees or business partners who violate our policies and break the law. In a community of 98,000 people and 640,000 partners, it isn't possible to say there will never be wrongdoing.[6]

The Microsoft example highlights that scrutiny and enforcement can be viewed in the following ways. Do companies subject to the FCPA do business in foreign markets:

- intent on engaging in bribery as a business strategy and without a commitment to compliance; or
- with a commitment to compliance, yet subject to unrealistic legal standards and/or difficult and complex business conditions?

Regrettably, there have been and will continue to be instances of the former. For instance, in the Siemens enforcement action the government stated that:

- "for much of its operations across the globe, bribery was nothing less than standard operating procedure for Siemens";
- the "pattern of bribery by Siemens was unprecedented in scale and geographic reach";
- Siemens had a "corporate culture in which bribery was tolerated and even rewarded at the highest levels of the company"; and
- "compliance, legal, internal audit, and corporate finance departments" of the company played a significant role in the conduct at issue.[7]

On a much smaller yet still egregious scale, an enforcement action against BizJet International (a small, privately held company) involved conduct by various executives at the highest levels of the company as well as the Board of Directors being specifically informed by certain executives that the company "would pay referral fees in order to gain market share" in various foreign countries.[8] In Siemens, BizJet and a few other enforcement actions the otherwise naïve and simplistic phrase "just don't bribe" accurately summarizes the conduct at issue.

However, not all companies that are under scrutiny and resolve enforcement actions deserve the "bad" or "unethical" label. Joseph Covington, a former DOJ FCPA Unit Chief, was spot-on when he observed: "rarely [has he] seen American companies affirmatively offering bribes in the first instance."[9] Rather, he observed that companies doing business in global markets are "reacting to a world not of their making" and that "as the world shrinks companies who seek to do the right thing can't help but confront corrupt officials – as customers, regulator and adjudicators – and confront them often." Indeed, one of the ironies of the FCPA's modern era is that several companies have resolved enforcement actions or have been the subject of scrutiny *during the same general time period* as being recognized as one of the "World's Most Ethical Companies,"[10] "Most Admired Companies,"[11] or "Companies That Are Changing the World."[12]

What often makes compliance difficult for even the most well-managed and well-intentioned business organization is that the basic question of what the FCPA even captures is seldom straightforward. For instance, various courts have found that the anti-bribery provisions contain ambiguous terms and the books and records and internal controls provisions are qualified through a reasonableness standard and good faith concepts. Thus, many of the FCPA's prohibitions are not rules-based but rather principle-based, making compliance difficult in much the same way traffic compliance would be difficult if the speed limit was "reasonable" and not a specific standard such as 65 miles per hour. Even the DOJ and the SEC acknowledge that difficult questions often arise under the FCPA. For instance, the U.S. Attorneys' Manual states: "The investigation and prosecution of particular allegations of violations of the FCPA will raise complex enforcement problems abroad as well as difficult issues of jurisdiction and statutory construction."[13] Likewise, as previously highlighted, the SEC's Director of Enforcement has stated that "FCPA law . . . is not well developed."[14]

Another reason compliance can be difficult for even the most well-managed and well-intentioned business organization is because of the shifting and often conflicting messages the enforcement agencies deliver to the business community. For instance, the FCPA Guidance (a non-binding policy document issued by the DOJ and SEC setting forth their FCPA enforcement approach and priorities) states:

> Devoting a disproportionate amount of time policing modest entertainment and gift-giving instead of focusing on large government bids, questionable payments to third-party consultants, or excessive discounts to resellers and distributors may indicate that a company's compliance program is ineffective. A $50 million contract with a government agency in a high-risk country warrants greater scrutiny than modest routine gifts and entertainment. Similarly, performing identical due diligence on all third-party agents, irrespective of risk factors, is often counter-productive, diverting attention and resources away from those third parties that pose the most significant risk.[15]

In connection with the FCPA Guidance, the Assistant Attorney General stated that the DOJ is "focused on bribes of consequence – ones that have a fundamentally corrosive effect on the way companies do business abroad."[16] Likewise, the Chief of the SEC Enforcement Division stated that the enforcement agencies "hope that [the Guidance] will clear up some myths about the type of conduct that gets prosecuted under the FCPA – that it is not the $5 cup of coffee, or the one off $50 gift to a public official, that companies need to be concerned about, but payments of real and substantial value that clearly represent an unambiguous intent to bribe a foreign official to obtain or retain business."[17] The SEC official further stated that the government was "interested in companies spending compliance dollars in the most sensible way" and hoped that the Guidance and the hypotheticals provided in it would help companies decide where they can "minimize investment and where they can maximize it."[18] The Assistant Attorney General added that the government wants compliance programs "to address real matters of concern."[19]

Notwithstanding sensible enforcement agency guidance and statements, recent enforcement actions have involved allegations about corporate hospitality, travel and entertainment, charitable donations, internships and hiring practices, and other inconsequential things of value such as perfume, dresses and handbags; a bottle of wine; a watch; a camera, kitchen appliances and business suits; television sets, laptops and appliances; tea sets and office furniture; and golf in the morning and beer drinking in the evening.[20] Do recognize that such inconsequential things of value are often *not the only allegations or findings* in an enforcement action. However, such non-determinative allegations or findings can be viewed in one of two ways: either the government was practicing its typing skills; or the government was sending a message to the business community of the types of conduct they view as being actionable under the FCPA.

Andrew Weissmann, who would later become Chief of the DOJ's Fraud Section, stated that a company that wants to do business in certain countries like China "is going to trip up on many of the provisions of the FCPA [and] will likely have an FCPA problem and it will make it very easy for the people in the DOJ and SEC to basically impose a tax for doing business in that country."[21]

FCPA practitioners, including a former DOJ FCPA enforcement attorney, have also stated:

> The world of business . . . frequently operates in territory that is somewhat grey: a world in which business persons strive to grow the company ethically in situations where the application of the existing rules are not entirely clear. For instance, in the current era of FCPA enforcement, international businesses struggle with their responsibilities to monitor and control the conduct of third parties with whom they do business: distributors and subdistributors, joint venture partners, dealers, and resellers. Even for companies that are firmly dedicated to compliance with the FCPA, it is not always clear when a third party amounts to an agent whose improper conduct might someday be ascribed to the company and its employees. Good and ethical companies struggle, every day, with the concept of defining an agent of the company as opposed to an independent customer who engages in an arm's-length transaction to purchase the company's products.[22]

Recognizing that the absolutist "good companies don't bribe – period" narrative is a fallacy is an important starting point for this book and gives you a better understanding for why compliance can be difficult for even the most well-managed and well-intentioned business organizations and why risk can't be eliminated when doing business in the global marketplace. Returning to the Microsoft example, some may ask how Microsoft, a company championed as a leader in ethical and compliant business conduct, became the subject of scrutiny? More sophisticated observers should recognize that it is for the same reasons that many ethically sound business organizations find themselves in the same position and that is because of the typical root causes of scrutiny and enforcement next discussed.

## Root causes of risk

This section highlights various real-world dynamics and conditions which often lead to scrutiny and enforcement under the FCPA and related laws, in other words the root causes of risk as demonstrated by the below visual.

As referenced earlier in this chapter, scrutiny and enforcement can be viewed the following ways: do companies subject to the FCPA do business in foreign markets

- intent on engaging in bribery as a business strategy and without a commitment to compliance; or
- with a commitment to compliance, yet subject to unrealistic legal standards and/or difficult and complex business conditions?

Regrettably, there have been and will continue to be instances of the former similar to the Siemens and BizJet International enforcement actions (often referred to as active bribery). However, the root causes of scrutiny and enforcement are more often the latter (often referred to as passive bribery). An examination of the root causes of scrutiny and enforcement, such as legal principles relevant to business organizations and various realities of the global marketplace, is not meant to excuse the conduct, but rather to understand how and why the conduct occurred in the first place. Moreover, understanding typical root causes of scrutiny and enforcement is an important foundational skill relevant to conducting the risk assessment in Chapter 6.

## Relevant legal principles

Risk under the FCPA and related laws arises when a business organization has points of contact with alleged "foreign officials" in the global marketplace. Business organizations are legal persons and thus can only have these points of contact through natural persons such as employees and agents hired or engaged by the organization. These natural persons may develop interests and motivations that do not always align with their employer or principal, not to mention being from different cultures, speaking different languages, and being located in different time zones thousands of miles from corporate headquarters. Even with compliance best practices, the practical reality of monitoring and supervising this vast and diverse network of individuals is difficult and no compliance program can prevent all misconduct.

In the minds of some, rogue actors who circumvent and act inconsistent with pre-existing compliance policies and procedures are a figment of the corporate apologist's imagination.[23] However, rogue actors actually do exist and no compliance program can ever prevent all wrongdoing by an organization's employees and agents. The DOJ recognizes this as a matter of policy in its U.S. Attorneys' Manual which states that "no compliance program can ever prevent all criminal activity by a corporation's employees."[24] In addition, high-ranking DOJ officials have recognized that "there will always be employees who decide to take matters into their own hands – they are a fact of life," and that "even the best compliance program may not stop fraud or corruption from occurring."[25] The former Assistant Chief of the DOJ's FCPA Unit candidly stated "most government attorneys realize that a company can take every reasonable step to prevent wrongdoing but ultimately is powerless if somebody really wants to break the law."[26]

Notwithstanding the existence of rogue actors who may circumvent and act inconsistent with pre-existing compliance policies and procedures, business organizations are often subject to scrutiny and enforcement because of the general U.S. legal principle of *respondeat superior* which states that employee and agent conduct can expose a business organization to legal liability, both criminal and civil, to the extent the individual: (i) acted within the scope of their duties; and (ii) the conduct was intended, at least in part, to benefit the organization.

For instance, software company SAP conducts business around the world through 272 subsidiaries, 280,000 individuals, and a network of 11,500 partners. Yet SAP resolved an enforcement action based on the conduct of Vicente Garcia (a former head of Latin America sales) based on government findings that:

- he "created a slush fund" that was used to pay the bribes and kickbacks;
- he "concealed his scheme from others at SAP";
- he "circumvented SAP's internal controls";
- he "justified the excessive discounting by falsifying SAP's internal approval forms";
- he "self-profited through kickbacks";
- he used his "personal e-mail" in connection with the scheme; and
- all of his accomplices were "others outside of SAP" (a term used by the government multiple times).[27]

Likewise, health science company Nordion resolved an enforcement action based on the conduct of Mikhail Gourevitch (a former engineer) who (along with his "childhood friend from Russia" who later became a Nordion agent) "conspired to use a portion of the funds Nordion paid the Agent to bribe Russian government officials to obtain approval for TheraSphere", a liver cancer therapy. According to the government, Gourevitch:

- received kickbacks from the Agent and "secretly enrich[ed] himself" and received "at least $100,000 for his role in the arrangement which was not disclosed to Nordion"; and
- "hid the scheme from Nordion" through, among other things, misrepresentations to his employer.[28]

Similarly, thermal imaging company FLIR Systems resolved an enforcement action based on the conduct of two individuals: Stephen

Timms (Head of FLIR's Middle East Office) and Yasser Ramahi (a business development employee who reported to Timm). According to the government, the individuals "concealed" the extent and nature of the travel and gifts provided to "foreign officials" which gave rise to the enforcement action as well as prepared false and misleading documents in connection with their bribery scheme. The conduct of the two individuals was inconsistent with FLIR's existing FCPA-related policies and internal controls as the government stated:

> During the relevant time, FLIR had a code of conduct, as well as a specific anti-bribery policy, which prohibited FLIR employees from violating the FCPA. FLIR's policies required employees to record information "accurately and honestly" in FLIR's books and records, with "no materiality requirement or threshold for a violation." FLIR employees, including Timms and Ramahi, received training on their obligations under the FCPA.

As these enforcement actions demonstrate, *respondeat superior* is an extremely flexible legal principle that serves as the root cause for many instances of scrutiny and enforcement. In thinking about *respondeat superior*, recall Microsoft's scrutiny and how the company has operations in 112 countries with nearly 98,000 employees and 640,000 business partners. Against this backdrop, the Microsoft executive was spot-on when observing "in a company of our size, it isn't possible to say there will never be wrongdoing."

Normally 99% success is rewarded. For instance, if a student scores 99% on a final exam, she will have the top grade in the class. If a basketball player makes 99% of his shots, or a soccer player scores a goal on 99% of her kicks, that player is destined for the hall of fame. In these real-world scenarios, we judge success holistically and not through the narrow lens of one question on an exam or one possession in a sports contest. However, 99% compliance success in a business organization means 1% non-compliance and instead of judging an organization's success holistically, government enforcement agencies seem to view an organization through the narrow lens of one employee, one business transaction, or one business unit or subsidiary. Because of *respondeat superior*, this means legal liability for the business organization and an FCPA practitioner stated:

> I think that companies' main frustration is that even with an outstanding compliance program and 99% of the employees maintaining strict adherence

> to the laws, you can still have violations which expose the entire company to extraordinarily serious penalties. I think the government has, at times, lost track of the main motivations for this statute and has become focused on the amounts of penalties, the imposition of compliance monitors, and exercising government control over what are basically private businesses. The vast majority of companies are absolutely committed to following the spirit and the letter of the FCPA, but when a company gets into trouble, the whole enterprise can be put at risk because of the conduct of a few people, and that doesn't seem right.[29]

As highlighted in this book's introduction, the legal principle of *respondeat superior* is controversial and materially different compared with corporate liability principles in other peer countries. While the DOJ and SEC have stated that they may consider the unique facts and circumstances relevant to the extent of wrongdoing as well as an organization's pre-existing compliance policies and procedures when determining how to resolve an action or how to calculate a settlement amount, the fact remains that a business organization's pre-existing good faith compliance efforts are not relevant as a matter of law to legal liability under the FCPA. This policy issue aside, the point here is that *respondeat superior* is often a root cause of scrutiny and enforcement for many business organizations.

Another common root cause of scrutiny and enforcement related to *respondeat superior* is the reality of parent–subsidiary relationships and expansive enforcement theories related to corporate hierarchies. For instance, many multinational companies are organized for practical and legal reasons through distinct corporate entities such as a parent corporation and various subsidiary companies in foreign countries. It is black-letter law that the legal liability of each distinct corporate entity is contained within that entity absent a finding of abuse of corporate form such as insufficient capitalization or failure to abide by certain formalities such as holding annual meetings or maintaining separate books and records. In other words, legal liability does not ordinary hop, skip and jump around a multinational company. However, in certain enforcement actions (particularly those charging or finding books and records and internal controls violations), the enforcement agencies seemingly advance the theory that a parent corporation is legally responsible for the acts of subsidiary employees even though there is no allegation or suggestion that the parent company was aware of, or participated in, the alleged improper conduct.

Commenting on this trend in connection with an enforcement action against Ralph Lauren Corporation ("RLC"), Philip Urofsky (a former DOJ Assistant Chief of the Fraud Section) asked "are there any limits to parent corporation liability" and stated:

> The facts of the case . . . point to the steady entrenchment of a more ominous prosecution theory: an approach that appears to approximate strict criminal and civil liability of parent corporations for their subsidiaries' corrupt acts. Although this disregard of corporate structures has been hinted at in previous SEC matters [. . .] the RLC case puts both agencies firmly in the camp of this aggressive and unprecedented expansion of corporate liability. [. . .] This approach, however, fails to honor the corporate form and the black-letter rule that to 'pierce the corporate veil' the government and other litigants must show that the parent operated the subsidiary as an alter ego, and itself paid no attention to the corporate form. Moreover, it is contrary to the language of the [FCPA's] original history. [. . .] It is disquieting [that in the RLC case] the DOJ appears to have jumped on the charge-the-parent bandwagon, bringing a bribery case against a parent without alleging any involvement by the parent in those violations. One can only speculate that it did so because it had no jurisdiction over the foreign subsidiary itself, given that it also did not allege any act by the subsidiary in U.S. territory. However, as always, the maxim that bad facts make bad law applies, and evidentiary weaknesses cannot excuse the distortion of the statute's previously clear and reasonable allocation of responsibility.[30]

While many enforcement actions against parent companies based on the conduct of foreign subsidiaries contain sparse allegations about the parent company itself, it is worth noting that a few enforcement actions do advance a plausible legal basis to hold the parent company liable for foreign subsidiary conduct by articulating so-called alter ego factors. For instance, an enforcement action against software company PTC based on travel and entertainment benefits provided to alleged Chinese "foreign officials" by foreign subsidiaries contained the following findings concerning the overlapping nature of the foreign subsidiary and the parent company:

- PTC exercised substantial control over PTC-China by creating functional reporting lines, approving PTC-China's key decisions, and setting PTC-China's business and financial goals.
- Both the Hong Kong and Shanghai subsidiaries shared common

directors, all of whom were senior members or officers of PTC's legal and finance departments.

Based on these factors, the government found: "under applicable agency principles, PTC-China and its employees acted as agents of PTC during the relevant time and were acting within the scope of their authority and for the benefit of PTC when participating in the bribery scheme."[31]

In sum, two main root causes of scrutiny and enforcement are parent – subsidiary issues and expansive enforcement theories related to corporate hierarchies as well as the previously discussed *respondeat superior* principle.

## Realities of the global marketplace

Whereas the above root causes of scrutiny and enforcement were generic, the specific realities of doing business in the global marketplace are also often root causes of scrutiny and enforcement. Referring back to the guiding question, do companies subject to the FCPA do business in foreign markets:

- intent on engaging in bribery as a business strategy and without a commitment to compliance; or
- with a commitment to compliance, yet subject to unrealistic legal standards and/or difficult and complex business conditions.

A close read of enforcement actions reveals that the origins of enforcement are often the latter category. In other words, business organizations subject to the FCPA and related laws must navigate difficult and challenging business conditions replete with trade barriers including customs procedures; import/export documentation and inspection requirements; arcane and complex licensing and certification requirements; quality standards that require product testing and inspection visits; and foreign government procurement policies. These conditions and barriers are seldom transparent and local law or practice may require a third party to navigate these bureaucracies. Using the below visual as guidance, well-intentioned companies doing business in many foreign countries are often funneled into an arbitrary world of low-paying civil servants who oversee "red tape" bureaucracies and may seek to supplement their often meager government salaries through payments common and seemingly condoned in the foreign country.

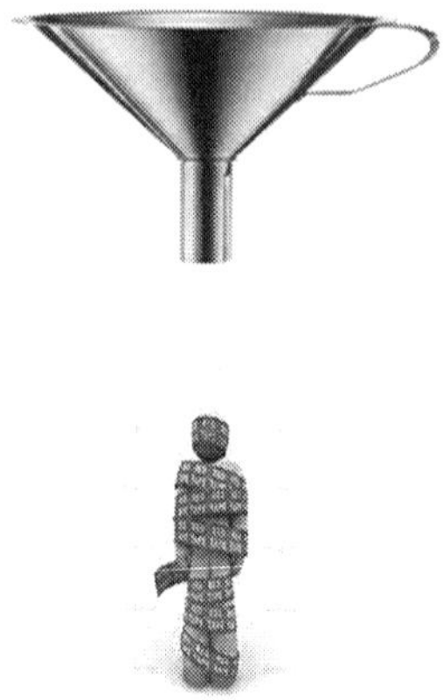

For instance, if a company wants to allow public access to its buildings in China, it must obtain a fire safety certificate and the process has been described as follows:

> To obtain a fire-safety certificate from a local fire department, a business owner must pass five 'checkpoints' in a complicated and lengthy administrative process. Each checkpoint is guarded by officials in charge of site inspections and reviewing construction blueprints, equipment and contingency plans. Bribes considerably expedite the process that officials might otherwise draw out for weeks, months or years. Bribes range from a few thousand yuan to hundreds of thousands, per official, depending on their rank and the size of the project. But money isn't everything – some officials must be wined and dined or given luxury cigarettes. Others request the services of prostitutes.[32]

Want to build a manufacturing facility in Russia? No problem, but a business organization may need 240 separate licenses and permits.[33] The risk formula is really not complex recognizing that the FCPA and related laws are implicated when real people, operating in real business environments, have real points of contact, with real "foreign officials."

- Foreign trade barriers, distortions and business conditions create bureaucracy.
- Bureaucracy creates points of contact with foreign officials.
- Points of contact with foreign officials create discretion.

- Discretion creates the opportunity for a foreign official to misuse their position by making bribe demands.

To successfully complete the risk assessment skills exercise in Chapter 6, it is critical to understand this basic, yet often overlooked, reality of doing business in the global marketplace. As discussed in greater detail in Chapter 6, while Transparency International's "Corruption Perception Index" tends to be a popular metric for business organizations to risk-rank countries, a better alternative may be the World Bank's "Ease of Doing Business" ranking which categorizes countries based on factors such as the ease of starting a business, obtaining permits, and otherwise dealing with regulatory officials. Not surprisingly, there is a clear overlap between foreign government bureaucracy and corruption and countries that have lower regulatory burdens tend to be less corrupt and countries with higher regulatory burdens tend to be more corrupt.[34]

The following enforcement actions highlight how foreign business conditions are often the root cause of enforcement actions.

- Helmerich & Payne, an oil and gas drilling company, resolved an enforcement action based on alleged payments made by second-tier subsidiaries to various officials and representatives of the Argentine and Venezuelan customs services in connection with the importation and exportation of goods and equipment. As alleged, the payments were made through agents or customs brokers, involved low dollar amounts, and were "made on an infrequent basis."[35]

- Seed company Delta & Pine Land Company resolved an enforcement action based on alleged payments made or offered by a subsidiary to officials of the Turkish Ministry of Agricultural and Rural Affairs to obtain government reports and certifications such as farm field inspections that were necessary to operate in Turkey.[36]

- Tyson Foods, a poultry producer, resolved an enforcement action based on alleged payments made by a subsidiary to Mexican veterinarians. As alleged, the veterinarians were required to be on-site at the company's facility to certify product for export and certain veterinarians were allowed to charge the facility for their work (to supplement their government salary) while certain other veterinarians were not. The resolution documents did not provide any detail how the payments sought to influence the veterinarians or suggest that the products were not qualified for export.[37]

Enforcement actions based on alleged conduct in high-growth markets like India and Nigeria further demonstrate how foreign business conditions often facilitate passive bribery. For instance, doing business in India often requires companies to navigate the "license raj" and practitioners have stated:

> As with other countries, a host of regulatory hurdles exists in India, including the need to obtain permits, licenses, and other regulatory approvals and to pay various application and registration fees. These types of low-level transactions provide opportunities for bribery.[38]

According to survey data, 54% of Indians pay bribes to receive basic services and India's Chief Economic Advisor has acknowledged that "harassment bribery is widespread in India."[39] Recent enforcement actions concerning business conduct in India demonstrate that harassment bribery is common and that business organizations operating in India face – just as locals do – difficult conditions simply to get things done.

- Mondelez International, a snack and beverage company, resolved an enforcement action in connection with an agent retained by an acquired entity to interact with officials to obtain approximately 30 licenses and approvals for a chocolate factory.[40]

- AB InBev, a beverage and brewing company, resolved an enforcement action based in part on it needing the approval of a state "Excise Minister" to extend brewery production time beyond 8 hours a day.[41]

- Diageo, a spirits company, resolved an enforcement action based in part on alleged payments made by a subsidiary in connection with product label registration and securing favorable product placement and promotion at state-owned liquor stores.[42]

- Wabtec, a brake manufacturer, resolved an enforcement action based on alleged payments made by a subsidiary in connection with scheduling pre-shipping product inspections, issuance of product delivery certificates, and tax audits.[43]

- Baker Hughes, an oilfield services company, resolved an enforcement action based in part on alleged payments made by a subsidiary to obtain shipping permits.[44]

In Nigeria, 142 separate signatures may be needed to clear cargo through customs and it is thus not surprising that several enforcement actions have involved business interactions with the notoriously corrupt Nigerian Customs Service (NCS) including a coordinated enforcement action involving several companies in the oil and gas industry.[45] These parallel actions largely involved alleged payments to NCS officials in connection with securing temporary importation permits for oil drilling rigs. In addition, the actions also involved payments through a freight forwarder to NCS officials to expedite the importation of goods and equipment into Nigeria and payments to circumvent customs clearance processes with respect to importation of certain tools and materials.[46]

The above root causes of enforcement all involved business organizations having points of contact with alleged "foreign officials" in connection with rather boring and mundane aspects of business. Yet another foreign business condition that often serves as a root cause of scrutiny and enforcement is the inability of a company to sell its product or service without a government-issued license. For instance, the root cause of enforcement actions against beauty and healthcare products companies Avon and Nu Skin Enterprises was the same: China prohibited direct selling of such products; the companies needed a government issued-license to do so; and in connection with securing the license various things of value were allegedly provided to regulatory officials.[47] Interestingly, several years prior to the enforcement action, Nu Skin publicly disclosed the following risks associated with direct selling in China:

> Our operations in Mainland China are subject to significant regulatory scrutiny. The legal system in Mainland China provides government authorities broad latitude to conduct investigations and many Chinese regulations, including those governing our business, are subject to significant interpretation, which may vary from jurisdiction to jurisdiction. Because of significant government concerns in Mainland China regarding improper direct selling activities, government regulators closely scrutinize activities of direct selling companies and activities that resemble direct selling. The government in Mainland China continues to inspect and interview the direct selling industry on a regular basis, which has and may continue to increase regulatory scrutiny of the industry and our business.[48]

Another frequent root cause of scrutiny and enforcement are forced business relationships that companies are often required to have pursuant to foreign law, regulation or practice. In other words, in certain countries and in certain sectors, a seller of products or services can't have a direct relationship with an interested buyer, but is required to work through a third party (whether an agent, representative, distributor, or joint venture partner) to interact with customers and potential customers. As discussed in greater detail in Chapter 3, because of the FCPA's third-party payment provisions, these relationships often serve as the root cause of enforcement as demonstrated by the following actions:

- Akamai Technologies resolved an enforcement action based on conduct in China pursuant to circumstances in which "under China's regulatory system, [the company was] required to contract with third-party channel partners to deliver its services to end customers."[49]
- Telia, a telecommunications company, resolved an enforcement action based on conduct in Uzbekistan pursuant to circumstances in which "before entering the Uzbek market, company management understood that they were required to have a Foreign Official as a 'local partner' to conduct business in Uzbekistan."[50]
- Conglomerate company Hitachi resolved an enforcement action based on conduct in South Africa pursuant to circumstances in which companies that partnered with a local black-owned entity enjoyed preferential status in government procurement and the local entity turned out to be a front for the country's ruling political party.[51]

Consider also the circumstances in which various oil and gas companies operate in Angola, the second largest oil-producing country in Africa. The sector is overseen by Sonangol (a state-owned/state-controlled enterprise) pursuant to local content regulations which require foreign companies to partner with Angolan companies. Given these circumstances, it is not surprising that this requirement has served as the root cause of several enforcement actions including against oil and gas service companies Halliburton and Weatherford International.

Even if business is legitimately secured in a foreign country, a dysfunctional foreign government may refuse to pay a company amounts legally owed providing yet another root cause of enforcement. For instance, several enforcement actions regarding conduct in Venezuela arose because the government was unable to pay its bills and alleged "foreign officials" at the state-owned oil company offered to pay outstanding bills (among a stack of many no doubt) in exchange for things of value.[52]

Likewise, a main feature of the $54 million enforcement action against agriculture company Archer Daniels Midland Co. (ADM) and related entities was that ADM and its shareholders were victims of a corrupt Ukraine government which refused to release value-added tax refunds legitimately owed to the company. In the words of the government "the Ukrainian government did not have the money to pay VAT refunds that it owed to companies that sold Ukrainian goods outside of Ukraine" and the "Ukrainian government determined to delay paying the VAT refunds owed or did not make any refunds payments at all."[53] One of the most dubious enforcement actions of all time was against Vitusa Corp. and its president under circumstances in which the company entered into a lawful contract to sell milk powder to the Dominican Republic government. According to the government:

> Although Vitusa delivered the milk powder to the Government of the Dominican Republic, the Dominican government did not pay Vitusa promptly for the milk powder received and, in fact, maintained an outstanding balance due for an extended period of time. Vitusa, therefore, made various efforts to collect the outstanding balance due, including contacting officials of the United States and Dominican Governments to obtain their assistance in securing payment in full.

Perhaps the Vitusa and ADM enforcement actions would not have occurred if foreign government were not dysfunctional. Perhaps the Halliburton and Weatherford enforcement actions would not have occurred if the companies were not subject to local content requirements in Angola. Perhaps the Akamai Technologies enforcement action would not have occurred if the company could have delivered its services directly to customers in China. Perhaps the AB InBev enforcement action would not have occurred if the company could have decided its production hours without Indian government approval.

To repeat, an examination of typical root causes of scrutiny and enforcement is not meant to excuse the conduct, but rather to understand how and why the conduct occurred in the first place. Against the backdrop of the simplistic "just don't bribe" narrative advanced by some is the fact that the overwhelming majority of business organizations subject to the FCPA and related laws do business in the global marketplace with a commitment to compliance yet subject to unrealistic legal standards and/or difficult and complex business conditions that result in real people, operating in real business environments, having real points of contact, with real "foreign officials."

From a compliance standpoint, it is imperative to understand and appreciate this basic reality of doing business in the global marketplace in order to minimize risk. Moreover, from a policy standpoint it is important to understand and appreciate this reality because ad hoc enforcement alone of FCPA and related laws against payors of alleged bribes will not reduce bribery and corruption. Rather, bribery and -corruption is best reduced through a reduction in foreign trade barriers, distortions and business conditions that often put business organizations in contact with alleged "foreign officials."

The omnipresent risk of doing business in the global marketplace discussed in this section is not the only reason why a diverse group of professionals need skills to spot risk under the FCPA and related laws. As the next section highlights, professionals also need the ability to spot risk because the failure to do so can have wide-ranging negative financial consequences for business organizations above and beyond any enforcement action brought by law enforcement.

## "Ripple effects" of scrutiny and enforcement

Obviously one reason to comply with the FCPA and related laws is because non-compliance can expose a company to an actual enforcement action brought by law enforcement. However, enforcement action settlement amounts are often only a relatively minor component of the overall financial consequences that often occur because of the "ripple effects" of scrutiny and enforcement. To guide your learning on this important topic, use the below visual and think of the drop of water as being scrutiny under the FCPA or related laws or an actual enforcement action brought by law enforcement.

This drop of water is going to cause numerous "ripple effects" just as scrutiny and enforcement under the FCPA and related laws often cause numerous "ripple effects" ranging from: pre- and post-enforcement action professional fees; and expenses to other negative impacts on a company's business operations and strategy from market capitalization, cost of capital, merger and acquisition activity, and impeding or distracting a company from achieving other business objectives. In addition, scrutiny and enforcement can also expose corporate directors and executives to private civil suits. Moreover, with increasing frequency business organization scrutiny and enforcement is being used "offensively" by others to achieve a business objective or to further advance a litigating position.

Discussion of these many other "ripples" is intended to shift the compliance conversation away from a purely legal issue to its more proper designation as a general business issue that needs to be on the radar screen of various professionals who can assist in risk management and who should view the importance of compliance more holistically and not merely through the narrow lens of actual enforcement actions.

## The three buckets of financial exposure

An obvious reason to comply with the FCPA and related laws is that non-compliance can expose a business organization to a criminal or civil enforcement action by government law enforcement. However, settlement amounts in an actual enforcement action are often only a relatively minor component of the overall financial consequences that can result from scrutiny or enforcement and the below visuals highlight the "three buckets" of financial exposure including the typical ratios between each separate category.

Pre-Enforcement Action Professional Fees and Expenses

Enforcement Action Day

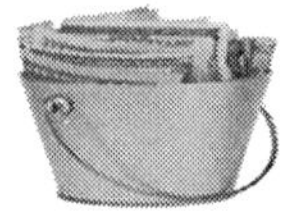

Post-Enforcement Action Professional Fees and Expenses

## Pre-enforcement action professional fees and expenses

Every instance of business organization scrutiny has a point of entry – in other words a set of facts which give rise to the scrutiny in the first place. This point of entry is often the beginning of a long and expensive journey for a business organization and the first bucket of financial exposure is pre-enforcement action professional fees and expenses. For instance, beauty products company Avon disclosed that it was conducting an FCPA internal investigation regarding compliance in China.[54] As is typical, the investigation soon spread to other countries and over the next several years the company disclosed approximately $550 million in pre-enforcement action professional fees and expenses – a figure that far exceeded the $135 million settlement amount in the actual enforcement action. Wal-Mart's scrutiny resulted in even higher pre-enforcement action professional fees and expenses after it disclosed that it was conducting an internal investigation concerning certain permitting, licensing and inspection issues in Mexico. Thereafter, Wal-Mart's investigation likewise expanded and the company's disclosed pre-enforcement action professional fees and expenses, as well as compliance enhancement costs, skyrocketed to approximately $880 million.[55]

It is not just large multinationals that are the subject of high-profile scrutiny that spend millions of dollars in pre-enforcement action professional fees and expenses. For instance, scientific instrument maker Bruker Corp. resolved an enforcement action for $2.2 million, but disclosed approximately $22 million (a 10:1 ratio) in pre-enforcement action professional fees and expenses. Likewise, telecommunications company Veraz Networks resolved an enforcement action for $300,000, but disclosed approximately $3 million (a 10:1 ratio) in pre-enforcement action professional fees and expenses. Similarly, oil and gas company Hyperdynamics resolved an enforcement action for $375,000, but disclosed approximately $12.7 million (a 33:1 ratio) in pre-enforcement action professional fees and expenses. Even more dramatic, oil and gas services provider NATCO Group resolved an enforcement action for $65,000, but disclosed approximately $11 million (a 170:1 ratio) in pre-enforcement action professional and expenses and also experienced cash-flow problems as a result of its scrutiny.[56]

Comparing pre-enforcement action professional fees and expenses to settlement amounts is not possible in all cases as companies have different disclosure requirements and practices. However, where a comparison is possible it is clear that pre-enforcement action professional fees and expenses are typically the greatest financial consequence to a business organization resolving an enforcement action. The question is why are pre-enforcement action professional fees and expenses so expensive?

Resolution documents from an enforcement action against telecommunications company Alcatel-Lucent provide some insight. In the resolution documents, it was noted:

> At the request of the government, [Alcatel-Lucent] undertook a 'Global Review' to evaluate its relationship with agents, interactions with government officials, and gifts, travel and entertainment provided in countries around the world. [. . .] In particular, Alcatel-Lucent and its outside counsel conducted investigations of 34 countries around the world to uncover potential misconduct. The internal investigation examined Alcatel-Lucent's agent and consultant approval, review, and termination processes, the activities of a number of terminated agents, and the knowledge and involvement of senior management in any potential wrongdoing. This effort was closely coordinated with the government. [. . .] [As part of its agent and consultant approval process review], Alcatel-Lucent retained an independent investigative firm to review all of Alcatel-Lucent's 300 then-existing agents and consultants. [. . .] Additionally, [. . .] Alcatel-Lucent commenced a review of its Board of Directors' and other senior management's knowledge of, and involvement in, any of the wrongdoing. As part of this review, interviews were conducted of 26 individuals who were either current high-ranking members of Alcatel-Lucent's management, former high-ranking members of Alcatel's management, or were in a position to provide information relevant to the review. Alcatel-Lucent and its counsel also reviewed documents collected from these individuals. [. . .] Overall, Alcatel-Lucent's outside counsel interviewed over 330 witnesses as part of these investigations, collected data from 201 individuals, and reviewed over 2 million documents, of which over 200,000 documents were produced to the government.[57]

As hinted at above, a main reason why pre-enforcement action professional fees and expenses are typically the most expensive aspect of scrutiny and enforcement is because of the "where else" question. The "where else" question generally happens as follows. A business organization becomes the subject of scrutiny for conduct that allegedly occurred in country *x*. Before the enforcement agencies resolve any enforcement action concerning the conduct in country *x*, they will often ask "where else?" In other words, if the conduct giving rise to scrutiny occurred in country *x*, how do the enforcement agencies know that similar conduct did not also occur in countries *a*, *b*, *c*, *d*, etc. Thus, the "where else" question typically asked results in a business organization conducting a much broader review of its operations.

Because cooperation with the government's investigation is an important factor that the enforcement agencies consider in deciding whether to bring an enforcement action, and if so on what terms, business organizations invariably, yet perhaps reluctantly, accept counsel's recommendation to broaden the internal investigation to best demonstrate cooperation. What happens next is that a business organization is paying for a team of lawyers (often accompanied by forensic accountants and other specialists) to travel around the world to answer the "where else" question even though the organization's scrutiny probably began with specific conduct in a specific country. For instance, the Magyar Telekom enforcement action focused on business conduct in Macedonia and Montenegro, but in resolving its scrutiny the company conducted a "thorough global internal investigation concerning bribery and related misconduct."[58] Likewise, the Tenaris enforcement action focused on business conduct in Uzbekistan, but in resolving the action, law enforcement cited the company's "voluntary investigation of [its] business operations throughout the world."

The "where else" question may even be asked in instances of scrutiny focused on conduct in foreign subsidiaries that comprise a meaningless percentage of the company's overall operations. For instance, the Tyson Foods enforcement action focused on conduct in Mexico involving a subsidiary company that "comprised less than one percent of Tyson's global net sales." Even though approximately 90% of Tyson's sales were domestic, in resolving the enforcement action Tyson "subjected to rigorous FCPA reviews" all of its wholly-owned production facilities, including those located outside of Mexico.

In short, a key take-away point is that scrutiny and enforcement under the FCPA and related laws will probably result in pre-enforcement action professional fees and expenses that far exceed settlement amounts in an actual enforcement action. Even though this is the factual take-away point, query whether FCPA and related scrutiny have simply turned into a boondoggle for many in FCPA Inc. and related industries. For instance, when scrutiny is prompted by board of director or senior executive conduct that raises the possibility of a culture of corruption within the organization, the "where else" question would seem like a legitimate law enforcement question. However, an FCPA practitioner (formerly an SEC FCPA enforcement attorney) stated as follows regarding the "where else" question:

> Q: What percentage of FCPA enforcement actions that you have been involved in have resulted in the 'where else' question being asked?
>
> A: In my time as a regulator at the Securities and Exchange Commission's Division of Enforcement and in private practice, the 'where else' question has been asked in virtually every single FCPA matter in which I have been involved. I have asked it and it has been asked of me.
>
> Q: Do you believe the 'where else' question was appropriate in these instances?
>
> A: In some instances it was entirely appropriate for the SEC, the DOJ, and other regulators to ask the 'where else' question. In others, however, the allegations did not support a 'where else' question and it appeared to be more of a fishing expedition and boiler plate question than a well-reasoned question under the facts. 'Where else' is a reasonable and appropriate question when the alleged misconduct appears to be systemic and/or the company under investigation appears to lack the controls necessary to prevent the payment of bribes to foreign government officials. It is not, however, an appropriate question where it is intended to force companies to conduct multi country internal investigations with little more than the uninformed hunch of a government official who has little or no experience in how businesses work around the world.

That the "where else" question is asked in the absence of any meaningful check or judicial oversight also raises a host of problematic policy issues. For instance, FCPA attorneys to whom the "where else" question is posed have little incentive to pushback as the question often leads to multi-year, multi-country billing bonanzas. As *Forbes* noted in an article titled "The Bribery Racket":

> A company that suspects bribery overseas hires a battery of lawyers, accountants and investigators who may then report any findings to Justice in hopes of some undefined leniency. More likely, the company pays out huge fines and then hires more lawyers as government-mandated compliance monitors, a job that can stretch into years of legal billing.[59]

The *Wall Street Journal* observed:

> [The FCPA] has become big business for the lawyers who delve into the operations of companies in response to an investigation by the Justice Department and the Securities and Exchange Commission – or to avoid one. The result is a mini-industry of investigators and white-collar criminal-law practices.[60]

Likewise, an article titled "Lawyers need to brake their bribe-case gravy train" observed:

> Lawyers need to pull the brake on their bribery-probe gravy train. [. . .] Wasteful scorched-earth legal tactics inflate costs, while potentially ruinous U.S. penalties make companies scared to skimp. Smarter lawyering could slow the runaway spending. Scrutiny under the FCPA typically throws multinationals into attorney-hiring overdrive. Having legal eagles delve into corporate innards helps a company look cooperative and thereby win leniency from the government. [. . .] Not only does the prospect of enormous fees encourage lawyers running an investigation to engage in overkill. A company's officers also don't want to be seen to cut corners or get in the attorneys' way. The usual healthy corporate tendency to police costs carefully doesn't apply.[61]

Relevant to pre-enforcement action professional fees and expenses, it was notable that the DOJ's FCPA Unit Chief called out the industry at an American Bar Association event and suggested that FCPA counsel often seeks to overdo it through a global search of operations for problematic conduct. Specifically, the FCPA Unit Chief discussed a case in which a company and its professional advisors came to a meeting with a global search plan and he said "no, no, no, that is not what I want."[62] Thereafter, the lawyers and other professional advisors in the room "looked unhappy," but the general counsel of the company was happy. Likewise, against the backdrop of eye-popping pre-enforcement action professional fees and expenses, the DOJ's Assistant Attorney General stated:

> All too often, criticism is leveled against the Justice Department for purportedly causing companies to spend years, and many millions of dollars, investigating potential violations. This is particularly true in the FCPA context where the need for international evidence can add to the expense and burden of an investigation. [. . .] There is no question that some cooperating companies spend large sums of money investigating potential misconduct

> and correcting internal controls issues that allowed the misconduct to occur. The decision to incur those costs, however, is one made by those companies, not a requirement of the department. [. . .] Although we expect internal investigations to be thorough, we do not expect companies to aimlessly boil the ocean. Indeed, there have been some instances in which companies have, in our view, conducted overly broad and needlessly costly investigations, in some cases delaying our ability to resolve matters in a timely fashion.[63]

For instance, in the previously mentioned Avon enforcement action, the resolution documents contained the notable statement that the company "without [DOJ] request or guidance" and "taking into account its own business interests, expended considerable resources on a company wide review" which "at times causes unintended delays in the progress of the [DOJ's] narrower investigations."[64] The government's observation about "boiling the ocean" in investigations became a sensitive topic because it implicitly called into question the decisions and motivations of FCPA Inc. participants and set off a war-of-words in the FCPA space. For instance, "defense attorneys . . . balked at the idea that they're spending too much time or money on investigations they're conducting in large part for the government's sake, saying they're not willfully adding unnecessary work to an FCPA probe."[65] The DOJ quickly shot back when asked about companies that "rack up massive legal bills and do massive worldwide investigations," saying "that's not us. That's the companies."[66] Regardless of who is most at fault for the extent of pre-enforcement action professional fees and expenses in a typical instance of scrutiny, the fact remains that such expenses are often the most serious financial consequence to a business organization under scrutiny.

## Settlement amounts

Failure to comply with the FCPA and related laws can obviously expose a business organization to a government enforcement action and resulting settlement demand. Because the focus of this section is the many other ripples of scrutiny and enforcement beyond settlement amounts in an actual enforcement action, this section does not discuss in detail the many legal and policy issues related to enforcement action settlement amounts.[67] However, to best understand the "three buckets" of financial exposure, it is useful to nevertheless highlight certain facts and figures concerning settlement amounts and Table 1.3 ranks the largest FCPA corporate settlement amounts.

*Table 1.3 Largest FCPA settlements*

| Company | Settlement amount | Year |
|---|---|---|
| Siemens | $800 million<br>($450 million DOJ)<br>($350 million SEC) | 2008 |
| Alstom | $772 million<br>($772 million DOJ) | 2014 |
| KBR/Halliburton | $579 million<br>($402 million DOJ)<br>($177 million SEC) | 2009 |
| Teva Pharma | $519 million<br>($283 million DOJ)<br>($236 million SEC) | 2016 |
| Telia | $483 million<br>($275 million DOJ)<br>($208 million SEC) | 2017 |
| Och-Ziff | $412 million<br>($213 million DOJ)<br>($199 million SEC) | 2016 |
| Total | $398 million<br>($245 million DOJ)<br>($153 million SEC) | 2013 |
| VimpelCom | $398 million<br>($230 million DOJ)<br>($168 million SEC) | 2016 |
| Alcoa | $384 million<br>($209 million DOJ)<br>($175 million SEC) | 2014 |
| Snamprogetti/ENI | $365 million<br>($240 million DOJ)<br>($125 million SEC) | 2010 |

The figures in Table 1.3 represent net FCPA settlement amounts after accounting for certain credits or deductions in a few enforcement actions involving foreign companies. For instance, in addition to the amounts listed above: Siemens also paid approximately $850 million in related German law enforcement actions,[68] Telia also paid approximately $483 million in related Swedish and Dutch law enforcement actions,[69] VimpelCom also paid approximately $398 million in a related Dutch law enforcement action[70] and Teva also paid approximately $22 million in a related Israeli law enforcement action.[71] In fact, several of the largest FCPA enforcement actions of all-time began, not with U.S. law enforcement investigations, but foreign law enforcement investigations.

For most of the FCPA's history, business organizations with exposure could sleep well at night after resolving a U.S. enforcement agency action. However, the landscape has changed and in the modern era U.S. enforcement actions are often just one consequence of scrutiny and enforcement. After resolving a corporate FCPA enforcement action the company may also become the subject of a foreign law enforcement investigation based on the same core conduct alleged in the FCPA enforcement action. After all, the U.S. action was based on allegations that the company, or someone on its behalf, made payments to a foreign official to obtain or retain business. Given the ease with which information now flows and the growing interest in cracking down on bribery and corruption, FCPA enforcement actions are frequently read around the world by foreign media, foreign-based non-governmental organizations, and even foreign governments themselves. Thus, it is not surprising that when the dust settles on corporate FCPA enforcement actions many remain interested in the conduct, including the foreign governments whose alleged "foreign officials" were implicated in the conduct at issue.

For instance, a few days after Ralph Lauren Corporation resolved an FCPA enforcement action based on the conduct of its subsidiary in Argentina, the head of Argentina's tax agency wrote to the U.S. Ambassador to Argentina stating that it was necessary for the Argentine government to have names and more detailed information about the alleged bribery to aid in a newly launched criminal investigation into the matter.[72] Likewise, tobacco companies Alliance One International Inc. and Universal Corporation resolved FCPA enforcement actions principally based on allegations of improper payments to Thai government officials to secure contracts with an alleged Thai government agency for the sale of tobacco leaf.[73] Soon thereafter, Thai law enforcement officials began an investigation of the conduct at issue.[74] Regarding law enforcement cooperation in international bribery schemes, the DOJ has stated:

> An international approach is being taken to combat an international criminal problem. We are sharing leads with our international law enforcement counterparts, and they are sharing them with us.
>
> It is safe to say that we are cooperating with foreign enforcement on foreign bribery cases more closely today that at any time in history.

In fact, one reason for the typically large pre-enforcement professional fees and expenses (as well as post-enforcement action professional fees and expenses highlighted next) is that business organizations under scrutiny often hire legal counsel and other professional advisors in multiple jurisdictions to interact with and report to the various law enforcement agencies investigating and prosecuting the underlying conduct.

Settlement amounts in an actual enforcement action will obviously be specific to the unique facts and circumstances at issue and it would be inaccurate to conclude from the above top 10 list of FCPA settlements that all corporate enforcement actions involve nine-figure settlement amounts. However, it is worth highlighting that settlement amounts have come a long way in a short amount of time. For example, in 2007 Baker Hughes resolved the largest FCPA enforcement action of all time by agreeing to pay a combined $44 million in DOJ and SEC enforcement actions.[75] According to the DOJ, the company made approximately $4.1 million in improper payments through an agent in connection with a "giant gas and oil field" in Kazakhstan. The DOJ's sentencing guidelines calculation noted that the "benefit received or to be received [from the alleged improper conduct was] approximately $19 million." The related SEC enforcement action against Baker Hughes was based on the same core conduct and the SEC's stated:

> Baker Hughes paid approximately $5.2 million to two agents while knowing that some or all of the money was intended to bribe government officials, specifically officials of State-owned companies, in Kazakhstan. . . . Baker Hughes engaged the agent and was awarded an oil services contract in the Karachaganak oil field in Kazakhstan that generated more than $219 million in gross revenues from 2001 through 2006.

In addition, the SEC stated:

- Baker Hughes authorized commission payments of nearly $5.3 million to an agent (who worked in Kazakhstan, Russia and Uzbekistan) under circumstances in which the company failed to determine whether such payments were, in part, to be funneled to government officials in violation of the FCPA;

- in Indonesia Baker Hughes paid certain freight forwarders to import equipment into Indonesia using a "door-to-door" process under circumstances in which the company failed to adequately assure itself that such payments were not being passed on, in part, to Indonesian customs officials;

- in Nigeria Baker Hughes authorized payments to certain customs brokers to facilitate the resolution of alleged customs deficiencies under circumstances in which the company failed to adequately assure itself that such payments were not being passed on, in part, to Nigerian customs officials; and

- in Angola Baker Hughes paid an agent more than $10.3 million in commissions under circumstances in which the company failed to adequately assure itself that such payments were not being passed on to employees of Sonangol, Angola's state-owned oil company, to obtain or retain business in Angola.

Since the then record-setting Baker Hughes enforcement action, comparatively minor enforcement actions, per the enforcement agencies' own allegations, have been resolved for larger settlement amounts. For instance, the Diebold enforcement action focused primarily on excessive travel and entertainment and government allegations that company subsidiaries provided various things of value (such as Las Vegas sightseeing, a dance show, a Grand Canyon tour, a Universal Studios tour and a Napa Valley tour) to alleged Chinese and Indonesian "foreign officials" at state-owned banks. As to the core conduct, the DOJ's sentencing guidelines calculation referenced a "value of benefit received [from the alleged improper conduct] of more than $7 million."

In other words, per the enforcement agencies' own allegations, the Diebold enforcement action involved significantly less egregious conduct than the Baker Hughes enforcement action. Yet the combined $48 million settlement amount in the Diebold was more than the record-setting $44 million Baker Hughes enforcement action just a short time ago. As FCPA practitioners have rightly observed: "an unmistakable characteristic of [recent] FCPA enforcement is that the market rate for resolving a corporate FCPA enforcement action [has] spiked precipitously."[76]

## Post-enforcement action professional fees and expenses

The negative financial consequences of scrutiny and enforcement continue even after enforcement action day because of post-enforcement action professional fees and expenses. Many corporate enforcement actions are resolved through non-prosecution agreements or deferred prosecution agreements (a resolution vehicle gaining acceptance in other countries as well) and a common clause in such agreements is a requirement that the company resolving the enforcement action report to the enforcement agencies during the typical 18 month to 3 year term of the agreement regarding, among other things, its implementation of a compliance program and its ongoing compliance efforts.[77] Such a requirement may seem simple and straightforward; however it often involves internal reviews, follow-up reviews and written reports and typically costs a business organization millions of dollars in additional professional fees and expenses. While post-enforcement action professional fees and expenses tend to be the smallest of the "three buckets" of financial exposure, such expenses can quickly mount even in garden-variety FCPA enforcement actions.

In addition to the above standard post-enforcement action compliance obligations, the enforcement agencies have also imposed "enhanced compliance obligations" on certain companies as a condition of settlement. For instance, healthcare company Johnson & Johnson (J&J) resolved an enforcement action focused on subsidiary conduct in Greece, Poland, and Romania. The enforcement action was resolved through a DPA and the government specifically noted: "J&J had a pre-existing compliance and ethics program that was effective and the majority of problematic operations globally resulted from insufficient implementation of the J&J compliance and ethics program in acquired companies."[78] The DPA contained the standard compliance obligations found in a typical FCPA DPA, but also included "enhanced compliance obligations" that J&J was required to abide by during the three-year term of the agreement. Even though the government stated that J&J, as part of the voluntary disclosure and cooperation process, "conducted an extensive, global review of all of its operations to determine if there were problems elsewhere," the "enhanced compliance obligations" nevertheless required J&J to "conduct risk assessments of markets where [the company] has government customers and/or other anticorruption compliance risks on a staggered, periodic basis."

In what seemed like an FCPA Inc. full employment act, the government also required J&J to "identify no less than five operating companies that are high risk for corruption because of their sector and location and [. . .] conduct FCPA audits of those operating companies at least once every three years." As stated in the DPA, "FCPA audits of other operating companies that pose corruption risk shall occur no less than once every five years" and "each FCPA audit should include" the following:

> (i) on-site visits by an audit team comprised of qualified auditors who have received FCPA and anticorruption training; (ii) where appropriate, participation in the on-site visits by personnel from the compliance and legal functions; (iii) review of a statistically representative sample appropriately adjusted for the risks of the market, of contracts with and payments to individual health care providers; (iv) creation of action plans resulting from issues identified during audits; and (v) where appropriate, feasible, and permissible under local law, review of the books and records of distributors which, in the view of the audit team, may present corruption risk.

From a policy perspective, were the "enhanced compliance obligations" truly necessary given the government's conclusion that J&J already had generally "effective" compliance policies and procedures and given that the company, prior to resolving the enforcement action, already "conducted an extensive, global review of all of its operations to determine if there were problems elsewhere"? Or were these "enhanced compliance obligations" an example of a business organization being required by the government to engage in fishing expeditions when the company already went fishing just for the sake of going fishing again? If so, the "enhanced compliance obligations" represented a boundless and unconstrained government-required transfer of shareholder wealth to FCPA Inc. Such fishing expeditions are of course lucrative for FCPA Inc. and hence one reason why few in the industry have raised concerns about "enhanced compliance obligations" or other post-enforcement action compliance requirements.

In addition to standard post-enforcement action compliance requirements or "enhanced compliance obligations," certain companies have also been required to engage an independent compliance monitor as a condition of settlement. As noted in the FCPA Guidance, "a monitor is an independent third party who assesses and monitors a company's adherence to the compliance requirements of an agreement that was designed to reduce the risk of recurrence of the company's misconduct." The term monitor is a bit misleading as it suggests a single person. The reality is that a monitor, while a single person, is more like the conductor of a large orchestra and a monitorship can become an expensive and distracting requirement of resolving an enforcement action. FCPA practitioners have observed:

> Few penalties imposed on a corporate criminal offender cause as much consternation as do compliance monitors. After the late-night crisis management meetings, after the invasive and expensive internal investigation,

> after the shakeup of senior managers, and after the protracted negotiations with federal authorities, companies just want to get back to business. They want to sell their goods and services, be profitable, invest, and grow. In short, they want to move on. Fundamentally, the corporate compliance monitor stands in the way of forgetting the past and going back to 'business as usual' – at least when it comes to obeying the law. The monitor's purpose is to see that the company follows applicable laws and regulations going forward and institutes the proper policies and procedures to help ensure compliance. Corporations will never welcome this "tail" to their criminal prosecutions. Monitorships inevitably involve significant expenditures of funds and time.[79]

As stated in FCPA Guidance, the enforcement agencies consider the following factors when determining whether a compliance monitor is an appropriate requirement of a corporate enforcement action: seriousness of the offense; duration of the misconduct; pervasiveness of the misconduct, including whether the conduct cuts across geographic and/or product lines; nature and size of the company; quality of the company's compliance program at the time of the misconduct; and subsequent remediation efforts.

Based on these factors, it was not surprising that Siemens (as well as certain other companies on the previously highlighted top ten FCPA settlement list) was required to engage a compliance monitor when resolving its enforcement action. The government's filing upon determining that Siemens satisfied its post-enforcement action obligations provided insight into the extent of the monitor's work and stated:

> In accordance with the plea agreement, the Monitor conducted an initial review and three subsequent reviews of Siemens's anti-corruption compliance program, and documented the Monitor's findings and recommendations in four annual reports [. . .]. Over the course of those four years, the Monitor conducted on-site or remote reviews of Siemens' activities in 20 countries; conducted limited or issue-specific reviews in or relating to an additional 19 countries; reviewed over 51,000 documents totaling more than 973,000 pages in 11 languages; conducted interviews of or meetings with over 2,300 Siemens employees; observed over 180 regularly scheduled company events; and spent the equivalent of over 3,000 auditor days conducting financial studies and testing.[80]

Siemens did not disclose its post-enforcement action professional fees and expenses, including its monitor costs, but one can safely assume that such fees and expenses were in the hundreds of millions of dollars and in addition to: (i) the approximate $1 billion dollars the company spent in pre-enforcement action professional fees and expenses; (ii) the $800 million the company paid to resolve the FCPA enforcement action; and (iii) the $850 million the company paid to resolve the related German enforcement action.

Even in less high-profile enforcement actions monitor costs can reach into the millions of dollars. For instance, oil and gas services company Willbros Group agreed to pay approximately $32 million to resolve an enforcement action and thereafter disclosed monitor expenses of approximately $10 million.[81] Likewise, Faro Technologies agreed to pay approximately $3 million to resolve an enforcement action and thereafter disclosed monitor expenses of approximately $2 million.[82]

Regardless of which of the "three buckets" the money falls into, the take-away point from this section is that scrutiny and enforcement under the FCPA and related laws typically result in wide-ranging negative financial consequences for a business organization, and as depicted in the below visual, settlement amounts in an actual enforcement action are often just the tip of the iceberg in terms of the company's overall financial exposure.

The "three buckets" of financial exposure highlighted above were all related to investigating conduct arising under the FCPA and related laws, responding to law enforcement inquiries, resolving actual enforcement actions, and abiding by post-enforcement action compliance obligations and reporting requirements. However, as next discussed there are also numerous other "ripples" of scrutiny and enforcement that are not as directly tied to law enforcement investigations and enforcement.

## Negative business effects of scrutiny and enforcement

To review, Chapter 1 has thus far focused on why a diverse group of professionals need skills to spot risk under the FCPA and related laws. In addition to the reasons highlighted above, professionals also need skills to spot risk because the failure to do so can have a variety of negative business effects. Legal scrutiny represents uncertainty and, as depicted in the below visual, is like a cloud hanging over a business organization. Because FCPA scrutiny concerns bribery and possible criminal sanctions, the cloud hanging over the organization is black or at the very least gray.

Combine this with the fact that scrutiny tends to last, on average approximately four years with longer periods possible, and it is not surprising that scrutiny often results in numerous other "ripples" for a business organization beyond those already highlighted.[83] As rightly noted by an FCPA commentator: "companies [under FCPA scrutiny] get stuck in FCPA limbo. [. . .] The threat of FCPA enforcement [. . .] casts a long shadow. It darkens the future for management, shareholders, lenders, customers, and suppliers."[84] As discussed in this section, these "ripples" can have a negative impact on a company's business operations and strategy ranging from market capitalization, credit ratings, merger and acquisition activity, and impeding or distracting a company from achieving other business objectives. Moreover, with increasing frequency scrutiny and enforcement is being used "offensively" by others to achieve a business objective or to further advance a litigating position.

It is particularly important for compliance professionals to understand and appreciate these numerous other "ripples" because their aggregate impact often exceeds even the "three buckets" of financial exposure previously highlighted. Moreover, compliance professionals often find themselves asking corporate management for additional resources for the compliance function. Surely, progress will be made when corporate management is warned that failure to devote sufficient resources to compliance with the FCPA and related laws can expose the organization to an actual law enforcement action and its attendant collateral effects.. Surely, progress will be made when corporate management is shown the previously highlighted top 10 list of FCPA settlements. Query, however, whether compliance professionals can best obtain the desired resources needed for compliance by highlighting the many negative business effects of scrutiny and enforcement in language that is most likely to resonate with corporate management such stock price, cost of capital, lost or delayed business opportunities, and perhaps even individual liability in related civil litigation. In other words, scrutiny and enforcement is not just a legal issue, but a business issue as well that needs to be on the radar screen of various professionals who can assist in risk management and who should view the importance of compliance holistically and not merely through the narrow lens of actual enforcement actions. It is these numerous other "ripples" of scrutiny and enforcement that are perhaps the most important reason why a diverse group of professionals need skills to spot risk and various case studies demonstrate this important, yet often overlooked, concept.

## Market capitalization

Market capitalization is an important data point for investors and an important metric by which business manager performance is judged and is calculated by multiplying a company's outstanding shares by the current market price of one share. Because FCPA or related scrutiny or enforcement can impact a company's share price, a company's market capitalization is likewise impacted, as highlighted by the following examples.

Wal-Mart's scrutiny, although disclosed in an SEC filing months earlier, escalated when the *New York Times* published a front-page article concerning alleged conduct in Mexico. The market reacted swiftly to the *Times* article and the first trading day after the *Times* article the stock dropped 4.7% and continued a downward trend for several days erasing approximately $20 billion in shareholder value). Shares of SciClone Pharmaceuticals Inc., a U.S.-based, China-focused specialty pharmaceutical company, plunged approximately 40% and closed down approximately 32% from its previous trading day. Such a dramatic decline in stock price is normally associated with a Chief

Executive Officer resigning, a declaration of bankruptcy, or other crisis-like events. However, the decline in SciClone's stock price was due to the following disclosure made by the company.

> SciClone was contacted by the SEC and advised that the SEC has initiated a formal, non-public investigation of SciClone. In connection with this investigation, the SEC issued a subpoena to SciClone requesting a variety of documents and other information. The subpoena requests documents relating to a range of matters including interactions with regulators and government-owned entities in China, activities relating to sales in China and documents relating to certain company financial and other disclosures. The Company [also] received a letter from the DOJ indicating that the DOJ was investigating FCPA issues in the pharmaceutical industry generally, and had received information about the Company's practices suggesting possible violations.[85]

Likewise, the share price of Cognizant Technology Solutions dropped approximately 13% on the day the company made the following disclosure (the same day the company also disclosed that its President has resigned):

> The Company is conducting an internal investigation into whether certain payments relating to facilities in India were made improperly and in possible violation of the U.S. Foreign Corrupt Practices Act and other applicable laws. The investigation is being conducted under the oversight of the Audit Committee, with the assistance of outside counsel, and is currently focused on a small number of Company-owned facilities. The Company has voluntarily notified the United States Department of Justice (the "DOJ") and United States Securities and Exchange Commission (the "SEC") and is cooperating fully with both agencies.[86]

Similarly, the share price of World Acceptance Corp., a small consumer finance company operating in the U.S. and Mexico, fell approximately 12% after the company made the following disclosure (the same day the company also disclosed that it was unable to file its annual report):

> The Company is conducting an internal investigation of its operations in Mexico, focusing on the legality under the U.S. Foreign Corrupt Practices Act and certain local laws of certain payments related to loans, the maintenance of the Company's books and records associated with such payments, and the treatment of compensation matters for certain employees.[87]

A company's stock price, and thus its market capitalization, can also be negatively impacted by institutional investor liquidations and investment analyst downgrades. As to the former, mutual fund Ohio National Fund disclosed the following regarding its investment in Petrofac Ltd (a U.K.-based oil and gas company with shares registered with the SEC and thus subject to the FCPA):

> Petrofac Limited – Shares of U.K. based oilfield services firm Petrofac Limited declined sharply after the U.K.'s Serious Fraud Office ("SFO") launched an investigation into bribery allegations related to the firm's past relationship with controversial Monaco-based consultancy Unaoil. While we had been constructive on the stock given its healthy pipeline of outstanding bids, strategic refocus on core assets, and prudent balance sheet deleveraging, the escalating fraud investigation seems to us a thesis changer. Over the past three years, nearly all of the SFO's investigations have led to charges being filed. Of particular concern, the executives currently running Petrofac Limited also ran the company when the alleged improprieties occurred. Any legal action against these individuals could materially impact Petrofac Limited's ability to win new business, without which the company's financial situation is tenuous. A change in circumstances requires a reassessment of the new reality, and we decided to liquidate our stake in Petrofac Limited given the rising risk profile.[88]

Regarding investment analyst opinions, the shares of technology company NCR Corp. fell approximately 8% after an investment analyst downgraded the company's stock to neutral from outperform because of the company's FCPA scrutiny. Among the concerns noted in the analyst's report were: "a multi-quarter investigation; potential fines and penalties from the single millions to tens of million; much of the company's share gains over the last two years came in emerging markets and such growth may be at risk if an FCPA investigation restricts current business practices; and that companies uninhibited by the FCPA, such as China-based competitors, could gain market share."[89]

Although investor reaction to FCPA related scrutiny and enforcement is not always as dramatic as the above examples, and even though the FCPA-induced stock price dips in the above examples were rather short lived as investors moved beyond the disclosures to focus more on long-term financial fundamentals, the take-away point here is that one negative business effect of scrutiny and enforcement is often a hit to the company's market capitalization.

## Credit ratings

A company's credit rating matters for a number of reasons. For instance, a company with a lower credit rating may be faced with a smaller pool of potential investors and thus may have to offer those investors a higher interest rate. Likewise, a company's credit rating will determine the interest rate at which the company can borrow money and certain institutional investors may be barred from owning non-investment grade bonds. Credit ratings can be impacted by FCPA and related scrutiny and enforcement and as stated by ratings agency Moody, "the wide range of potential outcomes and timing in [FCPA cases] can create substantial short-to-medium term uncertainty for credit investors, and we often view this uncertainty as credit negative."[90]

Likewise, a report titled "U.S. Foreign Corrupt Practices Act – No Minor Matter" by Fitch Ratings highlighted the variety of negative effects that can arise from scrutiny and enforcement.[91] The report noted that scrutiny can have ratings implications for companies with modest free cash flow and/or liquidity constraints. The report further noted that scrutiny can last for years and stated:

> In the interim, corporate credit profiles, liquidity, and ratings may weaken. The fine that could be easily paid with cash on hand today might not be readily payable years down the road if a company's credit profile has weakened and liquidity becomes constrained.

The Fitch report also highlighted the significant amount of pre-enforcement action professional fees and expenses typically incurred by companies under scrutiny and highlighted the previously mentioned Avon matter in which the company's bond rating was downgraded owing to "expenses related to the ongoing investigation under the FCPA."[92]

Although many FCPA settlements involve "large investment grade corporations whose substantial cash balances easily afford them the ability to absorb the payments with no or minimal increases in leverage," the Fitch report noted that "there have also been [FCPA] violations by non-investment grade companies." For instance, Willbros Group Inc. resolved a $32 million enforcement action and the report noted that the company's scrutiny required "several amendments on its bank credit facility" which was reduced from $150 million to $100 million.

## Mergers and acquisitions

In addition to market capitalization and credit ratings, scrutiny and enforcement can also negatively impact merger or acquisition activity. Such negative effects range from terminating planned merger or acquisition activity, to restructuring the terms and conditions of the planned transaction, to reducing the expected financial benefits of the transaction.

## Termination

In announcing a planned acquisition of Titan Corporation, the CEO of aerospace company Lockheed Martin Corp. stated:

> Titan provides additional presence within the U.S. Government customer base and expands our competencies. Titan is an excellent fit with Lockheed Martin, and its acquisition is consistent with our disciplined growth and cash deployment strategies. Titan's outstanding record of sales growth and the quality of its workforce made this transaction very attractive to us. This workforce, together with our highly skilled people, allows us to provide more cost effective and robust solutions to customers of both companies.[93]

Soon thereafter however, Lockheed announced that it had "learned of allegations that improper payments were made, or items of value were provided, by consultants for Titan Corporation or its subsidiaries to foreign officials." Lockheed stated:

> The allegations were identified as part of a review conducted with Titan of payments to Titan's international consultants in connection with the proposed acquisition of Titan. The alleged payments and provision of items of value, if true, raise questions concerning whether there has been a violation of the FCPA. [. . .] The review is ongoing. Titan is cooperating with this effort, as well as conducting its own review. Lockheed Martin and Titan have met with the SEC and the DOJ to discuss the allegations of improper payments. [. . .] Closing of the Titan transaction is subject to approval of Titan's stockholders, the absence of any material adverse change in Titan and other conditions set forth in the merger agreement. [. . .] Lockheed Martin will need to determine whether the conditions to the merger have been satisfied.[94]

Titan's scrutiny, which Lockheed could have inherited upon completion of the merger, resulted in a delay of the shareholder vote to approve the merger as well as an amended merger agreement extending the time period for the merger to occur. Ultimately, Titan's unresolved scrutiny caused Lockheed to abandon the merger and Lockheed stated:

> Under the terms of the amended merger agreement, either party could terminate the merger agreement if Titan either (i) had not obtained written confirmation from the DOJ that the investigation of alleged FCPA violations was resolved as to Titan and the Department did not intend to pursue any claims against Titan; or (ii) Titan had not entered into a plea agreement [by a certain date] ... Titan did not satisfy either requirement. [...] The corporation declined Titan's request for a further extension.[95]

In announcing termination of the merger, Lockheed said that the company "made every possible effort to make this happen, but it just reached a point where we didn't want the uncertainty surrounding this to continue indefinitely."[96] Termination of the merger had several adverse consequences for Titan. In addition to losing an acquirer, news of the merger termination caused Titan's shares to fall by approximately 20% and investment analysts downgraded the company's stock. Titan's scrutiny of course did not disappear and the company pleaded guilty to FCPA charges for, among other things, making more than $2 million in payments through an agent to the election campaign of Benin's then-incumbent President. In resolving its FCPA scrutiny, Titan agreed to pay approximately $28 million – at the time the largest FCPA settlement in history. [97]

Not all instances of FCPA scrutiny have as severe an impact on merger activity as in the Lockheed–Titan example. However, as demonstrated by the below examples, scrutiny and enforcement can also result in restructuring the terms and conditions of planned transactions and reduce the expected financial benefits of the transaction.

## Restructuring

Consider the following circumstances regarding diagnostic company Alere Inc. and what happened when it disclosed an SEC subpoena inquiring about its foreign business practices.[98] Thereafter, the company announced that it would be acquired by Abbott in a $5.8 billion transaction. However, Alere's troubles mounted as the company announced that it would be unable to timely file its annual report because it was "continuing to conduct an analysis of certain aspects of the timing of revenue recognition, more specifically, revenue cutoff, in

Africa and China." The company also disclosed at the same time that it "received a grand jury subpoena from the United States Department of Justice requiring the production of documents relating to, among other things, sales practices and dealings with third parties (including distributors and foreign governmental officials) in Africa, Asia and Latin America and other matters related to the U.S. Foreign Corrupt Practices Act." Alere's FCPA and related scrutiny complicated the planned acquisition by Abbott and Alere disclosed:

> In recent discussions between the parties, Abbott informed Alere that it has serious concerns about, among other things, the accuracy of various representations, warranties and covenants made by Alere in the parties' merger agreement. Abbott indicated that these concerns relate to the delay in filing the [annual report] and governmental investigations previously announced by Alere. Abbott has requested information from Alere about these and other matters, citing contractual rights to receive information under the merger agreement. In the initial meeting in which Abbott expressed its concerns to Alere, as part of a discussion about potential paths forward, Abbott requested that Alere agree to terminate the merger agreement in return for a payment by Abbott to Alere in the range of between $30 and $50 million in respect of Alere's transaction expenses. Alere's Board of Directors promptly rejected that request.[99]

Alere's FCPA and related scrutiny, and whether it represented a "material adverse change" in the company's business operations giving Abbott the potential right to terminate the planned acquisition, soon became the focus of separate civil litigation requiring Alere to engage additional counsel. In the end, Alere and Abbott agreed to complete the transaction; however the deal closed for $5.3 billion and not the originally contemplated $5.8 billion price. Alere's scrutiny of course did not disappear and it ultimately resolved a $13 million enforcement action (the FCPA portion of the settlement was approximately $3.8 million).[100]

A planned merger involving engineering companies PBSJ Corp. and WS Atkins also provides an instructive case study for how scrutiny can negatively impact the terms and conditions of a transaction. Pre-merger, PBSJ disclosed scrutiny in connection with certain projects undertaken by its subsidiary.[101] A few months later, PBSJ disclosed that its "Audit Committee completed the internal investigation [and] the results of that investigation suggest that FCPA violations may have occurred." Shortly thereafter, PBSJ announced that it entered into a definitive merger agreement in which WS Atkins planned to acquire

PBSJ in an all-cash transaction. Proxy materials filed by PBSJ in connection with the merger provided an informative insight into how its scrutiny impacted the terms and conditions by which PBSJ would attempt to sell itself.

Among other things, the proxy materials disclosed how interested purchasers of PBSJ: held meetings with PBSJ's outside counsel and its in-house counsel to discuss the investigation; requested the opportunity to meet with DOJ representatives regarding the investigation; and requested access to attorney-client privileged documents regarding the investigation.[102] In the end, PBSJ's board approved a merger agreement with Atkins even though PBSJ had received a higher offer from another company. However, the higher offer sought more stringent closing conditions concerning PBSJ's scrutiny and in approving Atkin's bid the proxy materials stated:

> Positive factors considered by the [PBSJ] board of directors included: [. . .] the terms of the merger agreement and the related agreements, including: the limited number and nature of the conditions to Atkins' obligation to consummate the merger, including its willingness not to impose special conditions related to our previously disclosed FCPA investigation beyond those developments that would independently constitute a material adverse effect.[103]

## Reduced financial benefits

Scrutiny and enforcement under the FCPA and related laws can also reduce the financial benefits expected from a merger by imposing significant post-closing expenses on the acquiring company for the target company's pre-closing scrutiny. For instance, facilities services company ABM Industries Inc. disclosed:

> [The] Company [has] begun an internal investigation into matters relating to compliance with the FCPA and the Company's internal policies in connection with services provided by a foreign entity affiliated with a Linc joint venture partner. Such services commenced prior to the Company's acquisition of Linc. As a result of the investigation, the Company has caused Linc to terminate its association with the arrangement. The Company [has] contacted the DOJ and the SEC to voluntarily disclose the results of its internal investigation to date. The Company cannot reasonably estimate the potential liability, if any, related to these matters.[104]

ABM's scrutiny thus did not involve anything it did but was based on a foreign entity affiliated with a joint venture partner of a company ABM acquired. The value of the merger was approximately $300 million and it was already reduced by the acquired company's scrutiny as ABM disclosed approximately $3.5 million in pre-enforcement action professional fees and expenses.[105] Factoring in ABM's potential exposure based on an actual enforcement action, 5% of the merger price could easily evaporate owing to the acquired company's FCPA issue.

In addition, post-enforcement action professional fees and expenses can further reduce the expected financial benefits of a merger. For instance, Alliance One International resolved an enforcement action by agreeing to pay $19.5 million in combined fines and penalties.[106] The entire enforcement action was based on the pre-merger conduct of acquired entities and pursuant to the resolution documents Alliance One was required to engage a compliance monitor for three years – a requirement that cost the company over $10 million in post-enforcement action monitoring costs.

The above examples of how scrutiny and enforcement can negatively impact merger and acquisition activity provide lessons for both an acquiring company and a target company. For an acquiring company, FCPA related due diligence of a target company should be part of the merger due diligence protocol so that potential issues can be learned in advance of closing. For a future target company, implementing the compliance policies and procedures discussed throughout this book can increase the value of the company and its attractiveness to a potential acquiring company. As further highlighted in Chapter 8, periodic assessment and continuous improvement are a component of compliance best practices, particularly when a company evolves, and one of the most dramatic ways a company can evolve – in terms of markets, products, services and personnel including third parties – is through merger and acquisition activity.

## Lost or delayed business opportunities

In addition to impacting market capitalization and credit ratings and having a wide range of negative effects on merger and acquisition activity, another "ripple" of FCPA and related scrutiny and enforcement is lost or delayed business opportunities.

For instance, Swiss logistics company Panalpina was under scrutiny for business conduct in Nigeria and in the midst of this scrutiny, during the company's annual meeting, a shareholder demanded that someone "step up and take responsibility" for the company's poor performance. In response, Panalpina's CEO stated, among other things, that "it is not easy being under investigation for two years, and [the FCPA investigation] is not making the situation any easier."[107] The company's Chief Operating Officer added:

> You can say the whole FCPA and Nigeria situation reflects badly on the management, but the fact is that as long as we are still involved in the investigation we will continue to lose market share, because our customers have internal regulations which prevent them from doing business with companies which are under investigation by the DOJ. As soon as this investigation is over, we will win some of this business back. Customers have told us "as soon as you have settled the FCPA, we will do business with you again."

While difficult to quantify, Panalpina's lost business opportunities during its scrutiny likely exceeded the $82 million the company paid to resolve its scrutiny in an actual enforcement action.[108] More dramatically, clients of hedge fund Och-Ziff withdrew $2.5 billion in assets from the firm in *just the month after* it resolved a $412 million enforcement action in connection with certain transactions in Africa countries.[109] In addition, the enforcement action negatively impacted Och-Ziff's ability to raise additional capital as it disclosed:

> Prior to the settlements, many of our funds raised capital relying on the exemption from registration provided by Rule 506 of Regulation D under the Securities Act ("Rule 506") in connection with a securities offering structured as a private placement. As a consequence of the settlements, many of our funds are currently disqualified from raising capital using Rule 506 offerings. This could negatively affect our ability to raise capital for these funds, and our ability to offer and sell fund interests to certain investors in certain U.S. states may be impaired. The inability of many of our funds to raise capital in Rule 506 offerings may also result in additional expenses. The potential negative impact of the FCPA settlements on our ability to raise or retain capital for our funds could adversely affect our business, financial condition or results of operations.[110]

Scrutiny under the FCPA and related laws often cause business organizations to become excessively risk averse and back away from potential deals because of the *potential* implications of bribery laws. For instance, in the immediate aftermath of JPMorgan's scrutiny concerning its internship and hiring practices in China (namely the allegation that the company hired the children of influential alleged Chinese officials), the company withdrew from several lucrative financial deals. The *Wall Street Journal* reported that JPMorgan withdrew "from underwriting midtier lender China Everbright Bank Co.'s $2 billion initial public offering in Hong Kong" because in the aftermath of the company's scrutiny "deals have faced intense scrutiny from the U.S. bank's compliance division."[111] Likewise, it was reported that JPMorgan "pulled out of a $1 billion initial public offering of a Chinese chemical company and won't seek a role in the IPO of a Chinese state-owned train maker, as the bank walks away from deals that could come under scrutiny from U.S. investigators probing its hiring practices in China." Investment bank IPO fees are typically 1.5–3% of the deal's size and JPMorgan's risk aversion, coupled with its pre-enforcement action professional fees and expenses, likely far exceeded the $203 million the company ultimately paid in the actual enforcement action regarding its internship and hiring practices.[112]

FCPA and related scrutiny can also crimp company growth and make general business conditions more difficult. According to the *Wall Street Journal*, Wal-Mart's growth plans in India stalled and one of "biggest reasons [was] a compliance crackdown" at the company following its scrutiny.[113] Among other things, the article noted that "developing and operating stores in India is complicated, even for locals" because "dozens of permits and licenses are required from various agencies down to the municipal level" and in response to its scrutiny Wal-Mart "enlisted a phalanx of lawyers from a U.S. firm to develop compliance procedures and train employees in India" and that "the company also has begun requiring its Indian landlords to attest that they haven't greased any government palms." In short, "running people through those hoops" slowed Wal-Mart's expansion plans in India.

Enforcement of the FCPA and related laws may also cause a company to exit a foreign country altogether.[114] For instance, Ralph Lauren resolved an enforcement action based on alleged conduct in Argentina and thereafter "ceased retail operations" in the country. Bio-Rad Laboratories resolved an enforcement actions based in part on alleged conduct in Vietnam and thereafter "closed its Vietnam office." Construction and drilling company Layne Christensen resolved an enforcement action based on alleged conduct in a variety of African countries and thereafter its Minerals Services division exited Africa. General Cable resolved an enforcement action based in part on alleged conduct in Thailand and during its scrutiny completed the sale of its Thai operations. To state the obvious, winding down operations in a foreign country and exiting the country altogether is not a time-free or cost-free exercise. In several of these examples, the DOJ/SEC seemingly viewed the country exits as a good thing and specifically mentioned them in the resolution documents as a "remedial measure." Yet from a policy standpoint, are such "country exits" in the aftermath of scrutiny or enforcement necessarily a good thing? Is a foreign country (including its government and citizens) in a better position when an otherwise ethically sound company (notwithstanding it resolving an enforcement action based on rather isolated conduct) leaves a country? Who takes that company's place and what if that company has less of a commitment to compliance and ethics?

## Management issues

Scrutiny can also be distracting for company management forced to focus on FCPA issues instead of other core business issues. For instance, Wal-Mart disclosed that its scrutiny "may require the involvement of certain members of the Company's senior management that could impinge on the time they have available to devote to other matters relating to the business."[115] Another instructive example involved gas detection company RAE Systems which resolved a $3 million enforcement action concerning alleged improper payments to Chinese officials made by employees of two joint ventures majority owned and controlled by RAE Systems.[116] In a subsequent revealing interview, the CFO at the time of the investigation and enforcement action discussed how the company's scrutiny came to derail his other job duties and caused him to have a falling out with the company's CEO.

Executive compensation is another "ripple" of scrutiny and enforcement that may uniquely impact corporate management. For instance, security systems company Diebold Inc. disclosed:

> While conducting due diligence in connection with a potential acquisition in Russia, Diebold identified certain transactions and payments by its subsidiary in Russia [. . .] that potentially implicate the FCPA, particularly the books and records provisions of the FCPA. While the company's current assessment indicates that the transactions and payments in question do not materially impact or alter the company's financial statements, the company continues to collect information and is conducting an internal review of its global FCPA compliance.[117]

Thereafter, Diebold's Compensation Committee reduced the cash bonus of the company's President and CEO, concluding that "given the CEO's ultimate responsibility for the oversight of the company, as a result of the impact to the company of the global FCPA investigation it was appropriate that [his] cash bonus be reduced."[118]

The negative business effects of scrutiny and enforcement have become so pronounced that FCPA and related risks are often included among the generic risks (such as loss of key personnel, global economic conditions, and currency fluctuations) companies disclose to investors as required in most SEC filings. The annual report of manufacturer Gardner Denver Inc. provides a representative example in that the company disclosed, among other risk factors:

> The risk of non-compliance with U.S. and foreign laws and regulations applicable to our international operations could have a significant impact on our results of operations, financial condition or strategic objectives. Our global operations subject us to regulation by U.S. federal and state laws and multiple foreign laws, regulations and policies, which could result in conflicting legal requirements. These laws and regulations are complex, change frequently, have tended to become more stringent over time and increase our cost of doing business. These laws and regulations include [. . .] anti-corruption and bribery laws such as the FCPA . . . and local laws prohibiting corrupt payments to government officials. We are subject to the risk that we, our employees, our affiliated entities, contractors, agents or their respective officers, directors, employees and agents may take actions determined to be in violation of any of these laws, particularly as we expand our operations geographically through organic growth and acquisitions. An actual or alleged violation could result in substantial fines, sanctions, civil or criminal penalties, debarment from government contracts, curtailment of operations in certain jurisdictions, competitive or reputational harm, litigation or regulatory action and other consequences that might adversely affect our results of operations, financial condition or strategic objectives.[119]

As the above examples demonstrate, FCPA and related scrutiny and enforcement often result in numerous "ripples" beyond an actual enforcement action. It is particularly important for compliance professionals to understand and appreciate these other "ripples" because their aggregate impact often exceeds even the "three buckets" of financial exposure previously discussed. Moreover, compliance professionals often find themselves asking corporate management for additional resources and success is most likely obtained by using the above concepts that resonate with corporate management. In short, the numerous other "ripples" of scrutiny and enforcement are perhaps the most important reason why a diverse group of professionals need skills to spot risk.

As if the numerous issues already discussed in this chapter were not enough, a final reason a diverse group of professionals need skills to spot risk is because failure to do so can also exposure a business organization, as well as corporate management, to FCPA-related civil litigation as well as "offensive" uses of the FCPA to achieve a business objective or to further advance a litigating position.

## FCPA-related civil litigation

Although courts have held that the FCPA does not provide a private right of action (i.e. only the DOJ or SEC can bring actual FCPA enforcement actions), plaintiffs' lawyers representing shareholders often target directors and executive officers of companies subject to scrutiny or enforcement with civil suits representing yet another "ripple" of scrutiny and enforcement. Two types of shareholder lawsuits often follow scrutiny or enforcement: derivative claims alleging director and officer breach of fiduciary duty and securities fraud class action claims. These lawsuits often follow a predictable pattern in that in the days and weeks following a business organization resolving an enforcement action or merely being the subject of scrutiny plaintiffs' firms representing shareholders launch purported investigations and lawsuits often begin to rain down on the company, its board of directors, or executive officers.

For instance, a feeding frenzy soon followed SciClone Pharmaceuticals' previously highlighted stock price drop upon disclosing scrutiny. The same day, four separate plaintiffs' firms announced investigations of SciClone on behalf of shareholders to determine whether securities laws were violated.[120] The next day, four additional plaintiff's firm announced similar investigations, the following days saw numerous other investigations, and within three days of the disclosure the first securities class action lawsuit was filed. A similar feeding frenzy also followed Wal-Mart's previously highlighted stock price drop after the *New York Times* front-page article regarding alleged conduct in Mexico. Within 48 hours, several plaintiffs' firms announced investigations on behalf of shareholders and within 10 days shareholder civil suits tracking the *Times* article began to pour in against the company and its directors and executive officers.[121] Approximately one month after the *Times* article, Wal-Mart disclosed:

> The Company is a defendant in several recently-filed lawsuits in which the complaints closely track the allegations set forth in a news story that appeared in the *New York Times* [. . .]. One of these is a securities lawsuit [. . .] in which the plaintiff alleges various violations of the [FCPA] . . . and asserts violations of [the securities laws] relating to certain prior disclosures of the Company. [. . .] In addition, eleven derivative complaints were filed [. . .] also tracking the allegations of the *Times* story, and naming various current and former officers and directors as additional defendants. The plaintiffs in the derivative suits [. . .] allege, among other things, that the defendants who are or were directors or officers of the Company breached their fiduciary duties in connection with oversight of FCPA compliance.[122]

In terms of derivative actions, the following context is important. The internal affairs of a corporation, such as the responsibilities of corporate directors and the rights of shareholders, are governed by state law. State law, including most prominently Delaware law, provides directors with broad discretion to manage the corporation subject to their fiduciary duties to the corporation and its shareholders. A director's fiduciary duties include the duty of care and the duty of loyalty including its subsidiary component the duty of good faith. In a notable case in the corporate director context, a court observed:

> The sentinel asleep at his post contributes nothing to the enterprise he is charged to protect [. . .] Shareholders have a right to expect that directors will exercise reasonable supervision and control over the policies and practices of a corporation. The institutional integrity of a corporation depends upon the proper discharge by directors of those duties.[123]

A corporate director's duty of good faith has evolved over time to include an obligation to attempt in good faith to assure that an adequate corporate information and reporting system exists. In the notable *Caremark* decision by the influential Delaware Court of Chancery, the court held that a director's failure to do so, in certain circumstances, may give rise to individual director liability for breach of fiduciary duty. In *Stone v. Ritter*, the Delaware Supreme Court provided the following necessary conditions for director oversight liability under the so-called *Caremark* standard: (i) a director utterly failed to implement any reporting or information system or controls; or (ii) having implemented such systems or controls, a director failed to monitor or oversee the corporation's operations.[124] The court held that both situations require a showing that a director knew that they were not discharging their fiduciary obligations and courts have widely recognized that a director's good faith exercise of oversight responsibility may not necessarily prevent employees from violating criminal laws or from causing the corporation to incur significant financial liability or both.

Derivative claims in the FCPA context are often based one or more of the following alleged actions or failures of directors and/or officers:

- participation in, concealment of, or failure to prevent the FCPA violations;
- preparation, review, and/or signing of false and misleading public statements;
- failure to comply with the company's code of business conduct or similar policy requiring FCPA compliance;
- failure to require the company to implement internal controls in compliance with the FCPA's antibribery provisions or books, records, and internal accounting provisions;
- failure to monitor the company's compliance with, or implement mechanisms for enforcement of, the company's anti-corruption policies and procedures;
- failure to implement information and reporting systems to ensure senior management and the board of directors have adequate information about the company's business and operations, material events, and compliance;
- failure to remedy any illegal conduct or direct the company to institute suit against current or former board members and officers for permitting FCPA violations;
- and failure to oversee, manage, and operate the company in a lawful and ethical manner.[125]

In terms of securities fraud actions, given how scrutiny and enforcement under the FCPA and related laws can impact a company's stock price, it is not surprising that such actions are another frequent form of shareholder litigation and the following context is important. The securities laws are based on the general premise that issuers make full and complete disclosure of all material facts relevant to its business. Although materiality is a murky concept, courts have construed this key concept to mean all information, whether positive or negative, that might be relevant to an investor's decision to buy, sell, or hold a security. The securities laws foundation of full and complete disclosure of all material facts is enforced through, among other provisions, Section 10(b) of the Exchange Act and its associated Rule 10b-5. Section 10(b) generally prohibits the use of "any manipulative or deceptive device or contrivance in contravention of such rules and regulations as the SEC may prescribe as necessary or appropriate in the public interest or for the protection of investors." Rule 10b-5 supplements Section 10(b) by making it unlawful for any person, directly or indirectly: (i) to employ any device, scheme or artifice to defraud; (ii) to make any untrue statement of a material fact or to omit to state a material fact necessary in order to make the statements not misleading; or (iii) to engage in any act, practice, or course of business which operates or would operate as a fraud or deceit upon any person – in connection with the purchase or sale of any security.

Securities fraud claims in the FCPA context generally allege that a company's public disclosures regarding potential FCPA violations and/or the potential settlement with the DOJ or the SEC were misleading in themselves or are proof of material misstatements in the company's prior public statements regarding one or more of the following topics:

- the nonexistence of FCPA violations and improper accounting of funds used in illegal activity;
- the quality of the company's internal controls;
- the company's general compliance with corporate policies, the FCPA, and other applicable laws;
- the risks and costs associated with an FCPA investigation, including legal and consulting fees and disruptions to the company's operations;
- predictions regarding the results, effects, or ultimate materiality of an FCPA-related investigation;

- the company's profitability or financial performance following the cessation of illegal activity and/or any decision to suspend certain operations due to illegal conduct; and
- the financial impact of increased monitoring expenses.[126]

In such cases, plaintiffs' typically assert that because of the issuer's false statements or omissions: "(1) the market price of the company's securities was artificially inflated and maintained; and (2) shareholders suffered losses when the stock price fell following the issuance of corrective disclosures and the materialization of risks previously concealed by the defendants (i.e., then the 'truth' was revealed)."[127]

Given the substantive elements, as well as procedural pleading requirements, of derivative and securities fraud actions a high percentage of these actions in the FCPA context fail to survive the motion to dismiss stage of litigation.[128] The few actions that do survive a motion to dismiss are typically settled and a trial on the merits rarely occurs because companies often make the business decision to settle for nuisance value and often backed by insurance coverage. A typical corporate position concerning settlement of FCPA-related civil litigation was articulated by the Chief Financial Officer of Maxwell Technologies, a company that resolved an approximate $14 million FCPA enforcement action based on conduct in China.[129] During an investor call, the CFO stated:

> As we have disclosed in past public filings . . ., two shareholders had alleged that certain of our past and current officers and directors failed to prevent us from violating the [FCPA]. [. . .] [M]ediation was held and a proposed settlement was reached wherein $3 million would be paid to plaintiff's counsels, with $2.7 million to be paid by our insurance carrier, and $290,000 would be paid by the Company. [. . .] Without admitting any wrongdoing, the defendants to this suit are willing to enter into this settlement in order to expedite resolution of the matter, and to relieve the defendants and the Company from further financial burden. We are pleased that this suit is near final settlement, and look forward to putting this matter behind us.[130]

Even though FCPA-related civil suits rarely survive the motion to dismiss stage of litigation, according to an analysis "a number of FCPA-related securities fraud suits have settled for amounts in excess of the penalty assessed by the DOJ and/or SEC" in the underlying enforcement action.[131] Most notably, in connection with its scrutiny under the FCPA and related laws Petrobras (a Brazilian oil and gas company with shares traded in the U.S.) agreed to pay $2.95 billion to resolve various private securities fraud actions based on alleged false or misleading statements or omissions in its securities filings related to its business practices. Even so, pursuant to the settlement Petrobras expressly denied liability and stated that the settlement was "in the company's best interest and that of its shareholders, given the risks of a verdict advised by a jury, particularities of US procedure and securities laws, as well its assessment of the status of the class action and the nature of such litigation in the United States".[132]

Given the frequency in which shareholder litigation follows FCPA scrutiny or enforcement and given the largely unsuccessful track record of such cases surviving the motion to dismiss stage, the question should be asked – does the majority of shareholder litigation in the FCPA context serve a purpose or are such actions merely parasitic attempts to feed-off of scrutiny and enforcement? For instance, a *Forbes* columnist wrote under the title "Plaintiff Lawyers Join The Bribery Racket":

> The Justice Department's unprecedented campaign to enforce a once-backwater statute called the [FCPA] has made corporate lawyers and accountants rich as big companies pay big law and accounting firms to investigate and defend potential violations. Plaintiff lawyers have noticed the enormous fees, which are often reaching into the hundreds of millions of dollars, enhanced FCPA enforcement is generating and are moving to extract their own cut. [. . .] The unintended consequences of the Justice Department's FCPA policy simply continue to mount. [. . .] Now the plaintiff lawyers are trying to join the fun. [. . .] What is clear is that the cost of enhanced FCPA enforcement on U.S. corporations keeps going up. And that more lawyers are finding ways to get rich off of it.[133]

When scrutiny or enforcement is the result of board of director or executive officer conduct, or the condoning or encouraging of such conduct by those with fiduciary duties, such civil suits or investigations would seem to be warranted and in the public interest. While there have been a few enforcement actions involving executive conduct at the highest levels of the company, the vast majority of enforcement actions do not allege any knowledge, participation or acquiescence in the conduct at issue by the board of directors or executive officers. In this typical scenario, shareholder litigation would seem to be merely an attempt by plaintiffs' lawyers to feed off scrutiny and enforcement. As with others things in the FCPA's modern era, shareholder litigation seems to have spiraled out of control and an FCPA practitioner rightly observed:

> Setbacks in court do not appear to have slowed the pace of new cases filed against corporations and their directors after FCPA disclosures. As the DOJ and SEC bring more cases, and as more companies voluntarily disclose potential FCPA violations, the trend of related civil litigation is likely to continue. In attempting to satisfy the expectations of the DOJ and SEC, a company's thorough internal investigation may also serve as the roadmap for a civil litigant. Companies negotiating with the DOJ and SEC must therefore balance the government's requests for the results of internal investigations with the risk of waiver of privilege and subsequent production to civil litigants. As a result of these practical considerations, reputational risk, and expenses involved in litigation, companies targeted by civil suits will feel pressure to settle, potentially even before the DOJ or SEC takes action.[134]

Regardless of the substantive merits of much FCPA related shareholder litigation, the take-away point here is that such civil litigation following an enforcement action or mere scrutiny represents yet another "ripple" and one can that may uniquely impact corporate management.

## "Offensive" use of the FCPA

Whether it's a DOJ or SEC enforcement action, a related foreign law enforcement action, or a related civil suit brought by plaintiffs' lawyers representing shareholders, business organizations are typically in a defensive posture when it comes to the FCPA. Even if a company is not involved in an enforcement action or related litigation, the FCPA still often impedes a business objective such as not acquiring a foreign target or not engaging a foreign agent because of risk. While such defensive positions continue to dominate, the FCPA is increasingly being used offensively to achieve a business objective or to advance a litigating position.

As to the former, Dish Network and Tokyo-based SoftBank were battling for control of wireless carrier Sprint Nextel. Among the regulatory approvals SoftBank needed to complete the transaction was Federal Communications Commission approval of a license transfer from Sprint Nextel to SoftBank. In opposing the transfer, Dish Network cited an FCPA enforcement action against UTStarcom in which the company agreed to pay $3 million "for the actions of UTS-China [its wholly-owned subsidiary] and its employees and agents, who arranged and paid for employees of Chinese state-owned telecommunications companies to travel to popular tourist destinations in the United States, including Hawaii, Las Vegas and New York City."[135] The link Dish Network made between the FCPA enforcement action and its battle with SoftBank for Sprint Nextel was that Softbank's founder Masayoshi Son was on the board of UTStarcom during certain time periods relevant to the conduct at issue in the enforcement action.[136] Dish Network asserted that the UTStarcom enforcement action was "relevant to the public interest analysis of the proposed transaction." In reply, Softbank stated that the UTStarcom enforcement action was not relevant to its attempt to gain control of Sprint Nextel and asserted:

> [The enforcement action did] not involve SoftBank or Mr. Masayoshi Son, Chairman and CEO of SoftBank. The settlement documents do not name, implicate, or otherwise relate to SoftBank or Mr. Son, and are legally and factually irrelevant to this proceeding.
>
> DISH suggests that these settlements raise a potential issue in this proceeding because Mr. Son at one time served as the Chairman of the Board of UTSI. Neither the DOJ or SEC settlement documents, however, even mention SoftBank or Mr. Son. This is hardly surprising. Mr. Son was not an operating officer of UTStarcom at any time and the alleged violations came to light years after Mr. Son left the Board, which he did in 2004.[137]

Another example of offensive use of the FCPA in a battle for corporate control involved Central European Distribution Corporation (CEDC), a large vodka producer headquartered in the U.S. that disclosed:

> There has been a breach of the books and records provisions of the [FCPA] and potentially other breaches of the FCPA. It was determined that payments or gifts were made in a foreign jurisdiction in which the Company operates, and that there was a failure to maintain documentation in respect of certain of these payments or gifts adequate to establish whether there was a valid business purpose in making the payments or gifts. Furthermore, our management also identified a material weakness in our internal control over financial reporting regarding the implementation of our policy on compliance with applicable laws [. . .]. Our conclusion that this deficiency is a material weakness in our internal control over financial reporting is not based on misstatements in our historical consolidated financial statements or our consolidated financial statements [. . .], but instead on the determination that we did not design or maintain sufficient policies, procedures, controls, communications or training to deter or prevent the risk of violations of law, including the [FCPA].[138]

Shortly thereafter, Russian billionaire Roustam Tariko (the founder of CEDC rival Russian Standard and CEDC's largest shareholder) claimed that CEDC executives themselves were the subject of an FCPA investigation. The claims of CEDC's largest shareholder caused the company to issue a letter to shareholders that stated:

> As you may be aware ... Mr. Roustam Tariko, Chairman of Russian Standard, published a letter to CEDC investors that has created anxiety and confusion in the marketplace. What you may not be aware of is that Mr. Tariko's letter was published less than 48 hours after the CEDC Board voted 5 to 3 (the 3 being Mr. Tariko and his Board designees) against Mr. Tariko's request that he be given total control over CEDC's operations and finance. This request follows repeated attempts by Russian Standard to remove the interim CEO. The purpose of this letter is to provide you with [among other things] correct information regarding FCPA matters.[139]

The letter then stated that "despite suggestions in the Russian Standard letter to the contrary, the company is NOT on notice that any of its current executives are under investigation with respect to FCPA violations or otherwise."

Perhaps the most high-profile instance of offensive use of the FCPA involved the boardroom battle between Wynn Resorts and its board member Kazuo Okada. Wynn Resorts disclosed:

> Wynn Macau, a majority owned subsidiary of Wynn Resorts, Limited (the "Company"), made a commitment to the University of Macau Development Foundation in support of the new Asia-Pacific Academy of Economics and Management. This contribution consists of a $25 million payment ... and a commitment for additional donations of $10 million each year for [ten years]. The pledge was consistent with the Company's longstanding practice of providing philanthropic support for deserving institutions in the markets in which it operates. The pledge was made following an extensive analysis which concluded that the gift was made in accordance with all applicable laws. The pledge was considered by the Boards of Directors of both the Company and Wynn Macau and approved by 15 of the 16 directors who serve on those boards. The sole dissenting vote was Mr. Kazuo Okada whose stated objection was to the length of time over which the donation would occur, not its propriety. Also as previously disclosed, Mr. Okada commenced litigation [...] in Nevada seeking to compel the Company to produce information relating to the donation to the University of Macau, among other things. [...] Following Mr. Okada's lawsuit, the Company received a letter from the [SEC] requesting that, in connection with an informal inquiry by the SEC, the Company preserve information relating to the donation to the University of Macau, any donations by the Company

> to any other educational charitable institutions, including the University of Macau Development Foundation, and the Company's casino or concession gaming licenses or renewals in Macau.[140]

While Wynn's disclosure did not specifically mention the FCPA, given that the company's disclosure of the SEC inquiry appeared to link the donation to the "Company's casino or concession gaming licenses or renewals in Macau," the disclosure seemingly implicated the FCPA. Indeed, Okada alleged in his complaint that "Wynn Macau's gaming concession expires – the last year of Wynn's donation commitment" and that he objected to the donation because the Chinese government owned the land on which the University is located.

Shortly thereafter, Wynn accused Okada of separate and distinct conduct that could implicate the FCPA. In a press release, Wynn announced that its "Compliance Committee has concluded a year-long investigation after receiving an independent report detailing numerous apparent violations of the [FCPA] by Aruze USA, Inc., its parent company Universal Entertainment Corporation, and its principal shareholder, Kazuo Okada."[141] In the release, Wynn noted that its Compliance Committee engaged a variety of experts, including Louis Freeh (the former Director of the FBI), who conducted "a thorough independent investigation" which "uncovered and documented more than three dozen instances over a three-year period in which Mr. Okada and his associates engaged in improper activities for their own benefit in apparent violation of U.S. anti-corruption laws and gross disregard for the Company's Code of Conduct." According to the release, "Mr. Okada and his associates and companies appear to have engaged in a longstanding practice of making payments and gifts to his two chief gaming regulators at the Philippines Amusement and Gaming Corporation, who directly oversee and regulated Mr. Okada's Provisional Licensing Agreement to operate in that country." The Wynn releases further stated:

> The Board has requested that Mr. Okada resign as a Director of Wynn Resorts. [. . .] The Freeh Report is the culmination of a year-long investigation by the Compliance Committee based on increasing concerns the Board had relating to the activities of Mr. Okada and Aruze USA, Inc. in the Philippines and statements made by Mr. Okada to Wynn Resorts' Directors that gifts to regulators are permissible in Asia. Mr. Okada is the only Director of Wynn Resorts who has continued to refuse to sign the Company's Code of Conduct or participate in mandatory Foreign Corrupt Practices Act training for Directors.

Wynn's FCPA allegations against Okada were used by the company to support its finding that Okada was an "unsuitable person" under Nevada gaming regulations and thus justified Okada's removal from Wynn's board.[142] The boardroom battle occurred in the context of Wynn's attempt to purchase Okada's 20% stake in the company at an approximate 30% discount. Okada ultimately resigned from Wynn's board and in doing so stated: "I no longer believe it is appropriate for me to serve on the Board of Directors of a company that is behaving in a manner that I deeply believe to be unethical."[143]

In addition to the FCPA being used offensively to achieve a business objective, with increasing frequency the FCPA is also being used offensively to advance a litigating position. As previously indicated, while certain courts have held that the FCPA does not contain a private right of action, plaintiffs nevertheless may attempt to use bribery-related conduct that could implicate the FCPA and related laws in bringing a cause of action under the Racketeer Influenced and Corrupt Organizations Act (RICO). To establish a violation of any of the substantive offenses under RICO, a plaintiff must show that a defendant engaged in a "pattern of racketeering," which requires at least two acts of racketeering activity and a violation of the Travel Act is one of the enumerated predicate offenses under RICO. The Travel Act, enacted prior to the FCPA, is part of the racketeering chapter of the criminal code and prohibits interstate and foreign travel or transportation in aid of racketeering enterprises. Specifically, the Travel Act prohibits travel in interstate or foreign commerce or use of the mail or any facility in interstate or foreign commerce with intent to, among other things, carry on "any unlawful activity," which is defined to include bribery in violation of state law. In short, conduct in violation of the FCPA is often in violation of state law, which in turn implicates the Travel Act, which in turn can implicate RICO given that a Travel Act violation is a predicate offense under RICO.

For instance, Aluminum Bahrain BSC ("Alba") (one of the largest aluminum smelters in the world and owned by, among others, the government of Bahrain) filed a civil lawsuit against Alcoa Inc. (the world's leading producer of primary aluminum products) alleging RICO violations. The complaint alleged that certain Aloca entities and their agents engaged in a conspiracy over a 15-year period to defraud Alba and specifically alleged that the defendants: (i) illegally bribed officials of the government of Bahrain and (or) officers of Alba in order to force Alba to purchase alumina at excessively high prices; (ii) illegally bribed officials of the government of Bahrain and (or) officers of Alba and issued threats in order to pressure Alba to enter into an agreement by which Alcoa would purchase an equity interest in Alba; and (iii) assigned portions of existing supply contracts between Alcoa and Alba for the sole purpose of facilitating alleged bribes and unlawful commissions.[144] After the judge denied the defendants' motion to dismiss, Aloca agreed to settle the case by paying Alba approximately $85 million and the action represented the "first time that a foreign-owned corporation has successfully sued a U.S. company in a federal court to recover losses suffered due to allegations of corrupt activity."[145]

As the following cases demonstrate, FCPA-related civil litigation often involves other causes of action as well.

- After Innospec resolved an FCPA enforcement action, NewMarket Corp. (a competitor company) learned of Innospec's conduct from the DOJ and SEC resolution documents including the allegation that Innospec's bribe payments in Iraq ensured that a field test of a competitor's product failed. Based on Innospec's acknowledgment of this conduct in resolving the enforcement action, the competitor filed a civil case against Innospec alleging violations of the Robinson-Patman Act, the Virginia Antitrust Act, and the Virginia Business Conspiracy Act. Innospec agreed to resolve the case by agreeing to pay NewMarket approximately $45 million.[146]

- In the aftermath of various FCPA enforcement actions alleging bribery and corruption at Venezuela's national oil company Petroleos de Venezuela, S.A. (PDVSA), Harvest Natural Resources Inc. alleged that various former high-ranking PDVSA officials and others "conspired to force American companies to pay-to-play in Venezuela's oil and gas industry." In filing a lawsuit asserting violations of RICO, the Sherman Act, the Robinson Patman Act, and the Texas Free Enterprise and Antitrust Act, Harvest alleged: "because Harvest and its business partners refused four separate $10 million bribe demands solicited by the Defendants, Venezuela's Ministerio del Poder Popular de Petroleo y Mineria withheld final approval for Harvest to sell its Venezuelan energy assets to two different buyers . . . (first for $725 million and then for $400 million). As a result, Harvest was forced to sell the same assets for approximately $255 million, at a loss of $470 million, and unexpectedly to cease doing business and wind up its affairs."[147]

- After medical products company Misonix disclosed FCPA scrutiny related to "the business practices of [an] independent Chinese entity that previously distributed its products in China," the former Chinese distributor filed a lawsuit against Misonix and certain officers and directors alleging that the company improperly terminated its contract. The civil complaint sought "various remedies, including compensatory and punitive damages, specific performance and preliminary and post judgment injunctive relief, asserts various causes of action, including breach of contract, unfair competition, tortious interference with contract, fraudulent inducement, and conversion."[148]

One of the most interesting "offensive" uses of the FCPA concerned civil litigation between Louis Berger International and Richard Hirsch (a former executive of the company who at times oversaw operations in Indonesia and Vietnam). After Louis Berger resolved a $17 million FCPA enforcement (based on the conduct of Hirsch and another employee) in connection with projects in Indonesia, Vietnam, India and Kuwait, it sued Hirsch for breach of fiduciary duty and the parties settled for undisclosed terms.[149]

"Offensive" use of the FCPA to advance a litigating position is not just limited to business organizations as individuals are also increasingly citing the FCPA to support claims of breach of contract or wrongful termination of employment as demonstrated by the below examples.

- Khaled Asadi (a former employee of a wholly-owned subsidiary of General Electric Company (G.E.)), filed a civil complaint alleging that G.E. harassed and pressured him to vacate his position, and ultimately terminated him after he informed his supervisor and G.E.'s Ombudsperson "regarding potential violations of the FCPA committed by G.E. during negotiations for a lucrative, multi-year deal with the Iraqi Ministry of Electricity."[150]

- Stephen Lowe (a former Allison Transmission Managing Director for operations in China, Japan, and Korea) filed a civil complaint against the company alleging that Allison fired him because he "refused to engage in violations of the FCPA."[151] Among other things, Lowe alleged that: (i) he witnessed Allison's Commercial Director of Asia Strategy deliver a cash-filled envelope to Beijing City Bus officials during dinner; (ii) he heard the Commercial

> Director describe how he purchased silver jewelry for Chinese government officials "in order to please the officials"; (iii) the Commercial Director bragged about winning a Beijing City Bus Olympics contract by doing "whatever it took to please the officials" "including giving gifts, money and prostitutes"; and (iv) the Commercial Director "deliberately lost" high-stakes card games to "key Beijing City Bus officials." According to Lowe's complaint, Allison's Vice President of International Sales and Marketing knew and approved of certain of the Commercial Director's conduct and Lowe further alleged that "a month before Allison fired him" he disclosed his concerns about the Commercial Director and the Vice President to Allison's Marketing Manager.

Such "noisy exits" by employees alleging wrongful termination of employment can also be the origins of high-profile corporate FCPA scrutiny. For instance, casino company Las Vegas Sands's scrutiny began when Steven Jacobs (the former President of the company's Macau operations) filed a civil complaint against the company alleging breach of contract and tort-based causes of action.[152] Jacobs alleged, among other things, that the company's "notoriously bellicose" CEO and majority shareholder made several "outrageous demands" upon him including "demands that Sands China continue to use the legal services of a Macau attorney [. . .] despite concerns that [the individual's] retention posed serious risks" under the FCPA. The conduct alleged in the civil lawsuit ultimately resulted in parallel DOJ and SEC enforcement action against Las Vegas Sands that the company resolved for approximately $16 million.[153]

Wrongful termination claims brought by individuals can also follow FCPA scrutiny and enforcement. A high-profile example concerned civil litigation initiated by Sanford Wadler (the former General Counsel and Secretary of Bio-Lab Laboratories) against the company in the aftermath of Bio-Rad resolving a $55 million FCPA enforcement action based on alleged conduct in Russia, Thailand and Vietnam. Wadler's civil complaint alleged that Bio-Rad and certain executive officers and board members engaged in various unfair employment practices including terminating him for blowing the whistle on certain potential FCPA issues. Wadler's claims were fully litigated and a jury awarded him $2.9 million in back pay and stock compensation and $5 million for punitive damages and the trial court doubled the compensatory award pursuant to applicable law for a total award of approximately $11 million.[154]

The take-away point from this section on the "ripple effects" of scrutiny and enforcement is that a business organization will experience wide-ranging financial consequences from FCPA and related scrutiny and enforcement beyond an actual government enforcement action. These "ripples" – ranging from pre- and post-enforcement action professional fees and expenses, various negative business effects, and FCPA-related civil litigation as well as various "offensive" uses of the FCPA – should make clear that compliance is not just a legal issue, but a general business issue that needs to be on the radar screen of various professionals who can assist in risk management and who should view the importance of compliance holistically and not merely through the narrow lens of actual enforcement actions.

More broadly, this chapter has highlighted why a diverse group of professionals need skills to spot risk and debunked the narrative that complying with the FCPA and related laws is easy given that the overwhelming majority of business organizations do business in the global marketplace with a commitment to compliance, yet subject to unrealistic legal standards and/or difficult and complex business conditions that often serve as the root cause of scrutiny and enforcement. With a clear understanding of why skills to spot risk are important, the next chapter begins to construct your "FCPA goggles" by analyzing the core elements of the FCPA's anti-bribery provisions as well as related risk management strategies.

NOTES

1 MarketWatch, "S&P 500 Companies Generate Barely Over Half Their Revenue at Home," (Aug. 19, 2015).
2 Jonathan Rockoff, "Abbott Looks to India for Shot in Arm", *Wall Street Journal* (Aug. 26, 2010).
3 SEC Release, "SEC Charges Smith & Wesson with FCPA Violations," (July 28, 2014).
4 Charles Denny & David Weissbrodt, "Business Forum: Good Companies Don't Bribe. Period", *Minneapolis StarTribune* (May 29, 2012).
5 Nick Wingfield, New York Times, "U.S. Said to Look Into Microsoft Bribery Allegations" (Mar. 19, 2013).
6 Microsoft Blog, "Our Commitment to Compliance" (Mar. 19, 2013).
7 Press Release, U.S. Department of Justice, "Transcript of Press Conference Announcing Siemens AG and Three Subsidiaries Plead Guilty to Foreign Corrupt Practices Act Violations" (Dec. 15, 2008).
8 FCPA Professor, "Where Was The BizJet Board?," (Apr. 11, 2013).
9 FCPA Professor, "Former DOJ FCPA Chief Supports FCPA Compliance Defense," (Oct. 4, 2011).
10 FCPA Professor, "Friday Roundup," (Mar. 8, 2013).
11 FCPA Professor, "Friday Roundup," (Feb. 28, 2014).
12 FCPA Professor, "Companies That Have Resolved FCPA Enforcement Actions Or Are Currently Under FCPA Scrutiny Are Helping To Change The World," (Sept. 7, 2016).

13 U.S. Attorneys' Manual, 9-47.000 – Foreign Corrupt Practices Act Of 1977.
14 FCPA Professor, "SEC Official – "FCPA Law .. Is Not Well Developed," (Dec. 5, 2013).
15 A Resource Guide to the U.S. Foreign Corrupt Practices Act.
16 FCPA Professor, "The Guidance Press Conference," (Nov. 15, 2012).
17 Id.
18 Id.
19 Id.
20 FCPA Professor, "Do Lanny Breuer And Robert Khuzami Actually Read FCPA Enforcement Actions?" (Dec. 13, 2012), containing links to original source documents.
21 FCPA Professor, "Andrew Weissmann On The FCPA – It Is "Very Easy For The People At The DOJ And SEC To Basically Impose A Tax For Doing Business" In Certain Countries," (Sept. 20, 2016).
22 Jones Day Commentary, "U.S. Department of Justice and Securities and Exchange Commission Guidance on the Foreign Corrupt Practices Act: What to Expect" (Sept. 2012).
23 Corruption, Crime & Compliance, "It Takes a Village . . . To Commit Bribery," (Oct. 29, 2017).
24 DOJ Principles of Federal Prosecution of Business Organizations, 9-28.800, Corporate Compliance Programs.
25 Press Release, U.S. Department of Justice, "Assistant Attorney General Lanny A. Breuer of the Criminal Division Speaks at the Annual Meeting of the Washington Metropolitan Area Corporate Counsel Association" (Jan. 26, 2011); Lanny A. Breuer, Assistant Attorney General, Criminal Division U.S. Department of Justice, Prepared Remarks to Compliance Week 2010 – 5th Annual Conference for Corporate Financial, Legal, Risk, Audit & Compliance Officers (May 26, 2010).
26 The Metropolitan Corporate Counsel, "Former Chief Of DOJ Fraud Unit Discusses Healthcare And FCPA Enforcement" (Sept. 29, 2012).
27 FCPA Professor, "2016 FCPA Enforcement Begins With SEC Action Against SAP," (Feb. 2, 2016).
28 In the Matter of Nordion (Canada) Inc., Release No. 77290 (Mar. 3, 2016).
29 FCPA Professor, "Q & A With Martin Weinstein" (May 18, 2010).
30 Philip Urofsky, "The Ralph Lauren FCPA Case: Are There Any Limits to Parent Corporation Liability?" Bloomberg BNA Securities Regulation & Law Report (May 6, 2013).
31 FCPA Professor, "The SEC's Recent Alter Ego Theories," (Feb. 29, 2016).
32 South China Morning Post, "Fire Officials Put the Nation at Risk as They Rake in Bribes" (June 9, 2013).
33 Peter Van Dyk, "From Iowa To Russia, Tractors Build Economic Bridge" National Public Radio (May 15, 2012).
34 FCPA Professor, "A Positive Correlation Between Bureaucracy And Corruption," (Jan. 12, 2018).
35 Letter from Steven A. Tyrell, Chief, Fraud Section, U.S. Department of Justice (Criminal Division), to Kimberly A. Parker, Attorney for Helmerich & Payne, Inc. (July 29, 2009).
36 Complaint, SEC v. Delta & Pine Land Co., No. 1:07-cv-01352 (D.D.C. July 25, 2007).
37 Information, U.S. v. Tyson Foods, Inc., No. 1:11-cr-00037-RWR (D.D.C. Feb. 10, 2011).
38 Foley & Lardner and Panag & Babu, "Anti-Bribery and Foreign Corrupt Practices Act Compliance Guide for U.S. Companies Doing Business in India".
39 Transparency International, Global Corruption Barometer 2010; Kaushik Basu, "Why, for a Class of Bribes, the Act of Giving a Bribe Should Be Treated as Legal" (Mar. 2011).
40 FCPA Professor, "The First FCPA Enforcement Action Of 2017 Is A $13 Million Joke," (Jan. 9, 2017).
41 FCPA Professor, "On National Drink Beer Day, AB InBev Agrees To Pay $6 Million To Resolve FCPA (And Related) Enforcement Action," (Sept. 29, 2016).
42 Diageo plc, Exchange Act Release No. 64978 (July 27, 2011).

43 Complaint, SEC v. Westinghouse Air Brake Techs. Corp., No. 08-cv-706 (E.D. Pa. Feb. 14, 2008).

44 Information, U.S. v. Baker Hughes, Inc., No. 4:07-cr-00130 (S.D. Tex. Apr. 11, 2007).

45 Nigeria Country Profile, Business Anti-Corruption Portal.

46 Press Release, U.S. Department of Justice, "Oil Services Companies and a Freight Forwarding Company Agree to Resolve Foreign Bribery Investigations and to Pay More than $156 Million in Criminal Penalties" (Nov. 4, 2010).

47 FCPA Professor, "Avon Resolves Long-Standing FCPA Scrutiny By Agreeing To $135 Million Settlement," (Dec. 19, 2014); A Blemish – Nu Skin Enterprises Resolves SEC FCPA Enforcement Action Based On Its Chinese Subsidiary's "Charitable Donation," (Sept. 21, 2016).

48 Nu Skin Enterprises Inc. Form 10-K filed February 16, 2018.

49 FCPA Professor, "Two For Tuesday In FCPA Enforcement Land – Akamai Technologies," (June 8, 2016).

50 FCPA Professor, "Next Up – Telia As DOJ And SEC Announce Contemplated $483 Million Net FCPA Enforcement Action," (Sept. 21, 2017).

51 FCPA Professor, "Issues To Consider From The Hitachi Enforcement Action," (Oct. 1, 2015).

52 FCPA Professor, "When A Government Customer Does Not Pay," (Feb. 15, 2018).

53 Id.

54 Avon 2009 annual report (filed March 2010).

55 FCPA Professor, "Checking In On Wal-Mart's Pre-Enforcement Action Professional Fees And Compliance Enhancements," (Feb. 21, 2018).

56 Nathan Vardi, "The Bribery Racket", Forbes (June 7, 2010).

57 Memorandum in Support of the Proposed Plea Agreements and Deferred Prosecution Agreement, U.S. v. Alcatel-Lucent France S.A., et al, Case No. 10-cr-20906 (S.D. Fl. May 23, 2011).

58 Id.

59 Forbes, "The Bribery Racket," (June 7, 2010).

60 Wall Street Journal, "FCPA Inc.: The Business of Bribery," (Oct. 2, 2012).

61 Reuters, "Lawyers Need to Brake Their Bribe-Case Gravy Train," (Aug. 27, 2013).

62 FCPA Professor, "Friday Roundup," (Sept. 20, 2013).

63 DOJ Release, "Assistant Attorney General Leslie R. Caldwell Delivers Remarks at New York University Law School's Program on Corporate Compliance and Enforcement" (Apr. 17, 2015)

64 FCPA Professor, "Issues To Consider From The Avon Enforcement Action," (Dec. 22, 2014).

65 Law360 "Mixed Messages On Internal FCPA Probes Exasperate Attys" (Apr. 27, 2015).

66 Joel Schectman, "DOJ Wants Faster Anti-Bribery Investigations, Too," *Wall Street Journal Risk & Compliance Journal* (May 19, 2015).

67 For instance, the composition of FCPA settlement amounts in many corporate enforcement actions is controversial. Many FCPA enforcement actions involving both a DOJ and SEC component include features of "double-dipping" (in which the company pays an amount representing the benefit received from the alleged improper payments twice – first to the DOJ and then to the SEC). See FCPA Professor, "Double-Dipping," (June 4, 2013). Likewise, it is common in FCPA enforcement actions for the SEC to seek a disgorgement amount even in the absence of anti-bribery violations (a practice known as no-charged bribery disgorgement). See FCPA Professor, "No-Charged Bribery Disgorgement," (Aug. 22, 2011).

68 SEC Release, "SEC Charges Siemens AG for Engaging in Worldwide Bribery," (Dec. 15, 2008).

69 FCPA Professor, "Next Up – Telia As DOJ And SEC Announce Contemplated $483 Million Net FCPA Enforcement Action," (Sept. 21, 2017).

70 FCPA Professor, "VimpelCom's Uzbekistan Bribery Scheme Nets $397.5 Million FCPA Enforcement Action," (Feb. 19, 2016).

71 The Times of Israel, "Teva to Pay NIS 75 Million to Israel Authorities to Settle Foreign Bribe Claims," (Jan. 15, 2018).

72 FCPA Professor, "Friday Roundup," (Apr. 26, 2013).
73 FCPA Professor, "More On Alliance One and Universal," (Aug. 25, 2010), containing links to original source documents.
74 FCPA Professor, "Friday Roundup," (Aug. 20, 2010).
75 FCPA Professor, "FCPA Settlement Amounts Have Come A Long Way In A Short Amount Of Time," (Dec. 3, 2013).
76 Gibson Dunn, "2013 Year End FCPA Update," (Jan. 6, 2014).
77 See for instance the Deferred Prosecution Agreement, U.S. v. Parker Drilling Co., Case 1:13-cr-00176 (E.D. Va., Apr. 16, 2013).
78 Deferred Prosecution Agreement, U.S. v. Johnson & Johnson, Case 1:11-cr-00099-JDB (D.D.C., Apr. 8, 2011).
79 Joseph Warin et al., "Somebody's Watching Me: FCPA Monitorships and How They Can Work Better," 13 University of Pennsylvania Journal of Business Law 321 (2011).
80 FCPA Professor, "The Work Of A Monitor And Checking In On Siemens" (Jan. 22, 2013), containing links to original source documents.
81 FCPA Professor, "Friday Roundup" (Apr. 13, 2012), containing links to original source documents.
82 FCPA Professor, "Faro's Monitor – Late and Expensive," (Dec. 27, 2010).
83 FCPA Professor, "The Gray Cloud Of FCPA Scrutiny Lasted Too Long In 2017," (Jan. 4, 2018).
84 FCPA Blog, "The FCPA's Long Shadow," (Aug. 6, 2012).
85 SciClone Pharmaceuticals Inc., Form 10-K (filed Aug. 9, 2010).
86 Cognizant Technology Solutions Corporation, Form 8-K (filed Sept. 30, 2016).
87 FCPA Professor, "Unable To File Its Annual Report Due In Large Part To An FCPA Investigation, World Acceptance Corp. Stock Drops 12.4%," (June 16, 2017).
88 Ohio National Fund Inc., Form N-CSR (Sept. 8, 2017).
89 Wall Street Pit, "NCR Corp (NCR): Downgraded as Potential FCPA Issues Add Meaningful Risk – Wedbush" (Aug. 14, 2012).
90 Moody's Investor Service, "Heightened Anti-Bribery and Corruption Enforcement Around FCPA to Continue," (May 2, 2016).
91 Fitch Ratings, "U.S. Foreign Corrupt Practices Act – No Minor Matter" (2010).
92 Reuters, "S&P cuts Avon Products Inc" (Mar. 16, 2012).
93 Press Release, "Lockheed Martin Announces Agreement to Acquire Titan Corporation" (Sept. 15, 2003).
94 Press Release, "Lockheed Martin Updates Status of Review of Titan's International Consultants" (Mar. 5, 2004).
95 Press Release, "Lockheed Martin Terminates Merger Agreement with the Titan Corporation" (June 26, 2004).
96 Los Angeles Times, "Lockheed Drops Titan Merger After Delays by Bribery Probe" (June 26, 2004).
97 Press Release, U.S. Department of Justice (Mar. 1, 2005).
98 FCPA Professor, "FCPA And Then Some As Alere Resolves SEC Enforcement Action," (Sept. 29, 2017).
99 FCPA Professor, "Friday Roundup," (May 6, 2016).
100 FCPA Professor, "FCPA And Then Some As Alere Resolves SEC Enforcement Action," (Sept. 29, 2017).
101 FCPA Professor, "The FCPA's Long Tentacles," (Aug. 3, 2010), containing links to original source documents.
102 Id.
103 Id.
104 FCPA Professor, "ABM Industries Discloses Merger Related Issue" (Dec. 26, 2011), containing links to original source documents.

105 ABM Industries, Inc., Form 10-K (filed Dec. 20, 2012).

106 FCPA Professor, "FCPA Issues Can Reduce The Value Of A Merger" (June 14, 2012), containing links to original source documents.

107 FCPA Professor, "It's Not Easy Being Under Investigation for Two Years . . ." (Mar. 15, 2010).

108 Press Release, U.S. Department of Justice, "Oil Services Companies and a Freight Forwarding Company Agree to Resolve Foreign Bribery Investigations and to Pay More Than $156 Million in Criminal Penalties" (Nov. 4, 2010).

109 Bloomberg, "Och-Ziff Saw $2.5 Billion of Outflows After Bribery Accord," (Nov. 2, 2016); FCPA Professor, "In Depth Into The Och-Ziff FCPA Enforcement Action," (Oct. 2, 2016).

110 Och-Ziff Capital Management Group LLC, Form 10-K (filed Feb. 23, 2018).

111 Prudence Ho & Yvonne Lee, "J.P. Morgan Exits China IPO," *Wall Street Journal* (Nov. 19, 2013).

112 FCPA Professor, "In Depth Into The JP Morgan FCPA Enforcement Action," (Nov. 18, 2016).

113 Megha Bahree, "Wal-Mart's Path to Power in India Hits Its Limits: The Lawyers" (Apr. 1, 2013).

114 FCPA Professor, "Merely A Coincidence Or FCPA-Related?," (Oct. 19, 2015).

115 FCPA Professor, "Scrutiny Alerts And Updates," (Apr. 3, 2013).

116 FCPA Professor, "The Former CFO Of RAE Systems Speaks," (Aug. 14, 2012), containing links to original source documents.

117 FCPA Professor, "Friday Roundup," (July 30, 2010).

118 FCPA Professor, "Business Effects," (Mar. 21, 2012).

119 GardnerDenver Inc., Form 10-K (filed Feb. 27, 2013).

120 FCPA Professor, "SciClone – An FCPA Feeding Frenzy" (Oct. 13, 2010).

121 FCPA Professor, "Friday Roundup," (May 4, 2012).

122 FCPA Professor, "Friday Roundup," (June 8, 2012).

123 432 A.2d 814 (1981).

124 911 A.2d 362 (2006).

125 Jeffrey Johnston and Erika Tristan, "The Next FCPA Battleground: Private Civil Lawsuits Following Foreign Corrupt Practices Act Settlements With U.S. Government Authorities," *Vinson & Elkins Securities Litigation Insights* (Fall 2010).

126 Jeffrey Johnston and Erika Tristan, Vinson & Elkins Securities Litigation Insights, "The Next FCPA Battleground: Private Civil Lawsuits Following Foreign Corrupt Practices Act Settlements With U.S. Government Authorities," (Fall 2010).

127 Id.

128 See e.g., FCPA Professor, "Development From The "Other Universe" – In Dismissing FCPA-Related Civil Claims, Judge Rejects The Notion That The FCPA "Establishes A Statutory Floor For Adequate Internal Controls," (June 22, 2017).

129 Press Release, U.S. Department of Justice, "Maxwell Technologies Inc. Resolves Foreign Corrupt Practices Act Investigation and Agrees to Pay $8 Million Criminal Penalty" (Jan. 31, 2011).

130 FCPA Professor, "Friday Roundup," (Mar. 2, 2012).

131 Amy Westbrook, "Double Trouble: Collateral Shareholder Litigation Following Foreign Corrupt Practices Act Investigations," 73 Ohio State Law Journal 1217 (2012).

132 Release, "Petrobras Signs Agreement in Principle to Settle Class Action in the U.S.," (Jan. 3, 2018).

133 Nathan Vardi, Forbes, "Plaintiff Lawyers Join The Bribery Racket" (Aug. 6, 2012).

134 James Tillen and Lauren Torbett, "Multiplying the Risks: Parallel Civil Litigation in FCPA Investigations," *Bloomberg Law Reports – White Collar Crime* (2010).

135 Press Release, U.S. Department of Justice, "UTStarcom Inc. Agrees to Pay $1.5 Million Penalty for Acts of Foreign Bribery in China" (Dec. 31, 2009).

136 FCPA Professor, "Offensive Use of the FCPA," (June 6, 2013).

137 Id.

138 FCPA Professor, "Friday Roundup," (Nov. 30, 2012), containing links to original source documents.

139 Id.

140 FCPA Professor, "Wynn Resorts $135 Million University of Macau Donation The Subject Of SEC Scrutiny," (Feb. 14, 2012).

141 FCPA Professor, "Wynn's Boardroom Battle Royale," (Feb. 20, 2012), containing links to original source documents.

142 Chris Sieroty, "Okada Claims Against Wynn Resorts Ruled Baseless," *Las Vegas Review-Journal* (Feb. 4, 2013).

143 Chris Sieroty, Las Vegas Review-Journal, "Kazuo Okada Resigns From Wynn Resorts Board of Directors" (Feb. 23, 2013).

144 FCPA Professor, "Alcoa Agent Charged in the U.K." (Oct. 25, 2012), containing links to original source documents.

145 Akin Gump Press Release, "Akin Gump Secures Settlement Valued at $447 Million in First-Ever RICO Claim by Foreign Company," (Oct. 9, 2012).

146 FCPA Professor, "Innospec Related News" (Aug. 10, 2010).

147 Complaint, Harvest Natural Resources, Inc. v. Juan Jose Mendoza Garcia, et al. (S.D. Tex. Feb. 16, 2018).

148 FCPA Professor, "Scrutiny Alerts and Updates," (May 8, 2017).

149 FCPA Professor, "Louis Berger Sues Former Executive For Exposing It To FCPA Liability," (June 21, 2016).

150 Christopher Matthews, "Former GE Exec Claims He Was Fired For Relaying FCPA Concerns," *Wall Street Journal Corruption Currents* (Feb. 7, 2012).

151 FCPA Professor, "Still Yet Another Noisy Exit," (Dec. 23, 2010).

152 FCPA Professor, "Another Noisy Exit," (Nov. 2, 2010).

153 FCPA Professor, "In An Unusual Development, The DOJ Brings A $7 Million FCPA Enforcement Action Against Las Vegas Sands Nine Months After The SEC's $9 Million Enforcement Action Based On The Same Conduct," (Jan. 20, 2017).

154 FCPA Professor, "Bio-Rad Appeals Approximate $11 Million FCPA-Related Civil Verdict In Favor Of Its Former General Counsel," (Oct. 19, 2017).

# 2 The FCPA's core anti-bribery provisions and related risk management strategies

This chapter begins to construct your "FCPA goggles" by analyzing the core elements of the FCPA's anti-bribery provisions. To competently conduct the risk assessment skills exercise in Chapter 6, you must first be familiar with the wide range of circumstances in which scrutiny and enforcement can arise. This requires you to have a comprehensive understanding of legal authority and non-legal sources of information of the following core elements: anything of value, corrupt intent, foreign official, and obtain or retain business.

Although a suitcase full of cash to a traditional foreign government official to obtain or retain a foreign government contract most certainly meets these elements, few modern enforcement actions concern this type of conduct. Rather, and the reason why the "just don't bribe" narrative is often simplistic and naïve, scrutiny and enforcement can also arise from things of value such as corporate hospitality, charitable donations, and internships or jobs. In other words, the underlying conduct is often legal and morally acceptable in most instances, yet when directed to a specific type of individual (i.e. a "foreign official"), government enforcement agencies might deem it bribery.

Throughout this chapter you will learn risk management strategies specific to certain core elements of the anti-bribery provisions that present the greatest compliance challenges for business organization and you will also have a chance to assess your acquired knowledge through several real-world issue-spotting scenarios.

## Anything of value

The anti-bribery provisions refer to the offer, payment, promise to pay, or authorization of the payment of any money, or offer, gift, promise to give, or authorization of the giving of "anything of value." While most enforcement actions concern things of value actually *given* to an alleged "foreign official," it is important to first recognize that the statutory language also includes *offers or promises* of things of value to "foreign officials."

For instance, an enforcement action against Innospec, a manufacturer of fuel additives and other chemicals, included allegations that the company "promised . . . additional [payments] to Ministry of Oil officials so as to garner good will with Iraqi authorities."[1] Likewise, an enforcement action against firearms company Smith & Wesson included allegations that the company "authorized improper payments to third party agents" and although the "contemplated deals in Nepal and Bangladesh were never consummated . . ., the company had obtained or attempted to obtain the contract by using third party agents as a conduit for improper payments to government officials."[2]

In certain enforcement actions, the "thing of value" is obvious and the compliance take-away point is actually "just don't bribe." For instance, in related enforcement actions against telecommunications companies VimpelCom and Telia the things of value were $114 million and $331 million in corrupt payments given to an Uzbekistan official with influence over the country's telecommunications market.[3] While few enforcement actions concern such suitcase-full-of-cash type scenarios, the above statutory language also captures less significant things of value provided or offered to a "foreign official" recognizing that such individuals – just like you and me – can be influenced in many different ways other than cash payments.

For instance, the thing of value in the Ashland Oil enforcement action was the purchase of a largely worthless mine owned by a "foreign official" for a substantial price.[4] In an enforcement action against individuals employed by Ports Engineering Consultants Corporation the thing of value included a "foreign official's" receipt of dividend and bearer shares in a corporation.[5] Travel and entertainment can also represent an attempt to influence a "foreign official" and an enforcement action against engineering firm Metcalf & Eddy represented the first enforcement action to focus exclusively on travel and entertainment issues. In the action, the government alleged that the company covered excessive travel and entertainment expenses for an Egyptian official "to induce the official to use his influence to effect and influence an act of the Government of Egypt" in connection with two contracts.[6] While judicial scrutiny of enforcement theories is sparse, in *U.S. v. Liebo* an appellate court concluded that there was sufficient evidence for the jury to convict an individual defendant based on payment of honeymoon airline tickets for a Niger official who was in a position of influence concerning a contract.[7]

Regarding "anything of value" the FCPA Guidance states:

> An improper benefit can take many forms. While cases often involve payments of cash [. . .] others have involved travel expenses and expensive gifts. Like the domestic bribery statute, the FCPA does not contain a minimum threshold amount for corrupt gifts or payments. Indeed, what might be considered a modest payment in the United States could be a larger and much more significant amount in a foreign country.

In recent speeches, enforcement officials have talked about enforcing the FCPA to its "fullest extent" and as stated by the SEC's Director of Enforcement:

> [T]he FCPA precludes the payment or provision of "anything of value" to a foreign official in order to induce that official to take official action or obtain an improper advantage for the purpose of obtaining or retaining business. And of course "anything" of value is, on its face, a broad term. Obviously, cash payments count. Similarly, tangible gifts to foreign officials undoubtedly qualify as things of value. But the Commission has also successfully brought FCPA cases where other, less traditional, items of value have been given in order to influence foreign officials.[8]

The "full extent" of the anything of value element is best demonstrated by Table 2.1, which highlights representative "things of value" alleged in recent enforcement actions.

In addition to the above, recent enforcement actions have also included allegations or findings about the following things of value: handbags; a bottle of wine; a camera; kitchen appliances and business suits; television sets, laptops and appliances; and tea sets and office furniture. In short, anything of value means just that – anything of value.

Returning to the above statutory language, recognize that there is no *de minimis* amount associated with the anything of value element.

*Table 2.1 "Anything of value" allegations*

| Enforcement action | Thing of value |
|---|---|
| Paradigm[9] | Travel and entertainment expenses, gifts, cash per diems, sightseeing, cash payments for shopping and a trip to Napa Valley that included visits to wineries and dinners that coincided with a foreign official's birthday |
| SciClone Pharmaceutical[10] | Attendance at a beer festival consisting of "golf in the morning and beer-drinking in the evening," vacations, gifts, expensive meals, foreign language classes, and entertainment |
| FLIR Systems[11] | Non-business travel, gifts including expensive watches, and entertainment |
| Bristol Myers Squibb[12] | A variety of benefits ranging from food and personal care items to shopping cards, jewelry, sightseeing, and cash payments as well as sponsorships for conferences and meetings |

This statutory concept seems to make sense in a world in which many "foreign officials" receive meager government salaries and thus may be influenced by otherwise small gifts or other things of value. Moreover, if the FCPA did specify a *de minimis* value (for instance $500), there would be a risk of "green-lighting" numerous things of value $499 and below being provided or offered to "foreign officials."

That the FCPA and related laws do not contain a *de minimis* value is best demonstrated by enforcement actions against Novartis and Layne Christensen. For instance, the Novartis enforcement action included allegations about a $1,154 receipt to purchase holiday gifts for 25 Chinese healthcare professionals (HCPs) when the proceeds were actually used to pay for spa and sauna sessions for the HCPs.[13] (*As highlighted later in this chapter, the government deems various employees of many foreign healthcare systems to be "foreign officials."*) Doing the math on the above figures, the value per HCP was approximately $45. Even more dramatic, the Layne Christensen enforcement action contained the following allegations:

> Layne Christensen made more than $10,000 in small payments to foreign officials through various customs and clearing agents that it used in Tanzania, Burkina Faso, Mali, Mauritania, and the DRC. These payments ranged from $4 to $1,700.[14]

Even though enforcement agency officials have stated that enforcement is only "focused on bribes of consequence," and payments of "real and substantial value," the above allegations in actual enforcement actions demonstrate otherwise. While it is true that the above enforcement actions were not based on $4 or "golf in the morning and beer-drinking in the evening," these actual allegations can be viewed in one of two ways.

Either the government was practicing its typing skills or the government was sending a message to the business community that even small payments or things of value need to be on the radar screen of business organizations. Compliance professionals would be wise to view the latter as the government's main motivation when including such allegations or findings in enforcement actions.

Enforcement actions concerning charitable donations further reflect the enforcement agencies' broad view of the "anything of value" element. The first enforcement action to focus on charitable contributions involved pharmaceutical company Schering-Plough and the Chudow Castle Foundation, "a charitable organization that was established . . . to restore castles and other historic sites in the Silesian region of Poland." In the action, the government found that a unit manager at a branch office of a foreign subsidiary made a donation to the foundation under circumstances in which the Founder and President of the foundation was also the Director of the Silesian Health Fund (one of 16 regional health authorities in Poland) that provided money to hospitals for the purchase of pharmaceutical products. The Schering-Plough enforcement action was rather remarkable given the following findings:

- The enforcement action was based on the conduct of one individual – a unit manager at a branch office of a foreign subsidiary.

- The individual structured his conduct to evade certain internal controls and otherwise provided false information on documents submitted to the company's finance department.

- The donations were made to a bona fide charitable organization.

- The aggregate donation amount (approximately $76,000) was not material (during the relevant time period Schering-Plough's net income was over $2 billion per year).

- The donations were recorded as "donations" on the company's books and records.

- The donations were made without the knowledge or approval of any Schering-Plough employee in the U.S.[15]

A subsequent enforcement action against pharmaceutical company Eli Lilly included the same core allegation regarding the Chudow Castle Foundation and FCPA practitioners rightly noted:

> The case is significant in suggesting that payments to a bona fide charity could violate the FCPA if made to influence the actions of a government official. Although thc SEC did not state that these payments were bribes within the meaning of the FCPA, in charging FCPA accounting violations for these payments, the SEC strongly signaled that it believes that charitable donations could violate the FCPA if made at the direction of a government employee to induce official action.[16]

The Nu Skin Enterprises, Alstom, and Stryker enforcement actions also contained allegations regarding charitable donations. For instance, in the Nu Skin enforcement action the government found that the nutritional products company violated the FCPA when its Chinese subsidiary transferred money to a bona fide charity to obtain the influence of a high-ranking Chinese official with discretion over its business.[17] Likewise, the Alstom enforcement action included the allegation that the transportation company violated the FCPA by, among other things, making a payment to "a U.S.-based Islamic education foundation associated with [an alleged 'foreign official' with decision-making responsibility.]"[18] Similarly, an enforcement action against medical device company Stryker found that the company violated the FCPA when its Greek subsidiary made a donation to a public university to fund a laboratory that was alleged to be a pet project of a public hospital physician.[19] In these enforcement actions, the government seems to have placed itself in the shoes of the alleged "foreign official" and asked whether the individual subjectively valued the donation and/or whether securing the donation provided the official with an intangible benefit of enhanced self-worth or prestige. In other words, the perception of the recipient and the subjective valuation of the thing of value conveyed may be a relevant factor in an enforcement agency analysis of whether "anything of value" has been given to a "foreign official."

This salient take-away point aside, it is worth pausing to reflect on the policy implications of charitable donation enforcement actions. For starters, it is well known that business organizations, directly or indirectly, make charitable donations to foundations or groups affiliated with U.S. officials or their spouses.[20] However, there is a slim chance the government will investigate these donations even though the U.S. domestic bribery statute has core elements similar to the FCPA. Yet why should the U.S. government subject business interactions with "foreign officials" to different standards than business interactions with U.S. officials? Why does the government seem to reflexively label a "foreign official" who receives "things of value" from private business interests as corrupt, yet generally turn a blind eye when it happens in the U.S.? Is the FCPA enforced too aggressively or is enforcement of the U.S. domestic bribery statute too lax? Ought not there be some consistency between enforcement of the FCPA and the domestic bribery statute?

Another issue to consider is whether enforcement actions based on foreign charitable donations represent a net positive or net negative? The FCPA Guidance contains the unobjectionable statement that companies "cannot use the pretense of charitable contributions as a way to funnel bribes to government officials." However, seldom are the circumstances as black and white as the government portrays and query whether certain business organizations, because of this guidance and because of the above enforcement actions concerning charitable donations, have become excessively risk averse and have stopped contributing to humanitarian causes or otherwise pulled back from supporting communities or institutions in need. For instance, Corporate Counsel at a well-known U.S.-based publicly traded company offered the following example and observation:

> Most people can agree that preventing corruption is a good thing, and that vigorous enforcement of the FCPA can help in advancing this compelling public policy aim. But can it go too far? Can vigorous enforcement create an environment that not only limits corruption but that also prevents businesses from acting altruistically, and potentially improving communities and lives, because of risk aversion made necessary by that enforcement?
>
> Here is a real world example, with names and locations omitted. Take the case of my company – a U.S.-based company that trades publicly on the New York Stock Exchange. My company operates principally in the US, but has an operational footprint that includes North America, Latin America, and Asia. As such, my company is aware that its operations implicate FCPA risk. Consistent with enterprise risk-ranking methodology, and on the advice of

external vendors specializing in FCPA compliance, my company categorizes vendor and third-party relationships based on degree of risk (whether low, medium, or high). My company further specifies that vendor and third-party relationships need to be managed in accordance with guidelines that are aligned to risk category. These guidelines run from sanctions/watch-list screenings, to contractual language requirements, enhanced due diligence, written certifications, training, and billing requirements. All of which looks objectively reasonable and which would seem to protect the company from FCPA risks while also providing operational flexibility.

But, let's look at a situation where one of my company's units operating in a high-risk jurisdiction was interested in making a modest charitable donation to a worthy humanitarian organization. Consistent with the aforementioned guidelines, the company considers foreign charities to be high risk relationships. Why? Because of the expansive way in which the "anything of value" element has been interpreted and enforced. We know that prosecuting authorities are likely to view foreign charitable contributions as a possible method for bribery. Accordingly, in order to mitigate against the risk of having a charitable donation being seen as corrupt, a prudent actor should follow the same steps for these relationships as it would for other high-risk relationships. In my company's case, the steps for vetting a high-risk relationship involve a strenuous due diligence requirement consisting of outsourced screening and internal review with follow up. All of this costs time and money.

Returning to our example, let's assume that the proposed donation is of surplus cleaning and office supplies which have little value to the company, but which might be assessed objectively at $500 USD. In order to follow protocol, however, the steps for vetting the charitable organization implicate many thousands of dollars in due diligence fees, and several hours of employee time. So what should my company do? Assume that there is no risk in making the donation and throw caution to the wind? Or should my company insist on following protocol thereby making the process of vetting and documenting the relationship so costly so as to remove any incentive for making the donation in the first place?

Is there a right answer? For my company, the business sponsors decided that making the donation was not worth the expenses of time and effort that would have been required to comply with the applicable compliance policies. In other words, the juice was simply not worth the squeeze.

As a result, a few things happened:

- A needy organization was deprived of useful goods and equipment;
- My company was deprived of the opportunity to act altruistically and to gain good will in the local community;
- Trust between the company's internal groups was affected because it was difficult for compliance to articulate the need to follow controls and procedures without seeming unreasonable.

Looked at another way, everyone lost out.

Is this the type of situation that the FCPA was enacted to address? It is hard to imagine that it was, or that a compelling argument can be advanced that preventing nominal value charitable donations is aligned with US foreign policy interests. But, in light of aggressive enforcement theories, this is the effect that the FCPA can have. Companies become risk-averse to the point that they avoid efforts with the potential to benefit all parties involved.[21]

Policy issues aside when it comes to enforcement actions based on charitable donations, it's time to try on your "FCPA goggles" and assess your knowledge of the "anything of value" element by reviewing the following issue-spotting scenario. All of the issue-spotting scenarios in the book are based on a hypothetical company T Systems and in this first scenario T Systems employees Nicole and Raphael are having a conversation.

Should T Systems offer the internship to the daughter of the China Mobile employee, would the conduct violate the FCPA's anti-bribery provisions? Surely the internship would be a thing of value to the daughter, but the FCPA's statutory provisions state that the thing of value must go "to" a foreign official. Yet then again, as highlighted in the charitable donation enforcement actions, the government would probably put itself in the shoes of the China Mobile employee (*you*

| | |
|---|---|
| Raphael: | So where are we with that contract proposal? Did you get any feedback from China Mobile? |
| Nicole: | No, he's been out of the office and I haven't been able to connect with him yet. I think he's actually in the U.S. right now visiting his daughter. |
| Raphael: | Oh yeah? Where's his daughter? |
| Nicole: | She's studying in Los Angeles – not sure where – and apparently looking for an internship. At least that's what he awkwardly hinted at. |
| Raphael: | Oh really? What kind of internship is she looking for. Do you know if we have one? |
| Nicole: | I can check with HR. |
| Raphael: | I mean, does it really matter? I mean, we want something from him – and we might be able to provide something for his daughter in return. |
| Nicole: | Good point. I'll let him know we might have an opening. If I do that today, then maybe he'll have the chance to tell her about it when he's here. |
| Raphael: | Yeah, I think that'll be the thing that gets us over the line. |

*will learn later in this chapter that the government is likely to deem this individual a "foreign official" because his employer is a state-owned or state-controlled enterprise*) and ask whether the China Mobile employee subjectively valued the internship for his daughter. In doing so, the government would probably conclude that the internship constituted a personal benefit to the alleged "foreign official." Recall, that the China Mobile employee "awkwardly hinted" that his daughter was looking for an internship and it appears that T Systems does not even have an internship opening, but is simply creating a position for the daughter as a way to perhaps curry favor with him at an important point in T Systems' contractual negotiations with China Mobile. In short, should T Systems offer or provide the internship to the daughter of the China Mobile employee, it is likely that this would be viewed by the government as a "thing of value" to a "foreign official" to assist in obtaining or retaining business.

Indeed, the above scenario is far from a hypothetical, but based on recent enforcement actions concerning internships and job opportunities for family members of alleged "foreign officials." For instance, in an enforcement action against financial services company BNY

Mellon, the government found that the company violated the FCPA's anti-bribery provisions by providing "valuable student internships to family members of foreign government officials affiliated with a Middle Eastern sovereign wealth fund."[22] As to the personal benefit issue discussed in the above issue-spotting scenario, the government stated: "the internships were valuable work experiences, and the requesting officials derived significant personal value in being able to confer this benefit on their family members." Likewise, in an enforcement action against Qualcomm the government found that the technology company violated the FCPA for "provid[ing] or offer[ing] full-time employment and paid internships to family members and other referrals of foreign officials with the purpose of trying to influence those officials to take actions that would assist Qualcomm in obtaining or retaining business in China."[23] Similarly, in an enforcement action against financial services company JPMorgan, the government found:

> [T]he firm provided valuable jobs and internships to the relatives and friends of certain key executives of its clients, prospective clients, and foreign government officials in the Asia-Pacific region ("APAC") as a personal benefit to the requesting officials in order to obtain or retain investment banking business or other benefits for the firm. Many of JPMorgan's clients were state-owned entities ("SOEs"), and therefore the client executives requesting employment for their relatives and friends were foreign government officials under the FCPA. The firm provided these jobs and internships with the intent to corruptly influence the foreign government officials making the requests.[24]

Even though all of the above internship and hiring actions were resolved in the absence of judicial scrutiny, in the aftermath of the JPMorgan enforcement action the SEC's Director of Enforcement boldly proclaimed:

> In the wake of some of the Commission's prior hiring practices cases, including our cases against Bank of New York Mellon and Qualcomm, some questioned whether providing internships could amount to an FCPA violation. But the JPMorgan case should put that debate to rest.[25]

This of course is a debatable point in that exercising leverage against risk-averse corporations to extract a settlement on a disputed legal theory in the absence of judicial scrutiny puts nothing to rest other than that the government possesses leverage. Indeed, around the same time that the JPMorgan enforcement action was resolved in the absence of judicial scrutiny, there was judicial scrutiny of a similar enforcement narrative in a case (outside the FCPA context) which found the narrative not to be viable. In a U.K. civil action brought by the Libyan Investment Authority (LIA) against Goldman Sachs to rescind certain transactions and to obtain the repayment of premiums from Goldman Sachs, the LIA alleged that Goldman Sachs improperly influenced the deputy chairman of the LIA by offering his younger brother an internship. However, the judge concluded that "although the offer of the internship may have contributed to a friendly and productive atmosphere . . . it did not have a material influence on the decision of [deputy chairman] and the LIA to enter into" the business transactions.[26]

Recall the two distinct questions that can be asked in connection with many instances of FCPA scrutiny and enforcement. The first question is whether Congress, in passing the FCPA, intended to capture the alleged conduct at issue and whether a court would find the alleged conduct in violation of the FCPA. The second question is whether the conduct at issue can expose a company to scrutiny and enforcement given government enforcement theories. Regarding the above internship enforcement actions, the first question remains unclear because the enforcement actions were resolved in the absence of judicial scrutiny. However, the answer to the second question is obviously yes and compliance professionals would be wise to recognize internship and employment decisions as yet another risk area for scrutiny and enforcement. To minimize this risk, human resources professionals should receive FCPA training so that they can spot risk relevant to their job function and be skilled at asking the following questions regarding internship and employment opportunities:

- is a "foreign official" requesting the internship or job opportunity;
- is there an actual open position;
- does the applicant possess the requisite skills and qualifications; and
- is the applicant subject to the company's normal HR process?

More broadly, the take-away point from the first element of the anti-bribery provisions is that "anything of value" means just that and includes more than suitcase full of cash type scenarios, but also a variety of direct and indirect ways of influencing a "foreign official" such as golf outings, meals and beverages, sport tickets, non-business travel and entertainment and charitable donations. As to certain of the indirect ways of influencing a "foreign official," the enforcement agencies appear to put themselves in the shoes of the alleged foreign official and ask how the recipient perceived the thing of value and whether he or she subjectively valued it. Another take-away point thus far is that there is no *de minimis value* associated with the anything of value element and many enforcement actions include allegations or findings about relatively small payments. As stated by the government:

> [B]ribes come in many shapes and sizes. So it is critical that we carefully scrutinize a wide range of unfair benefits to foreign officials when assessing compliance with the FCPA – whether it is cash, gifts, travel, entertainment, or employment of the family and friends of foreign officials.[27]

Because the government is scrutinizing a wide range of things of value offered or provided to alleged "foreign officials," it is important that such wide range of things of value be on the radar screen of compliance professionals. What makes compliance in this area tricky is that in many situations the thing of value (whether a golf outing, meals, entertainment or other corporate hospitality) will generally not be problematic if directed to a certain customer or potential customer. However, if directed towards a different type of person (i.e. a "foreign official") government enforcement agencies might deem it bribery. Thus, among other reasons, the meaning of "foreign official" (discussed later in this chapter in more detail) matters and is far from an academic exercise.

So what is a well-intentioned business organization supposed to do to minimize risk in this area recognizing that many of the above things of value are often provided in the ordinary course of business? Like most FCPA compliance issues, it all starts with training and making sure that all employees and third parties with points of contact with "foreign officials" in the global marketplace clearly understand the broad meaning and interpretation of "anything of value." This includes not just employees or agents involved in the sales process, but also others who may interact with "foreign officials" in connection with import/export, licensing, permitting or other regulatory issues.

From there, business organizations should implement and communicate written policies and procedures throughout the organization which operate to take authority or discretion away from rank and file employees to provide things of value to customers or potential customers without pre-approval by compliance professionals. When analyzing requests for pre-approval, the government has encouraged compliance professionals to ask the following questions:

- Was the thing of value requested by the foreign official?
- Does the company believe that providing the thing of value will advance a business interest?
- Is providing the thing of value consistent with company policy?
- Were normal company procedures followed in providing the thing of value?[28]

Query whether these government-suggested questions provide a useful guidepost, but one can imagine a situation being viewed differently:

- if a company, on its own initiative, took a customer or potential customer golfing or to an expensive dinner vs. being requested to do so by a "foreign official" with discretion over its business;
- if the thing of value was provided during the ordinary course of business vs. an important point in contractual negotiations; or
- if the thing of value was perhaps allowed under company policy, but only after various internal approvals vs. being inconsistent with company policy and/or not following normal company procedures.

In other words, the same thing of value may be provided to the same individual, but given the context the conduct may stick out and be viewed with suspicion. (*Note: corporate hospitality issues are also relevant to the FCPA's affirmative defense for so-called reasonable and bona fide expenditures and are discussed in more detail in Chapter 4 including risk management strategies.*)

In addition to the above compliance practices relevant to "anything of value", based on the charitable donation enforcement actions it is also important that company personnel involved in such practices and civic engagement more broadly be trained on the FCPA and have "FCPA goggles" so that they can also minimize risk in their job functions. Although several enforcement actions have been based on donations to charitable causes favored by "foreign officials," the DOJ has blessed certain other charitable donations and has self-identified the following Opinion Procedure Releases as being relevant to charitable contributions. (*Note: DOJ FCPA Opinion Procedure Releases are discussed in Chapter 6*).

| 80-01 | 95-01 | 97-02 | 06-01 | 09-01 | 10-02 | 13-01 |
|---|---|---|---|---|---|---|

For instance, in one Opinion Procedure Release the requestor was a U.S.-based energy company that planned to acquire and operate a plant in a country in South Asia that lacked modern medical facilities in the region where the plant was located. According to the release, a modern medical complex was presently under construction near the requestor's future plant and if the acquisition of the plant was completed the requestor planned to donate $10 million in a public ceremony to the medical facility for construction and equipment costs. The requester represented that, before releasing any funds, it would require certifications from all officers of the U.S. charitable organization that none of the funds would be used, promised or offered in violation of the FCPA. The requestor further represented that none of the persons employed by or acting on behalf of the charitable organization were affiliated with the foreign government and that it would also require audited financial reports from the U.S. charitable organization accurately detailing the disposition of the donated funds. Based on these facts and representations, the DOJ stated that it did not intend to take any enforcement action with respect to the prospective donation for the construction and equipment of the medical facility.[29]

Similar to other things of value, business organizations should implement and communicate written policies and procedures accessible throughout its organization relevant to charitable giving with the same goal of taking authority or discretion away from rank and file employees to make charitable contributions without pre-approval by compliance professionals. For instance, according to Walmart's Global Chief Ethics and Compliance Officer:

> [Walmart] has adopted enhanced controls for donations, including giving procedures that apply in all of our international markets. These procedures outline requirements for donations to municipal improvements and public works, corporate-level and store-level donations to government entities and non-governmental organizations, and emergency donations. The procedures also prohibit some types of donations and sponsorships.[30]

## Corrupt intent

For there to be a violation of the anti-bribery provisions, the thing of value to a "foreign official" to assist in "obtaining or retaining business" must be offered or provided with a corrupt intent and this section highlights legal authority and non-legal sources of information regarding this often murky element.

### Law

The corrupt intent requirement applies to both business organizations and individuals charged with violation the anti-bribery provisions. In addition, for an individual to be criminally liable proof of willfulness is also required. As with any white collar criminal law, the FCPA's *mens rea* requirements are often the most difficult to prove and analyze and that without incriminating documentary or other evidence it is hard to get inside the minds of defendants criminally charged with FCPA violations.

### Legislative history

Although the FCPA does not specifically define the terms "corrupt" or "willfully," legislative history is instructive. For instance, a House Report noted the following regarding corrupt intent:

> The word "corruptly" is used in order to make clear that the offer, payment, promise, or gift, must be intended to induce the recipients to misuse his

> official position; for example, wrongfully to direct business to the payer or his client, to obtain preferential legislation or regulations, or to induce a foreign official to fail to perform an official function. The word "corruptly" connotes an evil motive or purpose such as that required under 18 U.S.C. 201(b) which prohibits domestic bribery. As in 18 USC 201(b), the word "corruptly" indicates an intent or desire wrongfully to influence the recipient. It does not require that the act [be] fully consummated or succeed in producing the desired outcome.[31]

A Senate Report further stated:

> [The anti-bribery provisions] cover payments and gifts intended to influence the recipient, regardless of who first suggested the payment or gift. The defense that the payment was demanded on the part of a government official as a price for gaining entry into a market or to obtain a contract would not suffice since at some point the U.S. company would make a conscious decision whether or not to pay a bribe. That the payment may have been first proposed by the recipient rather than the U.S. company does not alter the corrupt purpose on the part of the person paying the bribe. On the other hand extortion situations would not be covered by this provision since a payment to an official to keep an oil rig from being dynamited should not be held to be made with the requisite corrupt purpose.[32]

In terms of "willfully," a House Report stated:

> The bill [states that a person] must be found to have violated the law "knowingly and willfully." Consistent with the often-reiterated holdings of the courts that have interpreted a similar standard in the few places it is included in the federal securities laws, the knowledge required is merely that a defendant be aware that he is committing the act which constitutes the violation – not that he knows his conduct is illegal or has any specific intent to violate the law. [. . .] Indeed, even in the criminal context, neither knowledge of the law violated nor the intention to act in violation of the law is generally necessary for conviction, and the Committee does not intend that either be required here in either civil or criminal proceedings.[33]

## Judicial decisions

Given that corrupt intent and willfulness are fact specific, it is not surprising that *mens rea* issues have been contested in the few litigated FCPA or related cases that exist. For instance, in *U.S. v. Liebo* the defendant argued that there was insufficient evidence to show that he acted "corruptly" by providing honeymoon airline tickets to a Niger official who was in a position of influence concerning a contract.[34] The court disagreed and was satisfied that sufficient evidence existed from which a reasonable jury could find that the airline tickets were given "corruptly." The court noted that the airline tickets were given to the foreign official shortly before a contract was approved and that the defendant classified the airline ticket as a "commission payment" for accounting purposes. In an interesting twist though, the court concluded that the trial court clearly abused its discretion in denying the defendant's motion for a new trial based on newly disclosed evidence. Specifically, the defendant argued that "two months after his conviction, a NAPCO employee provided [him] with a memorandum showing [a superior's] approval to the charge of the airline tickets" and that evidence of a superior's approval of the wedding trip was a determinative factor in the jury's verdict by "pointing to a question sent out by the jury during their deliberations asking whether there was 'any information regarding authorization for payment of wedding trip.'" The appellate court stated:

> [T]he evidence against Liebo, while sufficient to sustain the conviction, was not overwhelming. Indeed, we believe that the company president's approval of the purchase of the tickets is strong evidence from which the jury could have found that Liebo acted at his supervisor's direction and therefore, did not act "corruptly" by giving the tickets to [the foreign official].

Although not an actual FCPA enforcement action, *Stichting v. Schreiber* (a civil malpractice case alleging erroneous legal advice by counsel regarding payments to a Panamanian official that caused the entity to violate the FCPA) is also instructive on the corrupt intent element. In the case, an appellate court analyzed whether a company, in pleading guilty to FCPA anti-bribery violations, acknowledged acting with intent thus undermining its claims that the erroneous legal advice was the basis for its legal exposure.[35] The court stated:

> Knowledge by a defendant that it is violating the FCPA – that it is committing all the elements of an FCPA violation – is not itself an element of the FCPA crime. Federal statutes in which the defendant's knowledge that he or she is violating the statute is an element of the violation are rare; the FCPA is plainly not such a statute.

The court also stated that "corruptly" as used in the FCPA:

> [S]ignifies, in addition to the element of "general intent" present in most criminal statutes, a bad or wrongful purpose and an intent to influence a foreign official to misuse his official position. But there is nothing in that word or anything else in the FCPA that indicates that the government must establish that the defendant in fact knew that his conduct violated the FCPA to be guilty of such a violation.

FCPA *mens rea* issues were also the focus of an appellate decision in *U.S. v. Kay* (an enforcement action discussed in more detail later in this chapter in connection with the "obtain or retain business" element).[36] After a jury convicted the defendants of FCPA anti-bribery violations an appeal followed in which the defendants argued, among other things, that the trial court failed to adequately instruct the jury on *mens rea* issues. *Kay* is highlighted below in detail given that the appellate court squarely addressed corrupt intent and willfulness concepts.

As stated by the appellate court:

> The [district] court's instructions to the jury indicated that "corruptly" was an element of the offense and defined a corrupt act as one that is "done voluntarily and intentionally, and with a bad purpose or evil motive of accomplishing either an unlawful end or result, or a lawful end or result by some unlawful method or means." The [district] court also instructed the jury on the definition of an act done "knowingly" (thus incorporating the willfulness element into its instructions) and defined a knowing act as one "done voluntarily and intentionally, not because of accident or mistake."

The appellate court concluded:

> The FCPA does not define "willfully," and we therefore look to the common law interpretation of this term to determine the sufficiency of the jury instructions pertaining to the *mens rea* element. The definition of "willful" in the criminal context remains unclear despite numerous opinions addressing this issue. Three levels of interpretation have arisen that help to clear the haze. Under all three, a defendant must have acted intentionally – not by accident or mistake. The first and most basic interpretation of criminal willfulness is that committing an act, and having knowledge of that act, is criminal willfulness – provided that the actions fell within the category of actions defined as illegal under the applicable statute. In these cases, the defendant need not have known of the specific terms of the statute or even the existence of the statute. The defendant's knowledge that he committed the act is sufficient.

The second and "intermediate" level of criminal willfulness requires the defendant to have known that his actions were in some way unlawful. Again, he need not have known of the specific statute, but rather he must have acted with the knowledge that he was doing a "bad" act under the general rules of law. Under this intermediate level of criminal common law willfulness, "the Government must prove that the defendant acted with knowledge that his conduct was unlawful."

The strictest level of interpretation of criminal willfulness requires that the defendant knew the terms of the statute and that he was violating the statute. The courts have reserved this category to limited types of statutory violations involving "complex" statutes – namely those governing federal tax law and antistructuring transactions. Although [this court] has not addressed the FCPA under this category, [the *Schreiber* case discussed above] has determined that the FCPA does not fall within this narrow category of complex statutes, and we agree.

The district court's jury instructions captured both the first and second levels of criminal willfulness [. . .] We find the instructions sufficient, since the strictest interpretation of criminal willfulness is reserved for complex statutes. Under the first and broadest definition of criminal willfulness, the term "knowingly" in the context of willful criminal action "merely requires proof of knowledge of the facts that constitute the offense". [. . .]

The district court, by instructing the jury that a guilty verdict required a finding that defendant acted "voluntarily and intentionally, and with a bad purpose or evil motive of accomplishing either an unlawful end or result," and by including a separate "knowing" instruction, correctly indicated that the jury must identify evidence amounting to "knowledge of facts that constitute the offense" required by the traditional criminal definition of willfulness (which we have described as the first category of willfulness). The court's instructions also substantially covered the requested instruction that Defendants acted "corruptly," meaning they acted "knowingly and dishonestly, with the specific intent to achieve an unlawful result by influencing a foreign public official's action in one's own favor." The instructions suggested that illegal conduct under the FCPA defined the "unlawful end or result" to which the court referred, since the jury had to have some standard by which to gauge lawfulness. Additionally, the instructions correctly indicated that to be guilty under the Act, Defendants must have knowingly (i.e., voluntarily and intentionally) acted with awareness of these unlawful ends.

[. . .]

We find that the district court's jury instructions also capture our second, or intermediate, definition of criminal willfulness – a definition that we commonly follow – that a defendant knew that he was doing something generally "unlawful" at the time of his action. This level of interpretation is stricter than the first because it does not only require that the defendant knew that he was committing an act (an act which, incidentally, falls within the definition of the relevant statute); the defendant must have known that the act was in some way wrong. The district court's jury instructions captured this level of intent well with their requirement that the jury find that Defendants acted "with a bad purpose or evil motive."

[. . .]

The instructions' requirements that Defendants acted corruptly, with an "unlawful end or result," and committed "intentional" and "knowing" acts with a bad motive sufficiently captured the definition of criminal willfulness that we follow. They also allowed Defendants to effectively put forth adequate defenses: Defendants could have argued lack of intent and that they were not acting with knowledge of unlawful means or ends. The district court's jury instructions adequately conveyed the "willfulness" required for a conviction under the FCPA.

## Guidance

The FCPA Guidance states as follows regarding *mens rea* issues:

> As long as the offer, promise, authorization, or payment is made corruptly, the actor need not know the identity of the recipient; the attempt is sufficient. Thus, an executive who authorizes others to pay "whoever you need to" in a foreign government to obtain a contract has violated the FCPA – even if no bribe is ultimately offered or paid.
>
> The term "willfully" is not defined in the FCPA, but it has generally been construed by courts to connote an act committed voluntarily and purposefully, and with a bad purpose, i.e. with "knowledge that a defendant was doing a 'bad' act under the general rules of law." [. . .] "As a general matter, when used in the criminal context, a 'willful' act is one undertaken with a 'bad purpose.' In other words, to establish a 'willful' violation of a statute, 'the Government must prove that the defendant acted with knowledge that his conduct was unlawful.'"

Regarding extortion, the FCPA Guidance states:

> Situations involving extortion or duress will not give rise to FCPA liability because a payment made in response to true extortionate demands under imminent threat of physical harm cannot be said to have been made with corrupt intent or for the purpose of obtaining or retaining business.
>
> [. . .]

> Mere economic coercion, however, does not amount to extortion.
> [. . .]
> Businesses operating in high-risk countries may face real threats of violence or harm to their employees, and payments made in response to imminent threats to health or safety do not violate the FCPA. If such a situation arises, and to ensure the safety of its employees, companies should immediately contact the appropriate U.S. embassy for assistance.

In the FCPA Guidance the government also acknowledged how the corrupt intent element may limit application of the FCPA's anti-bribery provisions:

> The corrupt intent requirement protects companies that engage in the ordinary and legitimate promotion of their businesses while targeting conduct that seeks to improperly induce officials into misusing their positions. Thus, it is difficult to envision any scenario in which the provision of cups of coffee, taxi fare, or company promotional items of nominal value would ever evidence corrupt intent, and neither DOJ nor SEC has ever pursued an investigation on the basis of such conduct.

The DOJ has further provided, albeit perhaps indirectly, guidance on the corrupt intent element in several Opinion Procedure Releases which acknowledge that "the FCPA does not *per se* prohibit business relationships with, or payments to, foreign officials."[37] Rather, as stated by the DOJ, where an arrangement with a foreign official exists:

> the Department typically looks to determine whether there are any indicia of corrupt intent, whether the arrangement is transparent to the foreign government and the general public, whether the arrangement is in conformity with local law, and whether there are safeguards to prevent the foreign official from improperly using his or her position to steer business to or otherwise assist the company, for example through a policy of recusal.

## Enforcement actions

Notwithstanding the above legal authority as well as sensible government guidance that "the corrupt intent requirement protects companies that engage in the ordinary and legitimate promotion of their businesses while targeting conduct that seeks to improperly induce officials into misusing their positions," as highlighted earlier in this chapter several enforcement actions have included allegations or findings about relatively inconsequential things of value being offered or provided to alleged "foreign officials." In many of these enforcement actions, it would seem to be an open question whether the thing of value was provided with an evil motive or purpose or intended to induce the official to misuse their position. As FCPA practitioners have noted:

> Perhaps most interesting about [certain] recent cases is that the government's charging papers in some cases seem to lack any direct evidence that the benefits provided were provided as a *quid pro quo* to obtain a specific favorable decision from the official. The cases seem to simply conclude that if there were benefits provided to a government decision maker, the benefits must have been improper. Whether such allegations would be sufficient to satisfy the FCPA's "corruptly" standard in litigation remains to be seen.[38]

Reflective of the legislative history discussed above that corrupt intent "does not require that an act be fully consummated or succeed in producing the desired result," certain enforcement actions have been based on unsuccessful bribery schemes. For instance, in an enforcement action against agricultural company Monsanto, the government alleged in summary fashion:

> [A] senior Monsanto manager who was responsible for certain activities in the Asia Pacific region, authorized and directed an Indonesian consulting firm to make an illegal payment totaling $50,000 to a senior Indonesian Ministry of Environment official ("the Senior Environment Official"). This bribe was made to influence the Senior Environment Official to repeal an unfavorable decree that was likely to have an adverse effect on Monsanto's business. Although the payment was made, the unfavorable decree was not repealed.[39]

Likewise, the Smith & Wesson enforcement action included the following allegation:

> Smith & Wesson authorized improper payments to third party agents who indicated that parts of these payments would be provided to foreign officials in Nepal and Bangladesh in unsuccessful attempts to secure sales contracts in those countries. Although these contemplated deals in Nepal and Bangladesh were never consummated in each case, the company had obtained or attempted to obtain the contract by using third party agents as a conduit for improper payments to government officials.[40]

Perhaps most disheartening from a defendant's point of view, in an enforcement action against various individuals for an alleged bribery scheme to facilitate the sale of a commercial building in Vietnam, the scheme was unsuccessful because the third party intended to facilitate the scheme simply pocketed the money for himself. As the DOJ stated in connection with this enforcement action: "This alleged conduct proves the adage that there is truly no honor among thieves. The indictment alleges that two defendants wanted to bribe a government official; instead they were defrauded by their co-defendant."[41]

Regarding true extortion demands, recognize that although payments made in such situations may not violate the anti-bribery provisions because of the lack of corrupt intent, such payments still need to be properly accounted for on the company's books and records. For instance, in an enforcement action against oil field services provider NATCO Group the government acknowledged that the company's expatriate workers were the victims of extortion demands by Kazakistan officials – specifically that Kazakh immigration prosecutors threatened to fine, jail or deport the workers if the company did not pay cash fines. Believing the threats to be genuine, employees used personal funds to pay the prosecutors and then obtained reimbursement from the company. Despite these circumstances, the government found that the company violated the FCPA's books and records and internal controls provisions because the reimbursements were not accurately recorded on the company's books and records.[42]

While FCPA's *mens rea* requirements are fact specific and thus often murky, the following take-away points are clear:

- corrupt intent equates to an evil or wrongful motive and it does not matter if a payment is first proposed by a "foreign official";
- even unsuccessful bribery attempts may satisfy the corrupt intent element;
- to establish the willful requirement necessary for an individual FCPA criminal conviction it is not necessary that the individual knew of the FCPA or its specific elements;
- payments made in connection with true extortion demands involving imminent threat of physical harm or destruction of assets are not made with corrupt intent; and

- notwithstanding government statements that the corrupt intent requirement "protects" companies from scrutiny and enforcement, several enforcement actions have included allegations or findings about relatively inconsequential things of value being offered or provided to alleged "foreign officials" in circumstances in which it was an open question whether the thing of value was intended to induce the official to misuse their position.

It's time once again to try on your "FCPA goggles" and assess your knowledge of the corrupt intent element by listening in on a phone conversation T Systems employee Sally is having with a Russian vendor. After reviewing the scenario, in which Sally wants to show gratitude to an individual who recently assisted T Systems, consider whether anything of value is being given to a foreign official with a corrupt intent.

> Sally [on the phone]: Hello? Do you speak English? [pauses to listen] Oh, perfect. I was wondering if I could order a gift basket. It's to be delivered to the Moscow City Duma. [pauses to listen] Oh good. Her name is Natasha Petrovna and she's in the Accounts Chamber Department. [pauses to listen] Okay. And could you include a note on that also? Saying, "Thank you for all of your assistance the other day," from Sally Brown of T Systems. [pauses to listen] Perfect.
>
> [Natasha and her co-worker are approached by a delivery man in Moscow and Natasha receives the delivery, removes the card, and states] Wow! I wasn't expecting this. What a kind gesture!

- *Anything of value*: it is fairly obvious that the gift basket is a thing of value. Probably not a high-dollar thing of value, but recall that anything of value means just that and there is no *de minimis* amount associated with this element. Indeed, several enforcement actions have included allegations about small things of value.

- *Foreign official*: Likewise, it is obvious that Natasha, the recipient of the thing of value from T Systems, is a foreign official as she works in a Moscow government office.

- *Corrupt intent*: Does Sally have an evil motive in giving Natasha the gift basket? By providing the gift basket, is Sally intending to induce Natasha to misuse her official position? Based on the circumstances depicted in the scenario, no is probably the best answer to both questions. Rather, the scenario depicts a simple gesture in which T Systems wants to show gratitude for a service already rendered and in this regard the gesture is similar to giving a tip to a server in a restaurant.

Notwithstanding the above analysis, it is likely that many compliance professionals would be nervous in approving the gift basket if Sally first sought compliance approval before providing it to Natasha. After all, can it truly be said that many of the things of value previously highlighted, including "golf in the morning and beer drinking in the evening," were provided with an evil motive or intended to induce a "foreign official" to misuse their official position? If you are nervous about approving the gift basket, what does this say about the modern era of FCPA enforcement? Are business organizations so risk averse and so fearful of broad and expansive enforcement theories that personnel are unwilling to approve of the organization offering a simple gift basket to an individual that helped them? Has the current enforcement landscape caused people to view gift-giving (a commonly accepted way of showing gratitude and generosity throughout human history) through a bribery gaze in which:

- Any time someone wants to be generous – it could be bribery!

- Any time someone wants to be friendly – it could be bribery!

- Any time someone wants to display hospitality – it could be bribery![43]

Perhaps it has, even if the above scenario probably does not evidence corrupt intent. Yet consider the broader ramifications of this risk aversion no doubt based on enforcement theories. Does this "bribery gaze" have social and thus policy implications? It has been noted:

> Campaigns to eliminate these gift exchanges are at the same time campaigns to restrict the gamut of courtesy or ritual exchanges. The manifestations of

> courtesy, gratitude, and social bonds, which are so important as social glue in any cohesive society, are not just called into question, but criminalized.[44]

Policy issues aside, it is not too difficult to change the above scenario such that corrupt intent may be present. For instance, while the scenario is depicted as a one-off encounter between T Systems and the Russian official, what if the encounter was the beginning of a long-term relationship between T Systems and Natasha? What if Natasha is going to have discretion concerning some aspect of the company's business on a yearly or quarterly basis? If this were the situation, perhaps the thing of value T Systems provided to Natasha early in the relationship is an attempt to curry favor with her and an attempt to influence her discretion in the future.

Regardless of the answers, once again what makes compliance with the FCPA and related laws tricky for business organizations is that in many situations gifts will generally not be problematic if directed to a certain customer or potential customer, but if directed toward a different type of person (i.e. a "foreign official"), government enforcement agencies might deem it bribery. Because of this, business organizations often struggle with gift giving.

So what is a well-intentioned business organization supposed to do to minimize risk in this area? After all, in the FCPA Guidance even the government acknowledges:

> A small gift or token of esteem or gratitude is often an appropriate way for business people to display respect for each other. Some hallmarks of appropriate gift-giving are when the gift is given openly and transparently, properly recorded in the giver's books and records, provided only to reflect esteem or gratitude, and permitted under local law. [. . .] The FCPA does not

prohibit gift-giving. Rather, just like its domestic bribery counterparts, the FCPA prohibits the payments of bribes, including those disguised as gifts.

Similar to the risk management strategies highlighted earlier in this chapter regarding other things of value, compliance starts with training and making sure that all employees and third parties with points of contact with "foreign officials" clearly understand the potential FCPA implications of gift giving. From there, business organizations should implement and communicate written policies and procedures regarding gifts throughout the organization which operate to take authority or discretion away from rank and file employees to provide gifts to customers or potential customers without pre-approval by compliance professionals. When analyzing gift requests, compliance professionals should ask the same questions previously highlighted:

- Was the gift requested by the foreign official?
- Does the company believe that providing the gift will advance a business interest?
- Is providing the gift consistent with company policy?
- Were normal company procedures followed in providing the gift?

Hopefully your "FCPA goggles" now have you seeing the wide range of circumstances in which scrutiny and enforcement can arise. However, properly constructed "FCPA goggles" require more than just an understanding of the anything of value and corrupt intent elements and the next section discusses the all-important "foreign official" element of the FCPA's anti-bribery provisions.

## Foreign official

"Foreign official" is often viewed as the most important element of the anti-bribery provisions because even if something of value is offered or provided to an individual to obtain or retain business, the anti-bribery provisions apply only to the extent the recipient is a "foreign official." However, and similar to the "just don't bribe" narrative discussed earlier, some believe that the scope of "foreign official" is of little practical significance because a business organization should not bribe anyone

– whether a "foreign official" or an individual not a "foreign official." Indeed, certain commentators have stated:

> If you are trying to figure out whether [an individual is a "foreign official"] under the FCPA you are already in trouble. To reach that point in the FCPA analysis you've already paid a bribe, or are thinking of paying a bribe.[45]

However, this observation misses the mark because the meaning of "foreign official" determines whether an aggressively enforced law applies to an interaction in the global marketplace and as highlighted earlier many enforcement actions are based on internships, sports tickets, travel and entertainment, and other inconsequential things of value such as flowers, cigarettes, and visits to karaoke bars. In other words, the underlying activity is legal and socially acceptable in most situations, but if the same thing of value is offered or provided to an alleged "foreign official" the enforcement agencies may deem it bribery.

Nevertheless, still others claim that such things of value – even if provided to non-foreign officials – can still constitute commercial bribery under the Travel Act (a law enacted prior to the FCPA that is part of the racketeering chapter of the criminal code and prohibits interstate and foreign travel or transportation in aid of racketeering enterprises).[46] Specifically, the Travel Act prohibits travel in interstate or foreign commerce or use of the mail or any facility in interstate or foreign commerce with intent to, among other things, carry on "any unlawful activity" which is defined to include bribery in violation of state law. Such claims might have merit if there was robust enforcement of the Travel Act based on the above things of value being provided to non-foreign officials, but there is simply not much enforcement activity in this space.

In short, the meaning of "foreign official" matters and is of practical importance to business organizations and this section highlights legal sources of authority as well as non-legal sources of information relevant to the "foreign official" element including:

- what types of individuals may qualify as "foreign officials";
- whether the specific identity of a "foreign official" must be proven by the enforcement agencies; and

- whether a defendant must have knowledge that an individual is indeed a "foreign official" to be liable under the anti-bribery provisions.

As suggested by these issues, the "foreign official" element is subject to dispute and controversy in certain instances and legal development of this important element is still in its infancy.

## Law

What is not in dispute is what the FCPA says and the statute defines "foreign official" to mean:

> any officer or employee of a foreign government or any department, agency, or instrumentality thereof, or of a public international organization, or any person acting in an official capacity for or on behalf of any such government or department, agency, or instrumentality, or for or on behalf of any such public international organization.

The FCPA does not define "department," "agency," or "instrumentality."

## Legislative history

In passing the FCPA, the legislative history is clear that Congress was primarily concerned with the foreign policy implications of the discovered foreign corporate payments such as those to the Japanese Prime Minister, the President of the Republic of Korea, the President of Gabon, a Saudi Arabian General, and Italian political parties. The legislative history is also clear that Congress learned of a wide variety of corporate payments to a wide variety of foreign recipients for a wide variety of reasons.[47] As relevant to the disputed interpretation of "foreign official" in certain of the judicial decisions discussed below, Congress was aware of the existence of so-called state-owned or state-controlled enterprises (SOEs) and that certain of the questionable payments discovered may have involved such entities.[48]

Generally speaking, SOEs are profit-seeking enterprises that have many attributes of private business such as publicly traded stock or other private investors, and many SOEs do business outside a foreign country's borders and employ nationals and non-nationals alike. Nevertheless, and not often transparent, a foreign government may hold an ownership interest in an SOE or exert some level of control (such as through appointment of directors or officers) over the business enterprise. Several of the world's largest companies are considered SOEs and such entities are found in many foreign countries and are often most prevalent in certain Asian countries and the Middle East.

There is no express statement or information in the extensive legislative history to directly support the enforcement agencies' interpretation that alleged SOEs are "instrumentalities" (or "departments" or "agencies") of a foreign government such that employees of SOEs (regardless of rank, title, or position) are therefore "foreign officials" under the FCPA and occupy a position equal to that of a Prime Minister, President or other traditional government official.[49] However, there are several statements, events, and information in the legislative history that demonstrate that Congress did not intend the "foreign official" definition to include SOE employees. Among other things, in certain of the competing bills introduced in Congress to address the foreign corporate payments problem, the definition of "foreign government" expressly included SOEs and Congress was provided with an even more precise definition of "foreign government" to include SOEs.[50] However, despite being aware of SOEs, despite exhibiting a capability for drafting a definition that expressly included SOEs in other bills, and despite being provided a more precise way to describe SOEs, Congress chose not to include such definitions or concepts in the bill that ultimately became the FCPA.

From a comparative standpoint, recognize that certain other countries expressly include SOE concepts in their FCPA-like laws. For instance, the U.K. Bribery Act defines "foreign public official" to expressly include individuals who exercise a public function for any "public enterprise."[51] Similarly, Canada's "Corruption of Foreign Public Officials Act" defines "foreign public official" to expressly include a person who performs public duties or functions for a foreign state, including a person employed by a "corporation."[52] Likewise, the relevant provisions of Australia's Criminal Code Act expressly state that "foreign government body" includes "a foreign public enterprise," and the Act then contains a detailed definition of "foreign public enterprise."[53]

## Enforcement actions

For most of the FCPA's history, the "foreign official" element presented little controversy as enforcement largely focused on payments to bona fide "foreign officials" such as presidents, other heads of state, political leaders, and other foreign government regulatory officials. To be sure, certain enforcement actions in the modern era still focus on payments to such bona fide "foreign officials" – mostly various regulatory officials. However, interpretation of the "foreign official" element has led to dispute and controversy in certain instances as many recent enforcement actions have nothing to do with traditional, bona fide government officials. Rather, Table 2.2 highlights various enforcement agency "foreign official" allegations, in whole or in part, in recent corporate FCPA enforcement actions.

*Table 2.2 "Foreign official" allegations*

| Enforcement action | Alleged "foreign officials" |
|---|---|
| Rolls-Royce[54] | Employees at PTT Public Company Ltd [a Thai state-owned and state-controlled oil and gas company]; employees at Petrobras [a corporation in which the Brazilian government directly owned a majority of common shares with voting rights, while additional shares were controlled by the Brazilian Development Bank and Brazil's Sovereign Wealth Fund]; employees at Asia Gas Pipeline [AGP a joint venture between Kazakh and Chinese state-owned and state-controlled entities]; employees at SOCAR [the Azeri state-owned and state-controlled oil and gas company]; employees at SOC [South Oil Company, an Iraqi state-owned and state-controlled oil company]; employees at Sonangol [an Angolan state-owned and state-controlled oil company] |
| SciClone Pharmaceuticals[55] | Healthcare professionals employed by state-owned hospitals in China |
| PTC[56] | Employees of "Chinese state-owned entities" |
| Olympus[57] | Healthcare professionals in Brazil, Bolivia, Colombia, Argentina, Mexico, and Costa Rica |
| Pfizer/Wyeth[58] | Healthcare providers who worked at publicly-owned hospitals in Argentina, Brazil, and China, Greece, Poland, Romania, Bulgaria, Croatia, Kazakhstan, Czech Republic, Italy, Serbia, Indonesia, Pakistan and Russia |
| NORDAM Group[59] | Employees of Chinese state-owned and-controlled entities, including airlines created, controlled, and exclusively owned by the Chinese government |
| Aon[60] | Employees of Costa Rica's state-owned insurance company |
| Veraz Networks[61] | Employees of government-controlled telecommunications companies in China and Vietnam |

As indicated by the above chart, in many modern enforcement actions the "foreign officials" have been employed by alleged SOEs. Indeed, since 2010 approximately 50% of corporate enforcement actions have involved, in whole or in part, SOE employees.[62] As further reflected in the chart, another prominent enforcement theory is that various individuals associated with foreign healthcare systems (such as physicians, laboratory personnel, and even a mid-wife) are "foreign officials." Since first used in an enforcement action in 2002, this enforcement theory has since been used in approximately 25 corporate enforcement actions. However, and perhaps reflective of its validity and legitimacy, this enforcement theory has never been used to prosecute an individual for FCPA offenses. Given business organization risk aversion, none of the foreign official enforcement allegations in Table 2.2 were challenged or subjected to any meaningful judicial scrutiny.

## Judicial decisions

However, as the enforcement agencies began to bring more individual enforcement actions based on the enforcement theory that SOE employees are "foreign officials," individuals began to challenge this interpretation resulting in judicial decisions concerning the following issues: what types of individuals may qualify as "foreign officials"; whether the specific identity of a "foreign official" must be proven by the enforcement agencies; and whether a defendant must have knowledge that an individual is indeed a "foreign official" to be liable under the anti-bribery provisions.

## SOE employees as "foreign officials"

In *U.S. v. Esquenazi*, Joel Esquenazi and Carlos Rodriguez (former executives of Terra Telecommunications) were criminally charged for their alleged roles in a scheme to pay bribes to alleged "foreign officials" at Haiti Teleco.[63] After being convicted at trial of FCPA and other offenses, the defendants appealed challenging, among other things, the trial court's "foreign official" jury instruction and an issue presented to the appellate court was "[w]hether [defendants are] entitled to an acquittal because employees of Haiti Teleco were not 'foreign officials' within the meaning of FCPA simply because the National Bank of Haiti owned shares of Haiti Teleco and the Haitian government appoints board members and directors."

The appeal was historic in that it represented the first time in FCPA history in which an appellate court was presented with the opportunity to scrutinize the prominent enforcement theory that employees of alleged SOEs are "foreign officials." Because *Esquenazi* was a case of first impression, and given the previously highlighted prominence of the SOE "foreign official" interpretation as well as the general importance of the "foreign official" element, an extended discussion of the appellate court decision is warranted.[64] To state the obvious, the *Esquenazi* decision was based on the unique facts of the case and in terms of factual background the court stated:

> One of Terra's main vendors was [Haiti Teleco]. Because the relationship of Teleco to the Haitian government was, and remains, at issue in this case, the government presented evidence of Teleco's ties to Haiti. Former Teleco Director of International Relations Robert Antoine testified that Teleco was owned by Haiti. An insurance broker, John Marsha, testified that, when Messrs. Rodriguez and Esquenazi were involved in previous contract negotiations with Teleco, they sought political-risk insurance, a type of coverage that applies only when a foreign government is party to an agreement. In emails with Mr. Marsha copied to Messrs. Esquenazi and Rodríguez, Mr. Dickey called Teleco an "instrumentality" of the Haitian government.
>
> An expert witness, Luis Gary Lissade, testified regarding Teleco's history. At Teleco's formation in 1968, the Haitian government gave the company a monopoly on telecommunication services. Teleco had significant tax advantages and, at its inception, the government appointed two members of Teleco's board of directors. Haiti's President appointed Teleco's Director General, its top position, by an executive order that was also signed by the Haitian Prime Minister, the minister of public works, and the minister of economy and finance. In the early 1970s, the National Bank of Haiti gained 97 percent ownership of Teleco. From that time forward, the Haitian President appointed all of Teleco's board members. Sometime later, the National Bank of Haiti split into two separate entities, one of which was the Banque de la Republique d'Haiti (BRH). BRH, the central bank of Haiti, is roughly equivalent to the United States Federal Reserve. BRH retained ownership of Teleco. In Mr. Lissade's expert opinion, for the years relevant to this case, Teleco belonged "totally to the state" and "was considered . . . a public entity."
>
> Mr. Lissade also testified that Teleco's business entity suffix, S.A.M., indicates "associate anonymous mixed," which means the "Government put money in the corporation." Teleco's suffix was attached not by statute, but "de facto" because "the government consider[ed] Teleco as its . . . entity." In 1996, Haiti passed a "modernization" law, seeking to privatize many public institu-

> tions. As a result, Haiti privatized Teleco sometime between 2009 and 2010. Ultimately, Mr. Lissade opined that, during the years relevant to this case, "Teleco was part of the public administration." He explained: "There was no specific law that . . . decided that at the beginning that Teleco is a public entity but government, officials, everyone consider[ed] Teleco as a public administration." And, he said, "if there was a doubt whatsoever, the [anti-corruption] law [that] came in 2008 vanish[ed] completely this doubt . . . by citing Teleco as a public administration" and by requiring its agents – whom Mr. Lissade said were public agents – to declare all assets to avoid secret bribes.

Based on the above circumstances, the court concluded that Haiti Teleco "would qualify as a Haitian instrumentality under almost any definition [the court] could craft," and that the Haiti Teleco employees allegedly bribed were thus "foreign officials" under the FCPA. Elsewhere, the court stated that it had "little difficulty concluding sufficient evidence supported the jury's necessary finding that Teleco was a Haitian instrumentality." The court could have rendered its decision solely on this narrow issue, however "mindful of the needs of both corporations and the government for [future] direction about what an instrumentality is," the court went further and defined "instrumentality" as follows.

> An "instrumentality" [under the FCPA] is an entity *controlled* by the government of a foreign country that performs a *function* the controlling government treats as its own. Certainly, what constitutes control and what constitutes a function the government treats as its own are fact-bound questions. It would be unwise and likely impossible to exhaustively answer them in the abstract. Because we only have this case before us, we do not purport to list all of the factors that might prove relevant to deciding whether an entity is an instrumentality of a foreign government. For today, we provide a list of some factors that may be relevant to deciding the issue.
>
> To decide if the government "***controls***" an entity, courts and juries should look to the foreign government's formal designation of that entity; whether the government has a majority interest in the entity; the government's ability to hire and fire the entity's principals; the extent to which the entity's profits, if any, go directly into the governmental fisc, and, by the same token, the extent to which the government funds the entity if it fails to break even; and the length of time these indicia have existed.
>
> [. . .]
>
> We then turn to the second element relevant to deciding if an entity is an instrumentality of a foreign government under the FCPA – deciding if the entity performs a ***function*** the government treats as its own. Courts and juries should examine whether the entity has a monopoly over the function

> it exists to carry out; whether the government subsidizes the costs associated with the entity providing services; whether the entity provides services to the public at large in the foreign country; and whether the public and the government of that foreign country generally perceive the entity to be performing a governmental function. (Emphasis added)

The court apparently thought such answers would be easy to ascertain and stated:

> We think it will be relatively easy to decide what functions a government treats as its own in the present tense by resort to objective factors, like control, exclusivity, governmental authority to hire and fire, subsidization, and whether an entity's finances are treated as part of the public fisc. Both courts and businesses subject to the FCPA have readily at hand the tools to conduct that inquiry (especially because the statute contains a mechanism by which the Attorney General will render opinions on requests about what foreign entities constitute instrumentalities [the so-called FCPA Opinion Procedure Release Program].

However, it is difficult to envision how a compliance professional tasked with approving expenditures of things of value made in connection with a business purpose will find answers to certain issues identified by the court as being relevant. As FCPA practitioners noted:

> In practice, this analysis may be more difficult than the court allows because information on these factors is not always publicly available or easy to discern.[65]

> The boundaries between public and private entities are often blurred, particularly in developing countries where corruption risks are the target of heightened Justice Department scrutiny.[66]

> As companies long have known, it can be expensive and time consuming to make such determinations, particularly in countries such as Russia, China, and various countries in Central and Latin America and in Africa where information about companies and state ownership is less than transparent and objective.[67]

> Ten years ago, I would have been happy to bet anyone a doughnut that I could accurately define what a foreign official is. Now, with various court definitions and a lack of clarity from the DOJ, I fear I might actually lose my doughnut.[68]

Indeed, an irony of *Esquenzi*'s non-exhaustive, factor-based test for what constitutes an "instrumentality" under the FCPA is that elsewhere in the opinion the court itself recognized that it will be a "difficult task – involving divining the subjective intentions of a foreign sovereign, parsing history, and interpreting significant amounts of foreign law – to decide what functions a foreign government considers core and traditional." Moreover, the court recognized "there may be entities near the definitional line for 'instrumentality' that may raise a vagueness concern."

A further irony of the *Esquenazi* factor-based test is that it resorts to foreign government categorization and characterization of a business enterprise. However, in a previous Opinion Procedure Release, the DOJ rejected such an approach. Specifically, in Release 94-01 a company subject to the FCPA disclosed that its "foreign attorney has advised that under the nation's law, the individual [at issue] would not be regarded as either a government employee or a public official." Nevertheless, the DOJ stated that "the foreign attorney's opinion is not dispositive" and that it "considered the foreign individual to be a 'foreign official' under the [FCPA]."[69] By largely deferring to foreign government characterization of a business enterprise, the *Esquenazi* decision crafted an "instrumentality" definition with nearly 200 potential different meanings (the approximate number of sovereign countries in the world).

The soundness of the *Esquenazi* decision and its attendant practical compliance difficulties aside, *Esquenazi* is the leading case interpreting the "foreign official" element and compliance professionals should be well-versed on its two-factor control and function test which expanded the scope of the "foreign official" element beyond a "well-defined group of persons" (as correctly noted by another appellate court, albeit in dicta, in *U.S. v. Castle*) to a practically boundless category of persons. Consider the following examples of "foreign officials"/"instrumentalities" alleged in recent enforcement actions:

> A U.S. resident working for a U.S. company was a Russian "foreign official" because the company was a wholly-owned subsidiary of an entity indirectly owned and controlled by, and performed functions of, the Russian government.[70]

> A dual U.S./Egyptian citizen working for a U.S. company was an Egyptian "foreign official" because he was assigned by the company to be the general manager of a joint venture between the U.S. company and an Egyptian SOE.[71]

> A Texas incorporated, Texas based company was an "instrumentality" of the Angolan government because it was a "wholly-owned subsidiary of Sonangol . . . a state-owned and state-controlled oil company."[72]

> A subsidiary of an Italian oil and gas company was an "instrumentality" of the Kazakhstan government because it was granted a concession by the Kazakh government and was thus "acting in an official capacity for or on behalf" of the Kazakh government."[73]

Once again, some may react to the disputed scope of the "foreign official" element by saying "just don't bribe." However, as previously highlighted, the meaning of "foreign official" determines whether an aggressively enforced law applies to an interaction in the global marketplace and many recent enforcement actions have been based on allegations concerning internships, sports tickets, travel and entertainment, and other inconsequential things of value such as flowers, cigarettes, and visits to karaoke bars. In other words, the underlying activity is legal and socially acceptable in most situations, but if the same thing of value is offered or provided to an alleged "foreign official," the enforcement agencies may deem it bribery.

## Other types of foreign officials

While the above analysis largely focused on the meaning of "instrumentality," the FCPA's "foreign official" definition also includes the term "public international organization" and the proper meaning of this term has been subjected to judicial scrutiny. In *U.S. v. Harder*, the government criminally charged Dmitrij Harder (the former owner and President of Chestnut Consulting Group Inc. and Chestnut Consulting Group Co.) for allegedly bribing an official with the European Bank for Reconstruction and Development and the enforcement action was notable in that it invoked the rarely used "public international organization" prong of the FCPA's "foreign official" element.[74] Harder filed a motion to dismiss asserting, among other things, that the indictment was devoid of any allegations that he paid a corrupt payment to a "foreign official" and that the FCPA's use of the term "public international organization" was unconstitutional because it permits the President to expand this term pursuant to executive order. However, the judge disagreed and held that the term "public international organization" was not vague and that Congress's delegation to the President was narrowly circumscribed and thus constitutional. The take-away point here is that inclusion of "public international organization" in the definition of "foreign official" further expands the category of individuals deemed "foreign officials" such as those associated with the United Nations, World Health Organization and various development banks.

### Identity of foreign official

In addition to the disputed legal issue of what types of individuals may qualify as "foreign officials" are the related issues of whether the specific identity of a "foreign official" must be proven by the enforcement agencies and whether a defendant must have knowledge that an individual is indeed a "foreign official" to be liable under the anti-bribery provisions.

In *U.S. v. O'Shea*, the government alleged that the defendant violated the anti-bribery provisions by making payments to officials at a Mexican utility allegedly owned or controlled by the Mexican government. However, after the government's evidence, the judge granted a motion for acquittal and in commenting on the many flaws in the government's case stated:

> You can't convict a man promising to pay unless you have a particular promise to a particular person for a particular benefit. If you call up [somebody] and say, look, I'm going to send you 50 grand, bribe somebody, that does not meet the statute.[75]

However, the notion that the specific identity of a "foreign official" must be proven by the enforcement agencies has been rejected by two other trial courts in individual enforcement actions. In *SEC v. Jackson* (an enforcement action discussed in more detail in Chapter 4 concerning facilitating payments), the court concluded, in ruling on a pre-trial motion to dismiss, that the "government does not have to connect the payment to a particular official."[76] The court stated:

> The language of the statute does not appear to require that the identity of the foreign official involved be pled with specificity. [. . .] Nothing in the legislative history of the FCPA suggests that Congress intended to limit the application of [the FCPA] to those cases where the government could show that a defendant knew, either by name or job description, precisely which foreign officials would be receiving the illicit payments he had authorized. [. . .] It would be perverse to read into the statute a requirement that a defendant know precisely which government official, or which level of government official, would be targeted by his agent; a defendant could simply avoid liability

> by ensuring that his agent never told him which official was being targeted and what precise action the official took in exchange for the bribe.

Likewise in *SEC v. Straub* (an enforcement action discussed in more detail later in this chapter concerning jurisdiction issues as to foreign actors) the court agreed with the above analysis in *Jackson* and stated, in the context of a pre-trial motion to dismiss, that "the language of the [FCPA] does not appear to require that the identity of the foreign official involved be pled with specificity."[77] The court noted:

> Such a requirement would be at odds with the statutory scheme, which targets actions (such as making an "offer" or "promise") without requiring that the "foreign official" accept the offer or reveal his specific identity to the payer. Indeed, the fact that the FCPA prohibits using "any person" or an intermediary to facilitate the bribe to any "foreign official" or "any foreign political party" suggests that the statute contemplates situations in which the payer knows that a "foreign official" will ultimately receive a bribe but only the intermediary knows the foreign official's specific identity.

## Knowledge of foreign official

*U.S. v. Carson* is instructive regarding the issue of whether a defendant must have knowledge that an individual is indeed a "foreign official" to be liable under the anti-bribery provisions. In the enforcement action, various former employees of valve manufacturer Control Components Inc. were criminally charged with FCPA violations in connection with alleged payments to employees at alleged SOEs in China, Malaysia, and the United Arab Emirates. After the trial court denied the defendants' motion to dismiss challenging the government's "foreign official" enforcement theory in a manner similar to *Esquenazi,* the disputed "foreign official" issue moved to the jury instructions and the judge issued a jury instruction titled "knowledge of status of foreign official" which stated, in pertinent part:

> (4) The defendant offered, paid, promised to pay, or authorized the payment of money, or offered, gave, promised to give, or authorized the giving of anything of value to a foreign official;
> (5) The payment or gift at issue in element 4 was to (a) a person the defendant knew or believed was a foreign official or (b) any person and the defendant knew that all or a portion of such money or thing of value would be offered, given, or promised (directly or indirectly) to a person the defendant knew or believed to be a foreign official. Belief that an individual was a

> foreign official does not satisfy this element if the individual was not in fact a foreign official.[78]

After the judge issued this jury instruction and with trial looming, the government allowed the defendants to plead guilty to substantially reduced charges compared to the original indictment.

## Guidance

Relevant to "foreign official" issues, the FCPA Guidance states, in pertinent part:

> The FCPA broadly applies to corrupt payments to "any" officer or employee of a foreign government and to those acting on the foreign government's behalf. The FCPA thus covers corrupt payments to low-ranking employees and high-level officials alike.
>
> [. . .]
>
> Foreign officials under the FCPA include officers or employees of a department, agency, or instrumentality of a foreign government. When a foreign government is organized in a fashion similar to the U.S. system, what constitutes a government department or agency is typically clear (e.g., a ministry of energy, national security agency, or transportation authority). However, governments can be organized in very different ways. Many operate through state-owned and state-controlled entities, particularly in such areas as aerospace and defense manufacturing, banking and finance, healthcare and life sciences, energy and extractive industries, telecommunications, and transportation. By including officers or employees of agencies and instrumentalities within the definition of "foreign official," the FCPA accounts for this variability.
> The term "instrumentality" is broad and can include state-owned or state-controlled entities. Whether a particular entity constitutes an "instrumentality" under the FCPA requires a fact-specific analysis of an entity's ownership, control, status, and function.
>
> [. . .]
>
> While no one factor is dispositive or necessarily more important than another, as a practical matter, an entity is unlikely to qualify as an instrumentality if a government does not own or control a majority of its shares. However, there are circumstances in which an entity would qualify as an instrumentality absent 50% or greater foreign government ownership, which is reflected in the limited number of DOJ or SEC enforcement actions brought in such situations.

Regardless of the dispute and controversy regarding the FCPA's key "foreign official" element in certain instances, the take-away point from this section is that given the enforcement agencies' interpretations, scrutiny and enforcement can arise from business interactions with a wide scope of individuals in the global marketplace and not just bona fide foreign government officials.

So what is a well-intentioned business organization supposed to do to minimize risk in this area recognizing that the same thing of value can be provided to different people but only be deemed bribery by enforcement agencies if provided to a "foreign official"? For starters and practical difficulties with the *Esquenazi* two-factor test aside, a business organization needs to make good faith efforts to understand whether any of its customers or potential customers are foreign governments, departments, agencies or instrumentalities or public international organizations. With this understanding, a business organization can then prioritize the compliance policies and procedures already discussed regarding anything of value (as well as many more that will be discussed later in this book) to business interactions subject to the anti-bribery provisions. Like most aspects of compliance with the FCPA and related laws, training is important and a business organizations should train employees and agents and provide them with "FCPA goggles" so that they can spot risk in their specific job functions. This is particularly important when it comes to the "foreign official" element because the expansive interpretation of "foreign official" is not intuitive in all instances or an issue of common sense. Coupled with training, a business organization should also ensure that its written compliance policies and procedures accessible throughout the organization actually convey the broad interpretation of the "foreign official" element. However, in many cases actual codes of conduct fail in this regard by using language that refers to foreign officials by using narrow, traditional concepts of foreign government.

## Obtain or retain business

For there to be a violation of the FCPA's anti-bribery provisions something of value must be offered or provided with a corrupt intent to a "foreign official," not just for any reason but to influence or induce the recipient to assist in "obtaining or retaining" business. This section highlights legal authority and non-legal sources of information regarding this important qualifying element.

### Law

The FCPA's anti-bribery provisions apply to things of value offered or provided to "foreign officials" for purposes of:

> (A) (i) influencing any act or decision of such foreign official in his official capacity, (ii) inducing such foreign official to do or omit to do any act in violation of the lawful duty of such official, or (iii) securing any improper advantage; or
>
> (B) inducing such foreign official to use his influence with a foreign government or instrumentality thereof to affect or influence any act or decision of such government or instrumentality
>
> in order to assist . . . in obtaining or retaining business for or with, or directing business to, any person.

### Legislative history

Legislative history evidences that despite learning of a wide range of foreign corporate payments, Congress chose to limit the anti-bribery provisions to a narrow range of circumstances involving foreign government procurement or influencing foreign government laws or regulations. For instance, the Conference Report drafted immediately prior to the FCPA's passage stated:

> The scope of the prohibition [in the Senate bill] was limited by the requirement that the offer, promise, authorization, payment, or gift must have as a purpose inducing the recipient to use his influence with the foreign government or instrumentality, influencing the enactment or promulgation of

> legislation or regulations of that government or instrumentality or refraining from performing any official responsibilities, so as to direct business to any person, maintain an established business opportunity with any person or divert a business opportunity from any person.
>
> The House amendment was similar to the Senate bill; however, the scope of the House amendment was not limited by the "business purpose" test [. . .] The conferees clarified the scope of the prohibition by requiring that the purpose of the payment must be to influence any act or decision of a foreign official (including a decision not to act) or to induce such official to use his influence to affect a government act or decision so as to assist an issuer in obtaining, retaining or directing business to any person.[79]

For most of the FCPA's history, the "obtain or retain business" element presented little dispute or controversy as enforcement largely focused on payments in connection with foreign government procurement. However, in the modern era of enforcement the "obtain or retain" business element has led to dispute and controversy in certain cases as many enforcement actions have nothing to do with foreign government procurement. As the enforcement agencies brought more individual enforcement actions concerning conduct outside the context of foreign government procurement, individuals began to challenge this enforcement theory and judicial decisions followed.

## Judicial decisions

The enforcement theory that payments outside the context of foreign government procurement violate the anti-bribery provisions has been subjected to judicial scrutiny four times.

The first instance involved criminal charges against Alfred Duran and other various individuals associated with AEA Aircraft Recovery (a company in the business of recovery of seized aircraft).[80] According to the government, the defendants conspired to make payments to officials of the Dominican Republic in order to obtain the release of two aircraft seized by the government. All of the defendants pleaded guilty except for Duran, who put the DOJ to its burden of proof at trial. After the DOJ presented its evidence at trial, Duran filed a motion for judgment of acquittal and argued that "no reasonable jury could find that the purpose of any of the alleged intended payments was to assist [. . .] in obtaining or retaining business" and that the government "has failed to adduce sufficient evidence to prove any intended payments were not facilitating or expediting payments for the purpose of expediting or securing routine governmental action (i.e. grease payments)." The trial court judge granted the motion ending the case and according to media reports the judge said that "the government failed to prove the charges against [Duran] were a crime under the FCPA."

The second instance was in *U.S. v. Kay* in which David Kay and Douglas Murphy (the president and vice president of American Rice Inc. (ARI) were criminally charged with anti-bribery violations based on allegations that they made improper payments to Haitian foreign officials for the purpose of reducing customs duties and sales taxes owed by ARI to the Haitian government. The indictment, while specific as to other items, merely tracked the FCPA's "obtain or retain business" language and did not specifically allege how the alleged payments assisted ARI in obtaining or retaining business in Haiti or what business was obtained or retained. The trial court found the FCPA's "obtain or retain business" element ambiguous and thus consulted the legislative history and stated:

> A review of the legislative history confirms that in 1977, Congress chose to limit the scope of the prohibited activities under the FCPA and did not intend to cover payments made to influence any and all governmental decisions. This legislative history weighs against the Government's argument that the FCPA should be construed so broadly so as to encompass payments made to reduce customs duties or tax obligations. The Court thus determines that Congress has considered and rejected statutory language that would broaden the scope of the FCPA to cover the conduct in question here.[81]

Accordingly, the court granted the defendants' motion to dismiss the indictment and held, as a matter of law, that the alleged payments were not payments made to "obtain or retain business" and thus did not fall within the scope of the anti-bribery provisions.

Shortly after the trial court decision in *Kay* in the Southern District of Texas, a case in the same jurisdiction again considered whether payments made to foreign officials outside the context of foreign government procurement fell under the anti-bribery provisions. In *SEC v. Mattson*, a civil enforcement action against Baker Hughes Inc. employees Eric Mattson and James Harris, the government alleged that the FCPA captured goodwill payments to an Indonesian tax official for a reduction in a tax assessment.[82] The issue before the court in a pre-trial motion to dismiss was whether the FCPA prohibited goodwill payments for the purpose of reducing a tax assessment. The court noted that the *Kay* court already found that the FCPA did not prohibit goodwill payments to foreign officials to reduce a tax obligation. However, the SEC attempted to distinguish the *Kay* ruling by arguing that in the civil enforcement context the FCPA's language should be construed more liberally than in criminal cases. The court rejected the SEC's argument, followed the trial court's analysis in *Kay*, and held that the payments at issue to the Indonesian tax official did not violate the FCPA because it did not help Mattson's and Harris's employer "obtain or retain business."

Returning to the *Kay* enforcement action, the DOJ appealed the trial court dismissal and the appeal thus represented the fourth, and most recent, instance in which payments to foreign officials outside the context of foreign government procurement were subjected to judiciary scrutiny. Specifically, one issue on appeal was whether payments to foreign officials to obtain favorable tax and customs treatment can come within the scope of the FCPA's anti-bribery provisions.[83] Like the trial court, the appellate court's 2014 decision also found the "obtain or retain business" element ambiguous and stated:

> Perhaps our most significant statutory construction problem results from the failure of the language of the FCPA to give a clear indication of the exact scope of the business nexus element; that is, the proximity of the required nexus between, on the one hand, the anticipated results of the foreign official's bargained-for action or inaction, and, on the other hand, the assistance provided by or expected from those results in helping the briber to obtain or retain business. Stated differently, how attenuated can the linkage be between the effects of that which is sought from the foreign official in consideration of a bribe (here, tax minimization) and the briber's goal of finding assistance or obtaining or retaining foreign business with or for some person, and still satisfy the business nexus element of the FCPA?

Like the trial court, the appellate court also consulted the legislative history but came to a different conclusion than the trial court and stated:

> We surmise that, in using the word "business" . . . Congress intended for the statute to apply to bribes beyond the narrow band of payments sufficient only to "obtain or retain government contracts." [. . .] In short, the 1977 legislative history . . . convinces us that Congress meant to prohibit a range of payments wider than only those that directly influence the acquisition or retention of government contracts or similar commercial or industrial

> arrangements. [. . .] We cannot hold as a matter of law that Congress meant to limit the FCPA's applicability to cover only bribes that lead directly to the award or renewal of contracts. Instead, we hold that Congress intended for the FCPA to apply broadly to payments intended to assist the payer, either directly or indirectly, in obtaining or retaining business for some person, and that bribes paid to foreign tax officials to secure illegally reduced customs and tax liability constitute a type of payment that can fall within this broad coverage.
>
> [. . .]
>
> Thus, in diametric opposition to the district court, we conclude that bribes paid to foreign officials in consideration for unlawful evasion of customs duties and sales taxes could fall within the purview of the FCPA's proscription. We hasten to add, however, that this conduct does not automatically constitute a violation of the FCPA: It still must be shown that the bribery was intended to produce an effect – here, through tax savings – that would "assist in obtaining or retaining business."

Indeed, the appellate court emphatically stated that not all such payments to a foreign official outside the context of foreign government procurement violate the FCPA; it merely held that such payments "could" violate the FCPA. According to the court, the key question of whether the defendants' alleged payments constituted an FCPA violation depended on whether the payments were intended to lower ARI's costs of doing business in Haiti enough to assist ARI in obtaining or retaining business in Haiti. The court then listed several hypothetical examples of how a reduction in custom and tax liabilities could assist a company in obtaining or retaining business in a foreign country. On the other hand, the court also recognized:

> There are bound to be circumstances in which such a cost reduction does nothing other than increase the profitability of an already-profitable venture or ensure profitability of some start-up venture. Indeed, if the government is correct that anytime operating costs are reduced the beneficiary of such advantage is assisted in getting or keeping business, the FCPA's language that expresses the necessary element of assisting is obtaining or retaining business would be unnecessary, and thus surplusage – a conclusion that we are forbidden to reach.

After the appellate court remanded the *Kay* case back down to the trial court, and after the defendants were convicted at trial, the defendants renewed their legal challenge by arguing that the FCPA failed to give fair notice of its prohibitions and was thus unconstitutionally vague.[84]

However, the appellate court held that even though the FCPA's "obtain or retain business" language was ambiguous, the "imprecise general language [in one of the elements] for a bribery conviction under the FCPA does not draw a line so vague that defendants were not reasonably aware of their potential for engaging in illegal activity under the FCPA when they made payments to Haitian officials to reduce tax and duty burdens." In the words of the court: "a man of common intelligence would have understood that ARI, in bribing foreign officials, was treading close to a reasonably-defined line of illegality."

In short, there have been four instances of judicial scrutiny concerning the enforcement theory that things of value offered or provided to a foreign official outside the context of foreign government procurement fall under the anti-bribery provisions. The enforcement agencies lost three of those cases and the fourth case – the appellate court decision in *Kay* – is equivocal: the decision merely holds that payments to a foreign official outside the context of foreign government procurement can, under appropriate circumstances, fall within the statute. Given the facts and circumstances the *Kay* court found relevant, it is a highly fact-dependent question whether a payment to a foreign official outside the context of foreign government procurement falls within the scope of the anti-bribery provisions. The key portion from the *Kay* ruling would seem to be the following: "there are bound to be circumstances" in which payments outside the context of foreign government procurement do "nothing other than increase the profitability of an-already profitable venture or ensure profitability of some start-up venture" and thus presumably does not assist the payer in obtaining or retaining business.

## Guidance

Regarding the "obtain or retain business" element, the FCPA Guidance states:

> The FCPA applies only to payments intended to induce or influence a foreign official to use his or her position "in order to assist ... in obtaining or retaining business for or with, or directing business to, any person." This requirement is known as the "business purpose test" and is broadly interpreted. [...] The FCPA also prohibits bribes in the conduct of business or to gain a business advantage. For example, bribe payments made to secure favorable tax treatment, to reduce or eliminate customs duties, to obtain government action to prevent competitors from entering a market, or to circumvent a licensing or permit requirement, all satisfy the business

> purpose test. [. . .] In short, while the FCPA does not cover every type of bribe paid around the world for every purpose, it does apply broadly to bribes paid to help obtain or retain business, which can include payments made to secure a wide variety of unfair business advantages.

Elsewhere, the Guidance asserts that "in 1998, the FCPA was amended to conform to the requirements of the [OECD] Anti-Bribery Convention" and "these amendments expanded the FCPA's scope to: include payments made to secure 'any improper advantage.'" However, the government's position that the FCPA's 1998 amendments expanded the FCPA's scope to include payments made to secure "any improper advantage" is false. Indeed, its position on this specific issue was rejected by both the trial court and appellate court in *U.S. v. Kay*. The trial court decision stated:

> The OECD Convention had asked Congress to criminalize payments made to foreign officials "in order to obtain or retain business or other improper advantage in the conduct of international business. [. . .] Congress again declined to amend the 'obtain or retain business' language in the FCPA" [. . .] Congress did not insert the "improper advantage" language into the "obtain or retain business" provision of the FCPA.

Although as highlighted above the appellate court overruled the trial court's decision to grant defendants' motion to dismiss, the appellate court likewise stated as follows concerning the FCPA's 1998 amendments:

> When Congress amended the language of the FCPA, however, rather than inserting "any improper advantage" immediately following "obtaining or retaining business" within the business nexus requirement (as does the Convention), it chose to add the "improper advantage" provision to the original list of abuses of discretion in consideration for bribes that the statute proscribes.

The Guidance rightly discusses *Kay*, the only case law of precedent on the FCPA's "obtain or retain business element," and accurately states that its holding that payments outside the context of foreign government procurement "could" fall within the meaning of the FCPA. However the discussion of *Kay* in the Guidance is selective at best. For instance, the Guidance fails to mention that the appellate court specifically rejected the DOJ's broad interpretation of the "obtain or retain business" element when it stated:

> If the government is correct that anytime operating costs are reduced the beneficiary of such advantage is assisted in getting or keeping business, the FCPA's language that expresses the necessary element of assisting in obtaining business would be unnecessary, and thus surplusage – a conclusion that we are forbidden to reach.

Likewise, but not mentioned in the Guidance, the appellate court in *Kay* further stated "that there are bound to be circumstances" in which payments outside the context of foreign government procurement merely increase the profitability of an existing profitable company and thus, presumably, do not assist the payer in obtaining or retaining business. Further missing from the Guidance is any mention of the *Duran* or *Mattson* enforcement actions discussed above which represent the other instances in FCPA history in which the enforcement agencies were put to its burden of proof concerning payments to foreign officials outside the context of foreign government procurement.

In short, even though the Guidance boldly states that "payments made to secure favorable tax treatment, to reduce or eliminate customs duties, to obtain government action to prevent competitors from entering a market, or to circumvent a licensing or permit requirement, all satisfy the business purpose test," the legal authority discussed in this section demonstrates something much different when the government has actually been put to its burden of proof regarding such conduct.

## Enforcement actions

Notwithstanding the legal authority discussed above and despite *Kay*'s equivocal holding, there has been a significant increase in corporate enforcement actions post-*Kay* concerning alleged payments to foreign officials in connection with import/export, licensing, permitting, and other points of contact with regulatory officials. In addition to enforcement actions in this category previously discussed in Chapter 1 and those that will be discussed in Chapter 4 regarding the facilitating payment exception, Table 2.3 highlights certain additional representative corporate enforcement actions.

All of the above FCPA enforcement actions were resolved through resolution vehicles not subjected to any meaningful judiciary scrutiny and, as relevant to *Kay*'s holding, involved existing profitable

*Table 2.3 "Obtain or retain" business allegations*

| Enforcement action | "Obtain or retain business" allegations included |
|---|---|
| Biomet[85] | Payments to Mexican customs officials to facilitate the export of mislabeled products |
| Tyson Foods[86] | Payments to Mexican veterinarians to influence their decisions in certifying product for export |
| Nature's Sunshine Products[87] | Payments to Brazilian customs agents to import certain unregistered products into Brazil |
| Helmerich & Payne[88] | Payments to various officials and representatives of the Argentine and Venezuelan customs services in connection with the importation and exportation of goods and equipment related business operations |
| Con-Way[89] | Payments to Philippine customs officials to allow the firm to store shipments longer than otherwise permitted; to settle disputes with the Philippine Bureau of Customs; as well as payments to employees of state-owned airlines to induce the officials to improperly reserve space on airplanes |
| AGA Medical[90] | Payments to officials in the Chinese State Intellectual Property Office in order to cause the office to approve the company's patent applications |
| Bristow Group[91] | Payments to Nigerian tax officials to influence them to improperly reduce the amount of expatriate employment tax |
| Delta & Pine Land Co.[92] | Payments to officials of the Turkish Ministry of Agricultural and Rural Affairs to obtain government reports and certifications necessary to operate in the country |

companies. Regarding enforcement actions involving alleged payments to foreign officials to reduce certain regulatory costs, FCPA practitioners have noted that frequently the government's allegations make "no reference to how these reduced costs were used to obtain or retain business, rendering the [government's] charges facially deficient."[93] It was further noted:

> Whether the DOJ's and SEC's approach to the "obtaining or retaining business" element of the FCPA stems from a misinterpretation of *Kay* or is an attempt to challenge the Fifth Circuit's opinion, remains to be seen. Nevertheless, we are troubled by the lack of clarity in the DOJ's and SEC's approach as it ultimately disadvantages defendants who may otherwise be

pressured to settle charges over conduct which does not necessarily constitute a crime.

Regardless of the dispute and controversy regarding the obtain or retain business element in certain cases, the take-away point here is that, given the enforcement agencies interpretation, scrutiny and enforcement can arise *anytime* a business organization's employees or agents have points of contact with foreign officials, even if those points of contact have nothing to do with actually selling products or services to a foreign government. This interpretation, coupled with the enforcement agencies' seeming *de facto* repeal of the facilitating payment exception discussed in Chapter 4, has significantly expanded the scope of the FCPA to potentially include *any* point of contact a business organization has with a foreign official in the global marketplace including in connection with mundane, day-to-day business practices.

To assess your knowledge of the "obtain or retain business" element, it's time to again put on your "FCPA goggles" by reviewing the following issue-spotting scenario in which T Systems employees Mark and Tom are having a conversation (both are on assignment to a foreign country to oversee the building of a manufacturing facility). After reviewing the scenario, go through the elements of the FCPA's anti-bribery provisions covered thus far.

| | |
|---|---|
| Mark: | So, where are we in terms of our facility project? Do we even have a start date yet? [Tom laughs] The whole reason we moved the operation down here is so we can bring our products closer to our customers, but we need a manufacturing facility to do that. Look, I've got angry managers calling me, man. |
| Tom: | We're trying! But do you have any idea how much government bureaucracy we're having to deal with? National, regional, local – I mean, you name it! We have to get permits from several different agencies and I've been told it can take 6 to 9 months per permit. |
| Mark: | What?!? |

| | |
|---|---|
| Tom: | Yeah, however, a friend of mine recently went through the same problem when they opened their factory here and they said that there is a way that we can get permits overnight if you know the right person in the permitting agency. So ... what do you think? I mean, I can contact them. We can get this project started. |

*Anything of value*: while there is nothing in the scenario explicitly stating that money or other things of value are going to a foreign official in connection with the permitting process, the reference to knowing the right person in the permitting agency should cause some pause. Perhaps this person in the permitting agency is requesting money or something else of value to issue the permit promptly rather than the typical 6–9 month period.

*Corrupt intent*: if such a payment or thing of value were offered or provided, would it evidence corrupt intent? Recall, corrupt intent can be satisfied even if a foreign official requests the payment or thing of value. While there is not always concrete evidence of corrupt intent, law enforcement often establishes corrupt intent through circumstantial evidence including the chronology of events. In this regard, recall that Mark stated that the whole reason T Systems wants to move its manufacturing facilities to the foreign country is to be closer to its customers and that he has angry managers breathing down his neck. In other words, should a payment or thing of value be offered or provided to a foreign official in connection with the permitting process, it would be occurring at an important moment in time for T Systems and indeed a stressful time for its employees in the foreign country.

Relevant also to corrupt intent is perhaps the discretion of the foreign official in issuing the permit. Perhaps T Systems is truly entitled to the permit in that it has satisfied all permitting criteria and the only delay is getting the foreign official to actually issue the permit. On the other hand, perhaps T Systems is not entitled to the permit. For instance, perhaps a local law or regulation states that before issuing a permit for a manufacturing facility, a company has to have an environmental impact assessment done on the property. Perhaps T Systems has not satisfied this relevant criteria, but is trying to influence a foreign official to issue the permit anyway. These different scenarios would be relevant to corrupt intent (*as well as the facilitating payments exception discussed in more detail in Chapter 4 given that, in the words of a judge, the exception "is best understood as a threshold requirement to pleading that a defendant acted corruptly"*).

*Foreign official*: analysis of this required element of an anti-bribery violation is rather straightforward as the individual in the government permitting office would clearly be a foreign official and many enforcement actions have involved foreign officials with discretion over some ministerial or bureaucratic function such as issuing permits.

*Obtain or retain business*: this element is probably the trickiest element to analyze. For starters, it appears that T Systems is not selling goods or services to a foreign government and even if money or things of value would are offered or provided to a foreign official in connection with the permitting process, this is not a foreign government procurement type of case – the easiest type of case to analyze under the "obtain or retain business" element.

Rather, all T Systems wants to do is open a manufacturing facility in the foreign country, yet it is encountering various layers of bureaucracy all of which require a permit from a government office. As the *Kay* case instructs, the anti-bribery provisions can capture payments outside the context of foreign government procurement and the key issue would seem to be whether T Systems – even if money or things of value were offered or provided to a foreign official in connection with the permitting process to influence their discretion – secured an improper advantage to assist in obtaining or retain business compared with other similarly situated companies who may have to wait 6–9 months for the required permits. It is not too hard to imagine a scenario in which a promptly secured permit would allow T Systems to start manufacturing products sooner than competitors and thus gain an earlier foothold in a market. Thus, if T Systems does indeed make a payment or offer something of value to the right person in the permitting office such conduct could implicate the anti-bribery provisions as interpreted by the government.

So what is a well-intentioned business organization supposed to do to minimize risk in this area recognizing that even if it does not sell products or services to a foreign government it is still likely to have, in the aggregate, hundreds if not thousands of points of contact with foreign officials in connection with rather mundane, day-to-day business practices?

For starters, a business organization needs to categorize all of its points of contact with foreign officials in the global marketplace because each point of contact represents a risk area. Part of this task is to understand also who has the point of contact with the foreign official: is it an employee or a third party? To be sure, categorizing all points of contact will likely take a substantial amount of time as licenses, permits, certifications and other regulatory points of contact are often product specific and country specific. However, it will be time well spent because, upon learning the above information, a business organization can deliver specific training to employees or third parties in this high-risk job function and develop specific policies and procedures concerning oversight and supervision of relevant employees and agents.

For instance, according to Walmart's Global Chief Ethics and Compliance Officer:

> Walmart manages more than 50,000 licenses and permits for our facilities located outside of the United States. Given the scale and complexity of these licensing and permitting obligations, we made it a priority to strengthen the policies, procedures and processes in our licensing and permitting compliance program. Among other measures, we established a dedicated team in each of our retail markets to manage licensing and permitting. These teams are part of our independent ethics and compliance group, not market management. We also enhanced our licensing and permitting standards and controls by adopting a global licenses policy along with supporting procedures, mapping out the processes that must be followed to obtain and renew licenses and permits, and adopting comprehensive training, monitoring and tracking programs.
>
> Some examples of our enhanced controls include creating written work flows for our team members, obtaining documentation of the fees required for each permit, and requiring multiple approvals before any cash payments can be issued. With these controls, we strive to know as much as we can about how a license should be obtained and what the lawful fees may be, so we can spot any variances.

> To keep track of all these requirements and permitting processes for each of our retail markets and to provide a single repository for documentation, we created a global license management system. Our international ethics and compliance team uses this system to manage all license and permit information and activity, including applications, payments, and approvals, and to track the status of licenses and permits for each market. This centralized system provides consistency across markets and visibility at our home office.[94]

Your "FCPA goggles" should now be properly constructed as to the core elements of the FCPA's anti-bribery provisions and you should:

- understand the wide range of circumstances in which scrutiny and enforcement can arise;
- be familiar with risk management strategies specific to certain core elements; and
- have confidence in your acquired knowledge after completing the various real-world issue-spotting scenarios.

Other aspects of the FCPA's anti-bribery provisions are discussed in more detail in Chapter 3 (the third-party payment provisions) and Chapter 4 (the facilitation payment exception and affirmative defenses), but before turning to these issues this chapter closes by discussing jurisdiction and statute of limitations issues.

## Jurisdiction

In addition to the substantive elements of the anti-bribery provisions discussed above, the FCPA's jurisdictional elements must also be met in order for a business organization or individual to violate the provisions. Due to FCPA amendments in 1998 that provided for extraterritorial jurisdiction as to *U.S.* actors, there are few disputed or controversial jurisdictional issues in enforcement actions against *U.S.* companies or citizens. However, after highlighting legal authority and non-legal sources of information relevant to jurisdictional issues, this section discusses how there are disputed and controversial jurisdictional issues in certain enforcement actions against *foreign* actors given the enforcement agencies' expansive enforcement theories.

## Law

The FCPA's anti-bribery provisions apply to "issuers," "domestic concerns," and "persons" other than "issuers or "domestic concerns." As previously highlighted, an issuer is FCPA-speak for companies U.S. or foreign with securities traded on a U.S. exchange or otherwise required to file reports with the SEC. A "domestic concern" is generally any business form other than an issuer (e.g., private corporations, limited liability companies, partnerships, sole proprietorships) with a principal place of business in the U.S. or organized under U.S. law. A "domestic concern" also includes "any individual who is a citizen, national, or resident of the U.S." A "person" other than an "issuer" or "domestic" concern includes foreign non-issuer business organizations as well as foreign nationals not associated with issuers or domestic concerns.

Jurisdiction under the anti-bribery provisions depends on the type of business organization or person subject to the FCPA.

- As to *U.S.* "issuers" and "domestic concerns," the FCPA contains both territorial jurisdiction and nationality jurisdiction. Territorial jurisdiction refers to "use of the mails or any means or instrumentality of interstate commerce" in furtherance of an improper payment. Nationality jurisdiction means that an improper payment scheme is prohibited by the anti-bribery provisions "irrespective of whether [the U.S. person] makes use of the mails or any means or instrumentality of interstate commerce in furtherance" of an improper payment. Thus, as to *U.S.* "issuers" and "domestic concerns," the anti-bribery provisions have extraterritorial jurisdiction meaning that the FCPA can be violated even if an improper payment scheme is devised and executed entirely outside of the U.S. From a compliance standpoint, this means that a U.S. business organization should make clear to its employees that the FCPA will follow them no matter where in the world they are located. In other words, when flying to a business meeting in São Paulo, the FCPA will tag along for the ride or when packing for a business meeting in Shanghai, the FCPA will be in the suitcase along with the socks and toothpaste.

- As to foreign "issuers," the anti-bribery provisions apply only to the extent there is territorial jurisdiction, in other words "use of the mails or any means of instrumentality of interstate commerce" in furtherance of an improper payment scheme.

- As to "persons" other than an "issuer" or "domestic concern," the anti-bribery provisions apply to the extent that "while in the territory of the U.S.," the person "makes use of the mails or any means or instrumentality of interstate commerce" or engages in "any other act in furtherance" of an improper payment scheme.

The first take-away point from the above jurisdictional analysis is that, contrary to oft-repeated assertions that the FCPA applies only to *U.S.* companies and citizens, the FCPA can also apply to *foreign* companies or *foreign* nationals.

## Legislative history

The alternative nationality jurisdictional prong of the anti-bribery provisions applicable to *U.S.* "issuers" and "domestic concerns" became part of the FCPA as a result of the 1998 amendments and a relevant Senate Report stated:

> The OECD Convention calls on parties to assert nationality jurisdiction when consistent with national legal and constitutional principles. Accordingly, the Act amends the FCPA to provide for jurisdiction over the acts of U.S. businesses and nationals in furtherance of unlawful payments that take place wholly outside the United States. This exercise of jurisdiction over U.S. businesses and nationals for unlawful conduct abroad is consistent with U.S. legal and constitutional principles and is essential to protect U.S. interests abroad.[95]

Likewise, a relevant House Report stated:

> [The nationality jurisdictional prong] implements the OECD Convention by creating an additional basis for jurisdiction over foreign bribery by U.S. issuers [and domestic concerns] and U.S. persons that are officers, directors, employees, or agents, or stockholders of such issuers [or domestic concerns]. This section extends coverage for acts outside the United States to U.S. issuers [or domestic concerns] . . . and U.S. persons acting on such issuers' [or domestic concerns'] behalf.[96]

The 1998 amendments also added a new section to the FCPA's anti-bribery provisions applicable to "persons" other than an "issuer" or "domestic concern" and relevant Senate and House Reports stated

> [The amendment] creates a new section in the FCPA, providing for criminal and civil penalties over persons not covered under the existing FCPA provisions regarding issuers and domestic concerns. This section closes the gap left in the original FCPA and implements the OECD Convention's requirement that Parties criminalize bribery by "any person." The prohibited acts are the same as those covered by [the existing provisions in the FCPA] with two qualifications.
>
> First, the offense created under this section requires that an act in furtherance of the bribe be taken within the territory of the United States. The OECD Convention requires each Party to "take such measures as may be necessary to establish its jurisdiction over the bribery of a foreign public official when the offense is committed in whole or in party in its territory." The new offense complies with this section by providing for criminal jurisdiction in this country over bribery by foreign nationals of foreign officials when the foreign national takes some act in furtherance of the bribery within the territory of the United States. [. . .] As envisioned in the OECD the territorial basis for jurisdiction should be interpreted broadly so that an extensive physical connection to the bribery act is not required. [. . .] The second difference from the existing FCPA provisions is that this section expands the commerce nexus to include not only the use of the mails or any means or instrumentality of interstate commerce but "any other act" within the United States.[97]

## Judicial decisions

As mentioned above there are few disputed or controversial jurisdictional issues in enforcement actions against *U.S.* actors. However, there are disputed and controversial jurisdictional issues in certain enforcement actions against individual *foreign* actors. Such expansive jurisdictional theories have been subjected to judicial scrutiny several times and the enforcement agencies have an overall losing record when put to the burden of proof.

In the manufactured Africa Sting enforcement action, FBI agents (with the assistance of an individual who had already pleaded guilty to real, unrelated FCPA offenses) posed as representatives of the Gabon Minister of Defense, the end result being that 22 individuals in the military and law enforcement products industry were criminally charged with FCPA and other offenses. Among the defendants was U.K. citizen Pankesh Patel, who moved for a judgment of acquittal after the DOJ's evidence at trial that he sent a DHL package – containing a purchase agreement in furtherance of the alleged bribery scheme – from the U.K. to the U.S. The judge granted the acquittal from the bench and the hearing transcript evidences the following exchange between the judge and the DOJ prosecutor concerning the jurisdictional theory that an act by a foreign national need not be in the territory of the U.S. for the FCPA to apply.

> Judge: Has the Supreme Court said that?
>
> DOJ: Judge, no.
>
> Judge: Has the D.C. Circuit said that?
>
> DOJ: No.
>
> Judge: How about the 2nd Circuit, where you used to prosecute?
>
> DOJ: Judge, there's not a lot of case law on the FCPA, as Your Honor I think is well aware.
>
> Judge: So is this a novel interpretation you want me to take?
>
> DOJ: I don't know if it's a novel interpretation. I think it's an interpretation that's grounded in the law that's out there.
>
> Judge: Is it grounded in the legislative record?
>
> DOJ: We can go back and we can get Your Honor more particulars about the legislative history if Your Honor wants that.
>
> Judge: I would think the more cautious, conservative interpretation would be that each act has to be while in the territory of the United States, wouldn't it?[98]

The 2011 ruling in the Africa Sting case was significant in that it was the first instance of a foreign national defendant putting the DOJ to its burden of proof at trial on a jurisdictional issue. In 2013, the SEC was put to its burden of proof in two individual FCPA enforcement actions involving foreign national defendants and the pre-trial results were mixed.

*SEC v. Straub* involved allegations that Hungarian nationals employed by Hungary-based issuer Magyar Telekom violated the anti-bribery provisions in connection with a bribery scheme involving Macedonian "foreign officials."[99] The judge, ruling on a pre-trial motion to dismiss and issue of first impression, concluded that the FCPA's territorial jurisdiction element (use of the mails or any means of instrumentality of interstate commerce) could be met based on allegations that e-mails in connection with the alleged bribery scheme were routed through and/or stored on network servers located within the U.S. even if the defendants did not personally know where the e-mails would be routed and/or stored. In so holding, the judge found the territorial jurisdiction element ambiguous and thus turned to the legislative history and stated:

> The legislative history reveals that, although Congress intended to make an "intent" or *mens rea* requirement for the underlying bribery, it expressed no corresponding intent to make such a requirement for the "make use of . . . any means or instrumentality of interstate commerce" element.

In the same case, this time at the motion for summary judgment stage, the same judge confronted yet another issue of first impression: what does "use" of an instrumentality of interstate commerce mean in connection with the FCPA's jurisdictional element relevant to foreign issuers and those acting on its behalf?[100] In short, the judge held that Magyar clearly "used an instrumentality of interstate commerce (the Internet) when it made filings through EDGAR [the SEC's electronic submission system]" and that "Magyar's filings with the SEC were a foreseeable consequence of defendants' actions." Although a non-binding trial court opinion, this decision should send a word of caution to any foreign executive involved in an alleged bribery scheme who is also involved in a foreign issuer's SEC filings. The word of caution is that a U.S. court may find jurisdiction under the anti-bribery provisions based on the executive's participation in the SEC filings if the filings were in furtherance of an underlying bribery scheme that may otherwise lack a U.S. nexus.

*SEC v. Steffen* involved allegations that a German national formerly employed by Germany-based issuer Siemens violated the anti-bribery provisions in connection with a bribery scheme involving Argentine "foreign officials."[101] The judge granted the defendant's pre-trial motion to dismiss, concluding that personal jurisdiction over the defendant exceeded the limits of due process. This non-FCPA specific issue is an initial threshold question in all U.S. actions involving foreign defendants and because the judge found general jurisdiction lacking, she did not address the FCPA's specific jurisdictional provisions like in the *Straub* action.

Regarding the disputed issue of whether the SEC's complaint alleged sufficient facts to establish the two components of due process – minimum contacts and reasonableness – the judge stated as to minimum contacts:

> The SEC's allegations are premised on Steffen's role in encouraging [a co-defendant] to authorize bribes to Argentine officials that ultimately resulted in falsified [SEC[filings. While Steffen's actions may have been a proximate cause of the false filings – and that is a matter of some doubt – Steffen's actions are far too attenuated from the resulting harm to establish minimum contacts. Steffen was brought into the alleged scheme based solely on

his connections with Argentine officials. In furtherance of his negotiations with those officials, Steffen "urged" and "pressured" [a co-defendant] to make certain bribes. However, [a co-defendant] did not agree to make the bribes until he communicated with several "higher ups" whose responses he perceived to be instructions to make the bribes. Once [a co-defendant] agreed to make the bribes – following receipt of instructions from Siemens' management rather than Steffen – Steffen's alleged role was tangential at best. Steffen did not actually authorize the bribes. The SEC does not allege that he directed, ordered or even had awareness of the cover ups that occurred . . . much less that he had any involvement in the falsification of SEC filings in furtherance of those cover ups.

The judge further stated:

Neither [a co-defendant's] call to Steffen from the United States nor the fact that a portion of the bribery payments were deposited in a New York bank provide sufficient evidence of conduct directed towards the United States to establish minimum contacts. First, Steffen did not place the calls to [a co-defendant]. Further, Steffen did not direct that the funds be routed through a New York bank. [. . .] His conduct was focused solely on ensuring the continuation of the Siemens contract in Argentina. [. . .] If this Court were to hold that Steffen's support for the bribery scheme satisfied the minimum contacts analysis, even though he neither authorized the bribe, nor directed the cover up, much less played any role in the falsified filings, minimum contacts would be boundless. Illegal corporate action almost always requires cover ups, which to be successful must be reflected in financial statements. Thus, under the SEC's theory, every participant in illegal action taken by a foreign company subject to U.S. securities laws would be subject to the jurisdiction of U.S. courts no matter how attenuated their connection with the falsified financial statements. This would be akin to a tort-like foreseeability requirement, which has long been held to be insufficient. The allegations against Steffen fall far short of the requirement that he 'follow a course of conduct directed . . . to the jurisdiction of a given sovereign, so that the sovereign has the power to subject the defendant to judgment concerning that conduct. Absent any alleged role in the cover ups themselves, let alone any role in preparing false financial statements the exercise of jurisdiction here exceeds the limits of due process.

As to reasonableness, the judge stated:

The decision not to exercise jurisdiction in this case is bolstered by my conclusion that requiring Steffen to defend this case in the United States

> would be unreasonable. [. . .] When a defendant is not located in the United States, "great care and reserve should be exercised when extending our notions of personal jurisdiction into the international context." Steffen's lack of geographic ties to the United States, his age, his poor proficiency in English, and the forum's diminished interest in adjudicating the matter, all weight against personal jurisdiction.

Most recently, *U.S. v. Hoskins* involved allegations that Lawrence Hoskins, a U.K. national and former executive of France-based Alstom, violated the FCPA in connection with an Indonesian bribery scheme. However, Hoskins moved to dismiss certain charges on the basis that the indictment charged "a legally invalid theory that he could be criminally liable for conspiracy to violate the FCPA even if the evidence does not establish that he was subject to criminal liability as a principal, by being an 'agent' of a 'domestic concern.'" In 2015 the judge agreed, trimmed the government's case and stated: "based on the text and structure of the FCPA and the legislative history accompanying its enactment and its amendment, the Court concludes that Congress did not intend to impose accomplice liability on non-resident foreign nationals who were not subject to direct liability."[102] The government has appealed the ruling and framed the issue as follows, "whether a foreign person (who does not reside in the United States) can be liable for conspiring or aiding and abetting a U.S. company to violate the Foreign Corrupt Practices Act if that individual is not in the categories of principal persons covered in the statute."[103]

## Guidance

The FCPA Guidance states, under the heading "what jurisdictional conduct triggers the anti-bribery provisions," as follows:

> Placing a telephone call or sending an e-mail, text message, or fax from, to, or through the United States involves interstate commerce – as does sending a wire transfer from or to a U.S. bank or otherwise using the U.S. banking system, or traveling across state borders or internationally to or from the United States. [. . .] Those who are not issuers or domestic concerns may be prosecuted under the FCPA if they directly, or through an agent, engage in any act in furtherance of a corrupt payment while in the territory of the United States, regardless of whether they utilize the U.S. mails or a means or instrumentality of interstate commerce. Thus, for example, a foreign national who attends a meeting in the United States that furthers

a foreign bribery scheme may be subject to prosecution, as may any co-conspirators, even if they did not themselves attend the meeting. A foreign national or company may also be liable under the FCPA if it aids and abets, conspires with, or acts as an agent of an issuer or domestic concern, regardless of whether the foreign national or company itself takes any action in the United States.

## Enforcement actions

A 2006 enforcement action against Norway-based oil and gas company Statoil was the first criminal FCPA enforcement action against a foreign company. In the action, based on allegations the company made improper payments to Iranian officials including that certain payments in connection with the bribery scheme were wire transferred through U.S. banks, the DOJ stated:

> Although Statoil is a foreign issuer, the [FCPA] applies to foreign and domestic public companies alike, where the company's stock trades on American exchanges. This prosecution demonstrates the Justice Department's commitment vigorously to enforce the FCPA against all international businesses whose conduct falls within its scope.[104]

Since then, much of the largeness of the modern era of FCPA enforcement (in terms of both the number of enforcement actions brought and settlement amounts secured) has been the result of enforcement actions against foreign companies. Indeed, in certain years enforcement actions against foreign companies have comprised approximately 50% of overall corporate enforcement actions and approximately 90% of overall settlement amounts.[105]

Several of these enforcement actions are worth highlighting given that they involved sparse U.S. jurisdictional allegations. For instance, JGC Corporation of Japan was the subject of FCPA scrutiny given its participation in a joint venture operating in Nigeria. The joint venture operated through three Portuguese special purpose corporations and hired a U.K. citizen who, along with his Gibraltar corporation, allegedly paid bribes to Nigerian foreign officials. The FCPA could only apply to JGC to the extent the alleged bribery scheme had a U.S. nexus and given the above general factual scenario an obvious legal issue was whether the U.S. had jurisdiction over the Japanese company. However, the DOJ maintained that JGC was "declining to cooperate" with its investigation "based on jurisdictional arguments."[106]

Perhaps mindful of the adverse consequences of its perceived failure to cooperate (including the risk of an actual criminal indictment and associated business effects), JGC agreed to resolve its alleged scrutiny by paying approximately $218 million in criminal fines via a deferred prosecution agreement not subjected to any meaningful judicial scrutiny. The jurisdictional allegations in the enforcement action were that certain money in connection with the bribe scheme flowed through a U.S.-based account and that co-conspirators faxed or e-mailed information into the U.S. in furtherance of the bribery scheme.

A $519 million enforcement action against Teva Pharmaceuticals (an Israeli company) and Teva LLC (a related limited liability company incorporated in Russia) was likewise based on sparse jurisdictional allegations.[107] Regarding the conduct in Russia, the government alleged:

> Teva directly and indirectly made use of the mails and of the means and instrumentalities of interstate commerce in connection with and in furtherance of its illegal payments to Russian Official through Russian Distributor. Teva sent and responded to a number of *emails* to the Russian Distributor's President that were sent *through U.S. servers.* (Emphasis added.)

Regarding the conduct in Ukraine, the government alleged:

> Teva directly and indirectly made use of the mails and of the means and instrumentalities of interstate commerce in connection with and in furtherance of its illegal payments to Ukrainian Official. For example, although some of the compensation Ukrainian Official received from Teva was in cash, at least seven payments were *wired through U.S. correspondent banks.* (Emphasis added.)

Regarding the conduct in Mexico, the government alleged:

> Teva Mexico directly and indirectly made use of the mails and of the means and instrumentalities of interstate commerce in connection with and in furtherance of its illegal payments to Mexican officials. For example, a Teva Mexico manager corresponded with Teva Mexico's Copaxone distributor in Mexico about the delivery of cash to the Mexican officials using *emails sent and stored on U.S. servers.* (Emphasis added.)

A net $250 million FCPA enforcement action against Odebrecht (a Brazil holding company) and Braskem (a Brazil petrochemical company controlled by Odebrecht) concerned widespread bribery schemes in Angola, Argentina, Brazil, Colombia, Dominican Republic, Ecuador, Guatemala, Mexico, Mozambique, Panama, Peru, and Venezuela. It involved egregious conduct as the government alleged that Odebrecht established a standalone division within the company called the Division of Structured Operations that "effectively functioned as a bribe department within Odebrecht and its related entities."[108] Even so, for a foreign company to violate the anti-bribery provisions there needs to be jurisdiction and once again the U.S. jurisdictional allegations were sparse. Specifically, the government alleged that certain money in connection with the bribery schemes passed through a U.S.-based account and that an Odebrecht employee attended a meeting in the U.S. with the agent of a government official in which a bribe payment was discussed. Table 2.4 highlights certain other representative enforcement actions against foreign companies and the asserted U.S. jurisdictional allegations.

*Table 2.4 Jurisdictional allegations*

| Company | Jurisdictional allegations |
|---|---|
| Magyar Telekom (Hungary) | In connection with a bribery scheme, a company executive sent two e-mails to a Macedonian foreign official from his U.S. based e-mail address that passed through, was stored on, and transmitted from servers located in the U.S.<br>Certain electronic communications made in furtherance of the scheme and the concealment of payments, including drafts of certain agreements and copies of certain contracts with intermediaries, were transmitted by company employees and others through U.S. interstate commerce or stored on computer servers located in the U.S.[109] |
| Bridgestone (Japan) | Company employees sent and received e-mail and fax communications to/from the U.S. in connection with the bribery scheme involving Latin American "foreign officials."[110] |
| Tenaris (Luxembourg) | Payment to an agent via wire transfer through an intermediary bank located in New York in connection with a bribery scheme involving Uzbekistan foreign officials.[111] |

On one level, it seems odd that the FCPA can apply to business interactions between a Japanese company and Nigerian officials, between an Israeli company and Russian officials, between a Hungarian company and Macedonian officials, or between a Luxembourg company and Uzbek officials. However, the FCPA does allow for such jurisdiction over foreign actors in certain instances even though the legal contours of those instances have generally not been subject to judicial scrutiny. Yet just because the U.S. *can* bring enforcement actions against foreign actors for alleged bribery of non-U.S. officials, does not necessarily mean that the U.S. *should* bring such enforcement actions. Jurisdiction after all is the power to declare the law and expansive theories of jurisdiction raise various policy issues.

For instance, one notable feature of most enforcement actions against foreign companies is that the companies are headquartered in countries that, like the U.S., are parties to the OECD Convention on Combating Bribery of Foreign Public Officials in International Business Transactions (OECD Convention) and thus presumably have reputable legal systems to prosecute such offenses. Given this reality, as well as the specific provision in Article 4 of OECD Convention that

> when more than one Party has jurisdiction over an alleged offence described in this Convention, the Parties involved shall, at the request of one of them, consult with a view to determining the most appropriate jurisdiction for prosecution

can it truly be said that the U.S. was the most appropriate jurisdiction to prosecute certain foreign companies for alleged interactions with non-U.S. officials?[112]

As some commentators have rightly noted, perhaps "non-U.S. efforts to prosecute overseas bribery are hampered by the absence of clear, credible statements from U.S. prosecutors that they will desist from prosecuting if a local prosecutor does so in good faith."[113] Granted, in certain recent enforcement actions U.S. FCPA settlement amounts have been offset for related foreign law enforcement actions. However, the bigger question is whether these examples should have been instances in which the U.S. simply backed away from prosecution because of the related foreign law enforcement action? The U.S. did not, which raises the question of why the U.S. advances expansive jurisdictional theories in enforcement actions against foreign actors.

- Is it a moral obligation to hold bad actors accountable and help establish global norms as to corporate behavior and business ethics?

- Is it to score political points and make the U.S. government look good in the eyes of civil society organizations?

- Is it to make money for the U.S. treasury?

As to the latter point, in the minds of some FCPA enforcement has become a convenient cash cow for the U.S. government and the many lucrative enforcement actions against foreign companies based on sparse U.S. jurisdictional allegations only amplify these concerns.[114]

Yet expansive jurisdictional theories by U.S. law enforcement (in the FCPA context and otherwise) are not without geo-political consequences. For instance, in the aftermath of several high-profile U.S. enforcement actions against French companies, French politicians expressed concerns. According to one report, a French lawmaker stated: "we consider that today's situation amounts to abusive use of American law and we ask France and Europe to let it be known to the United States that we will no longer accept this type of behavior" which the lawmaker equated to "extortion."[115] Because of this, perhaps greater restraint by U.S. enforcement agencies is warranted. Indeed, during the 2010 Senate FCPA hearing Senator Coons stated: "Today we are the only nation that is extending extraterritorial reach and going after the citizens of other countries, we may someday find ourselves on the receiving end of such transnational actions." As a matter of law, the FCPA does not provide extraterritorial jurisdiction against foreign actors; however as a matter of practice this section has highlighted the expansive jurisdictional theories advanced by the enforcement agencies in bringing certain enforcement actions against foreign actors.

Relevant to Senator Coons's statement, consider again the Odebrecht/Braskem enforcement action, which is believed to be the first FCPA enforcement action in history against a foreign company for allegedly bribing its own *domestic* officials. In other words, a large portion of the action involved allegations that the *Brazilian* companies bribed (including through political donations) *Brazilian* officials. The equivalent would be Brazilian law enforcement bringing a multi-million dollar enforcement action against a *U.S.* company based on political donations to *U.S.* officials because a meeting occurred in Brazil or money flowed through a Brazil-based account in connection with the bribery scheme. How would U.S. politicians react to this? Policy issues aside, the take-away points from this section are that:

- as to U.S. actors, the anti-bribery provisions are extraterritorial and can be implicated even if a bribery scheme is devised and executed entirely outside the U.S.; and
- as to foreign actors, the anti-bribery provisions require a U.S. nexus, but this jurisdictional requirement is broadly interpreted by the enforcement agnecies.

## Statute of limitations

Statute of limitations is a fundamental legal principle which establishes a set period of time for an action to be brought after the alleged conduct occurred. In *Gabelli v. SEC* (an SEC enforcement action outside the FCPA context) the Supreme Court stated:

> Statute of limitations are intended to "promote justice by preventing surprises through the revival of claims that have been allowed to slumber until evidence has been lost, memories have faded, and witnesses have disappeared." They provide "security and stability to human affairs." [They] are "vital to the welfare of society" [and] "even wrongdoers are entitled to assume that their sins may be forgotten." [. . .] It "would be utterly repugnant to the genius of our laws if actions for penalties could 'be brought at any distance of time.'"[116]

The Supreme Court further stated that statute of limitations are even more important in a government enforcement action compared with a case brought by a private plaintiff.

> There are good reasons why the fraud discovery rule has not been extended to Government enforcement actions for civil penalties. [. . .] The SEC, for example, is not like an individual victim who relies on apparent injury to learn of a wrong. Rather, a central "mission" of the Commission is to "investigate potential violations of the federal securities laws." Unlike the private party who has no reason to suspect fraud, the SEC's very purpose is to root it out, and it has many legal tools at hand to aid in that pursuit. [. . .] Charged with this mission and armed with these weapons, the SEC as enforcer is a far cry from the defrauded victim the discovery rule evolved to protect. In a civil penalty action, the Government is not only a different kind of plaintiff, it seeks a different kind of relief. The discovery rule helps to ensure that the injured receive recompense. But this case involves penalties, which go beyond compensation, and are intended to punish, and label defendants wrongdoers.

The FCPA does not have a specific statute of limitations. Rather the 5 year "catch-all" provisions in 18 USC § 3282 (for criminal actions) and 28 USC §2462 (for civil actions) apply to FCPA enforcement actions. Despite this general 5 year limitations period, if you dig into the details of most corporate enforcement actions you quickly discover that the alleged conduct occurred 5–7, 7–10 and, in some instances, 10–15 years prior to the enforcement action.[117]

Why, despite the importance of statute of limitations and Supreme Court recognition that it "would be utterly repugnant to the genius of our laws if actions for penalties could be brought at any distance of time," do most corporate enforcement actions concern conduct well beyond the statute of limitations? Simply put, because in corporate enforcement actions this fundamental black-letter legal principle seems not to matter. Granted, counsel for a company under scrutiny can argue about statute of limitations issues around conference room tables behind closed doors in Washington, D.C. However, like many other FCPA issues, to truly challenge the enforcement agencies first requires that the company be criminally or civilly charged, something few corporate leaders are willing to let happen.

Rather, cooperation is often the name of the game in corporate inquiries and to raise bona fide legal arguments such as statute of limitations may not be viewed as cooperating. Indeed, one of the first steps a company under scrutiny often takes to demonstrate its cooperation is agree to toll the statute of limitations or waive statute of limitations defenses and the following corporate disclosure is an example.

> We are conducting an investigation, with the assistance of outside counsel, relating to certain business activities of the Company and its affiliates and contractors in countries outside the United States. The investigation includes a review of compliance with the requirements of the U.S. Foreign Corrupt Practices Act and other applicable laws and regulations. The Company is working with the U.S. Securities and Exchange Commission and the U.S. Department of Justice with respect to the investigation. [. . .] [T]he Company entered into a one-year agreement with the U.S. Securities and Exchange Commission tolling the statute of limitations relating to the investigation, and recently entered into a similar agreement with the U.S. Department of Justice.[118]

Regarding this common practice, a former DOJ enforcement attorney stated:

> As a practical matter, companies, especially publicly held companies [. . .], typically make a strategic decision to fully cooperate with a DOJ investigation. Despite the potential success of a statute of limitations defense, a company will often make the judgment that the negative press of a protracted investigation and the uncertainty of the outcome at trial make cooperation the more prudent business judgment. The company's hope is that it will be given credit for the cooperation and it will achieve a better outcome than if it went to trial (i.e., avoid charges, a DPA, or a reduced fine).[119]

Given this dynamic, the enforcement agencies face little to no time pressure in bringing corporate enforcement actions. The end result, as discussed in Chapter 1, is that the gray cloud of scrutiny often hangs over a company far too long and can result in a variety of negative financial consequences for a business organization. Commenting on this dynamic, a former high-ranking DOJ enforcement official called this "The Foreign Bribery Sinkhole at Justice" and stated:

> The Justice Department needs to do more than churn out resolutions to foreign bribery cases notable only for their record-breaking penalties. Rigorous and prompt FCPA enforcement can have a dramatic impact on the insidious and corrosive effect of corruption overseas and provide . . . restorative justice . . ..[120]

Regarding this issue, in 2017 it was notable that a high-ranking DOJ enforcement official stated the DOJ's "intent is for our FCPA investigations to be measured in months, not years."[121] But then again, in 2005 the DOJ's then Assistant Attorney General for the Criminal Division talked about "real-time enforcement" and stated:

> [I]n other words, punishing wrongdoers promptly after they commit their crimes. Simply put, speed matters in corporate fraud investigations. The days of five-year investigations, of agreement after agreement tolling the statute of limitations – while ill-gotten gains are frittered away and investor confidence sinks – are increasingly a thing of the past.

Once again, as you were warned early in the book, there are certain issues relevant to FCPA enforcement where one simply needs to accept the old adage "it is what it is" and when it comes to long-protracted government FCPA inquiries, "it is what it is." In addition to the enforcement agencies not facing any meaningful time pressure in bringing corporate enforcement actions, other reasons for the typical long periods of scrutiny can include: the "where else" question discussed in greater detail in Chapter 1; DOJ and SEC enforcement actions tend to be announced on the same day and it is common for one agency to wait for the other agency to conclude its investigation and deliberation; and attrition at the enforcement agencies tends to be high and it is not uncommon for employee turnover alone to prolong enforcement agency FCPA investigations.

Regarding the typical long periods associated with corporate scrutiny, an FCPA commentator stated:

> [Companies under FCPA scrutiny are] routinely asked to waive the statute of limitations. They could refuse but none do; refusal might trigger an instant enforcement action against the company or its people. So the waiver gives the feds limitless time to investigate, deliberate, or procrastinate. And no one can force the DOJ or SEC to move on, either with an enforcement action or a declination. The result? Companies [under FCPA scrutiny] get stuck in FCPA limbo. [. . .] But the DOJ and SEC should always keep one eye on the calendar. The threat of FCPA enforcement [. . .] casts a long shadow. It darkens the future for management, shareholders, lenders, customers, and suppliers. Exactly the problem the statute of limitations was supposed to fix.[122]

Regardless of the above dynamics and policy implications that arise from long protracted government inquiries, there are other ways in which statute of limitations may be extended in the FCPA context. The FCPA Guidance states as follows concerning criminal enforcement actions:

> In cases involving FCPA conspiracies, the government may be able to reach conduct occurring before the five-year limitations period applicable to conspiracies under 18 U.S.C. § 371. For conspiracy offenses, the government generally need prove only that one act in furtherance of the conspiracy occurred during the limitations period, thus enabling the government to prosecute bribes paid or accounting violations occurring more than five years prior to the filing of formal charges.
>
> Under 18 U.S.C. § 3292, the government may seek a court order suspending the statute of limitations posed in a criminal case for up to three years in order to obtain evidence from foreign countries. Generally, the suspension period begins when the official request is made by the U.S. government to the foreign authority and ends on the date on which the foreign authority takes final action on the request.

As to civil enforcement actions, the FCPA Guidance states:

> The five-year limitations period applies to SEC actions seeking civil penalties, but it does not prevent the SEC from seeking equitable remedies, such as an injunction or the disgorgement of ill-gotten gains, for conduct pre-dating the five-year period. In cases against individuals who are not residents of the United States, the statute is tolled for any period when the defendants are not "found within the United States in order that proper service may be made thereon."

As with most legal issues regarding FCPA enforcement, most of these enforcement agency positions regarding statute of limitations have not been subjected to judicial scrutiny. An exception was *SEC v. Kokesh*, a 2017 unanimous Supreme Court decision in which the court rejected the SEC's position and held that disgorgement "in the securities-enforcement context is a 'penalty' within the meaning of [28 U.S.C.] 2462 and so disgorgement actions must be commenced within five years of the date the claim accrues."[123] Although *Kokesh* was not an FCPA enforcement action, the decision *should be* FCPA relevant because disgorgement has become the dominant remedy sought by the SEC in corporate enforcement actions since the SEC first sought a disgorgement remedy in an FCPA enforcement action in 2004. Even though *Kokesh should be* FCPA relevant, the unanimous Supreme Court decision *will* only be relevant to the extent risk-averse business organizations do not roll over and play dead when subjected to FCPA scrutiny by waiving or tolling the statute of limitations.

In individual FCPA enforcement actions (where a defendant is much less likely to waive or toll the statute of limitations), the enforcement agencies have a mixed record when put to its burden of proof. For instance, in *U.S. v. Bourke* (an enforcement action discussed in greater detail in Chapter 3) the court dismissed certain criminal charges against various individuals.[124] The DOJ argued that the statute of limitations should be extended under 18 U.S.C. § 3292 based on the government's official requests for foreign evidence from the Netherlands and Switzerland. However, the court rejected this argument and noted that the government did not move to "suspend the running" of the statute of limitations until after it had expired and it was thus not entitled to any tolling. In so holding, the court noted that "this problem can easily be avoided – and easily could have been avoided in this case," but that "the government waited almost nine full months after making the official request to the Netherlands before applying for a section 3292 suspension." According to the court, "the mere fact that the government could have easily avoided this dismissal does not change the result here" and the court noted that "statutes of limitations must be enforced, even where it deprives society of its ability to prosecute otherwise viable criminal offenses; 'that is the price we pay for repose.'"

Likewise in the *SEC v. Jackson* enforcement action previously discussed, the court dismissed SEC civil FCPA charges seeking monetary damages against individuals in connection with an alleged bribery scheme in Nigeria. Among the reasons cited by the court was the SEC's failure to plead any facts to support an inference that it acted diligently in bringing the action.[125]

However, in *SEC v. Straub* the SEC's statute of limitations theory survived a pre-trial motion to dismiss. The action raised an issue of first impression under 28 USC §2462 which states:

> Except as otherwise provided by Act of Congress, an action, suit or proceeding for the enforcement of any civil fine, penalty, or forfeiture, pecuniary or otherwise, shall not be entertained unless commenced from the date when the claim first accrued if, within the same period, the offender or the property is found within the United States in order that proper service be made thereon.

The court noted that it was "undisputed that more than five years have elapsed since the SEC's claims first accrued."[126] However, the parties disagreed as to the plain meaning of section 2642 given that the Hungarian national defendants were not physically located within the United States during the limitations period. The court stated:

> The SEC argues that the statute of limitations has not run because the statute applies only "if within the same period, the offender . . . is found within the United States." Thus, according to the SEC, because Defendants were not "found" in this country at any point during the limitations period in question, the Court's inquiry should end. The Court agrees. [. . .] Here, the operative language in § 2462 requires, by its plain terms, that an offender must be physically present in the United States for the statute of limitations to run. In arguing otherwise, Defendants essentially seek to amend the statute to run against a defendant if he is either "found within the United States" or subject to service of process elsewhere by some alternative means. Such a reading would be a dramatic restatement of the statutory language

> and would render the clause "if . . . found within the United States" mere surplusage. [. . .] Additionally, reading the statute to require a defendant's physical presence in the United States is not inconsistent with § 2462's statement of purpose, as was originally understood.

Regarding the defendants' argument that the Hague Service Convention facilitated the serving of foreign defendants not found in the U.S., the court seemed to understand the logic of the position, yet exhibited restraint in concluding:

> [This] does not change the fact that Congress has maintained the statutory carve out for defendants not found within the United States. Indeed, although the purpose underlying the carve-out may no longer be as compelling as it might have once been in light of the possibilities opened by worldwide service of process, it is not for this Court to second-guess Congress and amend the statute on its own. Accordingly, the Court finds that the statute of limitations within § 2462 has not run on the SEC's claims.

The take-away point from this section is that while statute of limitations are a fundamental legal concept, in many enforcement actions this black-letter legal principle seems not to matter because risk-averse business organizations often waive or toll the statute of limitations and the end result is that many enforcement actions are based on conduct beyond any conceivable limitations period and raise significant policy issues. With a clear understanding of the core elements of the FCPA's anti-bribery provisions, the next chapter highlights the FCPA's expansive third-party payment provisions.

NOTES

1 Complaint, SEC v. Innospec Inc. (D.D.C., Mar. 17, 2010).
2 In the Matter of Smith & Wesson Holding Corp., Release No. 72678 (July 28, 2014).
3 FCPA Professor, "In Depth on VimpelCom," (Feb. 19, 2016).
4 SEC v. Ashland Oil, Inc., Case 86-1904 (D.D.C., July 8, 1986).
5 Indictment, U.S. v. Warwick, Case 3:09-cr-00449-HEH (E.D. Va., Dec. 15, 2009).
6 FCPA Professor, "The First Travel And Entertainment Enforcement Action," (June 16, 2014).
7 923 F.2d 1308 (8th Cir. 1991).
8 SEC Release, "ACI's 32nd FCPA Conference Keynote Address," (Nov. 17, 2015).
9 Letter from Steven A. Tyrell, Chief, Fraud Section, U.S. Department of Justice (Criminal Div.), to Saul Pilchen, Attorney for Paradigm B.V. (Sept. 21, 2007).
10 FCPA Professor, ""Golf In The Morning And Beer-Drinking In the Evening" – SciClone Pharmaceuticals Resolves $12.8 Million FCPA Enforcement Action For Subsidiary's Marketing And Promotional Activities," (Feb. 5, 2016).
11 FCPA Professor, "SEC Returns To "World Tour" Allegations In Administrative Action Against FLIR Systems," (Apr. 9, 2015).
12 FCPA Professor, "Next Up – Bristol Myers," (Oct. 6, 2015).

13 FCPA Professor, "Novartis Coughs Up $25 Million To Resolve FCPA Enforcement Action Based On Conduct Of Indirect Chinese Subsidiaries," (Mar. 24, 2016).
14 FCPA Professor, "Layne Christensen Company Resolves SEC Enforcement Action," (Oct. 28, 2014).
15 FCPA Professor, "Dubious As It Was, The Schering-Plough Enforcement Action Was Notable," (Feb. 5, 2018).
16 John Giraudo, "Charitable Contributions and the FCPA: Schering-Plough and the Increasing Scope of SEC Enforcement," The Business Lawyer Vol. 61, No. 1 (Nov. 2005).
17 FCPA Professor, "A Blemish – Nu Skin Enterprises Resolves SEC FCPA Enforcement Action Based On Its Chinese Subsidiary's "Charitable Donation," (Sept. 21, 2016).
18 Information at 23, United States v. Alstom S.A., No. 14-cr-00246-JBA (D. Conn. Dec. 22, 2014), http://www.justice.gov/criminal/fraud/fcpa/cases/alstomsa/DE-1-Information-for-SA.pdf [http://perma.cc/P7LN-65L3].
19 FCPA Professor, "Next Up – Stryker," (Oct. 25, 2013).
20 Mike Koehler, "The Uncomfortable Truths and Double Standards of Bribery Enforcement," 84 Fordham Law Review 2015.
21 FCPA Professor, "The Charitable Donation That Did Not Occur," (Mar. 26, 2018).
22 FCPA Professor, "BNY Mellon Becomes The First – Of What Is Expected To Be Several Financial Services Companies – To Pony Up Millions Based On Its Internship Practices," (Aug. 19, 2015).
23 FCPA Professor, "Qualcomm Caves – Pays $7.5 Million In Connection With Alleged Improper Hiring And Other Practices In China," (Mar. 2, 2016).
24 FCPA Professor, "In Depth Into The JP Morgan FCPA Enforcement Action," (Nov. 18, 2016).
25 Id.
26 FCPA Professor, "London Judge Rejects Link Between Goldman Sachs Internship And "Foreign Official" Decision-Making," (Oct. 19, 2016) *see also* FCPA Professor, "In A Domestic Corruption Case, The First Circuit Rejects The Narrative In Recent FCPA Enforcement Actions Concerning Internship And Hiring Practices," (Feb. 3, 2017).
27 FCPA Professor, "Analyzing The SEC's Recent FCPA Pharma Speech," (Mar. 5, 2015).
28 SEC Release, "ACI's 32nd FCPA Conference Keynote Address," (Nov. 17, 2015).
29 DOJ FCPA Opinion Procedure Release No. 95-01 (Jan. 11, 1995).
30 FCPA Professor, "Jay Jorgensen On Walmart's Enhanced Ethics & Compliance Program," (Oct. 24, 2017).
31 H.R. Rep. No. 95-640 (1977).
32 S. Rep. No. 95-114 (1977).
33 H.R. Rep. No. 95-640 (1977).
34 923 F.2d 1308 (8th Cir. 1991).
35 327 F.3d 173 (2d Cir. 2003).
36 513 F.3d 432 (5th Cir. 2007).
37 DOJ FCPA Opinion Procedure Release No. 13-01 (Dec. 19, 2013).
38 Wilmer Hale, Foreign Corrupt Practices Act Alert (Jan. 27, 2015).
39 Complaint, SEC v. Monsanto Co. (D.D.C., Jan. 2005).
40 In the Matter of Smith & Wesson Holding Corp., Release No. 72678 (July 28, 2014).
41 FCPA Professor, "Bahn, Et Al – Not A Typical FCPA Enforcement Action," (Jan. 16, 2017).
42 In the Matter of Natco Group Inc., Release No. 61325 (Jan. 11, 2010).
43 FCPA Professor, "Gifts And The "Bribery Gaze," (Sept. 3, 2014).
44 Id.
45 Compliance Building, "What is an "Instrumentality" under the FCPA?" (May 21, 2014).
46 18 U.S.C. § 1952.

47 Mike Koehler, "The Story of the Foreign Corrupt Practices Act," 73 The Ohio State Law Journal 2012.
48 The Activities of American Multinational Corporations Abroad: Hearings Before the Subcomm. on Int'l Econ. Policy of the H. Comm. on Int'l Relations, 94th Cong. (1975); Foreign and Corporate Bribes: Hearings Before the S. Comm. on Banking, Hous., and Urban Affairs, 94th Cong. (1976).
49 See Declaration of Professor Michael J. Koehler in Support of Defendants' Motion to Dismiss Counts One Through Ten of the Indictment, U.S. v. Carson, No. SACR 09-0007-JVS (C.D. Cal. Feb. 21, 2011).
50 Id.
51 Bribery Act 2010, c. 23, § 6 (Eng.).
52 Corruption of Foreign Public Officials Act 1998, c. 34, § 2 (Can.).
53 Criminal Code Act 1995, c. 4, Div. 70 25 (Austl.).
54 FCPA Professor, "Rolls-Royce Resolves $170 Million FCPA Enforcement Action," (Jan. 24, 2017).
55 FCPA Professor, "Golf In The Morning And Beer-Drinking In the Evening" – SciClone Pharmaceuticals Resolves $12.8 Million FCPA Enforcement Action For Subsidiary's Marketing And Promotional Activities," (Feb. 5, 2016).
56 FCPA Professor, "PTC Inc. And Related Entities Pay $28 Million In Yet Another FCPA Enforcement Action Involving Travel And Entertainment Provided To Alleged "Foreign Officials," (Feb. 17, 2016).
57 FCPA Professor, "Olympus Latin America Pays $22.8 Million In Latest FCPA Enforcement Action To Allege That Health Care Professionals Are "Foreign Officials," (Mar. 3, 2016).
58 FCPA Professor, "Next Up – Pfizer," (Aug. 8, 2012).
59 FCPA Professor, "NORDAM Group Resolves Enforcement Action Through A Non-Prosecution Agreement," (July 19, 2012).
60 FCPA Professor, "The FCPA Meets Insurance – Aon Resolves Enforcement Action," (Dec. 21, 2011).
61 FCPA Professor, "Former SEC FCPA Enforcement Attorney Critical of SEC's Recent Veraz Networks Inc. Enforcement Action," (July 14, 2010).
62 FCPA Professor, "The "Foreign Officials" Of 2017," (Jan. 22, 2018).
63 DOJ Release, "Two Florida Executives, One Florida Intermediary and Two Former Haitian Government Officials Indicted for Their Alleged Participation in Foreign Bribery Scheme," (Dec. 7, 2009).
64 752 F.3d 912 (11th Cir. 2014).
65 M. Witten et al., Eleventh Circuit Adopts Broad Definition of Government "Instrumentality" Under FCPA, Wilmer Hale (May 22, 2014).
66 Wendy Wysong et al., Eleventh Circuit Issues Much Anticipated Opinion Defining 'Foreign Official' Under FCPA, CLIFFORD CHANCE 1, 3 (May 20, 2014).
67 Sean Hecker et al., FCPA Update: U.S. Appellate Court Defines Government "Instrumentality" Under FCPA, DEBEVOISE & PLIMPTON LLP 1, 7 (May 2014).
68 Tom Webb, FCPA Enforcement Critic to Become DoJ Fraud Section Chief, Global Investigations Review (Jan. 13, 2015).
69 DOJ FCPA Opinion Procedure Release, No. 94-01, (May 13, 1994).
70 FCPA Professor, "DOJ Announces FCPA And Related Actions In Connection With Russian Nuclear Industry Bribe Scheme – Additional Actions Likely," (Sept. 2, 2015).
71 FCPA Professor, "Issues To Consider From The Alstom Action," (Jan. 2, 2015).
72 FCPA Professor, ""Foreign Official" Notable," (Dec. 4, 2017).
73 Id.
74 FCPA Professor, "Case Law Of Note," (Mar. 8, 2016).
75 Trial Tr. 227:19–23, U.S. v. O'Shea, No. 09-629 (S.D. Tex. Jan. 16, 2012).

76 908 F.Supp.2d 834 (S.D. Tex. 2012).
77 2013 WL 466600 (S.D.N.Y. 2013).
78 Order Re: Select Jury Instructions, U.S. v. Carson, No. SACR 09-0007-JVS (C.D. Cal. Feb. 16, 2012).
79 H.R. Rep. No. 95-831 (1977).
80 FCPA Professor, "An Important FCPA Case You've Likely Never Heard About," (May 7, 2012), containing links to original source documents.
81 200 F.Supp.2d 681 (S.D.Tex. 2002).
82 Memorandum and Order, SEC v. Eric Mattson et al., Case 4:01-cv-03106 (S.D.Tex. Sept. 9, 2002).
83 359 F.3d 738 (5th Cir. 2004).
84 513 F.3d 432 (5th Cir. 2007).
85 FCPA Professor, "Case Law Of Note," (May 8, 2016).
86 DOJ Release, "Tyson Foods Inc. Agrees to Pay $4 Million Criminal Penalty to Resolve Foreign Bribery Allegations," (Feb. 10, 2011).
87 SEC Release, "SEC Charges Nature's Sunshine Products, Inc. With Make Illegal Foreign Payments," (July 31, 2009).
88 DOJ Release, "Helmerich & Payne Agrees to Pay $1 Million Penalty to Resolve Allegations of Foreign Bribery in South America," (July 30, 2009).
89 SEC Release, "SEC Files Settled Enforcement Action Charging Con-way Inc. with Violations of the Foreign Corrupt Practices Act," (27 August, 2008).
90 DOJ Release, "AGA Medical Corporation Agrees to Pay $2 Million Penalty and Enter Deferred Prosecution Agreement for FCPA Violations," (June 3, 2008).
91 SEC Release, "SEC Institutes Settled Enforcement Action Against Bristow Group for Improper Payments to Nigerian Government Officials and Other Violations," (Sept. 26, 2007).
92 SEC Release, "Delta & Pine and Turk Deltapine Agree to Pay a $300,000 Penalty to Settle FCPA Charges," (July 26, 2007).
93 Shearman & Sterling "FCPA Digest" (Jan. 2015).
94 FCPA Professor, "Jay Jorgensen On Walmart's Enhanced Ethics & Compliance Program," (Oct. 24, 2017).
95 S. Rep. No. 105-277 (1998).
96 H.R. Rep. No. 105-802 (1998).
97 S. Rep. No. 105-277 (1998); H.R. Rep. No. 105-802 (1998).
98 FCPA Professor, "Significant dd-3 Development in Africa Sting Case," (June 9, 2011).
99 2013 WL 466600 (S.D.N.Y. 2013).
100 FCPA Professor, "FCPA Jurisprudence Alert," (Oct. 6, 2016).
101 2013 WL 603135 (S.D.N.Y. 2013).
102 FCPA Professor, "Judge Trims DOJ's FCPA Enforcement Action Against Lawrence Hoskins," (Aug. 17, 2015).
103 FCPA Professor, "Second Circuit Hears Oral Argument In U.S. v. Hoskins," (Mar. 6, 2017).
104 DOJ Release, "U.S. Resolves Probe Against Oil Company that Bribed Iranian Official" (Oct. 13, 2006).
105 FCPA Professor, "FCPA Enforcement Actions Against Foreign Companies From OECD Convention Peer Countries," (Jan. 23, 2018).
106 Deferred Prosecution Agreement, U.S. v. JGC Corp., Case 4:11-cr-00260 (S.D.Tex. Apr. 6, 2011).
107 FCPA Professor, "In Depth Into The $519 Million Teva FCPA Enforcement Action," (Dec. 22, 2016).
108 FCPA Professor, "Odebrecht / Braskem Bribery Schemes Net Approximate $420 Million FCPA Enforcement Action," (Dec. 21, 2016).

109 Deferred Prosecution Agreement, U.S. v. Magyar Telekom plc, Case No. 11-cr-597 (E.D. Va., Dec. 29, 2011).

110 Information, U.S. v. Bridgestone Corp., Case 4:11-cr-00651 (S.D. Tex., Sept. 15, 2011).

111 Letter from Dennis McInerney, Chief, Fraud Section, U.S. Department of Justice (Criminal Div.), to Robert Giuffra, Attorney for Tenaris (Mar. 14, 2011).

112 OECD Convention on Combating Bribery of Foreign Public Officials in International Business Transactions.

113 FCPA Professor, "Non-U.S. Efforts To Prosecute Overseas Bribery Are Hampered By The Absence Of Clear, Credible Statements From U.S. Prosecutors," (Nov. 6, 2017).

114 FCPA Professor, ""Total"ly Milking The FCPA Cash Cow?" (June 3, 2013).

115 Reuters, "U.S. Must Stop Judicial "Extortion" of Corporate Europe, French Lawmakers Say," (Oct. 11, 2016).

116 133 S.Ct. 1216 (2013).

117 For instance, in a 2012 enforcement action against pharmaceutical company Biomet the conduct at issue went back to 2000; in a 2012 enforcement action against pharmaceutical company Pfizer the conduct at issue went back to 1997; and in a 2012 enforcement action against trading and investment firm Marubeni the conduct at issue went back to 1995. Likewise, in a 2013 enforcement action against oil and gas company Total, the conduct at issue went back to 1995. So old was the conduct giving rise to the Total enforcement action that the DOJ made the unusual statement in the DPA that "evidentiary challenges" were present for both parties given that "most of the underlying conduct occurred in the 1990s and early 2000s."

118 Newmont Mining Corp. Form 10-Q (filed Apr. 20, 2016).

119 Breon Peace, Ryan Becker & Elizabeth Hanley, "The FCPA Statute of Limitations – a Way Out for Wal-Mart?," Bloomberg Law (2012).

120 Paul Pelletier, "The Foreign Bribery Sinkhole at Justice," Wall Street Journal (Apr. 21, 2015).

121 FCPA Professor, "DOJ's McFadden Makes Sense When Talking About "Declinations" And States That FCPA Investigations Should Be "Measured In Months, Not Years," (Apr. 19, 2017).

122 Richard Cassin, FCPA Blog, "The FCPA's Long Shadow" (Aug. 6, 2012).

123 FCPA Professor, "Supreme Court Benchslaps SEC Yet Again – Rules That Disgorgement Is A Penalty Subject To A Five Year Limitations Period," (June 6, 2017).

124 See 493 F.Supp.2d 693 (S.D.N.Y. 2007), affirmed 541 F.3d 166 (2d Cir. 2008).

125 908 F.Supp.2d 834 (S.D. Tex. 2012).

126 2013 WL 466600 (S.D.N.Y. 2013).

# 3 A focus on third parties and related risk management strategies

As discussed in Chapter 2, business organizations subject to the FCPA's anti-bribery provisions are prohibited from providing or promising money or anything of value, with a corrupt intent, to a foreign official, to assist in obtaining or retaining business. The FCPA prohibits such conduct directly, but if this was all that was captured there would be a substantial gap as things of value could be routed to "foreign officials" indirectly through third parties. Accordingly, the FCPA and related laws contain third-party payment provisions and this chapter highlights legal authority and non-legal sources of information relevant to these provisions as well as risk management strategies designed to minimize the risk of engaging and maintaining relationships with third parties in the global marketplace.

Prior to discussing these specific topics, it is important to generally understand how third-party relationships often present the greatest risk for business organizations. While some might respond to this risk by suggesting that business organizations not utilize third parties, recall from Chapter 1 and the representative enforcement actions discussed that in certain countries and in certain sectors business organizations may be required to engage various third parties. Even if not required, utilizing a third party is often an effective non-establishment form of doing business in a foreign country as the third party has an understanding and appreciation of the local business environment and has relationships with key business actors.

According to survey data, approximately 80% of U.S. business organizations partner with a third party when doing business abroad and survey respondents (senior compliance executives from a variety of industry sectors) reported:

- 37% of survey respondents reported working with between 100 and 1000 different third parties;
- 27% with between 1000 and 10,000 different third parties;
- 17% with between 10,000 and 100,000 different third parties; and
- a small percentage with more than 100,000 different third parties.[1]

The upside of utilizing third parties (an understanding and appreciation of the local business environment and relationships with key business actors) is also a downside and survey data suggests that by far the single greatest risk to an anti-bribery and corruption compliance program is third-party conduct.[2] Accordingly, an important component of having "FCPA goggles" is understanding the FCPA's expansive third-party payment provisions and highlighted next is relevant legal authority and non-legal sources of information.

## Third-party payment provisions

### Law

The anti-bribery provisions apply not only to direct payments or things of value offered or provided to "foreign officials" to assist in "obtaining or retaining" business, but also to payments or things of value offered or provided to:

> any person, while knowing that all or a portion of such money or thing of value will be offered, given, or promised, directly or indirectly, to any foreign official.

The FCPA defines "knowing" as follows:

> (A) A person's state of mind is "knowing" with respect to conduct, a circumstance, or a result if (i) such person is aware that such person is engaging in such conduct, that such circumstance exists, or that such result is substantially certain to occur; or (ii) such person has a firm belief that such circumstance exists or that such result is substantially certain to occur.
>
> (B) When knowledge of the existence of a particular circumstance is required for an offense, such knowledge is established if a person is

> aware of a high probability of the existence of such circumstance, unless the person actually believes that such circumstance does not exist.

In the language of the law, the above definition includes not only actual knowledge, but also so-called constructive knowledge, often referred to as conscious disregard or willful blindness.

## Legislative history

In the legislative history, Congress articulated what the third-party payment provisions were intended to capture as well as not capture. A Senate Report stated:

> [The provisions] are meant to prevent management from adopting "head-in-the-sand" approach to bribery in order to avoid liability by ignoring facts and circumstances underlying the subject transaction which would indicate the payment of a bribe. [. . .] On the other hand, the mere fact of doing business in a country where corrupt payments are common, or the employment of an agent with personal relationships with government officials in the country where the company seeks to do business, would not establish such a course of conduct. Similarly, the payment of a commission that is higher than customary would not by itself violate [the provisions] without other evidence that the increased amount of commission is to permit a corrupt payment to be made.[3]

A House Report likewise stated:

> The definition of "knowing" is intended to make it clear that a "head in the sand" approach to the payment of bribes through third parties will not be tolerated. Knowing is therefore defined to include conscious disregard of a high probability that a payment to a third payment will be transmitted by that party to a foreign official.[4]

The House Report further stated:

> [M]ere negligence will not give rise to a civil prosecution under the FCPA. There must be a showing of reckless disregard or knowledge. [. . .] [N]either mere negligence nor reckless disregard will give rise to a criminal prosecution under the FCPA. In order to bring a criminal prosecution for violation of the third party payments provisions, a showing of knowledge as defined in the [FCPA] would be required.

## Judicial decisions

The only judicial decision directly construing the FCPA's third-party payments provisions is *U.S. v. Bourke*. The factual background of the case was unique in that it did not involve traditional use of a foreign third party. Rather, Frederic Bourke (otherwise notable for being a founder of handbag maker Dooney & Bourke) participated in an investment consortium and the DOJ alleged that he and others conspired to purchase assets in the privatization of the Azerbaijan state-owned oil company by bribing various Azeri officials. After being convicted of FCPA and related offenses at trial, Bourke appealed and one issue on appeal was whether the trial court properly instructed the jury on conscious avoidance.[5]

The appellate court concluded that there was "ample evidence" to support Bourke's conviction at trial on a conscious avoidance theory under the third-party payment provisions. The court stated:

> The testimony at trial demonstrated that Bourke was aware of how pervasive corruption was in Azerbaijan generally. Bourke knew of [a co-defendant's] reputation [. . .] Bourke created the American advisory companies to shield himself and other American investors from potential liability from payments made in violation of FCPA, and joined the boards of the American companies instead of joining [a board of another company involved in the investment]. In so doing, Bourke enabled himself to participate in the investment without acquiring actual knowledge of [the other company's] undertakings. The strongest evidence demonstrating that Bourke willfully avoided learning whether corrupt payments were made came from tape recordings of a . . . phone conference with Bourke, [a] fellow investor . . . and their attorneys, during which Bourke voiced concerns about whether [a co-defendant] and company were paying bribes. [. . .] Finally, Bourke's attorney testified that he advised Bourke that if Bourke thought there might be bribes paid, Bourke could not just look the other way. Taken together, a rational juror could conclude that Bourke deliberately avoided confirming his suspicions that [co-defendant] and his cohorts may be paying bribes.

Using the below visual as a reference, the court aggregated various red flags regarding the issues identified.

Red flags can come in various shades – from pink, to light red, to deep red – and it is unlikely that the court would have affirmed Bourke's conviction (consistent with the previously mentioned legislative history) if

the evidence only showed that Bourke was aware of how pervasive corruption was in Azerbaijan. Yet, this "pink" flag was compounded by other evidence of knowledge and the court stated:

> It is not uncommon for a finding of conscious avoidance to be supported primarily by circumstantial evidence. Indeed, the very nature of conscious avoidance makes it unlikely that the record will contain directly incriminating statements. Just as it is rare to find direct record evidence of an employer stating, "I am not going to give you a raise because you are a woman," it is highly unlikely a defendant will provide direct record evidence of conscious avoidance by saying, "Stop! I think you are about to discuss a crime and I want to be able to deny I know anything about it!" Here, the evidence adduced by the government at trial suffices to support the giving of a conscience avoidance charge.

In so holding, the court specifically rejected Bourke's argument that the conscious avoidance charge improperly allowed the jury to convict him based on negligence rather than based on evidence that he avoided learning the truth. The court stated:

> The record contains ample evidence that Bourke had serious concerns about the legality of [co-defendant's] business practices and worked to avoid learning exactly what [co-defendant] was doing.

## Guidance

The FCPA Guidance states:

> The FCPA expressly prohibits corrupt payments made through third parties or intermediaries. [. . .] The fact that a bribe is paid by a third party does not eliminate the potential for criminal or civil FCPA liability. [. . .] Because Congress anticipated the use of third-party agents in bribery schemes – for

> example to avoid actual knowledge of a bribe – it defined "knowing" in a way that prevents individuals and businesses from avoiding liability by putting "any person" between themselves and the foreign officials. [. . .] A person has the requisite knowledge when he is aware of a high probability of the existence of such circumstance, unless the person actually believes that such circumstance does not exist. As Congress made clear, it meant to impose liability not only on those with actual knowledge of wrongdoing, but also on those who purposefully avoid actual knowledge.

Reflective of how third-party relationships often present the greatest risk in the global marketplace and how business organizations are often skittish about such relationships, a number of DOJ Opinion Procedure Releases address third parties and the DOJ has self-identified the following releases as being relevant to various third-party issues:

| 80-03 | 81-01 | 82-02 | 82-04 | 83-01 | 84-01 | 85-03 | 87-01 |
|---|---|---|---|---|---|---|---|
| 97-01 | 98-01 | 98-02 | 01-01 | 01-03 | 06-02 | 10-03 | 12-01 |

## Enforcement actions

While the third-party payment provisions do not set forth a strict liability standard, the knowledge standard, both as written and as enforced, is broad and includes concepts such as willful blindness and conscious disregard. Couple this with the frequent and sometimes required utilization of foreign third parties, and the end result is that the vast majority of enforcement actions concern, in whole or in part, the conduct of various third parties and Table 3.1 highlights representative examples.

*Table 3.1 Third-party allegations*

| Enforcement action | Type of third party and allegations |
|---|---|
| InVision Technologies | Company was aware of a high probability that its ***agents*** or ***distributors*** in Thailand, China and the Philippines paid or offered to pay money to foreign officials or political parties in connection with transactions or proposed transactions for the sale of airport security screening machines.[6] |
| Eli Lilly | Company sold drugs to ***distributors*** in Brazil at a discount; Lilly-Brazil approved "unusually large discounts" to certain distributors; the distributors used a portion of the purchase price to "bribe government officials from a Brazilian state so that the state would purchase Lilly product;" and the Lilly-Brazil sales and marketing manager who requested the discounts knew about the arrangement.[7] |

*Table 3.1 (continued)*

| Enforcement action | Type of third party and allegations |
|---|---|
| Data Systems and Solutions | Payments funneled to employees of alleged state-owned nuclear power plants in Eastern Europe through ***subcontractors*** who billed the company above market rates for services performed in connection with the projects.[8] |
| Various Oil and Gas Companies Doing Business in Nigeria | Company employees knew or were aware of a high probability that certain bribe payments were made by a ***customs agent (an entity that provided freight forwarding, customs clearing, haulage and general logistics services)*** to Nigerian Customs Service officials in connection with license and permit issues.[9] |
| Alcatel-Lucent | Senior executives of company and various subsidiaries knew bribes were being paid, or were aware of the high probability that many ***third-party consultants*** were paying bribes to Costa Rica foreign officials to obtain or retain business.[10] |
| RAE Systems | Payments through two ***joint venture entities*** to Chinese foreign officials to influence acts or decisions by them to obtain or retain business for the company; company was aware of significant indications of ongoing bribery but failed to effectively investigate these indications, or red flags, and to stop the bribery from continuing.[11] |
| SciClone Pharmaceuticals | Chinese ***travel companies*** were hired to provide services (such as arranging transportation, accommodations, and meals for alleged Chinese officials) in connection with what were ostensibly legitimate conferences, seminars, and other events; in addition to a lack of due diligence for these ***third-party vendors*** there was a lack of controls over the events to ensure they had an appropriate business purpose and that the events actually occurred.[12] |
| Keppel Offshore and Marine | To facilitate the payment of bribes and to conceal their purpose, company created and executed an agreement with a ***consulting company*** which then transferred money to bank accounts controlled by or for the benefit of Brazil foreign officials.[13] |

As these enforcement actions demonstrate, a broad range of third-party types (sales agents, distributors, joint ventures partners, and consulting companies) can expose a business organization to scrutiny and enforcement under the third-party payment provisions. In addition, a board range of third-party services, not just those in connection with the sales process, can expose a business organization to scrutiny and enforcement. In addition to the above types of third parties, compliance professionals should recognize that foreign lawyers and other professional service providers such as accounting firms can also be conduits for improper payments to "foreign officials." For instance, an enforcement action against Layne Christensen (a global water management, construction, and drilling company) was based in part on the conduct of a foreign lawyer. According to the government, a company subsidiary "reduced its tax liability by paying bribes through two lawyers retained at the suggestion of the tax authorities but who provided no services."[14] Even though business organizations often need to engage foreign counsel or other professionals when doing business in the global marketplace, such providers are also third parties that may expose the organization to scrutiny and enforcement.

Given the breadth of third-party types often engaged by business organizations, as well as the breadth of services that third parties provide, the compliance best practices discussed later in this chapter should be considered for all third parties with points of contact with foreign officials, even if those points of contact are outside the traditional sales function.

With knowledge of legal authority and non-legal sources of information relevant to the third-party payment provisions, it is time to once again put on your "FCPA goggles" and assess your knowledge of the third-party payment provisions.

Review the below issue-spotting scenario and determine, should the contemplated transaction go forward, whether: (i) Paul has actual knowledge of third-party improper conduct; and (ii) Paul has sufficient knowledge under the third-party payment provisions to expose himself, and thus T Systems, to scrutiny and enforcement?

T Systems sales employees Paul and Chris are at a bar after work.

Paul: All right, so, I'm about to close the biggest deal of my career. And not with a company, but with a government agency! If I close this, I've made my number for the year . . . and with a quarter left to go.

Chris: Sounds really good. Which one?

Paul: I'm not going to say. I don't want to jinx anything. But, I think I'm going to close. The only hiccup is that the head of the agency who

I've been negotiating with for a few months just said we should hire a consultant for $85,000. So he writes down the name and number of some guy he thinks would be good and gives me the info. I don't know what he thinks this consultant is going to do, but if he wants to give back to the local economy . . . I don't know . . . $85,000 to get a multimillion-dollar contract? Seems okay.

The first question you were asked to consider was whether Paul has actual knowledge of third-party improper conduct. Given the above information, it is unlikely that Paul has actual knowledge that the contemplated consultant is going to offer or pay money or anything of value to a foreign official to assist in obtaining or retaining business. Nevertheless, does Paul have sufficient knowledge under the third-party payment provisions to expose himself, and thus T Systems, to scrutiny and enforcement? Consider the red flags that even Paul seems concerned about in connection with the transaction.

- For starters, the head of the government agency recommended the consultant to Paul. It is a red flag when a third party is specifically recommended by a foreign official because it might suggest that the third party is merely a vehicle through which to funnel payments to the foreign official with discretion over some decision relevant to the business organization.

- Another red flag is the timing of the consultant being inserted into the business negotiations. Third parties obviously can provide legitimate value to business deals, but if that is the case the consultant should be involved in the transaction at an early stage and not at the "11th hour" before the deal is about to close. In such a situation, there is a serious question about what legitimate value the third party is actually providing.

- Another red flag is that Paul really has no idea why the consultant may be inserted into the business transaction. Indeed, he specifically says "I have no idea what this consultant is going to do." Again, third parties can indeed provide valuable and legitimate services in connection with foreign business transactions. However, Paul should have a clear understanding of the business justification, including the need for the consultant and what the consultant is going to do, prior to engaging the consultant.

- Another red flag perhaps is the contemplated $85,000 payment to the consultant. Again, to the extent a third party is providing valuable and legitimate services, the third party is deserving of some compensation often in the form of a commission. However, Paul should have a better understand how this amount compares with other similar business transactions. Presumably, this is not Paul's first business deal in the foreign country. How does $85,000 compare with other amounts paid by T Systems in the foreign country? Even if this is Paul's first deal in the foreign country, he needs to better understand, to the extent reasonably possible, how an $85,000 payment compares with industry norms in the foreign country. If an $85,000 payment is unusual, this would most certainly be a red flag.

In short, there are several red flags present in the above scenario. Some of these red flags (such as being recommended by a foreign official and at the "11th hour" of negotiations) are deeper shades of red than others. For instance, upon further investigation the contemplated $85,000 payment red flag may turn white, pink or remain red. Nevertheless, if this business transaction proceeds as set forth above, it is very likely that Paul has sufficient knowledge under the third-party payment provisions to expose himself, and thus T Systems, to scrutiny and enforcement. Similar to the *Bourke* case, the aggregate effect of the various red flags would probably mean that Paul is consciously disregarding or being willfully blind that the contemplated consultant may engage in improper conduct.

The above scenario highlights how business organizations can be exposed to scrutiny and enforcement under the FCPA and related laws not just through actual knowledge of third-party conduct, but also through the failure to identify and/or address red flags relevant to engaging and maintaining third-party relationships. Recognize that no single list is capable of capturing all possible red flags unique to specific circumstances; nevertheless the below list sets forth common red flags relevant to third-party relationships.

### *Third-party red flags*

A "yes" answer to any of these questions does not, in and of itself, suggest that a foreign third party is corrupt or likely to expose a company to scrutiny and enforcement. However, a "yes" answer to any of these questions should trigger concern and a more thorough review by a company.

- Does the country in which the third party operates have a history and reputation for corruption and bribery?
- Is the third party related to or connected to "foreign officials" or maintain close social or business relationships with "foreign officials" or their family members?
- Was the third party recommended by a "foreign official"?
- Does the third party place heavy reliance on foreign political or government contacts vs. knowledgeable staff and investment of time in assisting the company?
- Does the third party have inadequate facilities and unqualified staff? Does the third party lack a physical address? Does the third party lack experience with the company's product and/or industry?
- Does the third party lack a certificate of good standing or other foreign government required operational/business certificates?
- Is the third party's fee, commission or compensation unusual compared with the company's other third parties and/or compared with norms in the industry or country?
- Is the third party requesting an advance payment and/or payments to an account not owned by the third party or to an account not located in the third party's home country?
- Is the third party unwilling or unable to assist the company in developing or implementing a marketing plan?
- Is the third party unwilling to agree in writing to abide by the company's FCPA or related policies and procedures?
- Does the third party lack its own internal anti-corruption policies and procedures?
- Does the third party want to keep the nature of its relationship with the company secret?
- Has the third party ever had an unexplained or inadequately explained breakup with another company or other relationship problems with other companies?
- Has the third party ever been investigated, charged or convicted of corruption or similar allegations?
- Has the third party ever engaged in other suspicious conduct that would raise questions in the eyes of a rational, prudent person?

The answers to these questions are relevant not only to a business organization's scrutiny under the FCPA's third-party payment provisions, but also the FCPA's books and records and internal controls provisions discussed in Chapter 5.

So what is a well-intentioned business organization with a commitment to compliance supposed to do to minimize the risk of engaging and maintaining relationships with third parties? After all, in certain countries and in certain sectors business organizations may be required to engage various third parties. Even if not required, utilizing a third party is often an effective non-establishment form of doing business in a foreign country. Even so, there are compliance best practices relevant to third-party relationships and this chapter next highlights risk management strategies that business organizations should consider.

## Risk management strategies

Conceptually, think of risk management strategies relevant to third parties spanning all three phases of a third-party relationship: pre-engagement best practices; engagement best practices; and post-engagement best practices. Before highlighting the specifics of these various phases, it is important to understand (and this applies to all aspects of FCPA and related compliance not just third-party compliance) that no compliance program can *eliminate* the risk of engaging and maintaining relationships with third parties. However, a business organization that acts consistent with the risk management strategies highlighted can best minimize its risk and will likely be in a better position should a third party act inconsistent with its policies and procedures and expose the organization to scrutiny and enforcement. Recognize as well that a parent company should employ the strategies highlighted not just to its own third parties, but also – to minimize its exposure under the books and records and internal controls provisions discussed in Chapter 5 – third parties engaged by subsidiaries and affiliates over which the parent company exercises control and supervision.

A main goal of the third-party risk management strategies discussed is to negate the knowledge standard in the FCPA's third-party payment provisions. In other words, how could a government enforcement attorney conclude that a business organization was willfully blind or consciously disregard certain risks relevant to its third-party relationships if the organization conducted pre-engagement due diligence, properly engaged the third party pursuant to a written agreement with various representations and warranties, and thereafter implemented certain post-engagement monitoring and supervision policies relevant to the third party?

## Pre-engagement

Prior to engaging a third party, a business organization should: (i) require the third party to complete a detailed questionnaire; (ii) have the third party execute an acknowledgment letter; and (iii) use these materials and other information to assemble a complete and thorough due diligence file on the third party.

## Questionnaire

Prior to entering into a written agreement with a third party (there should be no third-party relationship without a written agreement), a business organization should have the prospective third party complete a questionnaire so that it can better understand the third party, its skills and qualifications, and its business structure. The purpose of this questionnaire is to uncover potential "red flags" that may need to be further investigated prior to entering into a formal, written agreement with the third party. A template questionnaire (that can be tailored to meet specific needs and circumstances of a business organization is set forth below).

*Third Party Questionnaire*

Third party name:

Third party contact information (address, telephone, e-mail, etc.):

Country/countries in which the third party will assist the company:

Estimated percentage of third party time that will be devoted to the company:

Date and place of third party incorporation/business organization:

Management information/executive officers of third party (name and title):

Owners/principals of third party (name and ownership interest):

Members of the board of directors of third party:

Other companies/businesses in which executive officers, owners/principals, members of the board of directors of third party are involved:

Does any current or former government official, political party official, candidate for political office, or employee of a state-owned or state-controlled enterprise have an ownership interest (whether direct or indirect) in the third party?

If so, identify the individual, his/her relation to the third party and provide the name and official position/duties of the individual:

Is any current or former government official, political party official, candidate for political office, or any employee of a state-owned or state-controlled enterprise an employee, officer, or director of the third party?

If so, identify the individual, his/her relation to the third party and provide the name and official position/duties of the individual:

Third party corporate relationships (parent company, subsidiary or affiliate companies, joint-ownership companies, etc.):

Third party relationships (whether currently active or inactive) with other companies during the past five years:

Third party business references (list three with contact information):

Third party banking/credit references (with contact information):

Historical information about third party (how long in business, how long in the specific area of business relevant to the company):

Describe the experience and qualifications of third party personnel who will assist the company and how this experience/qualifications may assist the company:

Attach financial statements (audited, if available) for the past three years, including balance sheets and profit and loss statements:

Provide any additional information that may be relevant to a relationship with the company:

Upon receipt of the completed questionnaire, a business organization should actually follow up with business, banking and credit references as well as seek clarification or further investigate answers such as those suggesting possible red flags common in third-party relationships.

## Acknowledgment letter

In conjunction with sending the questionnaire to the prospective third party, a business organization should also obtain the third-party's commitment to abide by its policies and procedures as set forth in a code of conduct or similar document. A template acknowledgment letter generally explaining the FCPA and the business organization's commitment to FCPA compliance is set out below.

*Third Party Acknowledgment Letter*

Dear [Third Party]

Re: Potential Business Relationship with Company

The purpose of this letter is to introduce you to certain policies and procedures of the Company that will govern our potential business relationship.

As a U.S. company, the Company is subject to the U.S. Foreign Corrupt Practices Act ("FCPA"). Briefly, the FCPA makes it a criminal offense for the Company and its officers, directors, and employees *or* for anyone representing the Company (including you and your employees) to:

> offer, pay, promise to pay, or authorize, the payment of money or anything of value;
>
> to an officer or employee of a foreign government or any department, agency, or instrumentality thereof, or any public international organization, or a foreign political party or official or any candidate for foreign political office (collectively "foreign officials"); *or*
>
> to any person while knowing that all or a portion of such money or thing of value will be offered, given, or promised, directly or indirectly, to any foreign official;
>
> for the purpose of influencing any act or decision of the foreign official to assist the Company in obtaining or retaining business.

For purposes of our relationship, you should assume that the term "foreign official" includes not only traditional government officials and those employed by government agencies, departments, or ministries, but also employees of companies that may be controlled by a foreign government and perform a government function.

The Company's FCPA policies and procedures require, among other things, that all foreign third parties engaged by the Company: (i) acknowledge and agree to comply with the Company's FCPA policies and procedures; (ii) complete a detailed questionnaire; and (iii) complete annual certifications relating to the FCPA.

> Because the FCPA is a criminal statute and the penalties and collateral effects which may be imposed on the Company and its personnel for non-compliance can be significant, the Company takes its FCPA compliance obligations seriously and the Company will expect that you and your employees do so as well. In fact, should you not agree to any of the Company's FCPA policies and procedures, or should the Company have reasonable cause to believe that you are unable to adhere to the Company's FCPA policies and procedures, the Company will not do business with you.
>
> For your benefit, enclosed is "A Resource Guide to the U.S. Foreign Corrupt Practices Act" issued by the U.S. government which provides detailed information about its FCPA enforcement approach and priorities. The Company expects you to familiarize yourself with the FCPA and to immediately inform the Company should you have any questions or concerns regarding compliance with the FCPA or related laws.
>
> [Signature Blocks]

The purpose of the acknowledgment letter is to provide a "meeting of the minds" and make clear to the prospective third party during the initial consideration phase that the business organization takes FCPA compliance seriously and that it will expect the same from the third party.

## Due diligence file

Once a business organization has obtained an FCPA acknowledgment from the third party, received responses to its questionnaire, followed up with references, and as warranted further investigated certain answers, the business organization can now better evaluate whether it should formally engage the third party. If the business decision is made to engage the third party, the organization should first prepare a written due diligence report on the third party and include as much background information as possible from the following checklist.

## Due diligence file checklist

- *Need for third party*: explain why the services of the specific third party are necessary and identify the qualifications of the third party. Also, explain how the company came to learn of the third party (for instance, was the third party recommended by a customer or potential customer or did the third party approach the company).

- *Experience*: identify the number of years the third party has been in business and specifically the number of years the third party has been involved in the particular business for which the company is engaging the third party.

- *Fees, commission, compensation*: identify the manner in which the third party will be paid and explain how the proposed third party fee, commission, or compensation compares with similar third parties engaged by the company and/or compares with typical terms in the industry and country.

- *General background*: generally describe the third party's current and prior activities and its primary areas of business activities.

- *Financial stability*: were financial statements obtained from the third party (audited if available) for the past three years, including balance sheets and profit and loss statements? If not, why not?

- *Ownership structure*: identify percentage of ownership of each of the principles of the third party.

- *Quantity of work to be performed*: estimate the percentage of time the third party's business will be devoted to the company. Estimate the time commitment required for the third party to assist the company.

- *Location*: identify the countries or territories within a country where the third party will perform on behalf of the company.

- *References*: identify the third party's business, banking and credit references and summarize the information obtained through reference checks.

- *Cooperation*: indicate whether the third party was willing to sign an FCPA acknowledgment letter and whether the third party has objected to any of the questions asked in the questionnaire.

- *Public records search*: identify various public records searches conducted of the third party and summarize any information learned.

- *Compliance verification*: identify company personnel who reviewed and discussed the FCPA and related laws with the third party.

- *Resolution of any "red flag"*: if any red flag appeared during the pre-engagement process, identify the red flag and steps taken to address the red flag. No agreement with a third party should be finalized until the company is reasonably certain that the red flag will not expose the company to scrutiny.

- *Other information*: identify other company personnel or outside vendors who participated in the pre-engagement due diligence process as well as specific dates in which certain tasks were performed.

These pre-engagement risk management strategies will certainly take time and resources to complete and given that many business organizations have hundreds, if not thousands, and in some cases tens of thousands of third parties, the question often arises: where to start and do these steps need to be used on all third parties?

Regarding the where to start question, Chapter 6 will teach you the fundamentals of conducting a risk assessment so that compliance policies can be specifically tailored to a business organization's unique risk points. As this skills exercise will instruct, different third parties will likely present different risk. Outside the context of a specific risk assessment, survey data suggests that business organizations use the following criteria to risk rank third parties:

- 82% type of third party (consultant, agent, distributor, etc.);

- 62% amount of contract;

- 61% geography of third party;

- 49% known government relationships;

- 29% other.[15]

Regarding whether pre-engagement strategies need to be used on all third parties, a specific risk assessment and the above criteria can help answer this question. However, recognize that law enforcement often has the benefit of hindsight when a business organization is under scrutiny. In other words, even if a business organization used the above practices on 99% of its 1000 third parties, this leaves ten third parties and if it turns out that one of these third parties is the source of scrutiny and enforcement, the government may view this as problematic. Further relevant to the breadth question is what to do with third parties already engaged who have had a long-term successful and compliant relationship with the business organization? While this type of third party may present less risk than a newly engaged third party, business organizations should consider employing the same strategies upon renewal of a third-party relationship and/or in connection with a roll-out of enhanced compliance policies and procedures.

Many of the above pre-engagement risk management strategies may seem obvious, but sometimes it takes learning of a real company, resolving a real enforcement action, with a real third-party failure in these areas to best drive home basic compliance points.

For instance, the government found in an enforcement action that a foreign official recommended that the company retain a specific third party. As previously mentioned, this is most certainly a red flag and in addition the government found that the company retained the third party without conducting due diligence and without entering into a written agreement detailing the services to be provided (as will be discussed shortly engagement best practice is to have a written agreement with a third party with a detailed description of the services to be provided).

In an enforcement action against software company Paradigm, the government was critical of the company because its agent requested that his commission be paid through five different entities. Further reflective of deficient pre-engagement practices, the company did not conduct due diligence on the agent or the five entities through which the agent requested payment.[16] Likewise, in the SBM Offshore enforcement action the government alleged that, at a third party's request, SBM "typically split its 'commission' payments to [the third party] into two accounts, transferring one portion to bank accounts in Brazil . . . and another, larger, portion of its 'commission' to bank accounts in Switzerland held in the names of [the third party's] shell companies."[17] According to the government, SBM "understood that the purpose of splitting payments [to the third party] was to facilitate the payment of bribes."

As these enforcement actions demonstrate, at a minimum business organizations need to have a basic understanding of where its money is being sent in connection with foreign business transactions facilitated by third parties. In this regard, the enforcement agencies are increasingly expecting financial gatekeepers such as finance, accounting and auditing personnel to play a meaningful role in compliance, including third party monitoring, and Chapter 7 discusses this holistic aspect of compliance in more detail.

As previously mentioned, the main purpose of the pre-engagement questionnaire is to allow a business organization to better understand a prospective third party, its skills and qualifications, and its business structure. If questionnaire answers reveal potential "red flags," further investigation should be conducted prior to entering into a formal written agreement with a third party.

**FAILURE**

Despite this best practice, in an enforcement action against Alstom (a company involved in large power, transportation and infrastructure projects) the allegations included:

> Certain consultants proposed for retention had no expertise or experience in the industry sector in which Alstom was attempting to secure or execute the project. Other consultants were located in a country different than the project country. At other times, the consultants asked to be paid in a currency or in a bank account located in a country different than where the consultant and the project were located. In multiple instances, more than one consultant was retained on the same project, ostensibly to perform the very same services. Despite, these "red flags," the consultants were nevertheless retained without meaningful scrutiny.

Specifically, the government found that Alstom entities: (i) retained a consultant on a transportation project even though the consultant's expertise was as a "wholesaler of cigarettes, wines and pianos;" and (ii) retained another consultant on a power project even though the consultant "sold furniture and leather products, and exported chemical products and spare parts." Based on these allegations, it was not surprising that Alstom was found liable under the third-party provisions for third-party conduct given that the provisions include concepts such as conscious disregard and willful blindness.

Even if a business organization acts consistent with best practices by sending a detailed questionnaire to a prospective third party and receiving back responses including a list of references, there is still more work to be done. For instance, in the Halliburton enforcement action concerning conduct in Nigeria the government was critical of the company for not actually checking the third party's references. In the words of the government, those conducting due diligence for the company "did not check all of the references provided by the UK Agent, some of which were in fact false."[18]

As highlighted above, a component of pre-engagement best practices is to document various information relevant to the third-party relationship in a written due diligence file including specific company personnel who were involved in the due diligence. However, in the Teva Pharmaceutical enforcement action the government was critical of the company's due diligence because it was essentially delegated to a subsidiary executive who had been pushing for the third-party agreement and who was also involved in the improper conduct.[19] Rather than having an individual with a vested interest in the third-party engagement perform due diligence, company personnel distanced from the third party and the underlying business transaction should conduct the due diligence and other pre-engagement compliance steps.

As these enforcement actions highlight, enforcement agencies often have the benefit of hindsight when a business organization is under scrutiny because of third-party conduct and a simplistic narrative is often advanced. In other words:

- if only the business organization had a written agreement with the third party;
- if only the business organization checked the third party's references; or
- if only appropriate personnel conducted the due diligence of the third party.

then the improper third-party conduct would not have occurred. Although this is simplistic and assumes causation, it is nevertheless the enforcement landscape that business organizations are subject to and mean that the above pre-engagement risk management strategies are all the more important. It is also important that business organizations actually follow through on these compliance practices and not just have them on paper.

**FAILURE**

For instance, in the Och-Ziff enforcement action the resolution documents contained a section titled "Och-Ziff Did Not Follow its Recommended Anti-corruption Policies" and noted that with the assistance of outside counsel the company had implemented an anti-corruption policy applicable to all subsidiaries and affiliates with required due diligence steps including:

- obtaining copies of the most recent financial statements for its business partners;
- identifying all shareholders owning or controlling each business partner, and the nature of that control;
- requesting references from financial institutions that have existing business relationships with business partners and clients;
- making all payments in the country in which an agent resides;
- accessing business partner books and records and utilizing a right-to-audit on a periodic basis;
- re-checking and confirming due diligence for business partners on an ongoing basis;
- reviewing all monies paid out by business partners as part of ongoing due diligence;
- conducting heightened due diligence in business transactions involving government officials or state-owned businesses, where the business partner's only contribution is influence, or where the partner refuses to put agreements or proof of expenditures in writing; and

- obtaining annual certifications by the chief financial officer and chief legal officer that all foreign business partners have complied with the firm's anti-corruption policies and procedures.

However, the government found that "Och-Ziff failed to follow its own recommended due diligence steps" in connection with the business transactions relevant to the enforcement action.[20]

In short, business organizations should implement various pre-engagement risk management strategies relevant to foreign third parties and actually follow through on those strategies prior to engaging third parties. As previously discussed, no compliance program can eliminate the risk of engaging and maintaining relationships with third parties and the above risk management strategies are not going to provide legal immunity for third-party conduct. However, the goal of third-party compliance is not only to minimize risk, but also negate the knowledge standard in the FCPA's third-party payment provisions. Should a business organization become the subject of scrutiny because of third-party conduct, law enforcement will likely ask about pre-engagement policies and procedures and the organization will look foolish if there are none. However, a business organization that acts consistent with the pre-engagement risk management strategies discussed will be able to tell the best story possible should a third party's conduct expose it to scrutiny and enforcement. As highlighted next, part of telling the best story possible is also adhering to engagement best practices relevant to third parties.

## Engagement

For a wide variety of reasons, not just those relevant to scrutiny and enforcement under the FCPA and related laws, relationships with third parties should be memorialized in a written agreement and company policy should prohibit third-party relationships from beginning with an oral agreement or handshake. As demonstrated by certain of the enforcement actions highlighted above, if a business organization becomes the subject of scrutiny because of third-party conduct, law enforcement will likely ask the organization to produce the written agreement with the third party and once again the organization will look foolish if there is none. However, just any written agreement is not going to suffice. Rather, the agreement with a third party should specifically describe the services the third party is going to perform and also include other FCPA-specific provisions as set forth in the sample agreement below.

*Third Party Contract Terms and Conditions*

*Include in the Representations and Warranties Section of the Third Party Contract*

The U.S. Foreign Corrupt Practices Act ("FCPA") makes it unlawful for Company, or anyone acting on behalf of Company including Third Party, to offer, pay, promise, or authorize to pay money, a gift, or anything of value to any officer or employee of a foreign government or any department, agency, or instrumentality thereof (including state-owned or state-controlled enterprises), or of a public international organization, or any foreign political party or official thereof or any candidate for foreign political office (collectively "foreign officials") with the intent of causing the foreign official to misuse their position to assist in obtaining, retaining or directing business to the Company. Third Party acknowledges and confirms its understanding of the FCPA and that it has received a copy of FCPA Guidance issued by the U.S. Government. Third Party agrees to comply with the FCPA and not in any way cause Company to be in violation of the FCPA or subject to FCPA scrutiny.

In connection with this AGREEMENT, Third Party hereby makes the following representations and warranties to Company, and covenants and agrees as follows:

(i) Third Party hereby represents, warrants and covenants to Company that Third Party has not, and covenants and agrees that it will not, in connection with business contemplated by this AGREEMENT or in connection with any other business involving Company, make or promise to make any payment or transfer anything of value, directly or indirectly, to a foreign official with the intent of causing the official to misuse their position to assist in obtaining, retaining or directing business to the Company. It is the intent of the parties that no payments or transfers of value shall be made which have the purpose or effect of bribery, acceptance of or acquiescence in kickbacks or other unlawful or improper means of obtaining or retaining business.

(ii) Third Party hereby represents, warrants, and covenants to Company that should it learn or have reason to know of: (a) any payment, offer, or agreement to make a payment to any foreign official for the purpose of assisting in obtaining, retaining or directing business to the Company; or (b) any other development that in any way makes inaccurate or incomplete the representations, warranties, and covenants of Third Party relating to the FCPA under the AGREEMENT, that Third Party will immediately inform Company, in writing, of such knowledge or suspicion and the entire factual basis known by Third Party.

(iii) Third Party hereby represents, warrants and covenants to Company that no ownership interest, direct or indirect, in Third Party or in the contractual relationship established by the AGREEMENT, is held or controlled by a foreign official. Third Party hereby agrees to inform Company, in writing, if at any time during the AGREEMENT this representation, warranty, and covenant changes.

(iv) Third Party hereby agrees: (a) that any payments to Third Party by Company under the AGREEMENT shall be made by check or wire transfer only, directly to Third Party or to a bank account in Third Party's name, and no requests for cash payments or other payments in non-bearer form shall be accepted; (b) that any payments to Third Party by Company shall be made in the foreign country where Third Party is to perform its duties under the AGREEMENT or in the U.S.; (c) that books and records showing expenses incurred in connection with the AGREEMENT shall reflect the purpose of each expenditure and for whose benefit the expenditure was made and that there will be written records of each and every service that Third Party performs for Company or on its behalf; (d) that Third Party shall retain accurate, detailed records of, and permit Company to review upon written request, any expenses or costs of Third Party which Company may be required to reimburse under the AGREEMENT; (e) that Company has the right, upon written request, to audit Third Party's compliance with the AGREEMENT; and (f) that the terms of the AGREEMENT may be disclosed to government agencies and other persons with a legitimate need for such information.

(v) Third Party agrees that it will, and will cause each of its directors, officers, employees, agents or other representatives who have any direct involvement with any of the management or operations of Third Party relevant to the AGREEMENT, at the request of Company and at least annually, to provide Company with a certification of FCPA compliance as provided by Company.

*Include, As a Cause for Termination in the Third Party Contract, the Following*
Company believes, in good faith, that Third Party has acted in a way that may subject Company to scrutiny or liability under the FCPA or related laws.

Regarding the suggested termination clause above, recognize how it grants a business organization more flexibility than a rigid termination clause that requires the organization to prove that a third party violated the FCPA or related laws. While potential legal exposure to a third party for wrongful termination may not be relevant in an actual FCPA enforcement, third parties have brought civil claims against business organizations for wrongful termination and related claims in connection with FCPA scrutiny and enforcement. In such actions, a business organization will have a better defense against such claims if it has a flexible termination clause.

Many of these suggested clauses may seem obvious, but others may not and once again it takes learning of a real company, resolving a real enforcement action, with real failures in these areas to best drive home basic compliance points.

For instance, in the above-referenced Halliburton enforcement action the compliance failures cited by the government included that the company's policies and procedures relevant to third party agents did not require "that the agent agree to any accounting or audit of fees received."[21] Recognize however that merely including audit rights in a third-party agreement may not be enough because the enforcement agencies will expect a business organization to actually exercise the audit rights. For instance, in the Akamai Technologies enforcement action based on third-party conduct in China the compliance deficiencies cited by the government included: "the failure to proactively exercise audit rights to ensure compliance with anti-bribery policies."[22]

As with the pre-engagement best practices previously discussed, adhering to engagement best practices relevant to third parties is not going to provide legal immunity for third-party conduct. However, a business organization that acts consistent with these risk management strategies will be able to tell the best story possible should a third party's conduct expose it to scrutiny and enforcement and this narrative flows into post-engagement strategies as well.

## Post-engagement

A business organization's good faith efforts to minimize risk associated with third parties along with its efforts to negate the knowledge standard in the FCPA's third-party payment provisions should continue even after formal engagement of the third party.

For starters, if not before engagement as soon as possible after engagement, a business organization should ensure that foreign third parties receive training specific to the organization's unique risks. As highlighted in Chapter 2, many of the FCPA's elements are broadly interpreted and thus third parties need to be educated on, among other things, the broad interpretation of: (i) anything of value and how it can include meals, entertainment and other common business courtesies; (ii) "foreign official" and how it can include employees of state-owned or state-controlled enterprises; and (iii) "obtain or retain business" particularly if third parties are used to navigate foreign bureaucracies. After the third party completes the training, a business organization should require the third party to sign a training acknowledgment letter and a template is set forth below.

*Third Party Training Acknowledgment*

I hereby acknowledge that:

On [date], I received FCPA specific training provided by Company. The training was comprehensive in nature and focused on, among other things, FCPA risk areas that may be encountered in doing business on behalf of Company. During the training session, I had the opportunity to ask questions or express concerns.

As a result of receiving the FCPA training, I hereby acknowledge an understanding of the FCPA's basic prohibitions and agree to abide by the FCPA in doing business on behalf of Company.

Comments:

____________________________________________________

Like other aspects of compliance best practices, training a third party and having the third party execute an acknowledgment letter is not going to provide a business organization with legal immunity for third-party conduct. However, in addition to minimizing risk, the training acknowledgment letter will once again allow a business organization to tell the best story possible should a third party's conduct expose it to scrutiny and enforcement. For instance, if a third party's conduct with an SOE employee is the source of scrutiny, the business organization can point to the specific portion of training that addressed this issue and demonstrate that the third party: received the training on a specific date; had the opportunity to ask questions about the training material; and acknowledged an understanding of the training content.

During the period of engagement with the third party, a business organization should also monitor and supervise the third party.

In other words, even if a third party passed the organization's pre-engagement due diligence process, was properly engaged through a written agreement, and received FCPA training unique to the organization's risks, none of this means that third parties can't change or that local business conditions can't change – both of which may warrant additional monitoring and supervision of the third party. At a minimum, a business organization should have the third party certify on an annual basis that it is in compliance with, and will continue to comply with, the organization's FCPA policies and procedures and a template annual certification is set forth below.

*Third Party Annual FCPA Certification*

I hereby certify that:

I have read and understand, and am presently in compliance with the Company's FCPA compliance policies and procedures as set forth in [formal name of the Company's code of conduct/other document provided to the third party];

Except as stated below, I confirm that I have no knowledge, belief or suspicion of any actual or potential violations of the FCPA compliance policies and procedures or conduct that could result in any scrutiny under the FCPA or related laws;

I am, and will continue to be, responsible for assuring that the FCPA compliance policies and procedures are understood and followed by personnel whom I supervise; and

I will continue to comply with the FCPA compliance policies and procedures while carrying out my job duties and functions on behalf of the Company.

Comments:

________________________________________________

Part of monitoring and supervising third-party conduct also includes being able to recognize "red flags" that may arise during the engagement, having the commitment and resources to investigate the red flags, and reassessing the relationship based on the results of the investigation.

This chapter has specifically focused on third parties and related risk management strategies because third parties often present the greatest risk for business organizations given the prominence of third-party relationships in the global marketplace coupled with the FCPA's broad third-party payment provisions. Although no compliance program can eliminate the risk of engaging and maintaining relationships with third parties, a business organization that acts consistent with the above pre-engagement, engagement, and post-engagement best practices can best minimize its risk and will likely be in a better position should a third party act in a manner inconsistent with its policies and procedures and expose the organization to scrutiny and enforcement. For example, consider the following compliance policies at Walmart as stated by Walmart's Global Chief Ethics and Compliance Officer:

> Much of the corruption risk that companies encounter stems from the use of third-party intermediaries (TPIs) to assist with functions such as licensing and permitting. Accordingly, Walmart has enhanced every aspect of our processes for managing TPIs, including measures to strengthen screening and diligence procedures, standardize anticorruption contractual commitments, expand risk-based TPI trainings, process compliance certifications, and conduct proactive targeted audits of TPIs.
>
> Under our program, Walmart's business units are required to identify all potential TPIs. Once identified, those TPI candidates must undergo a detailed due-diligence review. To assist with this review, we have developed a customized anticorruption portal with Dun & Bradstreet. The portal automates data collection and workflow, delivery of due-diligence reports, and the monitoring of TPIs' compliance with all of our contracting and certification requirements. The portal also allows for TPI monitoring more broadly, including alerts such as for new convictions or other red flags. [. . .]
>
> Finally, Walmart proactively audits our TPIs. These proactive audits are selected by Walmart not in response to allegations of any irregularities in the TPI's services, but based on factors such as risk ranking, TPI expenditures, input from relevant stakeholders, and monitoring results.

Although this chapter has rightly focused on risk management strategies relevant to engaging and maintaining relationships with foreign third parties, it closes with a policy issue worthy of consideration. The FCPA is certainly not unique in exposing a business organization to legal liability based on the acts of various third parties as there are countless other laws that have similar features. Yet do business organizations unleash the same compliance policies and procedures on a third party from Boston compared with Beijing, from Louisville compared with Luanda, from San Diego compared with São Paulo?

It seems that the starting point for a business organization's relationship with a *domestic* third party is that the third party is ethical until proven otherwise. Thus, a business organization is probably not going to devote its limited resources to engage in various compliance best practices and create extensive due diligence files so that it can tell the best story possible should a domestic third party act in a manner inconsistent with its compliance policies and procedures. This is a respectful and healthy way to begin and maintain a relationship with a human being – not to mention a cost- and time-efficient use of limited corporate resources.

On the opposite end of the spectrum, guided no doubt by the enforcement actions discussed above and the compliance take-away points from them, it seems that a starting point for a business organization's relationship with a *foreign* third party is that the third party is unethical. Thus, a business organization is likely to devote its limited resources to pre-engagement due diligence, create extensive due diligence files and engage in other compliance best practices so that it can tell the best story possible should a third party act in a manner inconsistent with the organization's compliance policies and procedures. Is this a respectful and healthy way to begin and maintain a relationship, recognizing that a human being is on the receiving end of the business organization's pre-engagement questionnaire, FCPA acknowledgment letter, training acknowledgment letter, and annual certification letter?

All of this begs the question of whether typical third-party compliance practices in the domestic context are too lax or whether typical third-party practices in the foreign context are too aggressive? Like many policy issues, the best answer is likely to be somewhere in between. Nevertheless, early in the book you were warned that on certain issues you simply need to accept the old adage "it is what it is" and when it comes to compliance best practices relevant to foreign third parties "it is what it is."

NOTES

1 Kroll/Compliance Week, Anti-Bribery and Corruption Benchmarking Report (2013).
2 Kroll/Ethisphere Anti-Bribery & Corruption Benchmarking Report (2017).
3 S. Rep. No. 100-85 (1987).
4 H.R. Rep. No. 100-40 (1987).
5 667 F.3d 122 (2d Cir. 2011).
6 Non-Prosecution Agreement Regarding In-Vision (Dec. 3, 2004).
7 Complaint, SEC v. Eli Lilly and Co., No. 1:12-cv-02045 (D.D.C., Dec. 20, 2012).
8 Deferred Prosecution Agreement, U.S. v. Data Systems & Solutions LLC, Case 1:12-cr-00262-LO (E.D.Va., June 18, 2012).
9 DOJ Release, "Oil Services Companies and a Freight Forwarding Company Agree to Resolve Foreign Bribery Investigations and to Pay More Than $156 Million in Criminal Penalties," (Nov. 4, 2010).
10 FCPA Professor, "Analyzing Alcatel-Lucent," (Jan. 6, 2011).

11 FCPA Professor, "RAE Systems Held Liable For The Acts Of Its Subsidiaries' Joint Venture Partners," (Dec. 13, 2010).
12 FCPA Professor, "Issues to Consider from the SciClone Enforcement Action," (Feb. 9, 2016).
13 FCPA Professor, "Keppel Offshore & Marine Resolves Net $105.5 Million FCPA Enforcement Action Based On Brazil Bribery Schemes," (Dec. 23, 2017).
14 FCPA Professor, "Layne Christensen Company Resolves SEC Enforcement Action," (Oct. 28, 2014).
15 FCPA Professor, "A Focus On Third-Party Practices," (Nov. 24, 2017).
16 Non-Prosecution Agreement, Paradigm B.V. (Sept. 21, 2007).
17 FCPA Professor, "Issues To Consider From The SBM Offshore Enforcement Action," (Dec. 4, 2017).
18 Complaint, SEC v. Halliburton Co. (S.D. Tex. Feb. 11, 2009).
19 FCPA Professor, "In Depth Into The $519 Million Teva FCPA Enforcement Action," (Dec. 22, 2016).
20 FCPA Professor, "In Depth Into The Och-Ziff FCPA Enforcement Action," (Oct. 2, 2016).
21 Complaint, SEC v. Halliburton Co. (S.D. Tex. Feb. 11, 2009).
22 FCPA Professor, "Two For Tuesday In FCPA Enforcement Land – Akamai Technologies," (June 8, 2016).

# 4 The FCPA's exception, affirmative defenses and related risk management strategies

Even if all of the substantive elements of the FCPA's anti-bribery provisions have been met, the final step in analyzing whether conduct violates the anti-bribery provisions is determining whether the facilitating payment exception or the so-called local law or reasonable and bona fide expenditures affirmative defenses apply and this chapter highlights legal authority and non-legal sources of information relevant to these provisions.

Before doing so, recall the two distinct questions posed at the beginning of this book that can be asked in connection with many instances of FCPA scrutiny and enforcement. The first question is whether Congress, in passing the FCPA, intended to capture the alleged conduct at issue and whether a court would find the alleged conduct in violation of the FCPA? The second question is whether, given the government's prevailing enforcement theories, the conduct at issue can expose a company to scrutiny and enforcement? These questions, specifically the second question, are particularly relevant to the facilitating payments exception because while the FCPA exempts facilitating payments, it is an open question whether this express statutory exception has any real meaning or whether the enforcement agencies, through their enforcement theories, have essentially repealed this exception. Regardless, prevailing best practices seem to be prohibiting facilitating payments except in cases of health and safety, and consistent with this approach, training best practices will be highlighted.

Along with third parties, corporate hospitality and related expenses often present the greatest challenges to a compliance program given that business organizations routinely incur expenses in connection with marketing, promotional and other legitimate business activities. Because of this, an additional component of having "FCPA goggles" is understanding the contours of the reasonable and bona fide expenditures affirmative defense and once again you will learn risk management strategies to minimize risk in this area and also have a chance to assess your acquired knowledge through a real-world issue spotting scenario.

## Facilitating payments exception

While some view facilitating or "grease" payments to be corrupt payments under a different name, the fact remains that the FCPA contains an express facilitating payments exception and it is this statute that the enforcement agencies are obligated to enforce (or not as with an exception).

### Law

The FCPA states that the anti-bribery provisions "shall not apply to any facilitating or expediting payment to a foreign official . . . the purpose of which is to expedite or to secure the performance of a routine governmental action by a foreign official . . .".

The FCPA defines "routine governmental action" as follows:

> The term "routine governmental action" means only an action which is ordinarily and commonly performed by a foreign official in:
>
> (i) obtaining permits, licenses, or other official documents to qualify a person to do business in a foreign country; (ii) processing governmental papers, such as visas and work orders; (iii) providing police protection, mail pick-up and delivery, or scheduling inspections associated with contract performance or inspections related to transit of goods across country; (iv) providing phone service, power and water supply, loading and unloading cargo, or protecting perishable products or commodities from deterioration; or (v) actions of a similar nature.
>
> The term "routine governmental action" does not include any decision by a foreign official whether, or on what terms, to award new business to or to continue business with a particular party, or any action taken by a foreign official involved in the decision-making process to encourage a decision to award new business to or continue business with a particular party.

## Legislative history

The legislative history is clear that in passing the FCPA Congress intended to capture only a narrow category of payments and chose not to capture so-called facilitating payments given the difficult and complex business conditions encountered in many foreign countries. Congressional leaders spearheading enactment of the FCPA were clear as to the scope of the law they envisioned. For instance, Senator Church stated:

> Let us be clear that we are not just talking about a little "baksheesh" to grease the palm of some petty clerk in order to speed needed documents on their way through the bureaucratic labyrinth. What we are talking about is a concerted effort by the petroleum industry to buy favorable tax and energy legislation in a European country in which one U.S. company alone made over $50 million in contributions to the government parties and members of the cabinet over a 9 year period. What we are talking about is an arms industry campaign to flood the Middle East with weapons, in which a U.S. aircraft company paid over $100 million in agents' fees in one country to sell an airplane which has no competitor.[1]

Senator Proxmire stated:

> I recognize it is hard [to define a bribe], but we are not concerned so much about the low level grease payments. What we are talking about is the payment, as I say, to make a sale. . . . What we are concerned about, as I say, and trying to get at . . . is bribery for the purpose of making sales abroad.
>
> [W]e define [a bribe] as a payment to an official of a foreign government for the purpose of inducing him to use his influence to secure business for the issuer or influence legislation or regulations of his government.[2]

Representatives Murphy and Eckhardt likewise stated during a House hearing:

> This bill is not concerned with so-called grease or facilitating payments, such as may be necessary to some petty clerk to speed documents through a bureaucracy. The bill does not address itself to "grease" or "facilitating" payments made to low-level clerical or ministerial government officials.[3]

Senate and House Reports evidence the limited scope of the FCPA and how it would not capture all foreign corporate payments Congress learned of during its multi-year investigation. A Senate Report stated:

> In drafting the bill ... the Committee deliberately cast the language narrowly, in order to differentiate between such payments [to a foreign official corruptly intended to induce the recipient to use his influence to secure business, influence legislation or regulations] and low-level facilitating payments sometimes called "grease payments." Thus, [the bill] would not reach a small gratuity paid to expedite shipment through Customs or the placement of a trans-Atlantic telephone call, to secure required permits, or to ensure that a corporation's warehouses were not put to the torch. In other words, payments made to expedite the proper performance of duties may be reprehensible, but it does not appear feasible for the United States to attempt unilaterally to eradicate all such payments. However, where the payment is made to influence the placement of government contracts or to influence the formulation of legislation or regulations, such payment is prohibited. ... The Committee fully recognizes that the proposed law will not reach all corrupt payments overseas.[4]

A House Report likewise stated:

> The scope ... is limited by the requirement that the offer, promise, authorization, payment, or gift must have as a purpose inducing the recipient to use influence with the foreign government or instrumentality, or to refrain from performing any official responsibilities, so as to direct business to any person, maintain an established business opportunity with any person, divert any business opportunity from any person or influence the enactment or promulgation of legislation or regulations of that government or instrumentality ... The bill's coverage does not extend to so-called grease or facilitating payments ... The language of the bill is deliberately cast in terms which differentiate between such payments and facilitating payments, sometimes called "grease payments". In using the word "corruptly", the committee intends to distinguish between payments which cause an official to exercise other than his free will in acting or deciding or influencing an act or decision and those payments which merely move a particular matter toward an eventual act or decision or which do not involve any discretionary action. In defining "foreign official", the committee emphasizes this crucial distinction by excluding from the definition of "foreign official" government employees whose duties are essentially ministerial or clerical. For example, a gratuity paid to a customs official to speed the processing of a customs document would not be reached by the bill. Nor would it reach payments made to secure permits, licenses, or the expeditious performance of similar duties of an essentially ministerial or clerical nature which must of necessity by performed in any event. While payments made to assure or to speed the proper performance of a foreign official's duties may be reprehensible in

> the United States, the committee recognizes that they are not necessarily so viewed elsewhere in the world and that it is not feasible for the United States to attempt unilaterally to eradicate all such payments. As a result, the committee has not attempted to reach such payments. However, where the payment is made to influence the passage of law, regulations, the placement of government contracts, the formulation of policy or other discretionary governmental functions, such payments would be prohibited. The committee fully recognizes that the proposed law will not reach all corrupt payments overseas.[5]

As suggested by the above legislative history, the FCPA originally contained an indirect facilitating payment exception embedded in the "foreign official" element by excluding from the definition of "foreign official" "any employee of a foreign government or any department, agency, or instrumentality thereof whose duties are essentially ministerial or clerical." In 1988, this indirect exception was removed from the definition of "foreign official" in favor of an express stand-alone exception. The House Report indicated that Congress did not seek to disturb Congress's original intent and stated:

> The policy adopted by Congress in 1977 remains valid, in terms of both U.S. law enforcement and foreign relations considerations. Any prohibition under U.S. law against this type of petty corruption would be exceedingly difficult to enforce, not only by U.S. prosecutors but by company officials themselves. Thus while such payments should not be condoned, they may appropriately be excluded from the reach of the FCPA. U.S. enforcement resources should be devoted to activities have much greater impact on foreign policy.[6]

## Judicial decisions

There is little case law construing the FCPA's facilitation payments exception and *U.S. v. Duperval* is the only appellate court decision to squarely address a component of the exception.[7] The case against Jean Rene Duperval, an official at Haiti Teleco, involved the same core conduct alleged in the *Esquenazi* "foreign official" decision previously highlighted in Chapter 2. Because "foreign official" bribe recipients are not subject to the FCPA's anti-bribery provisions, Duperval was charged with various money laundering offenses. However, a necessary predicate for those convictions was an underlying FCPA violation and after being convicted by a jury, among the issues Duperval appealed was whether the trial court erred in not instructing the jury on the

FCPA's facilitation payment exception. On appeal, Duperval admitted that he received money from the FCPA defendants, but asserted that the money was for doing a good job in the administration of the contracts at issue and was thus "routine governmental action." However, the Eleventh Circuit rejected this reasoning and held that the term "routine governmental action" in the facilitating payments exception should not be read to include "the government administering contracts with companies that provide telephone service."

An SEC enforcement action against Mark Jackson and James Ruehlen (individuals associated with Noble Corporation) is also notable in that a federal trial court judge interpreted various aspects of the facilitating payment exception during pre-trial proceedings. In terms of background, the DOJ and SEC brought parallel enforcement actions against several oil and gas companies doing business in Nigeria and a portion of the conduct focused on payments allegedly made to the notoriously corrupt Nigerian Customs Service in connection with securing or renewing temporary import permits so that oil rigs could remain in Nigerian waters. Other allegations in the so-called Customs Gate actions included payments made to Nigerian Customs Service officials "to expedite the delivery of goods and equipment into Nigeria." In a sign of the relevance of the facilitating payments exception to the conduct at issue, the DOJ twice stated in the Noble Corp. resolution documents that "the payments [at issue] . . . would not constitute facilitation payments for routine governmental actions within the meaning of the FCPA."[8] None of the Customs Gate corporate enforcement actions were subjected to any meaningful scrutiny, but were resolved through non-prosecution or deferred prosecution agreements in which the companies collectively paid approximately $236 million in combined settlement amounts.[9]

Perhaps signaling the weakness of the underlying enforcement theories, the *only* individuals charged in connection with Customs Gate were Jackson and Ruehlen and the individuals put the SEC to its burden of proof in the civil action. As relevant to facilitating payments, the defendants argued that the SEC had the burden of pleading the inapplicability of the facilitating payments exception, whereas the SEC argued that the defendants had the burden of pleading the inapplicability of the exception. In an issue of first impression, the judge held that the SEC "must bear the burden of negating the facilitating payments exception" and that the "exception is best understood as a threshold requirement to pleading that a defendant acted 'corruptly.'" Later in the pre-trial proceedings, even the SEC acknowledged that the facilitating payments exception is "a difficult area to understand, largely because of the wording of the exception and the statute overall." In denying competing motions for summary judgement, the judge stated:

> I have such trouble understanding the facilitating payment exception. [. . .] I mean, it almost swallows the rest of the statute. And I know it's in the legislative history that these, I think reference is made to grease payments, somehow to grease the skids. How do I separate those payments, which do seem to be contemplated, from the payments that [the SEC] alleges were made in this case, which you think are squarely within the FCPA's prohibition? [. . .] And I don't understand it. Whether we make the distinction based on size of payments, regularity of payments, purpose of payments, nature of the – of the favorable conduct elicited. I just really struggle with it.[10]

On the eve of trial and facing the prospect of having to negate the facilitating payments exception and otherwise prove its case, the SEC agreed to settle the matter on very favorable terms for the defendants and defense counsel subsequently stated:

> Due to the settlement [in the case], the court never had the opportunity to rule on the fate of the FCPA's facilitating-payments exception under the SEC's newfound interpretation. But the SEC's position on this issue signals a shift in policy toward the practical elimination of the exception. If the SEC continues down the road established in this case, it will be interesting to examine whether courts accept the SEC's position eliminating the exception. However, since most FCPA cases are not litigated, the SEC may seek to push its novel interpretation into law, without approval by the courts, by including it in settlement agreements going forward.[11]

Against this backdrop of actual legal authority relevant to the facilitating payment exception, this section next highlights non-legal authority relevant to the exception.

### Guidance

The FCPA Guidance calls the facilitation payments exception "narrow" and states:

> Whether a payment falls within the exception is not dependent on the size of the payment, though size can be telling, as a large payment is more suggestive of corrupt intent to influence a non-routine governmental action.

> But, like the FCPA's anti-bribery provisions more generally, the facilitating payments exception focuses on the purpose of the payment rather than its value. [. . .] Labeling a bribe as a "facilitating payment" in a company's books and records does not make it one. [. . .] As with any expenditure, facilitating payments may still violate the FCPA if they are not properly recorded in an issuer's books and records.

## Enforcement actions

Notwithstanding the above legal authority, many recent corporate FCPA enforcement actions concern payments made in connection with securing foreign permits, licenses or other official documents needed in connection with foreign country business activity. In addition to the Customs Gate enforcement actions previously mentioned as well as those highlighted in Chapter 1 in connection with passive bribery and foreign business conditions, the Layne Christensen enforcement action is instructive in that a significant portion of the alleged improper conduct concerned interactions with various regulatory officials in connection with permits, licenses or the expeditious performance of similar duties of an essentially ministerial or clerical nature.[12] For instance, the government alleged:

- In the Democratic Republic of Congo ("DRC") the company "encountered significant delays in obtaining customs clearance for the importation of its equipment" and that over a six month period approximately $125,000 was paid to Customs Clearance Agent that resulted in the company being "able to import equipment necessary to perform on its existing contracts."
- In the DRC, the company made approximately $7,000 in payments through an agent "to customs officials in order to secure the exportation of goods and equipment from the DRC to Zambia."
- In Burkina Faso, Guinea, Tanzania, and the DRC the company "made more than $23,000 in cash payments . . . to police, border patrol, immigration officials, and labor inspectors . . . to obtain border entry for its equipment and employees, to secure work permits for its expatriate employees, and to avoid penalties for noncompliance with local immigration and labor regulations."

Perhaps most notable are enforcement actions in which the government alleges bribery in connection with payments to a foreign official who refuses, in the absence of such payments, to release funds legitimately owed to the company. For instance, a principal feature of the $54 million enforcement action against Archer Daniels Midland Co. and related entities was that the company and its shareholders were victims of a corrupt Ukraine government which refused to release value-added tax refunds legitimately owed to the company.[13] In the words of the DOJ, "the Ukrainian government did not have the money to pay VAT refunds that it owed to companies that sold Ukrainian goods outside of Ukraine." Likewise, the SEC acknowledged that the "Ukrainian government determined to delay paying the VAT refunds owed or did not make any refunds payments at all." Relevant to the facilitating payment exception, how can seeking what one is legally entitled to receive not fit within the statutory exception for "secur[ing] the performance of a routine government action"?

Nevertheless, the above enforcement actions and many others that could also be cited raise the question of whether the facilitating payments exception has any real meaning or whether the enforcement agencies have essentially repealed this exception through its enforcement theories. Indeed, the SEC's former Assistant Director of Enforcement has called the exception "illusory" and stated:

> The drafters of the FCPA recognized that such demands for "grease payments" are a reality in many countries, and accordingly made clear that certain payments made to expedite the approval of permits or licenses, or to prompt the expeditious performance of similar low-level ministerial duties, fell outside the ambit of the statute's anti-bribery provisions. Yet that exception for "facilitating payments" [. . .] is becoming harder and harder to rely on. [. . .] The DOJ and SEC have pressed a narrow view of the exception in recent years . . . [. . .] Of course, the fact that the FCPA's twin enforcement agencies have treated certain payments as prohibited despite their possible categorization as facilitating payments does not mean a federal court would agree. But because the vast majority of enforcement actions are resolved through deferred prosecution agreements and non-prosecution agreements, and other settlement devices, these cases never make it to trial. As a result, the DOJ and the SEC's narrow interpretation of the facilitating payments exception is making that exception ever more illusory, regardless of whether the federal courts – or Congress – would agree.[14]

Further relevant to the *de facto* repeal of the facilitating payment exception, a current Senior Investigations Counsel with the SEC's FCPA Unit stated in his personal capacity:

> While the FCPA contains several core provisions that will always withstand the test of time, the facilitation payments exception is out of date in this modern-day era of commerce and sensibility.[15]

In some respects this may be a true statement as the U.K. Bribery Act does not contain a facilitating payments exception and Canada recently repealed the facilitating payments exception that had long been part of its Corruption of Foreign Public Officials Act.[16] Yet the facilitating payments exception remains part of the FCPA and it is this statute that the enforcement agencies are obligated to enforce (or not as with an exception). What is not out of date though is that the same foreign business conditions which motivated Congress to include a facilitation payment exception in the FCPA remain today. For instance, according to a business survey, "facilitation payments for routine government services are viewed as a common part of business" in various Southeast Asian countries.[17] It is this landscape that business organizations subject to the FCPA must navigate, and to assess your comprehension of the facilitating payment exception, as well as the core elements of the FCPA's anti-bribery provisions previously discussed, try on your "FCPA goggles" by reviewing the below issue-spotting scenario.

In the scenario, Sai (an employee of an Indian telecommunications company that also offers internet services) visits the local branch office of T Systems for a meeting with Chris, the office manager. To assist in your analysis, the 1000 Indian rupee amount mentioned is approximately $15.

| | |
|---|---|
| Chris: | Sorry to keep you waiting. |
| Sai: | Hello, sir. |
| Chris: | As I said in the message, we've been paying for Internet – broadband Internet connection – for the last several months and we still don't have any Internet, which is not good because we can't function without the Internet. |
| Sai: | Of course, sir. So it looks like your application appears to be incomplete, and therefore hasn't been processed. |

| | |
|---|---|
| Chris: | I don't understand. Our credit card has been charged every month, so something was processed because we're paying for something. |
| Sai: | Well, we do have your company registered in our system, and we do also have your payment information. But your application, like I said, is incomplete. You need to pay the initial registration and setup fee. |
| Chris: | We paid the initial fee and we're paying a monthly fee now. |
| Sai: | Okay, but there is also another registration fee of 1000 rupees. If you give it to me right now, I can get your Internet working right away. |
| Chris: | [pulls money from his back pocket]: Okay. All right. 1000 rupees. |

Before analyzing possible application of the facilitating payment exception, start with analyzing the core elements of the FCPA's anti-bribery provisions.

- *Anything of value*: money is obviously something of value and recall there is no *de minimus* amount associated with this element. Even though $15 is not a large amount of money, it is clearly something of value.

- *Corrupt intent*: does Chris have an evil motive or purpose in giving Sai $15? Probably not. Chris just wants T Systems' internet connected and this appears to be a shake-down, extortion type of situation given that the company has already been charged for this service. But then again, was there an evil motive or purpose in many of the things of value previously discussed in Chapter 2 including "golf in the morning and beer drinking in the evening"? Moreover, recall that it does not matter if the thing of value was first proposed by the "foreign official."

- *Foreign official*: although it's not expressly stated in the scenario, in many foreign countries telecommunications companies are owned or controlled by the government which then implicates the SOE enforcement theory previously discussed in Chapter 2. Indeed in several enforcement actions, including the *Esquenazi* action, the alleged "foreign officials" were employed by telecommunications companies. Thus, it is likely that the enforcement agencies would deem Sai to be a "foreign official."

- *Obtain or retain business*: even though T Systems is not seeking any sales with the telecommunications company, recall that a key take-away point regarding the "obtain or retain business" element is that many enforcement actions have nothing to do with sales, but rather other regulatory points of contact with alleged "foreign officials" in which an improper advantage is being sought. How far might this expansive enforcement agency interpretation of "obtain or retain business" go? Would it include a small payment to a "foreign official" to secure an internet connection (that T Systems appears to have already paid for) which would then allow Chris and his co-workers to more easily and efficiently go about their daily tasks? These are open questions of course, but given the expansive interpretation of "obtain or retain business" it may be that the enforcement agencies would deem this required element satisfied in the above scenario.

Even if the core elements of the anti-bribery provisions are satisfied, the FCPA expressly states that the anti-bribery provisions "shall not apply to any facilitating or expediting payment to a foreign official . . . the purpose of which is to expedite or to secure the performance of a routine governmental action by a foreign official." Recall also that in *SEC v. Jackson* the judge held that the government "must bear the burden of negating the facilitating payments exception" and that the "exception is best understood as a threshold requirement to pleading that a defendant acted 'corruptly.'" Relevant to the definition of "routine governmental action" in the facilitating payment exception, is a $15 payment to a "foreign official" to get the official to flip the switch and turn on the internet a "routine government action" given that T Systems appears to have already paid for the service, but Sai is claiming that its application is incomplete?

It would seem that the above conduct fits within the facilitating payment exception as written and as intended by Congress. However, if Chris alerted you to his predicament prior to his meeting with Sai, and sought your permission to make the $15 payment, would you have authorized the payment? Or might you be so fearful of potential scrutiny and enforcement that excessive risk aversion kicks in and you refuse to authorize the $15 payment even though it seems to fit within the facilitating payment exception? What might the consequences be for this excessive risk aversion? How long can the Indian branch office of T Systems go without having internet service? What impact will this have on Chris, his co-workers, and the company's business?

Thus far, the analysis of the above scenario has focused on the U.S. FCPA. However, what if T Systems is subject to the U.K. Bribery Act or other similar laws that do not, at least as written, exempt facilitating payments? What if this small payment to Sai is illegal under Indian law? Because of these issues, many business organizations prohibit facilitating payments except in situations involving employee health and safety.

Another issue to consider is the practical impact if Chris makes the $15 payment to Sai. Might Sai or others in his office come to view T Systems as their personal piggy bank and whenever in need of extra cash simply "flip the switch" and visit the company demanding a payment? Does one facilitating payment simply invite demands for future similar payments? Perhaps so, but then again how long can the Indian branch office of T Systems go without internet service?

Given the many difficult and challenging business conditions often encountered in the global marketplace, such as the one depicted above, what is a well-intentioned business organization with a commitment to compliance supposed to do to minimize risk in this area? For starters and for the reasons highlighted above, prevailing best practices seem to be prohibiting facilitating payments except in situations involving employee health and safety. However, if a business organization adopts this sensible policy, it is important that this concept not be defeated by training rank and file employees on the facilitating payments exception. In other words, to best minimize risk in this area business organizations should consider omitting discussion of facilitating payments (and perhaps even the FCPA's affirmative defenses discussed next) in rank and file employee training and other compliance materials provided to such employees.

To better emphasize this point, consider a parenting analogy. Imagine a parent having a long discussion with a child about the importance of cleaning their room. However, at the end of the conversation, the parent tells the child about a few circumstances in which they would *not* have to clean their room. Using this analogy, business organizations that train or otherwise alert rank and file employees to the facilitating payments exception (as well the affirmative defenses) may be providing employees with concepts and terms of art such "routine," "reasonable," and "bona fide" that they can use to rationalize and justify their conduct in the global marketplace. For instance, a foreign customs official may request a payment to clear goods and an employee might think: "no problem, that is routine governmental action." Likewise, a foreign SOE customer may enjoy high-priced liquor and fancy dinners and an employee might think: "no problem, that's reasonable and bona fide." This is not to suggest that legal and compliance professionals should be unaware of the facilitating payments exception or affirmative defenses, surely they should be. However, the goal of compliance is often to have difficult issues, such as those that arise under the facilitating payments exception and affirmative defenses, flow up to legal and compliance personnel and not to empower rank and file employees to make decisions that can expose the business organization to scrutiny and enforcement.

The above issue-spotting scenario and risk management strategies focused on the anti-bribery provisions and its facilitating payment exception. However, Chapter 5 focuses on the books and records and internal controls provisions and it is important to understand here that, even if a business organization determinates that a payment to a foreign official is indeed a facilitating payment and is comfortable making the payment, it still must be properly characterized as such on the company's books and records. In other words, the facilitating payment exception applies only to the anti-bribery provisions and not the books and records and internal controls provisions.

For instance, in the Noble Corp. enforcement action highlighted above concerning temporary import permits in Nigeria, the company, with the advice of legal counsel, booked the payments as facilitating payments. However, the SEC disagreed with this legal conclusion and thus concluded that Noble violated the books and records provisions. As stated by the SEC:

> Noble-Nigeria recorded the portion of the payments it made to its customs agent that certain Noble personnel believed were being passed on to Nigerian government officials in Noble's "facilitating payment" account and

> in some cases to other operating expenses accounts that consolidated into an expense item on Noble's Consolidated Statements of Income. Because these payments were not qualifying facilitating payments under the FCPA or otherwise legitimate expenses, Noble created false books and records by recording the payments as such.[18]

Of further note is the following exchange between the judge and the SEC attorney in the Jackson and Ruehlen matter when this enforcement theory was subjected to judicial scrutiny.

> Judge: What would they have needed to call it? That's what I am asking?
> SEC: Payments to government official – I can't speculate all the things that it possibly could have been called, but payments to government officials may have been – may have been adequate. However, they weren't designated payments to government officials in this case.[19]

## Affirmative defenses

In addition to the facilitating payments exception, the FCPA also contains two affirmative defenses. The first is for payments lawful under the written laws and regulations of a foreign country and the second is for payments of reasonable and bona fide expenditures directly related to promotion of products or services or the execution of a contract. As affirmative defenses, a business organization or individual under scrutiny has the burden of proving the elements of the defenses to be excused from liability for a payment that otherwise meets the requirements of the FCPA anti-bribery provisions.

### Local law defense

Highlighted below is legal authority and non-legal sources of information relevant to the FCPA's local law affirmative defense.

#### *Law*

The FCPA states that it shall be affirmative defense to an FCPA anti-bribery violation if:

> the payment, gift, offer, or promise of anything of value that was made, was lawful under the written laws and regulations of the foreign official's . . . country.

The key words from the statutory text are "written" laws and regulations. In other words, just because a payment otherwise in violation of the FCPA's anti-bribery provisions may be common, accepted or otherwise not prosecuted in a foreign country does *not* mean that the payment is "lawful under the written laws and regulations" of the foreign country as required for the affirmative defense to apply.

*Legislative history*

The local law affirmative defense was added to the FCPA by the 1988 amendments to the law. A Senate Report stated: "Under the affirmative defense provisions, a company must be able to defend its actions by documenting that they were in fact 'lawful' in the host country."[20] Likewise, the House Conference report stated: "The Conferees wish to make clear that the absence of written laws in a foreign official's country would not by itself be sufficient to satisfy this defense."[21]

*Judicial decisions*

Like other aspects of the FCPA, there is sparse judicial authority construing the local law affirmative defense, but in *U.S. v. Bourke* (an enforcement action previously discussed concerning an alleged bribery scheme in connection with the privatization of Azerbaijan's state-owned oil company), Bourke argued that the alleged payments were legal under Azeri law and thus under the FCPA given its local law affirmative defense.[22] Bourke's expert opined that under Azeri law a "person who has given a bribe shall be free from criminal responsibility if, [among other things] the person after giving the bribe voluntarily made a report of the occurrence." The judge framed the disputed issue as follows.

> As a threshold matter, I must determine the meaning of "relieved (or free) from criminal responsibility." Bourke contends that if an individual is relieved of criminal responsibility, his action was "lawful" and he may thus avail himself of the FCPA's affirmative defense.

The judge disagreed and concluded:

> For purposes of the FCPA's affirmative defense, the focus is on the payment, not the payer. A person cannot be guilty of violating the FCPA if the payment was lawful under foreign law. But there is no immunity from prosecution under the FCPA if a person could not have been prosecuted in the foreign country due to a technicality (e.g., time-barred) or because a

> provision in the foreign law "relieves" a person of criminal responsibility. An individual may be prosecuted under the FCPA for a payment that violates foreign law even if the individual is relieved of criminal responsibility for his actions by a provision of the foreign law.

As to the Azeri law at issue, the judge stated:

> The structure of the reporting exception to liability in [Azeri law] illustrates that the initial payment of a bribe was certainly not lawful. [Azeri law] relieves the payer of a bribe from criminal liability if the bribe is properly reported not because such an action retroactively erases the stain of criminality, but because the state has a strong interest in prosecuting the government official who received the bribe. By waiving liability for reporting payers, the state increases the likelihood that it will learn of the bribery. But at the moment that an individual pays a bribe, the individual has violated [Azeri law]. At that time, the payment was clearly not "lawful under the written laws" of Azerbaijan. If the individual later reports the bribe, she can no longer be prosecuted for that payment. But it is inaccurate to suggest that the payment itself suddenly became "lawful" – on the contrary, the payment was unlawful, though the payer is relieved of responsibility for it.

*Guidance*

The FCPA Guidance states as follows concerning the local law affirmative defense:

> The fact that bribes may not be prosecuted under local law is insufficient to establish the defense. In practice, the local law defense arises infrequently, as the written laws and regulations of countries, rarely, if ever, permit corrupt payments.

A DOJ FCPA Opinion Procedure release addressed, in part, the contours of the affirmative defense in the context of a requestor being a party to disputed legal proceedings in an Asian country relating to the disposition of property in a deceased relative's estate. As stated in the release, "the requestor proposes to make a payment [approximately $9,000] required by a family court judge in an Asian country to cover certain litigated-related costs" and the requestor represented, among other things, that: (i) nothing suggested that the requested payment was sought for the purpose of influencing the court, misusing the judge's official position, or inducing the judge or the estate administrator to do anything improper; (ii) that a lawyer who received law degrees in both the U.S. and the foreign country advised that the requested payment is not contrary to, and is in fact explicitly lawful under, the written law of the foreign country; and (iii) the requested payment would be made to the clerk's office of the family court, not to the individual judge presiding over the dispute. Based on this information, the DOJ stated that it did not intend to take any enforcement action because the requested payment would be made to a government entity rather than a foreign official and there was nothing to suggest that the presiding judge or the estate administrator would personally benefit from the funds after they are paid into the government account. As relevant to the local law affirmative defense, the DOJ stated that the requested payment was "lawful under the written laws and regulations of the foreign country according to an experienced attorney retained by the requestor in the Asian country."[23]

When Congress enacted the FCPA in 1977 and amended it in 1988 to include the local law affirmative defense it recognized that no foreign country permitted bribery of its officials in its written laws. Thus, the affirmative defense for payments lawful "under the written laws and regulations" of the foreign official's country has always been a curious portion of the FCPA and it is difficult to imagine a circumstance (save for unique situations addressed in the above opinion release) in which it could be successfully invoked by a business organization or individual subject to FCPA scrutiny.

## Reasonable and bona fide expenditures defense

Whereas the local law affirmative defense has little practical implication for business organizations, the FCPA's other affirmative defense for reasonable and bona fide expenditures has near daily implications, and along with third-party issues, often presents the greatest challenges to a compliance program. The reason is straightforward: business organizations routinely promote products, execute contracts, or otherwise sponsor brand building events and in connection with these common practices corporate hospitality, travel and entertainment, and other miscellaneous expenses are often incurred. It is here where the simplistic narrative "just don't bribe" really breaks down because most of these expenses are perfectly acceptable and legal when directed to a certain category of persons (i.e. non-"foreign officials"), yet when directed to an individual the enforcement agencies deem to be a "foreign official" such expenses may give rise to scrutiny and enforcement. An FCPA practitioner observed:

> Gifts, meals, entertainment and travel remain the part of the statute that companies still find the most vexing in terms of day-to-day compliance. Rarely a day goes by that I don't receive a call or email from a client with a question in this area.[24]

This is particularly true in many Asian countries where gift-gifting is a prominent feature of a business relationship. For instance, FCPA practitioners have noted:

> In China, building relationships, or guanxi, drives successful business development. These necessary relationships grow out of the exchange of favors and gifts, including meals and entertainment. Although not necessarily impermissible, these sorts of benefits, common in Chinese business, pose a serious corruption risk and serve to exacerbate what is already a very challenging anti-corruption compliance environment for foreign businesses in China.[25]

Accordingly, an additional component of having "FCPA goggles" is understanding the contours of the reasonable and bona fide expenditures affirmative defense and highlighted below is relevant legal authority and non-legal sources of information.

### *Law*

The FCPA states that it shall be an affirmative defense to an FCPA anti-bribery violation if:

> the payment, gift, offer, or promise of anything of value that was made, was a reasonable and bona fide expenditure, such as travel and lodging expenses, incurred by or on behalf of a foreign official . . . and was directly related to: (a) the promotion, demonstration, or explanation of products or services; or (b) the execution or performance of a contract with a foreign government or agency thereof.

### *Legislative history*

The reasonable and bona fide expenditures affirmative defense was also added to the FCPA by the 1988 amendments and a Senate Report stated:

> The exceptions for reasonable and bona fide expenditures associated with selling or purchasing goods, or the performance of a contract with a foreign government or agency thereof must encompass only legitimate expenses made to or for the foreign official in payment for or reimbursement of that

> foreign official's expenses. These terms should, of course, be interpreted in a common sense manner.[26]

The House Conference report stated: "If a payment or gift is corruptly made, in return for an official act or omission, then it cannot be a bona fide, good-faith payment, and this defense would not be available."[27]

### *Judicial decisions*

The FCPA's affirmative defense for reasonable and bona fide expenditures has never been directly addressed by a court. However, recall *U.S. v. Liebo* (previously discussed in Chapter 2 regarding "anything of value" and "corrupt intent") in which the defendant argued that there was insufficient evidence to show that he acted "corruptly" by providing honeymoon airline tickets to a Niger official who was in a position of influence concerning a contract. The court disagreed and was satisfied that sufficient evidence existed from which a reasonable jury could find that the airline tickets were given "corruptly." The court noted that the airline tickets were given to the foreign official shortly before a contract was approved and that the defendant classified the airline ticket as a "commission payment" for accounting purposes.[28]

### *Guidance*

Relevant to the reasonable and bona fide expenditures affirmative defense, the FCPA Guidance generically references several DOJ Opinion Procedure Releases and states:

> DOJ and SEC have consistently recognized that businesses, both foreign and domestic, are permitted to pay for reasonable expenses associated with the promotion of their products and services or the execution of existing contracts. In addition, DOJ has frequently provided guidance about legitimate promotional and contract-related expenses – addressing travel and lodging expenses in particular – through several opinion procedure releases. Under the circumstances presented in those releases, DOJ opined that the following types of expenditures on behalf of foreign officials did not warrant FCPA enforcement action:
>
> - Travel and expenses to visit company facilities or operations;
> - Travel and expenses for training; and
> - Product demonstration or promotional activities, including travel and expenses for meetings.

> Whether any particular payment is a bona fide expenditure necessarily reflects a fact-specific analysis. [. . .] Trips that are primarily for personal entertainment purposes, however, are not bona fide business expenses and may violate the FCPA's anti-bribery provisions. Moreover, when expenditures, bona fide or not, are mischaracterized in a company's books and records, or where unauthorized or improper expenditures occur due to a failure to implement adequate internal controls, they may also violate the FCPA's accounting provisions. Purposeful mischaracterization of expenditures may also, of course, indicate a corrupt intent

Reflective of the frequency in which the reasonable and bona fide expenditures affirmative defense may be implicated in ordinary business activity, much of the above guidance was originally articulated in DOJ Opinion Procedure Releases and the DOJ has self-identified the following releases as being relevant to "gifts, travel and entertainment," "reasonable, bona fide expenditures" and related compliance best practices.

| 80-01 | 81-01 | 81-02 | 82-01 | 83-02 | 83-03 | 85-01 | 92-01 |
|---|---|---|---|---|---|---|---|
| 96-01 | 04-01 | 04-03 | 04-04 | 07-07 | 07-02 | 08-03 | 11-01 |

At this point in the book, your "FCPA goggles" should be fitting nicely and you should have confidence in your ability to spot risk. Thus, instead of first highlighting enforcement actions that did not meet the standards set forth in the reasonable and bona fide expenditures affirmative defense, your final issue-spotting scenario relevant to the anti-bribery provisions is first presented.

Similar to the previous facilitating payment scenario, the below scenario may implicate the reasonable and bona fide expenditures affirmative defense, but you should also assess your comprehension of the core elements of the FCPA's anti-bribery provisions. Back at T Systems, Alicia and Kristen are having a meeting about next year's customer conference.

| | |
|---|---|
| Alicia: | So, it's time to start planning out our customer conference for next year. |
| Kristen: | Okay. |
| Alicia: | My initial goal is to select the dates and nail down the location, and then we can build on those ideas. |
| Kristen: | Okay. Do we have the same budget that we did last year? For the last conference? |
| Alicia: | No. I asked for and I got a bigger budget, since we're going to be launching a new product next year. So, it makes sense to spend more money on this next conference. |
| Kristen: | So, what if we host the conference in Vegas? |
| Alicia: | Oooh! I like that idea! |
| Kristen: | I mean, who doesn't want an excuse to go to Las Vegas. Right? The gambling, the golfing, the shows. Maybe we could sponsor a dinner and a show for all attendees. Maybe we should sponsor a golf outing for our VIP guests. |
| Alicia: | Oh, I like that! And we'll have some VIP customers coming from several foreign. So, for our foreign customers, Vegas is close to other destination spots like the Grand Canyon, Hollywood, and Disneyland. Okay, I think that works. Now we just need to nail down the right schedule that will work for most people. |

Before analyzing the reasonable and bona fide expenditures affirmative defense, start with analyzing the core elements of the FCPA's anti-bribery provisions.

- *Anything of value*: while Alicia and Kristen are not contemplating offering any money to attendees of the customer conference, T Systems is clearly thinking about offering numerous things of value to the attendees such as golf and shows, and for the VIP guests, side excursions to popular tourist destinations such as the Grand Canyon, Hollywood and Disneyland. Perhaps even the location of the conference in Las Vegas might constitute a thing of value to attendees, as Kristen says, "who doesn't want an excuse to go to Vegas?"

- *Corrupt intent*: there is nothing in the scenario to suggest that Alicia and Kristen have an evil motive or purpose in planning the customer conference. Rather, they seem excited about the job they have been asked to do and simply want to put on the best customer conference on behalf of T Systems. However, the enforcement agencies often allege corrupt intent through circumstantial evidence and query whether there is information in the above discussion suggesting corrupt intent? What about T Systems having a bigger budget for the upcoming customer conference because it is launching a new product? What about T Systems wanting to treat VIP guests to special excursions? Often, the chronology of events is relevant to corrupt intent and the timing of the upcoming customer conference along with the specifics of T Systems' anticipated product launch at least raise a question about this element.

- *Foreign official*: although the scenario does not explicitly state that "foreign officials" will be attending the customer conference, there is mention that VIP customers from several foreign countries may attend (and indeed be offered various side excursions). Thus, T Systems needs to better understand who these foreign customers are going to be because, given the extent of SOEs in many foreign countries, there is a possibility that the enforcement agencies will deem certain of the customers "foreign officials" under the *Esquenazi* control and function test. This scenario thus nicely reinforces an earlier "foreign official" take-away point and that is the meaning of "foreign official" matters because it can subject normal business activity to an aggressively enforced criminal law. In other words, there is generally no problem with T Systems' upcoming customer conference as it relates to certain customers or potential customers, but if those individuals are "foreign officials" the company suddenly has a potential issue.

- *Obtain or retain business*: application of this core element seems rather straightforward given that T Systems is planning the customer conference to demonstrate its capabilities and has a bigger budget given its new product launch.

However, even if the core elements of the anti-bribery provisions are satisfied, T Systems may have an affirmative defense to an anti-bribery violation if it can demonstrate that the various things of value were a "reasonable and bona fide expenditure" and "directed related to" (as relevant here) "the promotion, demonstration, or explanation of products or services."

Certain contemplated expenditures in connection with the customer conference seem to fall within the affirmative defense. For instance, there is probably nothing wrong with T Systems covering reasonable travel and hotel expenses for customers or potential customers attending the conference. Moreover, there is likely nothing wrong with T Systems providing meals, a cocktail party, or perhaps even a golf outing for conference attendees. Such reasonable expenses would seem to be directly related to the promotion, demonstration, or explanation of products or services.

For instance, in an opinion procedure release the DOJ stated that it did not intend to bring an enforcement action when an insurance company proposed to pay certain domestic expenses for approximately six officials of a foreign government to attend a five-day educational program at its U.S. headquarters. According to the requestor, the stated purpose of the trip was to familiarize the officials with the operation of the company and it proposed to cover air travel expenses (domestic economy class) as well as lodging, local transport, meals and incidental expenses (up to a modest set amount per day upon presentation of a receipt), and a modest four-hour city sightseeing tour for the officials. In addition, the requestor represented, among other things, that:

- it had no non-routine business under consideration by the relevant foreign government agency;
- it did not select the particular officials who would travel – that decision was made solely by the foreign government;
- it would host only the designated officials, and not their spouses or family members;
- it intended to pay all costs directly to the providers and in the event that an expense required reimbursement, it would only do so, up to a modest daily minimum, upon presentation of a written receipt;
- any souvenirs given to the visiting officials would reflect it business and/or logo and would be of nominal value, e.g., shirts or tote bags; and
- it would not compensate the foreign government or the officials for their visit, nor would it fund, organize, or host any other entertainment, side trips, or leisure activities for the officials, or provide the officials with any stipend or spending money.[29]

Scrutiny and enforcement might arise, however, for certain individuals attending the conference (i.e. "foreign officials") if T Systems paid for first class airfare, accommodations at the most expensive five-star hotel in Las Vegas and most certainly if the planned side excursions to the Grand Canyon, Hollywood, and Disneyland take place. For these potential expenditures, it would be difficult for T Systems to prove that the "reasonable and bona fide" and "directly related" standards of the affirmative defense are satisfied. The above issue-spotting scenario thus highlights the important take-away point that certain corporate hospitality expenditures may fall under the affirmative defense, but corporate hospitality can easily morph into conduct that may give rise to scrutiny and enforcement without proper risk management strategies (a topic discussed shortly).

## FAILURE

Like most issue-spotting scenarios in this book, the above corporate hospitality scenario was inspired by actual enforcement actions. For instance, an enforcement action against telecommunications company UTStarcom (UTS) was based on allegations that the company provided travel and other things of value to employees of state-owned telecommunications companies in China. According to the government:

> UTS spent nearly $7 million on approximately 225 trips [to places such as Hawaii, Las Vegas and New York] for customer employees pursuant to training provisions in systems contracts entered into between UTS-China and government-controlled municipal or provincial telecommunications companies.[30]

Like many enforcement actions that contain travel allegations, the UTS matter also included allegations that:

- "UTS provided other gifts and benefits to foreign government customers, including paying for them to attend executive training programs at U.S. universities;"
- "a general manager in Thailand spent nearly $10,000 on French wine as a gift to agents of the government customer, including rare bottles that cost more than $600 each"; and

- the manager "also spent $13,000 for entertainment expenses for the same customer in an attempt to secure the contract."

An FCPA enforcement action against telecommunications company Lucent Technologies was based on similar allegations as the government alleged:

> Lucent provided approximately 315 trips for Chinese government officials that included primarily sightseeing, entertainment and leisure. These trips were requested and approved with the consent and knowledge of the highest Lucent China officials and with the assistance of Lucent employees in the United States, including at corporate headquarters. Lucent improperly recorded expenses for these trips in its books and records and failed to provide adequate internal controls to monitor the provision of travel and other things of value to Chinese government officials.[31]

According to the government, although certain pre-sale trips included "brief stops" at certain Lucent facilities, the majority of the trips consisted of visiting Boston, Las Vegas, the Grand Canyon and Hawaii "for strictly entertainment, travel and leisure purposes." Other trips included hosting an alleged Chinese foreign official in California for "two and a half days of sightseeing, entertainment and leisure," approved by the company "after learning of the past and future revenues associated with this customer and [the] official's decision making role." Another trip included paying for an alleged Chinese "foreign official" and his wife and daughter to travel "to Thailand and Hong Kong for a seven-day vacation" and the planning for this trip indicated that the "vacation was aimed at influencing the [foreign official] and 'strengthening the customer relationship' to expand the business relationship with the customer." Other trips included post-sale visits termed "factory tours" which "consisted primarily or entirely of sightseeing to locations such as Disneyland, Los Angeles, San Francisco, Universal Studios, the Grand Canyon, Las Vegas, tours of Washington D.C., tours of New York City, and stop-overs in Hawaii." Additional allegations included that Lucent:

- "paid or offered to pay for educational opportunities for relatives or associates of Chinese government officials, some of whom were in a position to influence China's use of Lucent-compatible technologies;"
- "approved payments totaling over $71,000 to cover the tuition and living expenses of an employee of a Chinese government ministry,

who was obtaining a master's degree in international management" when that employee was "an assistant to a committee chairman at the ministry" and the "committee was at least partially responsible for choosing which mobile telecommunications platform China would adopt;"

- paid, upon the request of a "foreign official," approximately $22,000 so that the individual could obtain an MBA; and

- "provided a paid internship to the daughter of a Chinese government official working at the Chinese embassy in the United States" because "it [was] very important for Lucent to continue building a good relationship with the Chinese embassy, which has close ties to leaders in China when it comes to wireless standards and vendor selections."[32]

As highlighted by Table 4.1 below, numerous other business organizations have resolved enforcement actions based in whole or in part on corporate hospitality, travel and entertainment, or related expenses that the government did not believe fell within the FCPA's affirmative defense for "reasonable and bona fide" expenses "directly related" to the promotion, demonstration or explanation of products or services or execution of contracts.

*Table 4.1 Travel and entertainment allegations*

| Enforcement action | Relevant allegations |
|---|---|
| PTC | Travel and entertainment provide to alleged Chinese "foreign officials." While a component of the trips did involve a stop at the company's U.S. headquarters, the trips morphed to include sightseeing visits to New York, Las Vegas, Los Angeles, and Honolulu.[33] |
| Avon | Travel and entertainment provided to alleged Chinese "foreign officials." While a component of the trips did involve travel to the company's U.S. headquarters and its research and development facility, the trips morphed and the traveling delegation spent the rest of the 18-day trip sightseeing and being entertained by Avon China employees in New York, Vancouver, Montreal, Ottawa, Toronto, Philadelphia, Seattle, Las Vegas, Los Angeles, Hawaii, and Washington, D.C.[34] |
| GlaxoSmithKline | The payments to alleged Chinese "foreign officials" took varied forms, including gifts, improper travel and entertainment with no or little educational purpose, shopping excursions, family and home visits, and cash.[35] |

*Table 4.1 (continued)*

| Enforcement action | Relevant allegations |
|---|---|
| Diebold | "Diebold provided international leisure trips and entertainment to officials of government owned banks in China. This included trips to Europe, with stays in Paris, Amsterdam, Florence, Rome, and other European cities, and trips to the United States with travel to the Grand Canyon, Napa Valley, Disneyland, Las Vegas, and other popular tourist destinations. Diebold spent approximately $1.6 million on leisure trips, entertainment, and other improper gifts for government bank officials in China. During this same time period . . . Diebold spent over $147,000 on leisure trips and entertainment for officials of government owned banks in Indonesia."[36] |
| Teva Pharmaceuticals | To influence the discretion of a Ukrainian official, Teva paid for his vacations to Israel on at least five occasions in which the official traveled business class and on at least one occasion his wife traveled with him.[37] |
| NCH Corp. | Company provided things of value worth approximately $44,545 to alleged Chinese "foreign officials" including gifts, meals, and entertainment "including a 10-day trip to various cities in the U.S. and Canada, only one half-day of which involved business-related activities. The remainder of the trip involved sightseeing and other non-business activities."[38] |

As to the many enforcement actions based on corporate hospitality and travel and entertainment issues, FCPA practitioners have stated:

> [T]he settled cases give little guidance as to some of the gray areas that challenge compliance officers, such as the appropriate dollar amounts for business meals, or how much ancillary leisure activity is acceptable in the context of a business event. Perhaps most interesting about the recent cases is that the government's charging papers in some cases seem to lack any direct evidence that the benefits provided were provided as a quid pro quo to obtain a specific favorable decision from the official. The cases seem to simply conclude that if there were benefits provided to a government decision maker, the benefits must have been improper.[39]

In addition to the above, several corporate enforcement actions have also included allegations concerning items such as specialty foods, jewelry and handbags, karaoke bars, and spa treatments. The irony of course is that providing such items to certain customers would probably be deemed mere sales and marketing or maintaining goodwill with customers. However, the take-away point from this section is that providing such items to other customers (i.e. "foreign officials") may be deemed bribery by the enforcement agencies and give rise to scrutiny and enforcement.

So what is a well-intentioned business organization with a commitment to compliance supposed to do to minimize risk in this area given that there is nothing inherently wrong with wining and dining and treating customers and potential customers well and having some fun? Like many aspects of compliance with the FCPA and related laws, it all starts with training and providing employees in risk positions with "FCPA goggles" so that they can spot risk in their specific job function. As the above enforcement actions demonstrate, employees involved in corporate hospitality and/or planning travel and entertainment events are most certainly in risk positions. Thus, referring back to Alicia and Kristen at T Systems, the organization needs to make sure that these individuals receive training including on the "foreign official" element. The expansive interpretation of "foreign official" is not exactly intuitive or an issue of common sense for most people and Alicia and Kristen probably should not be faulted for not recognizing this risk area. Yet T Systems should be faulted if they did not provide Alicia and Kristen with the "FCPA goggles" so that they could minimize risk in their specific job functions.

In addition to training employees on the risks of corporate hospitality and related events, a business organization should also have specific written policies and procedures applicable to such expenditures as well as appropriate compliance and legal review of hospitality events and customer travel. For instance, the FCPA Guidance sets forth the following "non-exhaustive list of safeguards" in evaluating "whether a particular expenditure is appropriate or may risk violating the FCPA."

- Do not select the particular officials who will participate in the party's proposed trip or program or else select them based on predetermined, merit-based criteria.
- Pay all costs directly to travel and lodging vendors and/or reimburse costs only upon presentation of a receipt.
- Do not advance funds or pay for reimbursements in cash.
- Ensure that any stipends are reasonable approximations of costs likely to be incurred and/or that expenses are limited to those that are necessary and reasonable.
- Ensure the expenditures are transparent, both within the company and to the foreign government.
- Do not condition payment of expenses on any action by the foreign official.
- Obtain written confirmation that payment of the expenses is not contrary to local law.
- Provide no additional compensation, stipends, or spending money beyond what is necessary to pay for actual expenses incurred.
- Ensure that costs and expenses on behalf of the foreign officials will be accurately recorded in the company's books and records.

Furthermore, the enforcement agencies have stated that seldom, if ever, will any of the following be reasonable and bona fide and directly related to the business purposes identified in the FCPA: first class airfare; five star hotels; expensive food and drink; lavish entertainment; per diem spending money; and inclusion of spouses and children in travel or activities. However, query how helpful certain of this guidance really is to business organizations? For instance, what exactly is "expensive" food and drink? What is "lavish" entertainment? Moreover, with foreign customers often traveling long-distances is first class airfare (or even business class airfare mentioned in the above Teva enforcement action) really that unreasonable? These are all fact-specific and thus unanswered issues in government guidance, yet questions that business organizations often struggle with in attempting in good faith to comply with the FCPA and related laws.

Even though one of the safeguards highlighted above in the FCPA Guidance is paying all costs directly to travel and lodging vendors, a word of caution is warranted when using travel vendors to facilitate certain customer travel particularly in China. As you may have noticed, several of the enforcement actions highlighted above concerning problematic travel involved alleged Chinese foreign officials and in most of the enforcement actions the travel was facilitated through Chinese travel agencies. For instance, in one enforcement action, the government stated:

> Local Chinese travel companies were routinely hired to provide services (such as arranging transportation, accommodations, and meals for [alleged Chinese officials]) in connection with what were ostensibly legitimate conferences, seminars, and other events. In addition to a lack of due diligence for these third party vendors . . . there was a lack of controls over the events to ensure they had an appropriate business purpose and that the events actually occurred.[40]

As highlighted in Chapter 3, a broad range of third parties (not just those in connection with the sales activity) can expose a business organization to scrutiny and enforcement. Travel agencies are a third-party service provider and in certain circumstances the same pre-engagement, engagement, and post-engagement best practices previously highlighted should be used with such providers.

As highlighted in this section, even though the FCPA contains an affirmative defense for "reasonable and bona fide" expenses "directly related" to certain business purposes, without proper training and without proper controls, corporate hospitality and related expenditures can easily morph into conduct that can expose a business organization to scrutiny and enforcement. However, the risk management strategies highlighted above can minimize risk in this area as well as others. Indeed, as rightly noted by an FCPA practitioner, even though excessive travel and entertainment expenditures seldom yield high penalty enforcement actions "a disproportionate number of enforcement matters ultimately resulting in a high penalty for bribes unrelated to gifts/meals/travel/entertainment had their genesis in marketing/promotion expenses that soon turned out to be the 'tip of the iceberg' revealing more extensive and substantial corruption."[41] The practitioner noted:

> Companies who focus on keeping a clean FCPA house in the gifts/meals/entertainment/travel part of the statute stand a better chance of keeping big problems from occurring elsewhere among the statute's danger zones, both because it sends a strong "tone from the top" and because it keeps small problems from going undetected until they've morphed into big ones.

The focus of Chapters 2–4 has been analyzing legal authority and non-legal sources of information relevant to the FCPA's anti-bribery provisions as well as learning risk management strategies specific to certain issues that often present the greatest compliance challenges for business organizations. However, your "FCPA goggles" are not yet fully constructed and the next chapter focuses on the FCPA's books and records and internal controls provisions.

NOTES

1 Protecting the Ability of the United States to Trade Abroad: Hearing Before the Subcomm. on Int'l Trade of the S. Comm. on Fin., 94th Cong. (1975).

2 Foreign and Corporate Bribes: Hearings Before the S. Comm. on Banking, House., and Urban Affairs, 94th Cong. (1976).

3 The Activities of American Multinational Corporations Abroad: Hearings Before the Subcomm. on Int'l Econ. Policy of the H. Comm. on Int'l Relations, 94th Cong. (1975).

4 S. Rep. No. 94–1031 (1976).

5 H.R. Rep. No. 95–640 (1977).

6 H.R. Rep. No. 100–40 (1987).

7 U.S. v. Duperval (11th Cir., Feb. 9, 2015).

8 Letter from Dennis McInerney, Chief, Fraud Section, U.S. Department of Justice (Criminal Div.), to May Spearing, Attorney for Noble Corp. (Nov. 4, 2010).

9 Press Release, U.S. Department of Justice, "Oil Services Companies and a Freight Forwarding Company Agree to Resolve Foreign Bribery Investigations and to Pay More Than $156 Million in Criminal Penalties" (Nov. 4, 2010).

10 FCPA Professor, "Judge Grants Jackson And Ruehlen's Motion To Dismiss SEC's Monetary Claims – Finds That SEC Was Not Diligent In Bringing Case And That SEC Failed To Negate Facilitation Payments Exception – However Judge Allows SEC To File An Amended Complaint," (Dec. 12, 2012).

11 David Krakoff, "Writing the Facilitating Payments Exception Out of the FCPA," Corporate Counsel Business Crimes Bulletin (Feb. 9, 2015).

12 FCPA Professor, "Layne Christensen Company Resolves SEC Enforcement Action," (Oct. 28, 2014).

13 FCPA Professor, "Why You Should Be Alarmed By The ADM FCPA Enforcement Action," (Jan. 24, 2014).

14 Richard Grime & Sara Zdeb, "The Illusory Facilitating Payments Exception: Risks Posed By Ongoing FCPA Enforcement Actions And The U.K. Bribery Act" (2011).

15 Jon Jordan, "The OECD'S Call for an End to 'Corrosive' Facilitation Payments and the International Focus on the Facilitation Payments Exception Under the Foreign Corrupt Practices Act," 13 University of Pennsylvania Journal of Business Law 881 (2011).

16 Government of Canada New Release, "Canada Repeals Facilitation Payments Exception in Corruption of Foreign Public Officials Act," (Oct. 30, 2017).

17 U.S. Chamber of Commerce, "ASEAN Business Outlook Survey 2017," (Aug. 4, 2016).

18 Complaint, SEC v. Noble Corp. (S.D. Tex. Nov. 4, 2010).

19 FCPA Professor, ""I Have Such Trouble Understanding The Facilitating Payment Exception," (Dec. 9, 2014).

20 S. Rep. No. 100–85 (1987).

21 H.R. Rep. No. 100–40 (1987).

22 582 F.Supp.2d 535 (S.D.N.Y. 2008).

23 DOJ FCPA Opinion Procedure Release 07-03 (Dec. 21, 2007).

24 FCPA Professor, "Can We Make The Expenditure In The First Place? Practical Advice For Navigating Gift, Travel And Entertainment Issues," (May 22, 2013).

25 Joseph Warin, Michael Diamant & Jill Pfenning, "FCPA Compliance in China and the Gifts and Hospitality Challenge," 5 Virginia Law and Business Review 33 (2010).

26 S. Rep. No. 100–85 (1987).

27 H.R. Rep. No. 100–40 (1987).

28 923 F.2d 1308 (8th Cir. 1991).

29 DOJ FCPA Opinion Procedure Release 07–02 (Sept. 11, 2007).

30 Letter from Steven Tyrrell, Chief, Fraud Section, U.S. Department of Justice (Criminal Div.), to Leo Cunningham, Attorney for UTStarcom, Inc. (Dec. 31, 2009).

31 Letter from Steven Tyrrell, Chief, Fraud Section, U.S. Department of Justice (Criminal Div.), to Martin Weinstein, Attorney for Lucent Technologies Inc. (Nov. 14, 2007).

32 Complaint, SEC v. Lucent Technologies, Inc., Case No. 1:07-cv-02301 (D.D.C., Dec. 21, 2007).

33 FCPA Professor, "PTC Inc. And Related Entities Pay $28 Million In Yet Another FCPA Enforcement Action Involving Travel And Entertainment Provided To Alleged "Foreign Officials," (Feb. 17, 2016).

34 FCPA Professor, "Avon Resolves Long-Standing FCPA Scrutiny By Agreeing To $135 Million Settlement," (Dec. 19, 2014).

35 FCPA Professor, "GlaxoSmithKline Coughs Up $20 Million In SEC FCPA Enforcement Action Based On China Conduct," (Sept. 30, 2016).

36 FCPA Professor, "Diebold Resolves $48 Million FCPA Enforcement Action Based Primarily On Excessive Travel And Entertainment Payments By Subsidiaries," (Oct. 23, 2013).

37 FCPA Professor, "In Depth Into The $519 Million Teva FCPA Enforcement Action," (Dec. 22, 2016).

38 FCPA Professor, "DOJ Releases Two So-Called "Declination" Letters, Yet "Pursuant To" The Letters, HMT LLC And NCH Corp. Agree To Disgorge $2.7 Million And $335,000," (Sept. 30, 2016).

39 Wilmer Hale, "Global Anti-Bribery Year-in-Review: 2014 Developments and Predictions for 2015," (Jan. 27, 2015).

40 FCPA Professor, "Issues To Consider From The SciClone Enforcement Action," (Feb. 9, 2015).

41 FCPA Professor, "Can We Make The Expenditure In The First Place? Practical Advice For Navigating Gift, Travel And Entertainment Issues," (May 22, 2013).

# 5 The FCPA's books and records and internal controls provisions

The FCPA has always been a law much broader than its name suggests. The anti-bribery provisions that were the focus of Chapters 2–4 are just one prong of the FCPA. The other prong is the books and records and internal controls provisions (collectively the accounting provisions) and these provisions are applicable to issuers – FCPA speak for companies (both U.S. and foreign) with shares registered with the SEC or otherwise subject to SEC reporting requirements. These provisions, which operate independently of the anti-bribery provisions, state that issuers shall: "make and keep books, records, and accounts, which, in reasonable detail, accurately and fairly reflect the transactions and dispositions of the assets of the issuer" and that issuers shall: "devise and maintain a system of internal accounting controls sufficient to provide reasonable assurances" that certain specific financial objectives are met.[1]

This chapter discusses legal authority and non-legal sources of information relevant to the accounting provisions and highlights through actual enforcement actions the wide range of circumstances in which the enforcement agencies have used these flexible provisions to also address foreign bribery. Similar to Chapters 2–4, you will also have an opportunity to assess your acquired knowledge of the accounting provisions through real-world, issue-spotting scenarios.

## A law much broader than its name suggests

The FCPA has always been a law much broader than its name suggests. Unlike the FCPA's anti-bribery provisions which had, among other limiting features, a "foreign official" element, the books and records and internal controls provisions are generic and flexible. Indeed, most technical FCPA enforcement actions do not involve *foreign bribery* and to best understand this basic, yet important, take-away point, consider the following enforcement actions.

In an enforcement action against United Airlines, the SEC alleged that the CEO of the company unilaterally authorized, outside of the company's normal processes, a money-losing flight to a U.S. public official's vacation home at the same time the official had discretion over the approval of an airport maintenance hangar the company was seeking.[2] The thing of value was given to a U.S. official and *not* a "foreign official" and thus *not* a violation of the FCPA's anti-bribery provisions. Nevertheless, and reflective of how the books and records and internal control provisions operate independently of the anti-bribery provisions, the SEC alleged that: (i) United's books and records did not, in reasonable detail, accurately or fairly reflect the route transaction; and (ii) despite the significant potential corruption risks surrounding its dealings with public officials, United failed to design and maintain a system of internal accounting controls that were sufficient to prevent its officials from approving the use of company assets for corrupt purposes.

An SEC enforcement action against Gold Standard Mining is another example of a technical FCPA enforcement action *not* involving foreign bribery.[3] In the enforcement action, the SEC alleged that the company filed numerous materially false and misleading reports about its purported gold mining operations. Among other things, the SEC alleged that the company: failed to devise and maintain a system of internal accounting controls; did not have a means to verify the amount of gold produced; did not have a means to determine the costs of producing the gold that was sold; and did not maintain records of inventory.

Think of the United and Gold Standard Mining enforcement actions (for lack of a better term) as "non-FCPA FCPA enforcement actions" in that the FCPA books and records and internal controls violations were among the statutory provisions charged even though the alleged conduct did not involve *foreign bribery*.[4] Thus, an early take-away point from this chapter is that the accounting provisions, while making for a dull read, are among the most generic substantive legal provisions one can find. Because of this, and how these provisions are enforced, the accounting provisions are a potent supplement to the FCPA's anti-bribery provisions.

Another early take-away point and issue to be mindful of throughout this chapter is that while the accounting provisions technically apply only to issuers, all business organizations should act as if they are subject to the provisions. As rightly stated in the FCPA Guidance:

> Good internal controls can prevent not only violations of the FCPA's anti-bribery provisions [which are applicable to all forms of U.S. business organization] but also other illegal or unethical conduct by the company, its subsidiaries, and its employees.[5]

Likewise, the SEC Chairman stated:

> Corrupt practices by [an issuer] are generally indicators of larger problems within the business – problems with the potential to harm that business's shareholder-owners. Bribery and other corrupt practices may result in accounting fraud and falsified disclosures where shareholders are not getting an accurate picture of a company's finances in their regulatory filings. Bribery means losing control of – or deliberately falsifying – books and records. Often, key executives or board members are kept in the dark, limiting their ability to make informed decisions about the company's business. Obviously, engaging in corrupt practices means weakening or circumventing internal control mechanisms, leaving a company less able to detect and end not just corruption but other questionable practices. A company that has lost its moral compass is in grave danger of losing its competitive roadmap, as well – while shareholders are kept in the dark.[6]

In short, all business organizations should act as if they are subject to the accounting provisions and incorporate the risk management strategies discussed in the remaining chapters of this book because by doing so an organization is minimizing risk under the FCPA's anti-bribery provisions as well as a host of other laws which technically do apply to the organization.

## Legal authority and non-legal sources of information

This section highlights legal authority as well as non-legal sources of information concerning the FCPA's accounting provisions.

### Law

The FCPA's books and records provisions state that issuers shall:

> make and keep books, records, and accounts, which, in reasonable detail, accurately and fairly reflect the transactions and dispositions of the assets of the issuer.

The FCPA's internal controls provisions state that issuers shall:

> devise and maintain a system of internal accounting controls sufficient to provide reasonable assurances that:
> (i) transactions are executed in accordance with management's general or specific authorization;
> (ii) transactions are recorded as necessary (I) to permit preparation of financial statements in conformity with generally accepted accounting principles or any other criteria applicable to such statements, and (II) to maintain accountability for assets;
> (iii) access to assets is permitted only in accordance with management's general or specific authorization; and
> (iv) the recorded accountability for assets is compared with the existing assets at reasonable intervals and appropriate action is taken with respect to any differences.

The accounting provisions are typically enforced civilly by the SEC (a law enforcement agency with only civil enforcement authority), but do provide that "knowingly circumvent[ing] or knowingly fail[ing] to implement a system of internal accounting controls or knowingly falsif[ying] any book, record, or account" is subject to criminal prosecution by the DOJ.

Against this general statutory framework, the provisions set forth some important qualifications. For instance, the FCPA defines "reasonable assurances" and "reasonable detail" to mean "such level of detail and degree of assurance as would satisfy prudent officials in the conduct of their own affairs." In addition, the FCPA provides the following qualification:

> If an issuer "holds 50% or less of the voting power with respect to a domestic or foreign firm, [the books and records and internal controls provisions] require only that the issuer proceed in good faith to use its influence, to the extent reasonable under the issuer's circumstances, to cause such domestic or foreign firm to devise and maintain a system of internal accounting controls . . . Such circumstances include the relative degree of the issuer's ownership of the domestic or foreign firm and the laws and practices governing the business operations of the country in which such firm is located. An issuer which demonstrates good faith efforts to use such influence shall be conclusively presumed to have complied with the requirements of [the books and records and internal controls provisions].

Furthermore, the FCPA provides that "with respect to matters concerning the national security of the United States, no duty or liability [under the accounting provisions] shall be imposed upon any person acting in cooperation with the head of any Federal department or agency responsible for such matters if such act in cooperation with such head of a department or agency was done upon the specific, written directive of the head of such department or agency pursuant to Presidential authority to issue such directives."

In short, while the accounting provisions have a broad scope and often operate in tandem with the anti-bribery provisions to capture certain instances of corporate bribery, it is important to understand that the provisions are specifically qualified as a matter of law through concepts of reasonableness and good faith. These qualifications are best demonstrated through the below word cloud (a graphical representation of word frequency in a source text) of the accounting provisions which demonstrates that reasonable is the most prominent word in the provisions.

## Legislative history

Legislative history is another form of legal authority relevant to the accounting provisions and the following issues are addressed below: the origin of the provisions; what Congress hoped to accomplish with the provisions; and how Congress intended to qualify the provisions through concepts such as reasonableness and good faith.

During Congress's investigation and consideration of the foreign corporate payments problem, Congressional leaders were surprised to learn that existing corporate record-keeping and internal control requirements were deficient in preventing the discovered payments. The following exchange between Senator Proxmire and SEC officials is instructive:

> Senator Proxmire: "You stress the fact that in all nine of the SEC cases the corporate abuses were accompanied by false or inadequate corporate books and records and that most of the cases involved illegal or improper domestic and foreign payments. Does such falsification of corporate books and records constitute a violation of SEC's laws or regulations and do they constitute criminal violations?
> SEC Official: I can't say in all cases. There is no provision that prohibits just what you stated. There is no provision that provides, with respect to the kinds of companies we are talking about, that that could be a violation of law.
> Senator Proxmire: Well, then, it would seem to me that maybe we ought to consider . . . making it a violation of the law.[7]

Although the SEC wanted no part in enforcing what would become the FCPA's anti-bribery provisions, the SEC insisted that whatever legislation Congress enacted be supplemented by books and records and internal control provisions.

The 1976 SEC Report stated:

> We believe that any legislation ... should embody a prohibition against the falsification of corporate accounting records. The most devastating disclosure that we have uncovered in our recent experience with illegal or questionable payments has been the fact that, and the extent to which, some companies have falsified entries in their own books and records. [. . .] We believe that any legislation in this area should also contain a prohibition against the making of false and misleading statements by corporate officials or agents to those persons conducting audits of the company's books and records and financial operations. Finally, we believe that any legislation should require management to establish and maintain its own system of internal accounting controls designed to provide reasonable assurances that corporate transactions are executed in accordance with management's general or specific authorization; and that such transactions as are authorized are properly reflected on the corporation's books and records in such a manner as to permit the preparation of financial statements in conformity with generally accepted accounting principles or any other criteria applicable to such statements.[8]

The SEC Report proposed legislation which embodied the following goals: "(1) require issuers to make and keep accurate books and records; (2) require issuers to devise and maintain a system of internal accounting controls [. . .]; (3) prohibit the falsification of corporate accounting records; and (4) prohibit the making of false, misleading, or incomplete statements to an accountant in connection with an examination or audit."[9] The goal of the accounting provisions was thus to make explicit what was merely implicit in then existing securities laws. For instance, a Senate Report stated:

> While the Committee believes that the requirement that issuers maintain books, records, and accounts that accurately and fairly reflect the transactions and dispositions of the assets of the issuer is implicit in the existing securities laws, the Committee believes that such a basic requirement should be explicit.
>
> The committee recognizes that the SEC has broad authority to promulgate accounting standards for companies subject to jurisdiction under its existing authority. Nevertheless, the committee believes the Commission's current program for accurate accounting should be supplemented by an explicit statement of statutory policy. The accounting standards [. . .] are intended to operate in tandem with the criminalization provisions of the bill to deter corporate bribery [and express] a public policy which encompasses a unified approach to the matter of corporate bribery. This legislation imposes affirmative requirements on issuers to maintain books and records which accurately and fairly reflect the transactions of the corporation and to design an adequate system of internal controls to assure, among other things, that the assets of the issuer are used for proper corporate purposes. The committee believes that the imposition of these affirmative duties under our securities laws coupled with attendant civil liability and criminal penalties for failure to comply with the statutory standard will go a long way to prevent the use of corporate assets for corrupt purposes. Public confidence in the securities markets will be enhanced by assurance that corporate recordkeeping is honest.[10]

Even though Congress viewed the books and records and internal controls provisions as useful supplements to the FCPA's anti-bribery provisions, it is clear from the legislative history that Congress intended for these provisions to be qualified by concepts of reasonableness and good faith. A 1977 Senate Report stated:

> The establishment and maintenance of a system of internal controls and accurate books and records are fundamental responsibilities of management. The expected benefits to be derived from the conscientious discharge of these responsibilities are of basic importance to investors and the maintenance of

> the integrity of our capital market system. The committee recognizes, however, that management must exercise judgment in determining the steps to be taken, and the cost incurred, in giving assurance that the objectives expressed will be achieved. Here, standards of reasonableness must apply. In this regard, the term "accurately" does not mean exact precision as measured by some abstract principle. Rather it means that an issuer's records should reflect transactions in conformity with generally accepted accounting principles or other applicable criteria. While management should observe every reasonable prudence in satisfying the objections called for [in the accounting provisions] the committee recognizes that management must necessarily estimate and evaluate the cost/benefit relationships to the steps to be taken in fulfillment of its responsibilities ... The size of the business, diversity of operations, degree of centralization of financial and operating management, amount of contact by top management with day-to-day operations, and numerous other circumstances are factors which management must consider in establishing and maintaining an internal accounting controls systems.[11]

Regarding the "in reasonable detail" requirement of the provisions, a 1977 House Conference Report stated:

> The conference committee adopted the "in reasonable detail" qualification to the accurate and fair requirement in light of the concern that such a standard, if unqualified, might connote a degree of exactitude and precision which is unrealistic.[12]

In 1988, the then existing accounting provisions were amended to better address a parent company issuer's responsibility for the books and records and internal controls of minority-owned subsidiaries. A 1988 House Conference Report stated:

> [The provision] recognizes that it is unrealistic to expect a minority owner to exert a disproportionate degree of influence over the accounting practices of a subsidiary. The amount of influence which an issuer may exercise necessarily varies from case to case. While the relative degree of ownership is obviously one factor, other factors may also be important in determining whether an issuer has demonstrated good-faith efforts to use its influence.[13]

The accounting provisions were further amended in 1988 by defining the terms "reasonable assurance" and "reasonable detail" to mean such level of detail and degree of assurance as would satisfy "prudent officials in the conduct of their own affairs." Legislative history stated:

> The prudent man qualification [was adopted] in order to clarify that the current standard does not connote an unrealistic degree of exactitude or precision. The concept of reasonableness of necessity contemplates the weighing of a number of relevant factors, including the costs of compliance.[14]

## Judicial decisions

In addition to statutory text and legislative history, judicial decisions are also another form of legal authority concerning the accounting provisions. However, notwithstanding the broad scope of these provisions, *SEC v. World-Wide Coin Investments*[15] is the only judicial decision to directly address the substance of these provisions and is thus discussed below in detail.

Factually, *World-Wide Coin* was an egregious case and like many enforcement actions involving the accounting provisions it was a "non-FCPA FCPA enforcement action" in that the case had nothing to do with foreign bribery. Instead, the case involved a wide-ranging securities fraud involving a company engaged primarily in the wholesale and retail sale of rare coins. As the judge stated:

> The deterioration of World-Wide's internal controls and accounting procedures constituted the primary thrust of the SEC's complaint. The SEC contended that the combination of late filings, lack of internal controls, transactions unsupported by adequate documentation, and a total disregard for proper accounting procedures resulted in the precarious position of the company. [. . .] The company's accounting books were virtually ignored. General ledgers and general journals were not kept, and the checks written on World-Wide's five checking accounts were not reconciled.

The judge described the bookkeeper hired by the company as follows. "[She] was not a high school graduate; her only experience for this position consisted of five months of vocational school training and seven years of bookkeeping for a privately held lumber company." The judge's findings of fact further highlighted how the accounting firm retained by the company as an independent auditor wrote a letter to the company "expressing grave concern over certain accounting procedures and lack of internal controls that [it] considered to be detrimental to the company." Yet, as stated by the judge, company management "did nothing to remedy the situation" and the company had "total disregard for an adequate internal control system."

Turning to the accounting provisions, the judge noted that they were "short and deceptively straight-forward" and stated:

> The only express congressional requirement for accuracy is the phrase "in reasonable detail." Although [the books and records provisions] expect management to see that the corporation's recordkeeping system is adequate and effectively implemented, how the issuer goes about this task is up to management; the FCPA provides no guidance, and this court cannot issue any kind of advisory opinion. Just as the degree of error is not relevant to an issuer's responsibility for any inaccuracies, the motivations of those who erred are not relevant. There are no words in [the books and record provisions] indicating that Congress intended to impose a scienter requirement.
>
> Like the recordkeeping provisions of the Act, the internal controls provision is not limited to material transactions or to those above a specific dollar amount. While this requirement is supportive of accuracy and reliability in the auditor's review and financial disclosure process, this provision should not be analyzed solely from that point of view. The internal controls requirement is primarily designed to give statutory content to an aspect of management stewardship responsibility, that of providing shareholders with reasonable assurances that the business is adequately controlled.
>
> Internal accounting control is, generally speaking, only one aspect of a company's total control system; in order to maintain accountability for the disposition of its assets, a business must attempt to make it difficult for its assets to be misappropriated. The internal accounting controls element of a company's control system is that which is specifically designed to provide reasonable, cost-effective safeguards against the unauthorized use or disposition of company assets and reasonable assurances that financial records and accounts are sufficiently reliable for purposes of external reporting. [. . .] Internal accounting controls must be distinguished from the accounting system typically found in a company. Accounting systems process transactions and recognize, calculate, classify, post, summarize, and report transactions. Internal controls safeguard assets and assure the reliability of financial records, one of their main jobs being to prevent and detect errors and irregularities that arise in the accounting systems of the company. Internal accounting controls are basic indicators of the reliability of the financial statements and the accounting system and records from which financial statements are prepared.
>
> Among the factors that determine the internal accounting control environment of a company are its organizational structure, including the competence of personnel, the degree and manner of delegation and respon-

> sibility, the quality of internal budgets and financial reports, and the checks and balances that separate incompatible activities. The efficiency of the internal control system of a company cannot be evaluated without considering the company's organizational structure, the caliber of its employees, the strength of its audit committee, the effectiveness of its internal audit operation, and a host of other factors which, while not part of the internal control system itself, have an impact on the function of the system.
>
> Although not specifically delineated in the Act itself, the following directives can be inferred from the internal controls provisions: (1) Every company should have reliable personnel . . . and all should be supervised. (2) Account functions should be segregated and procedures designed to prevent errors or irregularities. The major functions of recordkeeping, custodianship, authorization, and operation should be performed by different people to avoid the temptation for abuse of these incompatible functions. (3) Reasonable assurances should be maintained that transactions are executed as authorized. (4) Transactions should be properly recorded in the firm's accounting records to facilitate control, which would also require standardized procedures for making accounting entries. Exceptional entries should be investigated regularly. (5) Access to assets of the company should be limited to authorized personnel. (6) At reasonable intervals, there should be a comparison of the accounting records with the actual inventory of assets, which would usually involve the physical taking of inventory, the counting of cash, and the reconciliation of accounting records with the actual physical assets. Frequency of these comparisons will usually depend on the cost of the process and upon the materiality of the assets involved.

Notwithstanding the above, the judge in *World-Wide Coin* struggled to articulate specific guidance for the accounting provisions and stated:

> The main problem with the internal accounting controls provision of the FCPA is that there are no specific standards by which to evaluate the sufficiency of controls; any evaluation is inevitably a highly subjective process in which knowledgeable individuals can arrive at totally different conclusions. Any ruling by a court with respect to the applicability of both the accounting provisions and the internal accounting control provisions should be strictly limited to the facts of each case.

Nevertheless, the judge offered the following key language:

> The definition of accounting controls does comprehend reasonable, but not absolute, assurances that the objectives expressed in it will be accomplished

> by the system. The concept of "reasonable assurances" contained in [the internal controls provisions] recognizes that the costs of internal controls should not exceed the benefits expected to be derived. It does not appear that either the SEC or Congress, which adopted the SEC's recommendations, intended that the statute should require that each affected issuer install a fail-safe accounting control system at all costs. It appears that Congress was fully cognizant of the cost-effective considerations which confront companies as they consider the institution of accounting controls and of the subjective elements which may lead reasonable individuals to arrive at different conclusions. Congress has demanded only that judgment be exercised in applying the standard of reasonableness. The size of the business, diversity of operations, degree of centralization of financial and operating management, amount of contact by top management with day-to-day operations, and numerous other circumstances are factors which management must consider in establishing and maintaining an internal accounting controls system. [. . .] It is also true that the internal accounting controls provisions contemplate the financial principle of proportionality – what is material to a small company is not necessarily material to a large company.

Consistent with the *World-Wide Coin* holding, various courts have held in the context of civil derivative actions that just because improper conduct allegedly occurred does not mean that internal controls must have been deficient.[16] As you read certain of the enforcement actions highlighted later in this chapter, ask yourself whether the allegations giving rise to books and records and internal controls violations were consistent with the above legal authority.

## Non-legal sources of information

In addition to the above legal authority, there are also non-legal sources of authority relevant to the accounting provisions and this section highlights in chronological order DOJ and SEC guidance regarding these provisions.

### *1979 SEC guidance*

Soon after the FCPA was enacted in 1977, the SEC adopted rules to supplement the FCPA's books and records and internal control provisions. In promulgating the rules, the SEC received numerous comments that "false entries of insignificant or nominal amounts would give rise to a violation" and that "in view of the large number of books, records and accounts kept by some corporations, particularly large corporations, application of the [provisions] to any falsification of such books, records and accounts would make compliance impossible."[17]

The SEC responded to these concerns by referencing congressional intent, specifically that the provisions were "qualified" by Congress "to make clear that issuers are required to "make and keep books, records and accounts, which *in reasonable detail,* accurately and fairly reflect the transactions and dispositions of the assets of the issuer."[18] The SEC concluded that the "presence of the words 'in reasonable detail' should alleviate much of the concern expressed in comments". In addition, the SEC concluded that concern expressed "with respect to inadvertent and inconsequential errors is unwarranted" because the FCPA "does not require perfection but only that books, records and accounts '*in reasonable detail*' accurately and fairly reflect the transactions and dispositions of the assets of the issuer." The SEC further stated that "the legislative history reflects that 'standards of reasonableness' are to be used in applying the provisions."

*1981 SEC guidance*

In 1981, the SEC issued additional formal guidance concerning the accounting provisions in the form of a speech by the SEC Chairman that was thereafter adopted by the SEC as a formal statement of policy.[19] Because this speech is the most extensive guidance ever issued by the enforcement agencies regarding these provisions, it is highlighted below in detail.

The SEC Chairman began his remarks as follows:

> When viewed from an abstract perspective, the Act's accounting provisions seem merely to codify a basic and uncontroversial management principle: no enterprise of any size can operate successfully without maintaining effective controls over its transactions and the disposition of its assets. Perhaps in part because these provisions were considered truisms, the Act was passed without Congressional dissent. However, practical experience with new legislation – even a law thought to be noncontroversial – often will reveal unanticipated problems. Newly enacted standards, for example, may be subject to differing constructions or raise compliance difficulties and ambiguities unforeseen by their draftsmen. And, until these problems are resolved by an agency, the courts or the Congress, those who are subject to these laws are often faced, unfortunately, with some disquieting circumstances. The

> anxieties created by the FCPA – among men and women of utmost good faith – have been, in my experience without equal.

The Chairman noted that "such uncertainty can have a debilitating effect on the activities of those who seek to comply with the law" and stated:

> My sense is that, as a consequence, many businesses have been very cautious – sometimes overly so – in assuring at least technical compliance with the Act. And, therefore, business resources may have been diverted from more productive uses to overly-burdensome compliance systems which extend beyond the requirements of sound management or the policies embodied in the Act. The public, of course, is not well served by such reactions.

As to the FCPA's books and records provisions, the Chairman stated:

> This provision is intimately related to the requirement for a system of internal accounting controls, and we believe that records which are not relevant to accomplishing the objectives specified in the statute for the system of internal controls are not within the purview of the recordkeeping provision. [. . .] Nor could a company be enjoined for a falsification of which its management, broadly defined, was not aware and reasonably should not have known.

As to the FCPA's internal control provisions, the Chairman stated:

> The Act does not mandate any particular kind of internal controls system. The test is whether a system, taken as a whole, reasonably meets the statute's specified objectives. "Reasonableness," a familiar legal concept, depends on an evaluation of all the facts and circumstances.
> [. . .]
> Private sector decisions implementing these statutory objectives are business decisions. And, reasonable business decisions should be afforded deference. This means that the issuer need not always select the best or the most effective control measure. However, the one selected must be reasonable under all the circumstances.
> [. . .]
> The accounting provisions principal objective is to reaching knowing or reckless conduct.

As to the "purposes of the Act," the Chairman provided a brief review of the "events which led to the [FCPA]" and stated:

> Clearly, Congress went further than determining whether the payments which gave the new law its name were ethically and commercially justifiable. It also chose to consider the corporate accounting and control deficiencies which had been breeding grounds for these practices. And, by doing so, it addressed the far more serious issues raised by these disclosures. [. . .] These payments and falsifications were not only previously unknown to public investors and independent auditors, but many were also unknown to the payer's board and, in numerous examples, even to its senior management. In some of these instances, internal controls existed, but they were shown to be ineffective or easily subverted. Unauthorized payments and related falsifications of corporate records seemed to evidence – indeed, were fostered by – a lack of adequate accounting records and controls. Consequently, in the legislation which ultimately emerged from Congress, prohibiting questionable payments and mandating control and recordkeeping were inexorably interconnected.
>
> [. . .]
>
> The primary thrust of the Act's accounting provisions, in short, was to require those public companies which lacked effective internal controls or tolerated unreliable recordkeeping to comply with the standards of their better managed peers. That is the context in which these provisions should be construed.

The Chairman then addressed "four of the most important" interpretative questions concerning the FCPA: "first, the degree of exactitude in recordkeeping mandated by the Act; second, the deference it affords business decisions concerning internal controls; third, whether a particular state of mind is necessary for a violation to exist; and finally, liability for compliance by subsidiaries."

As to the "degree of exactitude," the Chairman stated:

> I turn first to the question of whether the Act's text or purpose mandates that business records and controls conform to a standard of absolute exactitude or that a company's control system meet some absolute ideal. The answer is "no." Both of the Act's accounting provisions, it should be noted are modified by the key term "reasonable." [. . .] In essence, therefore, the Act does provide a de minimus exemption, though not in absolute quantitative terms.

The Chairman then noted that Congress specifically declined to adopt a materiality test and stated that "internal accounting controls are not only concerned with misconduct that is material to investors, but also with a great deal of misconduct which is not." He noted that while materiality is "appropriate as a threshold standard to determine the necessity for disclosure to investors, [it] is totally inadequate as a standard for an internal control system." The Chairman stated that "procedures designed only to uncover deficiencies in amounts material for financial statement purposes would be useless for internal control purposes" and noted that "systems which tolerated omissions or errors of many thousands or even millions of dollars would not represent, by any accepted standard, adequate records and controls." Indeed, he noted that many of the "questionable payments that alarmed the public and caused Congress to act [. . .] were in most instances of far lesser magnitude than that which would constitute financial statement materiality." According to the Chairman, "reasonableness, rather than materiality, is the appropriate test" and he further stated:

> Reasonableness, as a standard, allows flexibility in responding to particular facts and circumstances. Inherent in this concept is a toleration of deviations from the absolute. One measure of the reasonableness of a system relates to whether the expected benefits from improving it would be significantly greater than the anticipated costs of doing so. Thousands of dollars ordinarily should not be spent conserving hundreds. Further, not every procedure which may be individually cost-justifiable need be implemented; the Act allows a range of reasonable judgments.

As to the "specific recordkeeping requirement" in the FCPA, the Chairman stated:

> This provision is not an independent unrestrained mandate to the Commission to establish novel or unprecedented corporate recordkeeping standards; it is, rather, an integral part of Congress' efforts to assure that the business community records transactions and assets in such a way as to maintain adequate control over them. And this leads to two important conclusions: First, the Act does not establish any absolute standard of exactitude for corporate records. And, second, records which are not related to internal or external audits or to the four internal control objectives set forth in the Act are not within the purview of the Act's accounting provisions.

As to "deference" with respect to "issuer liability for recordkeeping violations," the Chairman stated that the SEC "will look to the adequacy of the internal control system of the issuer, the involvement of top management in the violation, and the corrective actions taken once the violation was uncovered." He then stated:

> If a violation was committed by a low level employee, without the knowledge of top management, with an adequate system of internal control, and with appropriate corrective action taken by the issuer, we do not believe that any action against the company would be called for.

The Chairman next turned to the "state of mind needed to violate the Act's accounting provisions," reiterated that the "Act's principal purpose is to reach knowing or reckless misconduct," and stated:

> Depending on the circumstances, intentional circumventions of a company's system of records and of accounting controls by a low-level employee would not always be considered violations of the Act by the issuer. No system of adequate records and controls – no matter how effectively devised or conscientiously applied – could be expected to prevent all mistaken and improper transactions and disposition of assets. Given human nature, regardless of the adequacy of the system, a bookkeeper may still erroneously post entries, an overzealous agent may make unauthorized payments, or an unscrupulous employee may falsify records for his own purposes. The Act recognizes each of these limitations. Neither its text and legislative history nor its purposes suggest that occasional, inadvertent errors were the kind of problem that Congress sought to remedy in passing the Act. No rational federal interest in punishing insignificant mistakes has been articulated. And, the Act's accounting provisions do not require a company or its senior officials to be the guarantors of all conduct of company employees.

In concluding this portion of the speech, the Chairman stated:

> The test of a company's internal control system is not whether occasional failings can occur. Those will happen in the most ideally managed company. But, an adequate system of internal controls means that, when such breaches do arise, they will be isolated rather than systemic, and they will be subject to a reasonable likelihood of being uncovered in a timely manner and then remedied promptly. Barring, of course, the participation or complicity of senior company officials in the deed, when discovery and correction expeditiously follow, no failing in the company's internal accounting system would have existed. To the contrary, routine discovery and correction would evidence its effectiveness.

As to the SEC's enforcement policy, the Chairman concluded his remarks:

> The genius – and challenge – of [the accounting provisions], it should be remembered, is their reliance on private sector decisionmaking – rather than specific federal edicts – to address an area of public concern. The Act's eventual success or failure will, therefore, depend primarily upon business's response. The Commission's obligation, in turn, is to provide a regulatory environment in which the private sector can address these issues meaningfully and creatively. In this regard, we must encourage public companies to develop innovative records and control systems, to modify and improve them as circumstances change, and to correct recordkeeping errors when they occur without a chilling fear of penalty or inference that a violation of the Act is involved.

In addition to the above 1981 formal statement of SEC policy, the SEC has also at various times affirmed statements of congressional intent relevant to the books and records and internal control provisions. For instance, in a 1999 SEC Staff Accounting Bulletin, the SEC cited with approval the following from the FCPA's legislative history:

> [Congress] adopted the prudent man qualification [in the FCPA's books and records and internal control provisions] in order to clarify that the current standard does not connote an unrealistic degree of exactitude or precision. The concept of reasonableness of necessity contemplates the weighing of a number of relevant factors, including the costs of compliance.[20]

In the same Bulletin, the SEC also cited with approval various aspects of its above highlighted 1981 formal statement of policy:

> The books and records provisions of the [FCPA] do not require registrants to make major expenditures to correct small misstatements. [. . .] As [the SEC] Chairman noted with respect to the internal control provisions of the FCPA, "thousands of dollars ordinarily should not be spent conserving hundreds. [. . .] Because the judgment of ["reasonableness" under the accounting provisions] is not mechanical, the [SEC] staff will be inclined to defer to judgments that "allow a business, acting in good faith, to comply with the Act"s accounting provisions in an innovative and cost-effective way.[21]

### *2012 FCPA guidance*

In 2012 the DOJ and SEC jointly issued FCPA Guidance setting forth its "FCPA enforcement approach and priorities" and a specific chapter concerned the accounting provisions. Like previous enforcement agency guidance, the FCPA Guidance cited legislative history or the FCPA itself for the following statements:

*Books and records provision*

> The "in reasonable detail" qualification was adopted by Congress "in light of the concern that such a standard, if unqualified, might connote a degree of exactitude and precision which is unrealistic."
>
> The term "reasonable detail" is defined in the statute as the level of detail that would "satisfy prudent officials in the conduct of their own affairs." Thus, as Congress noted when it adopted this definition, the concept of reasonableness of necessity contemplates the weighing of a number of relevant factors, including the costs of compliance."

*Internal controls provision*

> Like the "reasonable detail" requirement in the books and records provision, the Act defines "reasonable assurances" as "such level of detail and degree of assurance as would satisfy prudent officials in the conduct of their own affairs."
>
> The Act does not specify a particular set of controls that companies are required to implement. Rather, the internal controls provision gives companies the flexibility to develop and maintain a system of controls that is appropriate to their particular needs and circumstances.
>
> Companies may not be able to exercise the same level of control over a minority-owned subsidiary or affiliate as they do over a majority or wholly owned entity. Therefore, if a parent company owns 50% or less of a subsidiary or affiliate, the parent is only required to use good faith efforts to cause the minority-owned subsidiary or affiliate to devise and maintain a system of internal accounting controls consistent with the issuer's own obligations under the FCPA. In evaluating an issuer's good faith efforts, all the circumstances – including "the relative degree of the issuer's ownership of the domestic or foreign firm and the laws and practices governing the business operations of the country in which such firm is located" – are taken into account.

The above enforcement agency regarding the accounting provisions is instructive on many levels. First, the guidance demonstrates that these provisions have always presented compliance difficulties for issuers.

Second, the guidance demonstrates enforcement agency recognition of Congress's intent in enacting the provisions. Among other things, and in the words of the SEC:

- the "principal objective [of the provisions] is to reach knowing or reckless conduct";
- not all issuer books and records are "within the purview" of the provisions;
- the provisions are not "an independent unrestrained mandate to the Commission to establish novel or unprecedented corporate recordkeeping standards"; and
- "thousands of dollars ordinarily should not be spent conserving hundreds" in attempting to comply with the provisions.

With an understanding of both legal authority and non-legal sources of information relevant to the accounting provisions, this chapter next analyzes the wide range of circumstances in which the enforcement agencies have used these provisions.

## Enforcement action analysis

As previously mentioned, the accounting provisions are often enforced civilly by the SEC. However, like other securities law provisions, knowing and willful violations of the books and records and internal controls provisions can be enforced criminally by the DOJ.[22] Theoretically, as a criminal law enforcement agency the DOJ is subject to a higher burden of proof (beyond a reasonable doubt) compared with the civil burden of proof that guides SEC enforcement (preponderance of the evidence). As a practical matter, this generally means that the DOJ only charges books and records and internal controls violations that are egregious, meaning widespread (not isolated) violations, misrecording and inadequate internal controls over large (not relatively small) payments, and/or violations involving active conduct or significant oversight failures of board members, executives officers or other high-ranking corporate employees (not rank and file employees).

Relevant to enforcement, recall an important take-away point from earlier in this chapter: the accounting provisions operate independently of the FCPA's anti-bribery provisions and can be implicated even if all of the elements of the anti-bribery provisions are not met. Consider a circumstance in which payments are made to a foreign government and *not a foreign official* as required by the FCPA's anti-bribery provisions. Even though such payments directly to a foreign government may not violate the FCPA's anti-bribery provisions, such payments may under certain circumstances, violate other U.S. laws such as wire fraud and money laundering as well as the accounting provisions.

This was the case in a series of enforcement actions brought by the DOJ and SEC involving kickbacks to the Iraqi government through the United Nations Oil for Food Program. The Oil-for-Food Program (OFFP) was set up by the United Nations and provided certain limited exceptions to the Iraq sanctions regime by allowing Iraq to sell its oil on the condition that proceeds be used by the Iraqi government to purchase various humanitarian supplies for the Iraqi people.[23] Under the OFFP, a supplier of humanitarian goods contracted with a Iraqi government ministry or other department of the Iraqi government to sell goods. According to the allegations in the enforcement actions, the "Iraqi government demanded that the suppliers of humanitarian goods pay a kickback, usually valued at 10% of the contract price, to the Iraqi government in order to be awarded a contract by the government." The actions further alleged that these kickbacks were often termed "after sales service fees" (ASSFs), but did not represent any actual service being performed by the supplier. According to the government, "some suppliers labeled the ASSFs as such, thereby leading the U.N. to believe that actual after-sales services were being provided by the supplier," whereas "other suppliers disguised the ASSFs by inserting fictitious line items into the contracts for goods or services that were not being provided," and "other suppliers simply inflated their contract prices by 10% to account for the payments they would make, or cause to be made, to the Iraqi government." These enforcement actions represented a rather straightforward application of the books and records provisions given that issuers are required to maintain books and records which, in reasonable detail, accurately and fairly reflect issuer transactions and disposition of assets.

In terms of how the FCPA's internal controls provisions were implicated, consider an enforcement action against agriculture equipment manufacturer AGCO as a representative example.[24] At its core, the enforcement action involved approximately $6 million in kickback payments to Iraq, through a Jordanian agent in the form of ASSFs, to secure contracts worth approximately $14 million. Specifically, the government alleged several internal control deficiencies including:

- the "accrual account [where the kickback payments were recorded] was created by AGCO Ltd.'s marketing staff with virtually no oversight from AGCO Ltd.s' finance department";
- "no one questioned the existence of the dual accounts";
- "no one questioned why the [accrual account] contained approximately ten percent of the contract value despite the fact that there was no contract in place requiring that such ten percent be paid to the ministry or anyone else";
- "when the finance department authorized payments from the [accrual account], it did not ask for or receive any proof of service to warrant the payments";
- an employee cautioned the business manager for Iraq and his supervisor that "we don't want the auditors raising any questions on Iraq Business!";
- "sales and marketing personnel were able to enter into contracts without review from the legal or finance departments";
- "an accounting employee described the Finance Department employees as 'blind loaders' who input information into AGCO's books without any adequate oversight role";
- "marketing personnel were able to create accrual accounts [. . .] without any oversight and caused accounts to be created and payments to be made without proper documentation";
- "AGCO Ltd.'s structure at the time allocated inappropriate accounting and finance responsibilities to the marketing department";
- "turnover in the marketing department [. . .] was high and employees were forced to shoulder a great deal of the accounting burden";
- "AGCO did not conduct any due diligence on the [Jordanian] agent or require that the agent undergo FCPA training"; and

- "agent contracts with AGCO did not accurately explain the agent's services and payments, and lacked any FCPA language."[25]

Given the breadth of these allegations, it is understandable how the internal controls provisions were implicated given that issuers are required to devise and maintain a system of internal accounting controls sufficient to provide reasonable assurance that transactions are properly authorized, recorded, and accounted for by the issuer.

Numerous companies in various industries that participated in the OFFP (such as AkzoNobel, Johnson & Johnson, ABB, Innospec, Textron, El Paso, Weatherford, Flowserve, Ingersoll-Rand, Volvo, Chevron, General Electric, Fiat, and Novo Nordisk) also resolved FCPA books and records and internal controls enforcement actions based, in whole or in part, on the same core conduct highlighted above. As an aside, certain people often wonder about the reasons for the general increase in FCPA enforcement in the modern era. There are many practical (and certain provocative reasons) for the general increase, but for present purposes it is important to understand that OFFP enforcement actions are certainly one of the reasons. Indeed, during a five-year period such enforcement actions accounted for over 20% of corporate enforcement actions.[26]

Although the accounting provisions can be implicated by conduct that is not technically captured by the anti-bribery provisions, the accounting provisions are nearly always implicated in issuer anti-bribery violations as highlighted next. In many instances, the books and records and internal controls violations seem clear and represent non-controversial "on target" enforcement actions. Yet in many FCPA enforcement actions, the alleged books and records and internal controls violations are less clear and may represent controversial "off-target" enforcement actions in which it is difficult to reconcile the enforcement theories advanced with the previously highlighted legal authority, as well as even enforcement agency guidance. The next section analyzes enforcement actions that fit both categories starting with "on target" enforcement actions.

## Siemens

Siemens AG, a German company with shares listed on a U.S. exchange and thus subject to the FCPA, resolved parallel DOJ and SEC enforcement actions by agreeing to pay an FCPA record $800 million settlement.[27] According to the DOJ, Siemens made payments totaling approximately $1.4 billion through various mechanisms and, of this amount, approximately $555 million was paid for unknown purposes including approximately $341 million in direct payments to business consultants for unknown purposes. The remaining $805 million was intended, in whole or in part, as payments to foreign officials through various payment mechanisms including cash desks and slush funds. The DOJ stated that "for much of its operations across the globe, bribery was nothing less than standard operating procedure for Siemens" and "compliance, legal, internal audit, and corporate finance departments" were areas of the company that played a significant role in the conduct at issue.

The DOJ specifically alleged:

> Siemens engaged in systematic efforts to falsify its corporate books and records and circumvent existing internal controls. These systematic efforts included, but were not limited to: (a) using off-book accounts for corrupt payments even after compliance risks associated with such accounts were raised at the highest levels of management; (b) entering into purported business consulting agreements with no basis, sometimes after Siemens had won the relevant project; (c) engaging former Siemens employees as purported business consultants to act as conduits for corrupt payments to government officials; (d) justifying payments to purported business consultants based on false invoices; (e) mischaracterizing corrupt payments in the corporate books

> and records as consulting fees and other seemingly legitimate expenses; (f) limiting the quantity and scope of audits of payments to purported business consultants; (g) accumulating profit reserves as liabilities in internal balance sheet accounts and then using them to make corrupt payments through business consultants as needed; (h) using removable Post-It notes to affix signatures on approval forms authorizing payments to conceal the identity of the signers and obscure the audit trail; (i) allowing third party payments to be made based on a single signature in contravention of Siemens' [policy]; (j) drafting and backdating sham business consulting agreements to justify third party payments; and (k) changing the name of purported business consulting agreements to agency agreements or similar titles to avoid detection and conceal noncompliance.[28]

The SEC likewise stated that the "pattern of bribery by Siemens was unprecedented in scale and geographic reach."[29] At the press conference announcing the charges, government officials stated that: "Siemens engaged in a systematic and widespread effort to make and hide hundreds of millions of dollars in bribe payments across the globe"; Siemens employees "sometimes carried . . . cash in suitcases across international borders to pay bribes"; and Siemens had a "corporate culture in which bribery was tolerated and even rewarded at the highest levels of the company."[30] The SEC specifically alleged that "the success of Siemens' bribery system was maintained by lax internal controls over corruption related activities and an acceptance of such activities by members of senior management and the compliance, internal audit, legal and finance departments."[31] In short, violations of the accounting provisions in the Siemens enforcement action were rather clear and fully consistent with the above-highlighted legal authority as well as enforcement agency guidance.

## Daimler

Daimler AG, also a German company with shares listed on a U.S. exchange and thus subject to the FCPA, resolved parallel DOJ and SEC enforcement actions by agreeing to pay an approximate $185 million settlement.[32] According to the DOJ, the company and certain of its subsidiaries "brazenly offered bribes in exchange for business around the world" and the company "saw foreign bribery as a way of doing business." The DOJ specifically alleged:

> Daimler's longstanding violations of the FCPA resulted from a variety of factors, including: (1) an inadequate compliance structure; (2) a highly decentralized

> system of selling vehicles through a myriad of foreign sales forces, subsidiaries, and affiliates, with no central oversight; (3) a corporate culture that tolerated and/or encouraged bribery; and (4) the involvement of certain key executives, such as the then head of its overseas sales division, the then head of internal audit, and the then CEO's of several subsidiaries and affiliates.[33]

The DOJ also alleged improper conduct at the highest levels of the company. For instance, during a Board of Management meeting, Daimler's then head of internal audit proposed that the company adopt an integrity code that included anti-bribery provisions. However, the DOJ alleged that "participants in the meeting discussed that adopting such policies (and stopping the practice of making 'useful payments') would result in Daimler losing business in certain countries." Even though the company did adopt "an integrity code with anti-bribery provisions," the DOJ alleged that Daimler, among other things, "failed to make sufficient efforts to enforce the code, train employees on compliance with the FCPA or other applicable anti-bribery statutes," or "otherwise attempt to ensure that the company was not continuing to make improper payments in order to obtain or retain government business overseas." Elsewhere, the DOJ alleged that "Daimler's internal audit department was aware that Daimler employees had made and could make bribe payments" and that the department drafted a document identifying fourteen separate improper payment mechanisms. According to the DOJ, the same document noted that "payment of 'useful expenditures' through these methods was subject to criminal prosecution in countries such as the United States." However, the document also noted the "level of difficulty" law enforcement authorities would have in "proving corruption carried out through the various methods."

Similar to the DOJ, the SEC likewise stated:

> It is no exaggeration to describe corruption and bribe-paying at Daimler as standard business practice. [. . .] The bribery was so pervasive in Daimler's decentralized corporate structure that it extended outside of the sales organization to internal audit, legal, and finance departments. These departments should have caught and stopped the illegal sales practices, but instead they permitted or were directly involved in the company's bribery practices.[34]

The SEC's specifically alleged that Daimler's "improper payments were made possible in part as a result of the falsification of corporate records" and specifically alleged that Daimler:

- internally referred to various of the improper payments as "N.A." payments (a German abbreviation for "useful expenditures" or "useful payments");

- used bogus pricing mechanisms such as "price surcharges," "price inclusions," or excessive commissions, "discounts" or "rebates"; and

- otherwise improperly booked corrupt payments in several expense accounts designated as "key accounts," "costs of goods sold," "gifts line," "petty cash" and "broker commissions."[35]

Like the Siemens enforcement action, violations of the accounting provisions in the Daimler enforcement action were rather clear and fully consistent with legal authority as well as enforcement agency guidance.

## VimpelCom

VimpelCom Ltd, a Bermuda company headquartered in the Netherlands with shares listed on a U.S. exchange and thus subject to the FCPA, resolved parallel DOJ and SEC enforcement actions by agreeing to pay approximately $398 million in net FCPA settlement amounts. According to the DOJ, VimpelCom and a related entity conspired with others to provide bribes in exchange for an Uzbekistan official's influence to obtain necessary government approvals and to obtain and retain Uzbek telecommunications business. According to the DOJ, VimpelCom "built their business in Uzbekistan on over $114 million in bribes funneled to a government official" and throughout the time period of the bribery scheme it "failed to implement adequate internal accounting controls and failed to enforce the internal accounting controls it did have in place, which permitted the . . . bribe payments to occur without detection or remediation." Among other internal controls deficiencies alleged were the following:

- VimpelCom "failed to implement a system for conducting, recording, and verifying due diligence on third parties, including joint venture partners, consultants, reseller companies, and suppliers to uncover their true nature, beneficial ownership, and possible corruption risks. Time and again, board members, executives, and employees of VimpelCom identified serious concerns with third parties, and VimpelCom still failed to undertake adequate due diligence."

- VimpelCom showed failure "to enforce price thresholds that determined the required level of approval authority, failure to retain documentation of deliverables for contracts, and failure to adequately classify and obtain approvals for purported charitable contributions that were made in exchange for state-provided assets."

In addition, the DOJ alleged that VimpelCom executive officers as well as various VimpelCom corporate committees were engaged in the improper conduct and the allegations painted a picture of a culture of corruption at VimpelCom with high-level executives seeking legal cover at nearly every turn to facilitate the alleged bribery scheme. Similar to the DOJ, the SEC likewise alleged:

> [T]hese payments were primarily made through sham contracts, but were also, in certain instances, made under the guise of legitimate charitable contributions or sponsorships. These payments were improperly characterized in the books of records of VimpelCom's subsidiaries as legitimate expenses, and consolidated in VimpelCom's financial statements which were filed with the Commission throughout the relevant period.[36]

Once again, violations of the accounting provisions in the VimpelCom enforcement action were rather clear and fully consistent with legal authority as well as enforcement agency guidance.

## Embraer

Embraer, a Brazil-based aircraft manufacturer with shares listed on a U.S. exchange and thus subject to the FCPA, agreed to pay $187 million in net FCPA settlements to resolve parallel DOJ and SEC enforcement actions concerning wide-spread bribery schemes in the Dominican Republic, Saudi Arabia, and Mozambique. According to the DOJ, "Embraer paid millions of dollars in bribes to win government aircraft contracts in three different continents,"[37] and the SEC likewise stated that "these bribes were authorized by senior executives at Embraer and its subsidiaries while knowing or recklessly ignoring red flags which indicated a high probability that such payments were intended for, or would be passed to, foreign officials."[38] Under the heading "Embraer's Internal Accounting Controls," the DOJ alleged:

> During the relevant period, Embraer knowingly and willfully failed to devise and maintain an adequate system of internal accounting controls. In particular ... Embraer had no internal accounting controls that, among

> other things: (a) required adequate due diligence for the retention of third-party consultants and agents; (b) required a fully executed contract with a third-party before payment could be made to it; (c) required documentation or other proof that services had been rendered by a third-party before payment could be made to it; or (d) implemented oversight of the payment process to ensure that payments were made pursuant to appropriate controls.

In addition, the SEC alleged:

> Embraer's legal department was responsible for approving the consultants its senior legal executive engaged ... As a result, senior Embraer executives in Brazil, including a senior legal executive at the time, at least two other senior Embraer executives, and several Embraer managers, circumvented the Company's internal accounting controls by, among other things, approving the engagement of third parties through sham contracts to act as conduits for bribes to foreign officials, and concealing bribe payments as legitimate expenses under contracts obtained in countries that bore no relation to any legitimate services rendered and that were intended largely to pay bribes to foreign government officials.

Once again, violations of the accounting provisions in the Embraer enforcement action were rather clear and fully consistent with legal authority as well as enforcement agency guidance.

## Odebrecht/Braskem

A final example of an "on-target" enforcement action involved Odebrecht (a Brazil holding company) and petrochemical company Braskem (an entity controlled by Odebrecht with shares listed on a U.S. exchange and thus subject to the FCPA). The entities agreed to pay approximately $250 million in net FCPA settlement amounts to resolve parallel DOJ and SEC enforcement actions concerning widespread bribery schemes in Angola, Argentina, Brazil, Colombia, Dominican Republic, Ecuador, Guatemala, Mexico, Mozambique, Panama, Peru, and Venezuela. According to the DOJ, Odebrecht established a standalone division within the company called the Division of Structured Operations that "effectively functioned as a bribe department within Odebrecht and its related entities." Specifically, the DOJ alleged:

> To conceal its activities, the Division of Structured Operations utilized an entirely separate and off-book communications system called "Drousys," which allowed members of the Division of Structured Operations to

communicate with one another and with outside financial operators and other co-conspirators about the bribes through the use of secure e-mails and instant messages, utilizing codenames and passwords.[39]

Likewise, the SEC alleged:

> Braskem and its subsidiary, at the direction of these senior executives, created false books and records to conceal the bribe payments. These payments were improperly recorded as legitimate commission expenses in Braskem's books and records and were consolidated into Braskem's financial statements.[40]

The widespread and systematic internal controls breakdowns and booking deficiencies in the Siemens, Daimler, VimpelCom, Embraer and Odebrecht/Braskem enforcement actions represented obvious "on-target" books and records and internal controls violations. Yet these types of enforcement actions (mostly involving foreign issuers) are not typical. In many enforcement actions, the alleged violations of the accounting provisions are less obvious and may represent controversial "off-target" enforcement actions in which it is difficult to reconcile the enforcement theories advanced with legal authority as well as even enforcement agency guidance. Certain representative actions are analyzed next.

Before highlighting various potential "off-target" enforcement actions, recall from the legal sources of authority discussed earlier that the accounting provisions do not require an unrealistic degree of exactitude and precision. Rather, the provisions are qualified by concepts such as reasonableness and good faith and reasonableness means the weighing of a number of factors including the cost of compliance. As stated in *World-Wide Coin,* the provisions contemplate "reasonable, but not absolute assurances" and the "costs of internal controls should not exceed the benefits expected to be derived." The legal decision further stated that neither "the SEC or Congress . . . intended that the statute should require that each affected issuer install a fail-safe accounting control system at all costs." Further, the FCPA clearly states, as to issuers which hold 50% or less of the voting power with respect to a firm, that the books and records and internal controls provisions "require only that the issuer proceed in good faith [. . .] to cause such [firm] to devise and maintain a system of internal accounting controls" and that an "issuer which demonstrates good faith efforts to use such influence shall be conclusively presumed to have complied with the requirements."

Recall as well that the enforcement agency guidance previously highlighted stands for the following propositions:

- not all books and records are within the purview of the provisions;
- issuers should not face liability when management was not aware and reasonably should not have known of the conduct at issue;
- the principal objective of the provisions is to reach knowing or reckless conduct;
- thousands of dollars ordinarily should not be spent conserving hundreds;
- the provisions are not an independent unrestrained mandate to establish novel or unprecedented corporate recordkeeping standards;
- if conduct was engaged in by a low-level employee, without the knowledge of top management, and with appropriate corrective action taken, an enforcement action against the issuer is not warranted; and
- the provisions do not require a company or its senior officials to be guarantors of all conduct of company employees.

As you read the following enforcement actions, ask yourself whether it is possible to reconcile the enforcement theories advanced with legal authority as well as even enforcement agency guidance relevant to the books and records and internal controls provisions.

## Schering-Plough

In the Schering-Plough enforcement action previously discussed in Chapter 2, the SEC charged the company with violating the accounting provisions based on payments made to a bona fide Polish charitable foundation because the founder and president of the foundation was also associated with a government health fund that, among other things, provided money for the purchase of pharmaceutical products.[41] The action was based on the conduct of one individual (a unit manager at a branch office of a foreign subsidiary) and the SEC acknowledged in the enforcement action:

- the individual structured his conduct to evade certain internal controls and otherwise provided false information on documents submitted to the company's finance department;
- the donations were made to a bona fide charitable organization;
- the aggregate donation amount (approximately $76,000) was not material (during the relevant time period Schering-Plough's net income was over $2 billion per year); and
- the donations were recorded as "donations" on the company's books and records.

Even though the SEC further acknowledged that "the payments to the Foundation were made without the knowledge or approval of any Schering-Plough employee in the U.S.," the SEC nevertheless charged the company with accounting violations because the donations were "to induce the purchase of Schering-Plough's pharmaceutical products" and "none of the payments to charity [were] accurately reflected in Schering-Plough's books and records" and its "system of internal accounting controls [were] inadequate to prevent or detect the improper payments."

## NATCO Group

In the NATCO Group enforcement action previously discussed in Chapter 2, the SEC charged the company with violating the accounting provisions based on the conduct of its subsidiary TEST Automation

& Controls, Inc., which maintained a branch office in Kazakhstan (TEST Kazakhstan).[42] The SEC acknowledged that TEST Kazakhstan's expatriate workers were the victims of extortionate demands by Kazakhstan officials, specifically that Kazakh immigration prosecutors "threatened to fine, jail or deport the workers if TEST Kazakhstan did not pay cash fines." "Believing the prosecutor's threats to be genuine," the SEC alleged that TEST Kazakhstan employees "used personal funds to pay the prosecutors" and "then obtained reimbursement" from the company. According to the SEC, even though there was no allegation that NATCO Group participated in or had knowledge of the conduct at issue, NATCO Group nevertheless violated the accounting provisions because its subsidiary described the reimbursements as "an advance against bonus" or "payroll advance" in its wire instructions to the bank.

## Oracle

The SEC charged Oracle with books and records and internal controls violations based on the conduct of its Indian subsidiary and alleged in summary fashion:

> This matter involves violations of the books and records and internal controls provisions of the FCPA by Oracle Corporation. [. . .] Certain employees of Oracle's Indian subsidiary ["Oracle India"] secretly "parked" a portion of the proceeds from certain sales to the Indian government and put the money to unauthorized use, creating the potential for bribery or embezzlement. These Oracle India employees structured more than a dozen transactions so that a total of around $2.2 million was held by the Company's distributors and kept off Oracle India's corporate books. The Oracle India employees would then direct its distributor to disburse payments out of the unauthorized side funds to purported local "vendors." Several of the "vendors" were merely storefronts that did not provide any services. Oracle failed to accurately record these side funds on the Company's books and records, and failed to implement or maintain a system of effective internal accounting controls to prevent improper side funds in violation of the FCPA, which requires public companies to keep books and records that accurately reflect their operations.[43]

More specifically, the SEC alleged:

> On approximately 14 occasions related to 8 different government contracts . . . certain Oracle India employees created extra margins between the end

> user and distributor price and directed the distributors to hold the extra margin in side funds. Oracle India's employees made these margins large enough to ensure a side fund existed to pay third parties. At the direction of the Oracle India employees, the distributor then made payments out of the side funds to third parties, purportedly for marketing and development expenses. Some of the recipients of these payments were not on Oracle's approved local vendor list; indeed, some of the third parties did not exist and were merely storefronts. Because the Oracle India employees concealed the existence of the side fund, Oracle did not properly account for these side funds. These funds constituted prepaid marketing expenses incurred by Oracle India and should have been recorded as an asset and rolled up to Oracle's corporate books and records. These marketing expenses should then have been reflected in the income statement once they were used. Instead, the parked funds were not reflected on Oracle India's books and were not properly recorded as prepaid marketing expenses. This incorrect accounting in turn affected Oracle's books and records.

The SEC further alleged:

> Oracle lacked the proper controls to prevent its employees at Oracle India from creating and misusing the parked funds. For example, Oracle knew distributor discounts created a margin of cash from which distributors received payments for their services. [. . .] However, the company failed to audit and compare the distributor's margin against the end user price to ensure excess margins were not being built into the pricing structure. In addition, although Oracle maintained corporate policies requiring approvals for payment of marketing expenses, Oracle failed to seek transparency in or audit third party payments made by distributors on Oracle India's behalf. This control would have enabled Oracle to check that payments were made to appropriate recipients.

The SEC stated:

> Through its subsidiary's use of secret cash cushions, Oracle exposed itself to the risk that these hidden funds would be put to illegal use. It is important for U.S. companies to proactively establish policies and procedures to minimize the potential for payments to foreign officials or other unauthorized uses of company funds.[44]

The only allegations against Oracle itself were that it failed to audit distributor margins against end user prices and that it failed to audit third-party payments made by distributors. Consider however that it is common for large multinational companies like Oracle to engage thousands of third parties around the world to assist in business development. Because of this, audits that Oracle was held liable for not conducting are not practical or cost-effective *absent* red flags suggesting improper conduct. However, the SEC did not allege any red flags; in fact the SEC alleged that Oracle's Indian subsidiary "concealed" and kept "secret" the conduct from Oracle. As stated by the DOJ's former assistant chief of FCPA enforcement: "Oracle is the latest example of the SEC's expansive enforcement of the FCPA's internal controls provision, and it potentially paints a bleak picture – one in which the provision is essentially enforced as a strict liability statute that means whatever the SEC says it means (after the fact)."[45]

## Hewlett-Packard

The SEC found that Hewlett-Packard (HP), a technology company with over 300,000 employees worldwide, violated the accounting provisions based on the following summary allegation:

> HP Co.'s indirect, wholly-owned subsidiaries in Russia, Mexico and Poland, by and through their employees, agents and intermediaries, made unlawful payments to various foreign government officials to obtain business. These payments were also falsely recorded in the subsidiaries' books and records and, ultimately, in HP Co.'s books and records.[46]

As to the company's internal controls, the SEC found:

> HP failed to devise and maintain an adequate system of internal accounting controls sufficient to provide reasonable assurance that: (1) access to assets was permitted only in accordance with management's authorization; (2) transactions were recorded as necessary to maintain accountability for assets; and (3) transactions were executed in accordance with management's authorization.[47]

In announcing the enforcement action, the SEC stated:

> Hewlett-Packard lacked the internal controls to stop a pattern of illegal payments to win business in Mexico and Eastern Europe. The company's books and records reflected the payments as legitimate commissions and expenses. Companies have a fundamental obligation to ensure that their internal controls are both reasonably designed and appropriately implemented across

> their entire business operations, and they should take a hard look at the agents conducting business on their behalf.[48]

Yet elsewhere in the resolution documents of the $108 million parallel DOJ and SEC enforcement action, the government acknowledged the following about HP's internal control environment at the time of the alleged improper conduct:

- HP had existing FCPA and related policies and procedures in place and all relevant employees received training on the policies;
- HP had existing policies and procedures in place related to commission payments to channel partners, due diligence of channel partners, and other tracking policies regarding channel partners;
- HP had an existing approval process in place that applied to all service-related projects valued at greater than $500,000 anywhere in the world and as part of that process HP managers questioned relevant subsidiary employees about questionable information; and
- HP had an existing SOX certification and sub-certification process in place as relevant to the referenced subsidiaries.[49]

It would seem quite clear that the government would have found violations of the internal controls provisions if:

- HP did *not* have FCPA policies relevant to all employees;
- HP did *not* have policies relevant to third party commission payments and due diligence of third parties; or
- HP did *not* have an approval process or SOX certification and sub-certification process.

However, according to even the government HP did these things and yet the government still found HP to be in violation of the accounting provisions because, in the words of the government, a "small fraction" of employees at certain foreign subsidiaries engaged in covert means to willfully circumvent HP's internal controls. Among the covert means used by this "small fraction" of employees was communicating through anonymous e-mail accounts and prepaid mobile telephones. Moreover, the government alleged that a subsidiary employee and alleged foreign official drove around in vehicles in "remote locations" and typed "messages in a text file, passing the computer between themselves." According to the government, "communications were made in this fashion to avoid possible audio recording of the discussions by hidden devices, and to circumvent HP's internal controls." The HP enforcement action thus seems to represent a "damned if you, damned if you don't" theory of enforcement and would seemingly result in every issuer violating the internal controls provisions when a "small fraction" of employees take drastic measures to willfully circumvent existing internal controls.

## Nu Skin Enterprises

A final enforcement action, and recognize there are many more that could also be highlighted, that raises the question of whether prevailing books and records and internal controls enforcement theories even "hit the target" concerns Nu Skin Enterprises (a small Utah-based company involved in the manufacturing and marketing of cosmetic and nutritional products primarily through direct selling, or multilevel marketing, channels). The SEC specifically noted the following regarding Nu Skin's internal controls at the time of the alleged improper conduct involving a charitable donation made "to obtain the influence of a high-ranking Chinese Communist party official to impact an ongoing provincial agency investigation."[50]

- Nu Skin identified the FCPA risks inherent in the charitable donation and advised its Chinese subsidiary to consult with outside U.S. legal counsel based in China to ensure that the donation complied with the FCPA; and

- Nu Skin's outside counsel made recommendations to the Chinese subsidiary, but employees at the subsidiary acted contrary to counsel's recommendations and otherwise failed to disclose certain relevant information to the company.

Once again, it would seem quite clear that the government would have found violations of the internal controls provisions if Nu Skin did *not* pro-actively identify the FCPA risks inherent in a charitable donation and did *not* advise its Chinese subsidiary to consult with U.S. legal counsel in China concerning the donation. However, Nu Skin did these things and yet the SEC still found in the approximate $765,000 enforcement action that:

- Nu Skin violated the books and records provisions because: "in its wholly-owned subsidiary's expenditure authorization form, the purpose of the payment to the charity was inaccurately and/or unfairly described as a donation rather than an improper payment to obtain the Party Official's influence"; and

- Nu Skin violated the internal controls provisions because: it "did not ensure that adequate due diligence was conducted by Nu Skin China with respect to charitable donations to identify links to government or political party officials and to prevent payments intended to improperly influence such persons in violation of the company's anticorruption policy and the FCPA."[51]

The Nu Skin enforcement action also seems to represent a "damned if you, damned if you don't" theory of enforcement and would seemingly result in every issuer being in violation of the internal controls provisions when its instructs a foreign subsidiary to consult legal counsel regarding a specific issue, but the foreign subsidiary acts contrary to legal counsel's recommendations and otherwise fails to disclose certain relevant information to the parent company.

A few pages ago, you were asked whether it is possible to reconcile the enforcement theories advanced in certain enforcement actions with legal authority as well as even enforcement agency guidance relevant to the books and records and internal controls provisions. Regardless of your answer, it should now be clear that the accounting provisions are potent supplements to the FCPA's more glamorous anti-bribery provisions and a key take-away point is that the provisions, as currently enforced, are practically boundless. As stated by an FCPA practitioner:

> The government – and especially the SEC – has settled on an interpretation of the internal controls provision that is at odds with the understanding of many in-house finance professionals about what internal controls are intended to address. Ask corporate finance professionals about internal controls at their companies and you will likely get an answer about processes designed to protect the company's assets at a level that would materially impact the company's financial statements. Ask your friendly neighborhood SEC investigator about internal controls and you will instead get inquiries about the exponentially smaller level of amounts of money that would be enough to influence a low-paid public official in a poor third-world country. Not only is the SEC looking at controls on a more microscopic level, but its

> predilection to pursue internal controls charges sometimes seems based on an interpretation of the FCPA that borders on strict liability.[52]

Regarding the books and records provisions, in nearly every instance of issuer FCPA scrutiny the alleged improper thing of value offered or provided to a "foreign official" (often corporate hospitality, gifts, and other items not material to an issuer's overall financial condition) will be recorded *somewhere* in a book or record within the corporate hierarchy even if that somewhere is a foreign subsidiary that contributes less than 1% of the issuer's overall business, a fifth-tier minority-owned subsidiary, or even a joint venture partner. For example, in a $6 million enforcement action against Anheuser-Busch InBev (a Belgium brewer with shares traded on a U.S. exchange and thus subject to the FCPA) the SEC found, without alleging the absence of good faith concerning InBev's oversight, books and records and internal controls violations even though the alleged misconduct focused on InBevIndia International Private Limited, a non-consolidated joint venture in which AB InBev held a 49% interest.[53]

Moreover, as the Schering-Plough enforcement action demonstrated, even if the thing of value was accurately recorded (as a donation in that action), that SEC may nevertheless conclude that the recording was inaccurate because of the real purpose or motivation for making the payment. Moreover, an expense may be accurately recorded on a company's books and records, but the SEC may nevertheless disagree with the company's good faith legal conclusion about the expense. For instance, in the previously highlighted enforcement actions involving temporary importation permits for oil drilling rigs in Nigeria, Noble Corporation in good faith recorded the payments in an account labeled "facilitating payments" after consulting with legal counsel. However, without elaborating the SEC nevertheless found that "because these payments were not qualifying facilitating payments under the FCPA or otherwise legitimate expenses, Noble created false books and records by recording the payments as such."[54]

Regarding the internal controls provisions, the enforcement agencies seemingly take an "if/then" approach to enforcement. In other words, if anything of value was offered or provided to an alleged "foreign official" (even if by an employee in a distant subsidiary or affiliate and without the knowledge of the parent company), then issuer internal controls must have been deficient because, if the issuer had sufficient internal controls, the conduct would not have occurred. Here again, it is important to keep in mind that the key statutory term in the internal controls provisions is "reasonable" and that Congress intended this term to mean that internal controls do not connote an unrealistic degree of exactitude or precision and that the concept of reasonableness contemplates the weighting of a number of relevant factors including the costs of compliance. Recall as well that prior enforcement agency guidance states that the internal controls provisions "do not require a company or its senior officials to be guarantors of all conduct of company employees" and that "inherent in the concept of reasonableness is a toleration of deviation from the absolute."

Another important point to keep in mind when assessing certain books and records enforcement theories is that the provisions are intended to address "financial" books and records. As highlighted earlier in this chapter, the SEC has stated:

> records which are not relevant to accomplishing the objectives specified in the statute for the system of internal controls are *not* within the purview of the recordkeeping provision. (Emphasis added.)
>
> [T]his provision is not an independent and unrestrained mandate to the [SEC] to establish novel or unprecedented corporate recordkeeping standards; it is, rather, an integral part of Congress' efforts to assure that the business community *records transactions and assets* in such a way as to maintain adequate control over them. And, this leads to two important conclusions: First, the [FCPA] does not establish any absolute standard of exactitude for corporate records. And, second, records which are not related to internal or external audits or to the four internal control objectives set forth in the [FCPA] are *not* within the purview of the [FCPA's] accountingprovisions.[55] (Emphasis added.)

Likewise, in the 2012 FCPA Guidance the government stated:

> The FCPA's accounting provisions operate in tandem with the anti-bribery provisions and prohibit off-the-books *accounting*. Company management and investors rely on a company's *financial* statements and internal accounting controls to ensure transparency in the *financial* health of the business, the risks undertaken, and the *transactions* between the company and its customers and business partners. The accounting provisions are designed to "strengthen the accuracy of the corporate books and records and the reliability of the audit process which constitute the foundations of our system of corporate disclosure.[56] (Emphasis added.)

Notwithstanding this guidance (which is after all consistent with the FCPA's actual provisions), the enforcement agencies seemingly take the position that *any* false or misleading record at an issuer (not just "financial" records) is actionable under the books and records provisions. For instance, a $25 million enforcement action against BHP Billiton (an Australian mining company with shares listed in the U.S. and thus subject to the FCPA) focused on the company being an official sponsor of the summer Olympics and as such receiving priority access to tickets, hospitality suits, and accommodations. Not surprisingly, the company invited people to attend the Olympics and some of the individuals who attended were alleged "foreign officials." The false and misleading books and records according to the SEC, were not financial books and records, but rather "internal forms" that employees prepared in order to invite "foreign officials" to the Olympics that did not "in reasonable detail, accurately and fairly reflect pending negotiations or business dealings with the government official at the time of the invitation."[57] As FCPA practitioners rightly noted: "this settlement represents one of the most expansive assertions of the SEC's authority under the FCPA's accounting provisions in its enforcement practice to date."[58]

The SEC's enforcement action against financial services company JPMorgan further demonstrates its practically boundless theory of enforcing the books and records provisions. The core allegation in the enforcement action was that JPMorgan's Chinese subsidiary provided internships and jobs to so-called Chinese princelings (the family members of alleged Chinese officials) as a way to curry favor with the officials. According to the SEC, the false and misleading books and records consisted of subsidiary personnel submitting, reviewing, and approving "inaccurate compliance questionnaires" containing false and misleading information which failed to disclose the intended, improper purpose of making certain client referral hires.[59] Once again, seemingly lost in the enforcement action was that the internal compliance questionnaires had nothing to do with financial reporting and commenting on recent SEC enforcement actions including the JPMorgan action an FCPA practitioner rightly observed:

> In passing the Foreign Corrupt Practices Act, Congress did not authorize SEC enforcement actions for the failure of issuers to prevent wrongdoing writ large. [. . .] If [the SEC's enforcement theories are] allowed to persist, this expansion not only is unlawful, but it also hands the SEC the capacious

> authority to regulate by enforcement almost any aspect of the operations of any issuer.[60]

Perhaps most troubling, in a number of enforcement actions the SEC invokes a statutory standard that *does not even exist in the FCPA*. For instance, in an enforcement action against Mead Johnson regarding the business practices of its Chinese subsidiary which allegedly provided various things of value to healthcare professionals, the government acknowledged that Mead Johnson "established internal policies to comport with the FCPA and local laws, and to prevent related illegal and unethical conduct" including internal policies "against providing improper payments and gifts to healthcare professionals that would influence their recommendation of Mead Johnson's products."[61] Yet when Mead Johnson China acted inconsistent with those policies, the SEC concluded that: "Mead Johnson failed to devise and maintain an adequate system of internal accounting controls over Mead Johnson China's operations *sufficient to prevent and detect the improper payments that occurred over a period of years*" (emphasis added). As you know from the beginning of this chapter, the internal controls provisions do not require issuers to have internal controls sufficient to "prevent and detect" improper payments, but rather require that issuers "devise and maintain a system of internal accounting controls sufficient to reasonable assurances that" certain financial objectives are met.

Based on the above information and analysis of various FCPA enforcement actions you should now clearly understand that the accounting provisions are extremely flexible, and as currently enforced, are practically boundless and thus a potent supplement to the FCPA's more glamorous anti-bribery provisions.

To assess your comprehension of the books and records and internal controls provisions, it's time again to put on your "FCPA goggles" by reviewing the below issue-spotting scenario which contains two parts. The first part is a conversation between finance personnel at T

Systems' U.S. headquarters and the second part consists of a manager at T Systems' South America subsidiary sharing a secret. As to the second part, keep in mind that the finance professionals at company headquarters are not privy to what the manager in South America is about to say.

After reviewing the scenario, ask yourself the following questions:

- Given the discussion at corporate headquarters, does T Systems have a system of internal accounting controls sufficient to provide reasonable assurances that transactions are properly authorized, recorded and accounted for?
- What additional steps should T Systems take to act consistent with this statutory standard?
- If the South America manager proceeds as he says, has T Systems violated the books and records and internal controls provisions?
- Given the discussion at corporate headquarters, does T Systems have a system of internal accounting controls sufficient to provide reasonable assurances that transactions are properly authorized, recorded and accounted for?
- What additional steps should T Systems take to act consistent with this statutory standard?
- If the South America manager proceeds as he says, has T Systems violated the books and records and internal controls provisions?

Company Headquarters

| | |
|---|---|
| Linda | [finance supervisor shuffling papers and appearing stressed]: I am never going to get done with this stuff. |
| Melissa | [Linda's direct report]: Hey Linda, can I run something by you real quick? |
| Linda: | I am really swamped! But go ahead. |
| Melissa: | I've been going over the expenses for the South America team and the manager there has a bunch of expenses marked meals and entertainment, but there are no people or projects associated with the expenses and I don't see any receipts. This is real money we are talking about here – thousands of dollars – so what do you think? |

South America Subsidiary

Carlos [manager of T Systems' subsidiary in South America]: Somebody in Finance at our parent corporation called me the other day, asking me to explain my expenses the last two quarters and wanting me to detail them out and people want from me. Our division makes a lot of profit for the parent company. I get some big utility contracts requiring multiple government approvals and licenses. No one up there wants to know the details. They just look at the bottom line. But now they're second-guessing my expenses. We do business differently down here and it's all about personal relationships. The Northerners don't get it and they won't understand my expenses. So, I'll just say "meals and entertainment" and leave it at that. We'll see if they push it further.

The first question to consider is given the discussion at corporate headquarters, does T Systems have a system of internal accounting controls consistent with the statutory standard – that is controls sufficient to provide reasonable assurances that transactions are properly authorized, recorded and accounted for?

For starters, it is quite clear that T Systems does indeed have *some* internal controls relevant to subsidiary expenses. After all, Melissa spotted certain red flags regarding Carlos's expenses including that the expenses were marked "meals and entertainment," but there were no people or projects associated with the expenses or any receipts. If corporate headquarters would have blindly processed these expenses it would probably be an internal controls problem, but that is not what the company did. Rather, we learn that Carlos was contacted by corporate headquarters and asked to provide greater detail regarding his expenses including specific references to people and projects. This is what you would expect from a company with a control environment consistent with the FCPA's statutory requirement. But is this enough?

If Carlos does as he says – that is lie and say meals and entertainment – what should the company do? Is it reasonable to simply accept Carlos's response? Recall, that the FCPA's definition of "reasonable" means such a level of detail and degree of assurance as would satisfy a prudent official in the conduct of their own affairs? Is trusting Carlos's response prudent?

On some level this may depend on whether there has been any previous issues or concerns regarding Carlos's expenses or other conduct. If the answer is no, this is literally the first time anyone at corporate headquarters had a concern regarding Carlos, is trusting his response prudent? From the enforcement actions previously highlighted, it would seem clear that the enforcement agencies would say no.

Thus, another question to consider is perhaps most important: what additional steps should T Systems take? The company probably wants to learn additional information about Carlos's expenses and not simply accept his response. For instance, does Carlos frequently wine and dine customers or potential customers or is this a one-off type of situation and thus an unusual expense for Carlos? Who does Carlos report to? What does Carlos's supervisor know about his past practices, reputation, and integrity?

Indeed, having an individual at the South American subsidiary with supervisory authority over sales and marketing personnel is an additional control and thus an important check against potential improper conduct by Carlos and other employees. However, in several enforcement actions the hoped-for supervisory check was actually involved in the improper conduct. For instance, the previously highlighted FLIR Systems enforcement action was based on the conduct of two individuals (Stephen Timms – the head of FLIR's Middle East office in Dubai during the relevant time period; and Yasser Ramahi – who reported to Timms and worked in business development in Dubai) and involved allegations that they provided expensive travel, entertainment, and personal items to Saudi foreign officials to obtain or retain business with the Saudi Arabia Ministry of the Interior. According to the SEC, "sales managers, such as Timms, were solely responsible for expense approvals for their sales staff," but what happened is that both individuals "concealed" the extent and nature of the travel and gifts to "foreign officials" which gave rise to the enforcement action.[62] In other words, FLIR's hoped-for-check did not provide any additional layer of protection, but rather a false sense of security.

Some large companies may have an in-country or regional finance and auditing team that could further investigate Carlos's expenses. However, in many small to medium-size companies this may not be a practical option. In other words, does the size of T Systems affect your answer as to what additional steps the company should take? The books and records and internal controls provisions make no explicit distinction regarding the size of the company, but the FCPA Guidance acknowledges that a factor the enforcement agencies consider when evaluating an organization's compliance program is the size of the organization and the DOJ's "FCPA Corporate Enforcement Policy" likewise states that "implementation of an effective compliance and ethics program . . . may vary based on the size and resources of the organization."[63] If T Systems is a large company that has the personnel and resources to conduct a more extensive investigation of Carlos's expenses, what additional steps do you suggest? At a minimum, it would seem prudent for the company to demand that Carlos produce receipts for the claimed expenses. But if he did, is this the end of it? In many foreign countries there is a black market for "fake receipts" and receipts can be made after the fact for just about anything.[64]

Should T Systems review Carlos's e-mails? Might this investigative step implicate privacy issues in the foreign country? Given that several improper payment schemes, such as the previously highlighted HP enforcement action, are executed by employees through personal e-mail accounts and personal phones (as opposed to company e-mail and phones), would a search of Carlos's work e-mail or phone uncover any relevant information?

If T Systems is a small company that does not have an in-country or regional finance and auditing team, what are Linda and Melisa supposed to do – fly down to South America and personally interview and investigate Carlos? This obviously will not be a time-free or cost-free exercise.

What makes these types of scenarios difficult for issuers making good faith efforts to comply with the FCPA is that while we (as well as the enforcement agencies) have the luxury of looking at this scenario in isolation as if it is the only questionable expense at T Systems, the reality is that most issuers have other similar questions about other employee expenses on a frequent basis. In other words, when one knows the end of the story (including Carlos's secret), it is very easy to look back with the perfect benefit of hindsight and say that the issuer woulda, coulda, shoulda done more, and if only the company did more in real time, the improper conduct could have been averted. However, the reality of fluid, real-world situations is that detection and prevention are challenging given the size of many business organizations. To demonstrate this point, consider the challenge law enforcement often has in detecting and preventing terrorism activity or other violent acts.

Often, when the perpetrator is identified it turns out that the individual had previous contact with law enforcement and with the perfect benefit of hindsight and knowing the end of the story we might be tempted to say that law enforcement woulda, coulda, shoulda done more.[65]

The questions and concerns about Carlos's expenses are not unique and there are probably dozens or hundreds or perhaps even thousands of people like him at T Systems who are submitting expenses to corporate headquarters on a frequent basis. Thus, whatever time and expense it takes to investigate Carlos's expenses, should we expect the company to spend the same amount of time and expense on the dozens or hundreds of other similar situations? In thinking about these questions, recall that legal authority and prior enforcement agency guidance stand for the notion that the internal controls provisions were never intended to provide absolute assurances or a fail-safe accounting control system at all costs. Recall as well enforcement agency guidance which stated that the costs of internal controls should not exceed the benefits expected to be derived and that thousands of dollars ordinarily should not be spent conserving hundreds.

So what is T Systems supposed to do if its investigation of Carlos is inconclusive? Should the company discipline or terminate Carlos because of its suspicions even if the company is unable to find definitive evidence that he engaged in improper conduct? If the answer is yes, fire him, recall that Carlos is doing well for the company. Even if the answer is not to fire him, on a practical level, do you really want to upset Carlos too much recognizing that he could voluntarily leave the company at any time? These are all difficult issues to consider, but issues business organizations frequently encounter in the global marketplace.

Depending on your answers to some of the above questions, including whether more was expected of a large company compared with small company, it might be that T Systems' conduct as depicted in the scenario was indeed consistent with the statutory standard of having internal accounting controls sufficient to provide reasonable assurances that transactions are properly authorized, recorded and accounted. Whether the enforcement agencies would agree with this and recognize the company's good faith efforts is of course an open question. If the company did engage in all or most of the additional steps discussed above, perhaps the government would still find violations based on a "damned if you, damned if you don't" enforcement theory similar to the Oracle, HP and Nu Skin Enterprises enforcement actions. Recall that in those actions, foreign subsidiary employees concealed and lied about their conduct to corporate headquarters, but that did not stop the enforcement agencies from finding books and records and internal controls violations by the parent company issuer.

Once again, the issues raised in the above scenario highlight a key take-away point from the FCPA's accounting provisions and that is as currently enforced the provisions are practically boundless and thus a potent supplement to the FCPA's more glamorous anti-bribery provisions.

Congratulations. You should now also have a pair of "FCPA goggles" relevant to the FCPA's accounting provisions and understand the wide range of circumstances in which scrutiny and enforcement can arise given how these provisions are interpreted by the enforcement agencies. With your "FCPA goggles" properly constructed, you are now ready to graduate to the next level of compliance proficiency by learning the fundamentals of conducting a risk assessment and thereafter confidently completing the risk assessment skills exercise that follows.

NOTES

1 FCPA Professor, "In Depth Into The $519 Million Teva FCPA Enforcement Action," (Dec. 22, 2016).
2 SEC Release, "United Settles Charges in Case of Flight Route to Benefit Public Official" (Dec. 2, 2016).
3 SEC Release, "SEC Charges Gold Standard Mining Corp. and Others for False and Misleading Statements Concerning Russian Gold Mining Operations" (July 3, 2012).
4 Since the FCPA's enactment in 1977, there have been over 1,200 "non-FCPA FCPA enforcement actions. See Searle Civil Justice Center, "The Foreign Corrupt Practices Act: An Empirical Examination of Enforcement Trends" (Sept. 2012).
5 A Resource Guide to the U.S. Foreign Corrupt Practices Act at p. 41.
6 SEC Release, "Opening Remarks at Foreign Bribery and Corruption Training Conference" (Feb. 11, 2013).
7 Abuses of Corporate Power: Hearings Before the Subcomm. on Priorities and Econ. in Gov't of the Joint Econ. Comm., 94th Cong. (1976).
8 SEC, "Report of the Securities and Exchange Commission on Questionable and Illegal Corporate Payments and Practices," (1976), reprinted in Special Supplement, Sec. Reg. & L. Rep. (BNA) No. 353 (May 19, 1976).
9 Id.
10 S. Rep. No. 114 (1977).
11 S. Rep. 95-114 (1977).
12 H. Conf. Rep. 94–831 (1977).
13 H. Conf. Rep. 100–576 (1988).
14 Id.
15 567 F.Supp. 724 (N.D. Ga. 1983).

16 2009 WL 6799492 (S.D. Tex. 2009); 803 F.Supp.2d 630 (S.D. Tex. 2011); Horman, et al. v. Abney, et al., C.A. No. 12290–VCS (Del. Ch. Jan. 19, 2017).
17 44 Fed. Reg. 10, 968 (Feb. 23, 1979).
18 Id.
19 SEC Release No. 17500 (Jan. 29, 1981).
20 SEC Staff Accounting Bulletin: No. 99 – Materiality, 17 CFR Part 211 [Release No. SAB 99], Staff Accounting Bulletin No. 99 (Aug. 12, 1999).
21 Id.
22 For representative examples of criminal books and records and internal controls cases, see FCPA Professor, "Criminal Internal Controls Charges Against Individuals," (Mar. 16, 2017); FCPA Professor, "Criminal Books And Records And Internal Controls Enforcement Actions," (July 20, 2016).
23 See e.g., Information, U.S. v. AGCO Limited, No. 1:09-cr-00249-RJL (D.D.C., Sept. 30, 2009).
24 Id; Complaint, SEC v. AGCO Limited, No. 1:09-cv-01865 (D.D.C., Sept. 30, 2009).
25 Id.
26 FCPA Professor, "Keeping FCPA Enforcement Statistics In Perspective," (Jan. 23, 2013).
27 Press Release, U.S. Department of Justice, "Siemens AG and Three Subsidiaries Plead Guilty to Foreign Corrupt Practices Act Violations and Agree to Pay $450 Million in Combined Criminal Fines" (Dec. 15, 2008).
28 Information, U.S. v. Siemens, No. 08-cr-367-RJL (D.D.C., Dec. 12, 2008).
29 Press Release, SEC, "SEC Charges Siemens AG for Engaging in Worldwide Bribery" (Dec. 15, 2008).
30 Press Release, U.S. Department of Justice, "Transcript of Press Conference Announcing Siemens AG and Three Subsidiaries Plead Guilty to Foreign Corrupt Practices Act Violations" (Dec. 15, 2008).
31 Complaint, SEC v. Siemens, No. 1:08-cv-02167 (D.D.C., Dec. 12, 2008).
32 Press Release, U.S. Department of Justice, "Daimler AG and Three Subsidiaries Resolve Foreign Corrupt Practices Act Investigation and Agree to Pay $93.6 Million in Criminal Penalties" (Apr. 1, 2010).
33 Information, U.S. v. Daimler, No. 1:10-cr-00063-RJL (D.D.C., Mar. 22, 2010).
34 Press Release, SEC, "SEC Charges Daimler AG With Global Bribery" (Apr. 1, 2010).
35 Complaint, SEC v. Daimler, No. 1:10-cv-00473 (D.D.C., Mar. 22, 2010).
36 SEC Release, "VimpelCom to Pay $795 Million in Global Settlement for FCPA Violations," (Feb. 18, 2016).
37 DOJ Release, "Embraer Agrees to Pay More than $107 Million to Resolve Foreign Corrupt Practices Act Charges," (Oct. 24, 2016).
38 Complaint, SEC v. Embraer S.A., (S.D. Fl., Oct. 24, 2016).
39 FCPA Professor, "Odebrecht / Braskem Bribery Schemes Net Approximate $420 Million FCPA Enforcement Action," (Dec. 21, 2016).
40 Complaint, SEC v. Braskem S.A. (D.D.C., Dec. 21, 2016).
41 Complaint, SEC v. Schering-Plough Corp. (D.D.C., June 9, 2004).
42 Complaint, SEC v. Natco Group, No. 4:10-cv-00098 (S.D. Tex., Jan. 11, 2010).
43 Complaint, SEC v. Oracle Corp., No. CV1204310 (N.D. Cal., Aug. 16, 2012).
44 Press Release, SEC, "SEC Charges Oracle Corporation With FCPA Violations Related to Secret Side Funds in India" (Aug. 16, 2012).
45 FCPA Professor, "Former Assistant Chief Of The DOJ's FCPA Unit Blasts Aspects Of SEC FCPA Enforcement," (Feb. 4, 2014).
46 In the Matter of Hewlett-Packard Co., Release No. 71916 (Apr. 9, 2014).
47 Id.
48 SEC Release, "SEC Charges Hewlett-Packard with FCPA Violations" (Apr. 9, 2014).

49 FCPA Professor, "HP And Related Entities Resolve $108 Million FCPA Enforcement Action," (Apr. 10, 2014).

50 In the Matter of Nu-Skin Enterprises, Inc., Release No. 78884 (Sept. 20, 2016).

51 Id.

52 FCPA Professor, "Friday Roundup," (Jan. 16, 2015).

53 In the Matter of Anheuser-Busch InBev SA/NV, Release No. 78957 (Sept. 28, 2016).

54 Complaint, SEC v. Noble Corp. (S.D.Tex. Nov. 4, 2010).

55 The Accounting Provisions of the Foreign Corrupt Practices Act: An Analysis An Address by Harold M. Williams, Chairman Securities and Exchange Commission (Jan. 13, 1981).

56 A Resource Guide to the U.S. Foreign Corrupt Practices Act (p. 3).

57 In the Matter of BHP Billiton Ltd. and BHP Billiton Plc, Release No. 74998 (May 20, 2015).

58 Lucinda Low & Tom Best, "Does SEC's Enforcement Action Against BHP Billiton Take the FCPA's Accounting Provisions Too Far?," (May 27, 2015).

59 In the Matter of JP Morgan Chase & Co., Release No. 79335 (Nov. 17, 2016).

60 Michael N. Levy and Amanda L. Fretto, "The SEC's Unlawful and Dangerous Expansion of the Exchange Act," (Nov. 2017).

61 In the Matter of Mead Johnson Nutrition Company, Release No. 75532 (July 28, 2015).

62 In the Matter of FLIR Systems, Inc. Release No. 74673 (Apr. 8, 2015).

63 U.S. Attorneys' Manual, 9-47.000 – Foreign Corrupt Practices Act Of 1977.

64 FCPA Blog, "Fapiaos (Part 3 of 4): Fakes and Frauds Abound," (May 20, 2015).

65 FCPA Professor, "The Challenges Of Detection And Prevention," (Nov. 8, 2017).

# 6 Compliance best practices and the fundamentals of conducting a risk assessment

This chapter begins by highlighting the wide body of so-called "best practices" sources. At first blush, these numerous sources may seem a bit overwhelming, but the risk management strategies are then broken down into bite size pieces that are easier for compliance professionals to digest.

A common thread in all sources of best practices is the importance of conducting a risk assessment. After all, rarely does a compliance professional receive questions tied to specific FCPA elements such as "is this customer an instrumentality of a foreign government such that its employees will be deemed a 'foreign official' under the FCPA" or "does this planned corporate hospitality event represent a 'reasonable' and 'bona fide' expenditure 'directly related' to a business purpose." Rather, compliance professionals listen to generic stories or receive generic information and from these real-world stories and information are expected to spot risk. In this chapter, you will graduate to the next level of compliance proficiency by learning the fundamentals of conducting a risk assessment. Thereafter, and with your "FCPA goggles" on, you will conduct a risk assessment by reviewing a real company's generic business information and categorizing the company's unique risk points.

Before highlighting the specifics of FCPA and related best practices, it is important to once again understand that no compliance program can prevent all misconduct and risk can't be eliminated. As discussed in this book's introduction, anyone who markets compliance products and services as a way to eliminate risk is selling a false dream and this dream was shattered in various enforcement actions previously highlighted in which business organizations did engage in several compliance best practices, but the alleged improper conduct still occurred. Even though risk can't be eliminated, a business organization that acts consistent with best practices can best minimize risk and will likely be in a better position should non-compliance occur. In other words, should a business organization become the subject of scrutiny, the consequences of that scrutiny are likely to be less severe if the organization can demonstrate to the enforcement agencies that prior to the alleged conduct occurring it conducted a risk assessment; provided risk-specific training to its employees and agents; translated its compliance policies and procedures into relevant local languages; and otherwise engaged in the compliance best practices discussed throughout this book.

## Overview of best practices

There has been frequent mention already throughout this book of the term "best practices," but you might be thinking what does this even mean? It is a good question to ask because there are a wide number of potentially relevant sources. Highlighted below are relevant sources of best practices specific to the topic of bribery and/or internal controls designed to minimize the risk of bribery as well as a number of broader sources relevant to risk management strategies.

### FCPA Opinion Procedure Releases

One source of compliance best practices is so-called FCPA Opinion Procedure Releases in which the DOJ provides responses to specific inquiries submitted by so-called requestors subject to the FCPA concerning conformance of contemplated conduct with the DOJ's "present enforcement policy." Pursuant to the governing regulations, "specified, prospective – not hypothetical – conduct" is subject to a DOJ opinion and while the DOJ's opinion has no precedential value, its opinion that contemplated conduct conforms with the FCPA is entitled to a rebuttable presumption should an enforcement action be brought against the requestor. Often, the DOJ's opinion is based on specific representations by the requestor and these representations can be converted into a *de facto* compliance checklist relevant to the topic addressed in the Opinion Procedure. Since the Opinion Procedure program was enacted, the DOJ has issued approximately 60 releases (all publicly available on the DOJ's FCPA website) on a wide range of issues including, as previously highlighted in Chapters 3 and 4, third party and corporate hospitality issues.[1]

## FCPA Resolution Documents

Another relevant source of compliance best practices is documents used to resolve corporate FCPA enforcement actions that are publicly available on the DOJ's and SEC's FCPA websites.[2] Obviously each enforcement action is fact-specific, but nearly all corporate resolution documents include an attachment titled "Corporate Compliance Program" that sets forth various minimum elements of a compliance program that the resolving company agrees to implement. Moreover, compliance professionals should read these actual enforcement actions and develop the skill to "flip" the relevant allegations or findings into compliance best practices. When doing so, recognize that from a compliance take-away standpoint large, egregious bribery schemes (such as Siemens and VimpelCom) are often the least instructive and the "just don't bribe" narrative actually applies. Rather, enforcement actions that seemingly take the law in new directions (albeit in the absence of judicial scrutiny) or involve unique enforcement agency interpretations (such as the internship and hiring practices and charitable donations actions previously highlighted or the prominent enforcement theory that individuals associated with various healthcare systems are "foreign officials) provide the most instructive compliance take-away points.

## FCPA Guidance (2012)

Another relevant source of compliance best practices discussed throughout this book at various times is the FCPA Guidance jointly issued by the DOJ and SEC.[3] The Guidance contains a specific section titled "Hallmarks of Effective Compliance Programs" that is "meant to provide insight into the aspects of compliance programs that DOJ and SEC assess, recognizing that companies may consider a variety of factors when making their own determination of what is appropriate for their specific business needs." Among other things, the Guidance acknowledges that a factor the enforcement agencies consider when evaluating a business organization's compliance program is the size of the organization and the fact that small-to-medium size organizations will probably have different compliance programs compared with large multi-national organizations.

## DOJ FCPA Corporate Enforcement Policy (2017)

This policy document "is aimed at providing additional benefits to companies based on their corporate behavior *once they learn of misconduct*" (such as voluntarily disclosure, cooperation and timely and appropriate remediation).[4] Nevertheless, the document contains a list of factors that "will be required for a company to receive full credit for timely and appropriate remediation" that can be converted into a *de facto* compliance checklist relevant to certain best practices issues and certain of these factors will be highlighted later in this book.

## OECD Guidance (2010, 2013)

Another relevant source of compliance best practices specific to internal controls is the OECD Good Practice Guidance on Internal Controls, Ethics, and Compliance.[5] The OECD Guidance "is addressed to companies for establishing and ensuring the effectiveness of internal controls, ethics, and compliance programs or measures for preventing and detecting the bribery of foreign public officials in their international business transactions." In addition, the OECD, United Nations and World Bank released a document titled "Anti-Corruption Ethics and Compliance Handbook for Business," which originated in "companies' observation that the myriad of existing anti-corruption principles for business can be confusing."[6] As stated in the Handbook, it is "not intended to create new standards or represent any form of legally binding requirement for businesses," but rather to "serve as a useful, practical tool for companies seeking compliance advice in one, easy-to-reference publication."

## ISO 37001 (2016)

Another potential source of compliance best practices is the so-called ISO 37001 released by the International Organization for Standardization (ISO). Unlike the other sources highlighted in this section, ISO 37001 is not publicly available but has to be purchased and is being marketed by some as a tool "designed to help organizations combat bribery risk in their own operations and throughout their global value chains." ISO 37001 is probably the least important source of best practices highlighted in this section because it largely duplicates the other sources previously mentioned, but in certain instances falls short of these other metrics. Nevertheless, as Jay Jorgensen (Wal-Mart's Global Chief Ethics and Compliance Officer) has noted:

"while a number of governmental agencies have provided guidance on how compliance programs should be structured, businesses often don't adopt recommendations of a government that is not their own."[7] Therefore, Jorgensen observed, "promoting increased standardization of corporate anti-corruption efforts [as ISO 37001 seeks to accomplish] would benefit everyone who is working against the plague of corruption."

Each of the sources of compliance best practices highlighted above is specific to the topic of bribery and/or internal controls designed to minimize the risk of bribery. In addition to these specific sources, there are also a number of broader sources relevant to risk management strategies.

## DOJ "Evaluation of Corporate Compliance Programs" (2017)

This policy document highlights 11 factors relevant to the DOJ's evaluation of a corporate compliance program.[8] Although not FCPA specific, the document "provides some important topics and sample questions that the Fraud Section has frequently found relevant in evaluating a corporate compliance program." As stated in the document "the topics and questions . . . form neither a checklist nor a formula" and "in any particular case, the topics and questions set forth . . . may not all be relevant, and others may be more salient given the particular facts at issue."

## DOJ Principles of Prosecution

The DOJ's Principles of Federal Prosecution of Business Organizations may also be relevant to FCPA and related compliance best practices as it contains a section titled "Corporate Compliance Programs" which lists various factors that the DOJ considers in deciding whether to prosecute alleged instances of corporate crime and if so the form of resolution.[9] Even so, the Principles of Prosecution state that the DOJ "has no formulaic requirements regarding corporate compliance programs."

## U.S. Sentencing Guidelines

Last, but certainly not least, the U.S. Sentencing Guidelines contain a section titled "Effective Compliance and Ethics Program."[10] Like other sources just mentioned, the Sentencing Guidelines are not FCPA specific, but the metrics may be relevant to certain corporate governance issues, including maintaining an FCPA compliance program.

In short, there are a number of potentially relevant sources (some more specific than others and some more helpful than others) that address FCPA and related risk management strategies. Not surprisingly, there is substantial overlap in many of these sources. For instance, the FCPA Guidance incorporates several Opinion Procedure Releases as well as compliance lessons from resolved enforcement actions; the DOJ's Evaluation of Corporate Compliance Programs cites to the FCPA Guidance and the OECD Guidance and Handbook; and the DOJ's Principles of Prosecution cite to the U.S. Sentencing Guidelines. Because of this, at first blush compliance best practices may seem a bit overwhelming and if you were to print off all of the sources highlighted above you would have hundreds of pages on your desk. However, what follows is a comprehensive topical aggregation of risk management strategies from these various sources in bite size pieces that are easier for compliance professionals to digest. Thereafter, the remainder of this book goes in-depth into these risk management strategies to the extent not previously discussed.

*Table 6.1 Overview of risk management strategies*

| | |
|---|---|
| Risk assessment | The business organization should understand all of its points of contact with "foreign officials" in the global marketplace. |
| Implementation of a compliance program | Based on the risk assessment, an organization should implement policies and procedures uniquely tailored to its risks and designed to minimize risk under the FCPA and related laws.<br>The policies and procedures should be in a written form, clearly articulated, accessible throughout the organization, translated into relevant local languages, and use localized examples.<br>Regarding the organization's points of contact with "foreign officials" (whether direct or indirect through various third parties), it should implement a system of accounting controls requiring that transactions are accurately and fairly documented (including as to the specific topics highlighted below) as well as internal controls to provide reasonable assurances that such transactions are subject to managerial authorization. |
| Specific policies and procedures | Based on the risk assessment, the organization should implement specific policies and procedures to address: (i) gifts; (ii) corporate hospitality; (iii) travel and entertainment issues; (iv) internship and hiring practices; (v) charitable donations and sponsorships; and (vi) facilitating payments. *(See Chapters 2 and 4 for various risk management strategies related to these topics.)* |

*Table 6.1 (continued)*

| | |
|---|---|
| Specific policies and procedures | Based on the risk assessment, the organization should implement pre-engagement, engagement, and post-engagement policies and procedures relevant to third parties. *(See Chapter 3 for various risk management strategies related to third parties.)* |
| Application | The organization's policies and procedures should apply to all directors, officers, and employees of the company, as well as third parties engaged by the organization. |
| Training and guidance | The organization should implement protocols to ensure that its FCPA and related policies and procedures are effectively communicated to all directors, officers and employees as informed by the risk assessment, and third parties. When new individuals or entities in these positions are hired or engaged, the organization should ensure that these individuals or entities are subject to the protocols as soon as practical.<br>At a minimum, the protocols should include:<br>• Periodic training for all directors and officers; all employees in positions of leadership; various financial gatekeepers (such as internal audit and finance positions); employees whose job functions present risk as informed by the risk assessment; and third parties.<br>• Periodic certification of compliance with the training requirements.<br>• Internal systems to adequately document and track the above training and certification requirements.<br>In addition, the organization should implement a system for providing guidance and advice to relevant individuals regarding its policies and procedures including when such persons need advice on an urgent basis or in any foreign jurisdiction in which the organization operates. |
| High-level commitment | The organization's directors and senior managers should be knowledgeable about its policies and procedures and provide strong, explicit, and visible support and commitment to the policies and procedures. This includes ensuring that the organization has sufficient resources (both in terms of money and personnel) devoted to the compliance function to best manage and minimize risk.<br>The organization should consider making FCPA and related compliance a relevant factor in determining director and senior manager compensation, bonuses, and promotion. |
| Oversight responsibility and resources | The organization should assign, to one or more competent senior managers with knowledge and understanding of the organization's business, responsibility for the implementation and oversight of its policies and procedures.<br>To best minimize risk, the oversight function should be reasonably centralized to ensure appropriate monitoring of all international activities. |

*Table 6.1* (continued)

| | |
|---|---|
| Oversight responsibility and resources | Managers with oversight responsibility should have direct reporting obligations to independent monitoring bodies (such as internal audit, the Board of Directors, or any appropriate committee of the Board) and should have an adequate level of autonomy from management as well as sufficient resources and authority to maintain such autonomy. |
| Internal reporting and investigation | The organization should maintain an effective system for internal reporting (including possible confidential reporting) by relevant individuals concerning alleged violations of its policies and procedures. To maximize effectiveness, the internal reporting system should be available in relevant local languages.<br>Upon receiving such reports, the organization should ensure that appropriate personnel have sufficient resources for investigating and documenting the alleged violations. Among other things, the organization should: (i) investigate all facts relevant to the wrongdoing including involvement by officers, directors, employees and third parties; and (ii) collect and preserve all relevant documents including those located overseas consistent with local law. |
| Enforcement, discipline, and incentives | If the organization's policies and procedures have been violated, it should promptly implement remedial measures designed to stop the alleged violations. Moreover, the organization should analyze the underlying "root causes" of the alleged violation and take reasonable steps including enhancements to existing policies and procedures to minimize the risk of future similar violations.<br>As to violations of policies and procedures, the organization should appropriately discipline culpable individuals including through termination as warranted. This includes not just individuals directly responsible for the violation, but also those deficient in their oversight or supervisory responsibilities. Such disciplinary procedures should be applied consistently and fairly throughout the organization regardless of the position held by, or perceived importance of, the relevant individual(s).<br>The organization should also consider ways to appropriately incentivize compliance including through personnel evaluations and promotions and rewards for developing improved policies and procedures. |
| Periodic assessment and continuous improvement | The organization should periodically and reasonably assess its policies and procedures to learn of their effectiveness in minimizing risk.<br>Moreover, the organization's policies and procedures should evolve as the organization's business evolves. Risk is a function of points of contact with "foreign officials" and new markets, new products and services, and new employees and third parties may result in the organization having new points of contact and new risk areas that need to be managed through new policies and procedures. |

*Table 6.1* (continued)

| | |
|---|---|
| Periodic assessment and continuous improvement | Another way in which the organization may evolve is through merger and acquisition activity. When such activity occurs, the organization should conduct appropriate risk-based due diligence on potential new entities and once the transaction closes the organization should ensure that its policies and procedures apply as quickly as practical to the newly acquired entity and its employees and agents. |
| Record keeping | As to all of the above risk management strategies, the organization should adopt systems for the appropriate retention of business records including a prohibition on destruction or deletion of business records such as through software that generates but does not appropriately retain business records. |

## The fundamentals of conducting a risk assessment

A common thread in all sources of compliance best practices is the importance of starting with a risk assessment. A risk assessment is based on the notion that FCPA and related compliance is not a one size-fits-all proposition, but rather uniquely tailored to a specific business organization. As the FCPA Guidance states:

> One-size-fits-all compliance programs are generally ill-conceived and ineffective because resources inevitably are spread too thin, with too much focus on low-risk markets and transactions to the detriment of high-risk areas.
>
> When assessing a company's compliance program, DOJ and SEC take into account whether and to what degree a company analyzes and addresses the particular risks it faces.

Likewise, the DOJ's "Evaluation of Corporate Compliance Programs" asks:

> Risk Management Process – What methodology has the company used to identify, analyze, and address the particular risks it faced?

Risk assessments are thus important, but you might be thinking what does this term of art actually mean? Terms of art tend to make things more complex than they really need to be and you should take a deep breath because with an understanding of the FCPA's elements, legal sources of authority and non-legal sources of information including common enforcement theories (i.e. your "FCPA goggles"), conducting a risk assessment is not a complex task. Rather, it is based on fundamental questions we learned long ago in terms of gathering information: where, who, how, and what?

## Where

Starting with the where question: in which countries does the company do business or plan to do business in the future? As to each country, what is known about the country's business conditions including corruption? Granted, this sounds rather basic, but if a company does business in numerous foreign countries, implementing risk management strategies needs to start somewhere and that somewhere is often prioritizing compliance to countries or regions of the world that have high perceived levels of corruption. Recall in the *U.S. v. Bourke* case previously highlighted in Chapter 3 that among the red flags providing ample evidence to affirm Bourke's criminal conviction was his general knowledge of how pervasive corruption was in Azerbaijan.

Even though a country's reputation for corruption is a relevant question when conducting a risk assessment, do not become too reliant on various rankings of corruption in foreign countries. For instance, Transparency International's Corruption Perception Index (CPI) is often mentioned (largely because it was the first such metric) when ranking corruption in foreign countries.[11] Query however whether the CPI (or any ranking for that matter) is a reliable or meaningful measure of the *specific* risks *specific* business organizations face when competing in *specific* countries for the following reasons.

- The CPI is merely a survey, and a survey of perceptions at that. Transparency International itself recognizes the limitations of the CPI and states "there is no meaningful way to assess absolute levels of corruption in countries or territories on the basis of hard empirical data." Moreover, Transparency International rightly acknowledges that the CPI does not tell the full story of corruption in a country because it "is limited in scope, capturing perceptions of the extent of corruption in the public sector from the perspective of business people and country experts."

- The CPI likely tells you what you already know or is otherwise composed of distinctions without differences. Each country in the CPI is assigned a numerical score between 100 (the best score) and 0 (the worst score). Sure there is a meaningful distinction between a country that scores, for example 91, vs. a country that scores, for example 8, but you probably did not need the CPI (or any other ranking for that matter) to alert you that Denmark is probably less corrupt than Somalia. In this way, the corruption rankings are similar to "best places to live" or "best places to retire" lists. They are interesting to read, but likely do not tell you things that you did not already know. Moreover, because the CPI numerically ranks countries, there is a meaningful ranking distinction between a country that scores, for example 39, and a country that scores, for example 30, but as a practical matter this is a largely a distinction without a difference.

- The CPI is country specific, not province or region specific, and this methodology deficiency is important because in certain countries corruption may be province or region specific. In other words, corruption is often localized and the CPI can thus both induce complacency (i.e. the belief that the business organization has low risk because the country's overall score is good even though a specific region in which the organization operates may have higher levels of actual or perceived corruption) as well as result in needless worry (i.e. the belief that the business organization has high risk because the country's overall score is bad even though the specific region in which the organization operates may have substantially lower levels of actual or perceived corruption).

At its core, FCPA and related risk is a function of *specific* business actors (employees and agents), coming into contact with *specific* alleged foreign officials, in connection with *specific* foreign business conditions and none of these factors are adequately captured by the CPI or other rankings. Moreover, just because Nigeria may have higher levels of perceived corruption than Finland in rankings, the fact remains that the vast majority of Nigerians are ethical, law-abiding people. On the flip side, even though Finland has lower levels of perceived corruption in rankings, the fact remains that there are some unethical people in Finland. Indeed, given the other questions relevant to conducting a risk assessment highlighted below, one can imagine a situation in which Finland might present more risk than Nigeria given the industry, the company's product or services, or the company's go-to-market strategy.

Even though compliance professionals should not become too obsessed with a country's reputation for corruption, as the *Bourke* case illustrates, general knowledge of corruption in a foreign country may be relevant and thus asking the "where" question is often a good place to start in terms of prioritizing FCPA and related compliance. In terms of prioritizing compliance to specific countries, a compliance professional may want to review the World Bank's Ease of Doing Business rankings which categorizes countries based on factors such as the ease of starting a business, obtaining permits, and otherwise dealing with regulatory officials.[12] Indeed, these rankings intersect more directly with the all-important "what" question discussed shortly (i.e. what licenses, permits, or certifications does a business organization need to do business in a country). Other resources relevant to a foreign country's business conditions include U.S. Department of Commerce Country Commercial Guides[13] and U.S. State Department Investment Climate Statements.[14]

## Who

The next question that should be asked in conducting a risk assessment is the "who" question. In other words, given where the company does business or plans to do business in the future who are the customers or potential customers in each country?

Even if a business organization is not doing any business with a foreign government *per se*, recall that a key take-away point from Chapter 2 was that the "foreign official" element of the FCPA's anti-bribery provisions is broadly interpreted to include individuals associated with so-called SOEs as well as foreign healthcare systems. Thus, scrutiny and enforcement can arise from business interactions with a broad category of individuals and not just a narrow category of bona fide foreign government officials. As further highlighted in Chapter 2, this scrutiny can arise when various things of value are provided or offered to "foreign officials" such as corporate hospitality, sports tickets, and gifts. In other words, the underlying conduct is often legal and morally acceptable in most instances, yet when directed to a specific type of individual, government enforcement agencies might deem it bribery.

Because the interpretation of "foreign official" determines if an aggressively enforced law applies to an interaction in the global marketplace, business organizations need to understand whether any customers or potential customers are controlled by a foreign government or perform a government function under the *Esquenazi* factor-based test (difficult as it may be to apply in practice). In terms of the "who" question, it is also important to understand that different products or services offered by the same business organization may target different customers and thus this question may need to be asked in certain organizations as to each relevant subsidiary, division or business unit.

## How

With an understanding of the "where" and "who" questions, a risk assessment next moves to the "how" question. In other words, how does the company do business and/or interact with customers or potential customers in the global marketplace? Specifically, does the company use third parties (whether agents, representatives, distributors or joint venture partners) as part of its go-to-market strategy or to facilitate other business tasks? If so, because of the FCPA's third-party payment provisions and its broad knowledge standard including concepts such as willful blindness and conscious disregard, a business organization is likely to have risk in connection with its third-party relationships. Indeed, as discussed in Chapter 3, the vast majority of corporate enforcement actions involve, in whole or in part, the conduct of various third parties and thus the pre-engagement, engagement, and post-engagement risk management strategies previously highlighted should be used based on the risk-ranking of the third parties.

Another important "how" question in conducting a risk assessment is understanding how the company's product, or perhaps raw materials used to manufacture the product, enter and exit a foreign country. Ports and other points of entry in foreign countries are often high-risk areas because bureaucratic and ministerial "foreign officials" levy customs duties or import or export taxes and in doing so may request improper payments. Such payments, even though outside the sales context, may be actionable for the reasons previously discussed in Chapter 2 and thus the simple process of moving product or raw materials from Point A to Point B in a foreign country can present risk. To best minimize this risk, a business organization needs to understand who within the organization is in these high-risk positions so that compliance policies and procedures including training can be targeted toward them. Furthermore, a business organization needs to understand if it uses the services of a customs broker or freight forwarder in connection with moving product or raw materials and/or interacting with customs and other regulatory officials. Customs brokers or freight forwarders are of course third parties and the same risk management strategies apply to such third parties even though they may not necessarily be involved in the sales process. Similar to other questions relevant to a risk assessment, in certain business organizations the "how" question may need to be asked as to each relevant subsidiary, division or business unit.

## What

A thorough risk assessment should next address the all-important "what" question. In other words, what licenses, permits, certifications and other regulatory requirements is the business organization subject to in a foreign country? This may seem like a mundane question and answering it will probably take a substantial amount of time as licenses, permits, and certifications are often product specific and country specific. However, as previously discussed in Chapter 2, numerous enforcement actions have been based on interactions with "foreign officials" outside the sales context and each license, permit, or certification that a business organization needs provides a point of contact with a "foreign official" with discretion and can thus implicate the FCPA and related laws. Related to this, a business organization needs to understand who obtains the licenses, permits, or certifications on its behalf. Is it an employee, in which case compliance policies and procedures including training need to be targeted to this high-risk job function, or is it a third party, in which case the organization needs to utilize its third-party compliance policies and procedures.

Another question relevant to a risk assessment is what other points of contact, broadly speaking, does the business organization have with "foreign officials"? Once again, answering this question will probably take a substantial amount of time given that, like other risk assessment questions, the answers are probably subsidiary, division or business unit specific as well as country specific. However, as previously highlighted in Chapter 2, several enforcement actions have been based on tax, immigration, labor, or other bureaucratic officials having points of contact with a business organization. Moreover, charitable donations and even hiring and internship practices can provide, directly or indirectly, points of contact with "foreign officials."

As these fundamental risk assessment questions demonstrate, FCPA compliance is not a one-size fits all proposition as the answers to specific risk assessment questions will be different for a defense contractor compared with an industrial manufacturer compared with a pharmaceutical company. While the term "risk assessment" may sound like a complex term of art, the reality is as simple as asking the basic where, who, how and what questions.

Another way to conduct a risk assessment is perhaps even more simple and informal but often just as effective. This involves gathering in the same room and without the distraction of laptop computers or smart phones all key business managers knowledgeable about the company's products, services, and business operations around the world. Once gathered, ask the following question: "an FCPA violation is occurring today in the company – where do you think it is occurring and why do you think it is occurring there?"

After some time for reflection, go around the room and listen to the answers. If there are common threads in the answers (for instance several managers think the most likely source of an FCPA violation is the China operations or this business unit or division and not another) then drill down the specific reasons for these answers. With China, is it the country itself, is it perhaps the personnel on the ground, or is it perhaps some unique form of regulation in China relevant to the company's products or services that is the problem? The answers to the rather simple and straightforward initiating question can often be revealing and just like the other risk assessment questions previously discussed can assist a business organization in prioritizing FCPA and related risk management strategies to unique risks.

In short, conducting a risk assessment in whatever form works best for a business organization is a critical first step in terms of best minimizing risk. To be sure, a risk assessment will take time and resources and should be a collaborative effort recognizing that individuals in the middle to lower tiers of the organization are likely to have the most informed answers to certain of the questions posed above. Moreover, a thorough risk assessment may require a compliance professional to travel to various foreign subsidiaries or business units to learn relevant information. Nevertheless, by breaking down the risk assessment into basic questions this section has hopefully de-mystified the process and you should now have greater confidence to competently conduct a risk assessment of a real company.

## Risk assessment skills exercise

Set out below is factual information from a real issuer company as disclosed in its SEC filing. After reading this information and with your "FCPA goggles" on you should be able to identify the unique risks the company has under the FCPA and related laws.

> The Company's diversified industry-leading portfolio of specialty chemicals, advanced materials, agrosciences and plastics businesses delivers a broad range of technology-based products and solutions to customers in approximately 160 countries and in high growth sectors such as electronics, water, energy, coatings, and agriculture. The Company has annual sales of $56.8 billion and employs approximately 54,000 people worldwide on a full-time basis with approximately 50% located in North America, 25% located in Europe, Middle East and Africa, and 25% located in other locations. The Company's more than 5,000 products are manufactured at 188 sites in 36 countries across the globe. The Company derives 68% of its sales and has 49% of its property investment outside the United States.
>
> The Company conducts its worldwide operations through global businesses, which are reported in six operating segments: Electronic and Functional Materials, Coatings and Infrastructure Solutions, Agricultural Sciences, Performance Materials, Performance Plastics and Feedstocks and Energy.
>
> **Business Products and Segments**
>
> *Electronic and Functional Materials*
>
> Electronic and Functional Materials develops and markets customized materials using advanced technology and unique chemistries for specialty applications ranging from semiconductors and liquid crystal displays to microbial protection for the oil and gas industry and cellulosics for innovative pharmaceutical drug formulation and healthier foods. These businesses serve the needs of market segments as diverse as: electronics and entertainment; healthcare and medical; energy; water; and consumer and home goods. The

segment's commitment to continuous innovation and rapid new product development enable it to maximize opportunities in emerging geographies and high-growth industries.

*Coating and Infrastructure Solutions*

Coatings and Infrastructure Solutions comprises an industry-leading portfolio of businesses utilizing advanced technology to deliver products ranging from low volatile organic compound coatings to building insulations and adhesives to next-generation solar and water technologies. The segment has broad geographic reach with sales in nearly 140 countries and R&D and manufacturing facilities located in key geographic areas.

The Building and Construction business is comprised of three global businesses – Building Solutions, Construction Chemicals, and Solar Solutions – that offer extensive lines of industry-leading insulation, housewrap, sealant and adhesive products and systems, as well as construction chemical solutions and building-integrated photovoltaics.

The Coating Materials business manufactures and delivers solutions that leverage high-quality, technologically advanced product offerings for architectural paint and coatings, as well as industrial coatings applications, including packaging, pipelines, wood, automotive, marine, maintenance and protective industries.

Water and Process Solutions is a leading provider of purification and separation technologies. The business provides the critical technology, including reverse osmosis membranes and ion exchange resins, to help customers with a broad array of needs such as reusing waste water streams, making fresh drinking water from sea water, creating a closed-loop water system for oil-field operations, making controlled release drugs possible, and removing impurities in dairy processing.

*Agricultural Sciences*

The Agricultural Sciences segment is a global leader in providing crop protection and plant biotechnology products, urban pest management solutions and healthy oils. The business invents, develops, manufactures and markets products for use in agriculture, industrial and commercial pest management, and food service. The segment has broad global reach with sales in more than 130 countries and R&D and manufacturing facilities located in all geographic areas.

Agricultural Sciences has significant technology-driven growth, led by plant biotechnology traits and crop protection products that utilize proprietary formulations. As a result, the Company uses patents, trademarks, licenses and registrations to protect its investment in germplasm, traits and proprietary chemistries and formulations. The Company also licenses plant biotechnology traits from third parties and engages in research collaborations with global industry, academia, and governments.

Agricultural Sciences has a diverse worldwide network which markets and distributes the Company's brands to customers globally. This network consists of the Company's sales and marketing organization partnering with distributors, independent retailers and growers, cooperatives and agents throughout the world.

*Performance Materials*
The Performance Materials segment comprises 11 market-focused, technology-driven, customer-centric businesses that are advantaged through integration and driven by innovative technology and solutions. Products produced by this segment are back-integrated into feedstocks, supporting a low-cost manufacturing base and consistent, reliable supply. The Performance Materials segment is positioned for growth through diverse markets and product offerings.

The segment has broad geographic reach with sales in over 140 countries and manufacturing facilities located in all geographic areas. Performance Materials serves customers in a large number of industries, including automotive, consumer, construction, infrastructure, oil and gas, appliance and electronics. The Performance Materials segment markets its products primarily through the Company's sales force and also utilizes distributors worldwide.

Key joint ventures that impact the Performance Materials segment are listed below:

- Map Ta Phut Olefins Company Limited – effective ownership is 33% of which the Company directly owns 20% and indirectly owns 13% through its equity interest in Siam Polyethylene Company Limited and Siam Synthetic Latex Company Limited. This Thailand-based company manufactures propylene and ethylene.
- A portion of the results of Sadara Chemical Company – a development-stage Saudi Arabian company that will manufacture chlorine, ethylene and propylene for internal consumption and will produce and market high-value added chemical products and performance plastics; owned 35% by the Company.

*Performance Plastics*
The Performance Plastics segment is a solution-oriented portfoliolio composed primarily of four businesses: Elastomers, Electrical and Telecommunications, Hygiene and Medical and Performance Packaging. The segment has broad geographic reach with sales in more than 100 countries and manufacturing facilities located in all geographic areas.

Joint ventures play an integral role within the Performance Plastics segment by dampening earnings cyclicality and improving earnings growth. Key joint ventures are listed below:

- EQUATE Petrochemicals Company K.S.C. – a Kuwait-based company that manufactures ethylene, polyethylene and ethylene glycol; owned 42.5% by the Company.
- The Kuwait Olefins Company K.S.C. – a Kuwait-based company that manufactures ethylene and ethylene glycol; owned 42.5% by the Company.
- The SCG Group consists of Siam Polyethylene Company Limited – owned 50%; Siam Polystyrene Company Limited – owned 50%; Siam Styrene Monomer Co., Ltd. – owned 50%; and Siam Synthetic Latex Company Limited – owned 50%. These Thailand-based companies manufacture polyethylene, polystyrene, styrene and latex.
- Sadara Chemical Company – a development-stage Saudi Arabian company that will manufacture chlorine, ethylene and propylene for internal consumption and will produce and market high-value added chemical products and performance plastics; owned 35% by the Company.

*Feedstocks and Energy*

The Feedstocks and Energy segment is the largest global producer of ethylene, chlorine, caustic soda and purified ethylene oxide. This segment is also a leading purchaser and producer of propylene and one of the world's largest industrial energy producers.

Joint ventures play an integral role within the Feedstocks and Energy segment by dampening earnings cyclicality, improving earnings growth and enabling access to high growth markets. Key joint ventures are listed below:

- MEGlobal – headquartered in Dubai, United Arab Emirates and manufactures and markets monoethylene glycol, diethylene glycol and polyethylene terephthalate resins; owned 50% by the Company.
- EQUATE Petrochemicals Company K.S.C. – a Kuwait-based company that manufactures ethylene, polyethylene and ethylene glycol; owned 42.5% by the Company.
- The Kuwait Olefins Company K.S.C. – a Kuwait-based company that manufactures ethylene and ethylene glycol; owned 42.5% by the Company.

**Patents, Licenses, and Trademarks**

The Company continually applies for and obtains U.S. and foreign patents and has a substantial number of pending patent applications throughout the world. At present, the Company owns 3702 active U.S. patents and 15,546 active foreign patents.

**Properties**

The Company operates 188 manufacturing sites in 36 countries. The Company's major production sites outside of the U.S. are located in Canada, Germany, the

Netherlands, Spain, Argentina, Brazil and Thailand. The Company also has plants and holdings in the following geographic areas: Canada (five manufacturing locations in three provinces); Europe, Middle East and Africa (53 manufacturing locations in 18 countries); Latin America (30 manufacturing locations in five countries); and Asia Pacific (42 manufacturing locations in 11 countries).

**Taxes**

Tax years that remain subject to examination for the Company's major foreign tax jurisdictions are as follows: Argentina, Brazil, Canada, France, Germany, Italy, the Netherlands, Spain, Switzerland, and the U.K.

## Risk assessment skills exercise guidance

The above risk assessment concerned Dow Chemical and your "FCPA goggles" should have provided clear insight as to the company's unique risks under the FCPA and related laws given its various points of contact with "foreign officials" in the global marketplace.

Before categorizing these risks, recall from Chapter 1 that in the minds of some, compliance should be easy for Dow and other business organizations: "just don't bribe." However, with 54,000 employees worldwide (including approximately 50% outside of North America) doing business in approximately 160 countries through various subsidiaries and numerous third parties, is it really that simple? Of course not, and even if Dow is 99% compliant on a daily basis, this means 1% non-compliance which can expose Dow to legal liability because of the *respondeat superior* principle previously highlighted as well as the reality of parent–subsidiary relationships and expansive enforcement theories related to corporate hierarchies.

### *Where*

Dow does business in several regions of the world with high perceived or actual levels of corruption such as Asia, Africa, and the Middle East. Moreover, these regions and certain specific countries therein such as Kuwait and Saudi Arabia rank relatively low on the World Bank's Ease of Doing Business Index in terms of obtaining permits and otherwise dealing with regulatory officials. Although compliance professionals should not become too reliant on any one ranking, Dow clearly does business in various regions of the world that present corruption and other compliance challenges due to high levels of bureaucracy. Recall, however, that Dow should not become too complacent in other regions of the world it does business in (such as Canada, the U.K., France, Germany etc.) because risk under the FCPA and related laws can arise anywhere. Nevertheless, in terms of prioritizing compliance policies and procedures, your "FCPA goggles" are working well if you focused on certain regions of the world in which Dow is active.

*Who*

Dow has a diverse range of customers or potential customers given its many business segments and products. While Dow engages in research collaborations with academia and governments, there is little else in the generic information highlighted above explicitly stating that it does business directly with foreign government *per se*. However, recall from Chapter 2 that the "foreign official" element is broadly interpreted to include individuals associated with SOEs as well as foreign healthcare systems. Thus, it is likely that the enforcement agencies would deem the two-factor *Esquenazi* "control" and "function" test satisfied in the following industries in many countries: oil and gas and other energy; chemical; water; healthcare and medical; agriculture; and telecommunications. Accordingly, numerous of Dow's business relationships in the global marketplace will be subject to the FCPA and related laws, including when it provides or offers corporate hospitality or other things of value to alleged "foreign officials." In short, your "FCPA goggles" are working well if you recognized that Dow may engage in the same conduct with certain customers and in most cases the underlying conduct is likely to be legal and socially acceptable, but if the same conduct involves an alleged "foreign official" the enforcement agencies may deem it bribery.

*How*

Dow relies on numerous third parties as part of its go-to-market strategy or to facilitate other business tasks in various high-risk industries and/or high-risk countries. For instance, the Agricultural Services segment has a "diverse worldwide network" including distributors, retailers and growers, cooperatives and agents which "market and distribute" product. Likewise, the Performance Material segment "utilizes distributors worldwide" and has "key joint ventures" in Thailand and Saudi Arabia. Furthermore, "joint ventures play an integral role" within the Performance Plastics segment, including "key joint ventures" in Kuwait, Thailand, and Saudi Arabia. Your "FCPA goggles" are fitting well if you recognized that Dow can be exposed to scrutiny and enforcement under the FCPA's third-party payment provisions, including through concepts such as willful blindness and conscious disregard based on the conduct of these various third parties. Accordingly, the previously discussed pre-engagement, engagement, and post-engagement risk management strategies relevant to third parties should be used based on the risk-ranking of the third parties.

Another how question relevant to the risk assessment relates to Dow's 188 manufacturing sites in 36 countries. In other words, how are Dow's products or the raw materials used in the manufacturing process entering and exiting a foreign country? Your "FCPA goggles" are fitting well if you recognized that these rather mundane logistical issues present risk because they provide yet further points of contact with "foreign officials" at port facilities who levy customs duties or otherwise oversee import or export regulations. If Dow utilizes the services of a third-party customs broker of freight forwarder to facilitate these logistical issues, these third parties although outside the sales process, need to be subject to the same third-party compliance policies and procedures previously highlighted.

### *What*

This is likely to be the area in which Dow has the greatest risk. As highlighted above, given the industries Dow is active in it already has many points of contact with alleged "foreign officials." Given the company's 188 manufacturing facilities in numerous foreign countries, Dow will also have numerous additional points of contact with "foreign officials" in terms of building and running the facilities. Such "foreign officials" are likely to include zoning, environmental, and tax officials. Moreover, these facilities employ people meaning that Dow will have additional points of contact with labor and immigration officials. Given the highly regulated nature of many of its products, Dow will also have numerous additional points of contact with "foreign officials" with discretion over various aspects of its business. Specifically, Dow's many chemical, agricultural and pest management products will be subject to licensing, permitting, certification or other regulatory regimes. Related to the "what" question of conducting the risk assessment is also categorizing other points of contact that Dow is likely to have with "foreign officials." Recall that Dow uses patents, trademarks, and licenses to protect its intellectual property and it owns 15,546 active foreign patents. Each of these patents provided a point of contact with a "foreign official" with discretion in terms of both securing the patent and perhaps patent renewals. Moreover, Dow has open tax examinations in several foreign countries, which provides yet another point of contact with "foreign officials" with discretion over this aspect of Dow's business.

Your "FCPA goggles" are fitting well if you recognized these many additional points of contact with "foreign officials" and how they present risk because of the broad meaning of the "obtain or retain business" element highlighted in Chapter 2 as well as the *de facto* repeal of the facilitation payments exception discussed in Chapter 4. Accordingly, compliance policies and procedures need to cascade down to the employees (or third parties) who interact with "foreign officials" in connection with these rather mundane, yet important aspects of Dow's underlying business.

Up until this point, this risk assessment guidance has focused on issues relevant to the FCPA's anti-bribery provisions, but recall that Dow is an issuer subject to the FCPA's accounting provisions which, as discussed in Chapter 5, are extremely flexible and represent a potent supplement to the more glamorous anti-bribery provisions. Given how these provisions are enforced, Dow's risk management strategies should apply to all entities within its corporate hierarchy. In other words, an inaccurate recording in a book or record of a consolidated entity for purposes of financial reporting or a control deficiency anywhere in its corporate hierarchy will likely become Dow's liability under the books and records and internal controls provisions given how these provisions are enforced.

As this risk assessment demonstrates, Dow (like most business organizations competing in the global marketplace) has numerous points of contact with "foreign officials" that may give rise to scrutiny and enforcement. Many of these risk areas may not have been obvious when you first picked up this book, but hopefully came into clearer focus with each additional chapter leading up to this skills exercise.

Given where Dow does business and the number of employees and third parties operating on its behalf, the industry sectors in which it is involved, the foreign laws and regulations it is subject to, and the many other points of contact it has with "foreign officials," it should not come as a surprise that Dow previously resolved an FCPA enforcement action based on the alleged conduct of DE-Nocil Crop Protection Ltd, a "fifth-tier subsidiary" in India.[15] According to the SEC, DE-Nocil, through third parties, made payments to "Indian government officials to register several agro-chemical products slated for marketing in time for India's growing season." Without making a single allegation that Dow participated in or had knowledge of the conduct at issue (indeed, the SEC specifically stated that "the payments were made without knowledge or approval of any Dow employee"), and without alleging the absence of good faith concerning Dow's oversight of DE-Nocil, the SEC nevertheless charged Dow with violating the FCPA books and records and internal control provisions.

Conducting a risk assessment is a critical first step in minimizing risk under the FCPA and related laws and thus a fundamental skill for compliance professionals. However, you can perform the most competent and thorough risk assessment ever, but without more, risk is not going to be effectively minimized. There is more work to be done and the next chapter focuses on using the results from the risk assessment to implement a compliance program and effectively communicate compliance expectations throughout a business organization.

NOTES

1 DOJ FCPA website "FCPA Opinions".
2 DOJ FCPA website "Related Enforcement Actions," SEC FCPA website "FCPA Cases".
3 A Resource Guide to the U.S. Foreign Corrupt Practices Act.
4 U.S. Attorneys' Manual, 9–47.120 – FCPA Corporate Enforcement Policy.
5 OECD, "Good Practice Guidance on Internal Controls, Ethics, and Compliance," (Feb. 18, 2010).
6 OECD – UNODC – World Bank "Anti-Corruption Ethics and Compliance Handbook for Business," (2013).
7 Jay Jorgensen, Texas Lawyer, "Increased Standardization Would Benefit the Global Anti-Corruption Effort," (Dec. 1, 2017).
8 U.S. Department of Justice, Criminal Division, Fraud Section, Evaluation of Corporate Compliance Programs.
9 U.S. Attorneys' Manual, 9–28.000 – Principles of Federal Prosecution Of Business Organizations.
10 U.S. Sentencing Guidelines, Chapter Eight – Sentencing of Organizations.
11 Transparency International, Corruption Perceptions Index.
12 World Bank, Doing Business Rankings.
13 Export.gov, Country Commercial Guides.
14 U.S. Department of State, Investment Climate Statements.
15 Complaint, SEC v. Dow Chemical (D.D.C. Feb. 13, 2007).

# 7 Implementing a compliance program and effectively communicating compliance expectations

There is more to FCPA and related compliance than just identifying risk unique to a business organization through a risk assessment. Consider a sports analogy in which a coach has devoted hours to studying an opponent to learn of its deficiencies and vulnerabilities. This is a great start, however, the success of a sports team will largely depend on the coach's ability to implement a specific game strategy and effectively communicate it to players who will be interacting with the opponent. Likewise, the success of a business organization in minimizing risk will depend upon implementing a compliance strategy and effectively communicating it to employees and agents in the global marketplace and this chapter highlights how to best implement written compliance policies and procedures throughout a business organization in a way that resonates with the intended audience. Next, training best practices will be highlighted (both in terms of who to include in training and how best to convey important concepts) as well as the importance of holistic compliance in which various personnel should play a meaningful role in minimizing risk.

## Written policies and procedures

The goal of conducting a risk assessment is to identify risks *unique* to a business organization so that the organization can implement *specific* written policies and procedures to minimize the risk. Think of this best practice through the below visual reference and building a wall.

Based on a risk assessment, different organizations are going to have different risks and because of this, different sections of the wall may need to be stronger for certain organizations compared with others. For starters, business organizations should have specific written policies and procedures relevant to its specific risk areas. For instance, many of Dow's points of contact with "foreign officials" occur because of the highly regulated nature of its products. Accordingly, an organization like Dow should have specific written policies and procedures relevant to securing licenses, permits and other regulatory approvals similar to those discussed in Chapter 2. A business organization with different products or services not subject to extensive government regulation may not need to fortify its compliance "wall" in this area to the extent that Dow does.

Recall as well from Chapter 2 that given the broad interpretation of anything of value, many instances of scrutiny and enforcement arise from corporate hospitality, travel and entertainment, gifts, charitable donations, and employment decisions. Business organizations can best minimize these risks through specific written policies and procedures that are accessible throughout the organization. Risk management strategies relevant to these issues were previously discussed in Chapter 2, but are worthy of brief mention here again.

Regarding corporate hospitality, a business organization should clearly communicate that all corporate hospitality potentially involving "foreign officials" needs to be pre-approved by legal or compliance personnel well versed on the FCPA who can ensure that the controls discussed in Chapter 4 are being followed. The same goes for gifts and charitable giving and rank and file employees should not have the authority or discretion to offer such things of value without pre-approval by legal or compliance personnel. In this regard, think of these specific written policies and procedures as taking discretion away from rank and file employees with the likely points of contact with "foreign officials" and moving the decision-making authority to a less-interested individual with a better understanding of the FCPA and related laws.

Employment decisions are increasingly presenting risk for companies based on the enforcement theory that providing employment or internships (even unpaid internships) to family members of alleged "foreign officials" may constitute something of value to a "foreign official" and thus a potential FCPA violation. To minimize this emerging risk, a business organization should have specific policies and procedures relevant to employment decisions as previously discussed in Chapter 2.

Third parties are often the largest source of risk for business organizations and as previously discussed business organizations should have specific pre-engagement, engagement, and post-engagement policies and procedures relevant to third parties. Pre-engagement policies and procedures should include a questionnaire completed by the third party designed to identify potential red flags, an acknowledgment letter signed by the third party evidencing the third party's understanding of the organization's commitment to compliance, and completion of a due diligence file by the organization documenting, among other things, the need for a third party, the third party's skills and experience, and resolution of any potential red flags. As to engagement, all agreements with third parties should be in writing with specific clauses concerning payment terms, record keeping and audit rights, and termination. Even after engagement of the third party, there is still work to be done and business organizations should have policies and procedures requiring the third party to be trained on the FCPA and related laws as well as monitoring and supervision of the third party through annual certifications, acknowledgment letters, and perhaps periodic audits.

Specific written policies and procedures are an important next step in minimizing a business organization's specific risks as informed by a risk assessment. However, these efforts may be wasted unless a business organization can clearly and effectively communicate its unique risks and its specific policies and procedures throughout its organization in a way that resonates with the intended audience. In short, effective communication is a key factor in minimizing risk under the FCPA and related laws.

## Effective communication strategies

A sports analogy is again useful in highlighting the importance of effective communication because what often makes a sports team successful can also inform compliance in a business organization. Consider the playbook of a sports team.

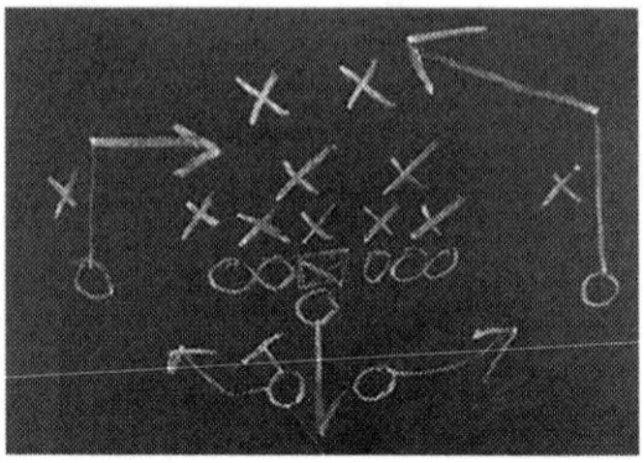

For starters, sports teams obviously want their players to understand the playbook and to do so the coaches drafting the playbook need to communicate in a way that resonates with players. The same is true when it comes to communicating the compliance playbook in a way that resonates with employees and agents. However, often FCPA and related policies and procedures are written in legalese instead of plain English. On one level, this is not surprising given that the FCPA is a law and because of this lawyers typically draft compliance policies and procedures. Yet on a more important level, query whether legalese will resonate with a non-legal audience? Consider the following actual language from a real company's publicly available compliance policy.

> The Foreign Corrupt Practices Act ("FCPA") makes it a criminal offense to pay, offer, or give anything of value to a foreign official or employee of a foreign government who has discretionary authority with the intent to improperly influence the business decisions of that official. Civil penalties for violations of the FCPA can include fines up to \$500,000.00. Criminal penalties can exceed \$2,000,000.00 and may include imprisonment for up to five years. The FCPA also contains certain recordkeeping requirements and prohibits the use of false records or accounts in the conduct of foreign business. Certain foreign laws and international treaties make it a criminal offense to pay, offer, or give anything of value to any individual, regardless of that person's private or governmental status, with the intent to improperly influence the business decisions of that individual.

This policy largely just restates the FCPA's statutory language. How would you respond if you were on the receiving end of such legalese? Is this an effective way to communicate with a non-legal audience? Surely not and perhaps the following language, written in plain English, would better resonate with a non-legal audience.

> When conducting business in various countries, the company, its employees, and others acting on behalf of the company may have contact with various foreign officials regarding various aspects of the company's business. It is important to recognize that the term "foreign official" means more than just traditional government officials, but also employees of various government agencies or departments as well as employees of certain entities controlled by a foreign government that perform a government function. It is the company's policy not to offer, authorize, or merely promise to provide, anything of value to any "foreign official." Anything of value means just that, anything of value and enforcement actions have included things of value as small as $4 as well as sports tickets, golf, gifts, meals, and travel and entertainment being offered or promised to "foreign officials."

Another important factor in minimizing risk that can also be highlighted with the sports playbook analogy is instructing players to steer clear of gray areas because much of what happens on the field of play falls into gray areas with referees having a tremendous amount of discretion. A team that plays too aggressively may find itself on the wrong end of that referee's discretion. The same is true when it comes to FCPA and related compliance because the practical reality is that much of what happens in the global marketplace can also fall into gray areas.

For instance and as highlighted in Chapter 4 in more detail, in the minds of many, the FCPA's facilitating payments exception has essentially been read out of the statute through certain enforcement actions that focused on permitting, licensing or other routine regulatory actions performed by ministerial or clerical officials. Also recall from Chapter 4 that several enforcement actions have focused on meals, entertainment, and other corporate hospitality. Nevertheless, many business organizations specifically mention the facilitation payments exception as well as the reasonable and bona fide expenses affirmative defense in written policies and procedures accessible throughout its organization. Consider the additional excerpt from the same real company's compliance policy:

> There is an exception to the FCPA anti-bribery prohibition for payments made to facilitate or expedite performance of a "routine governmental action." The statute lists the following examples: obtaining permits, licenses, or other official documents; processing governmental papers, such as visas and work orders; providing police protection, mail pick-up and delivery; providing phone service, power and water supply, loading and unloading of cargo, or protection of perishable products; and scheduling inspections associated with contract performance or transit of goods across country.
> [. . .]
> Employees may provide [company] products, advertising or promotional items of nominal value, such as a coffee mug, calendar, or similar item displaying the [company] logo; and may provide food and refreshments in connection with business activities.

Query whether communicating the facilitation payment exception and the reasonable and bona fide expenses affirmative defense to rank and file employees actually increases a business organization's risk by giving employees with points of contact with alleged "foreign officials" terms of art that they can use to justify their conduct. For instance, a foreign customs official may request a payment to clear goods and an employee might think "no problem, that is routine governmental action and my compliance policy says that such payments are allowed under the FCPA." Likewise, a foreign SOE customer may enjoy high-priced liquor and fancy dinners and an employee might think "no problem, that's reasonable and bona fide and my compliance policy says that I may provide food and refreshments in connection with business activities."

By training rank and file employees on the FCPA's exception and affirmative defenses, the above company probably increased, not decreased, its FCPA risk. Because of this, most business organizations prohibit facilitation payments except perhaps in cases of personal health and safety. Moreover, the rationale for prohibiting facilitation payments and not mentioning the statutory exception in written compliance policies and procedures is further supported by the fact that other FCPA-like laws such as the U.K. Bribery Act and Canada's Corruption of Foreign Public Officials Act do not exempt such payments.

The above discussion has focused on communicating statutory exceptions and affirmative defenses to *rank and file* employees. This does not mean that legal and compliance personnel within a business organization should be *unaware* of such concepts. Surely they should be aware of these statutory concepts. However, the goal of compliance, particularly when it relates to gray areas, is to implement and communicate policies and procedures which funnel these difficult issues to legal and compliance personnel and *not* to empower rank and file employees to make decisions in the global marketplace that can expose the business organization to scrutiny and enforcement.

Returning to the sports analogy and the importance of understanding the playbook, imagine a sports team with players from several different countries, not all of whom fluently speak or understand English. Such a team could have a playbook full of winning plays, but success is dependent on all players being able to understand the playbook. Accordingly, the team should provide the playbook in languages best understood by individual players. Again, the same holds true for compliance in a business organization given that most business organizations have employees located all over the world, not all of whom fluently speak or understand English. Accordingly, communicating compliance policies and procedures in local languages is a best practice, as is using localized examples in policies and procedures that resonate with the intended audience. For instance, sports tickets to a high-profile college sporting event or gifts during the Christmas season might resonate with a U.S. audience, but perhaps not with a foreign audience. As stated by a compliance officer at a leading company:

> Gift cards aren't commonly used in Mexico. Golf outings don't really happen in Brazil. Therefore, mentioning either as part of anti-bribery training to workers in these countries won't resonate.[1]

To best resonate with a foreign audience, compliance policies and procedures should incorporate local customs and practices, local forms of entertainment, and culturally significant holidays. In other words, a business organization should consider tweaking its compliance policies and procedures to resonate with its *entire* employee or agent base, not just a *portion* of its base.

Enforcement agencies clearly expect business organizations to have a compliance playbook that is effectively communicated and understood by all employees. For instance, the FCPA Guidance states:

> Compliance policies cannot work unless effectively communicated throughout a company. [. . .]

> [I]nformation should be presented in a manner appropriate for the targeted audience, including providing training and training materials in the local language. For example, companies may want to consider providing different types of training to their sales personnel and accounting personnel with hypotheticals or sample situations that are similar to the situations they might encounter.

Likewise, the DOJ's Evaluation of Corporate Compliance Programs asks:

> Has the training been offered in the form and language appropriate for the intended audience?

Communicating the compliance playbook in a way that resonates with all employees and agents may seem like an obvious best practice, but sometimes it takes learning of a real company, resolving a real enforcement action, with a real failure in this area to best drive home this basic compliance point.

**FAILURE**

For instance, among the internal control failures highlighted in an enforcement action against medical device company Orthofix International were the following:

> [Company] did not have an effective FCPA compliance policy or FCPA related training. Although Company disseminated some code of ethics and anti-bribery training to the subsidiary employees, the materials were only in English, and it was unlikely that subsidiary employees understood them as most subsidiary employees spoke minimal English.[2]

Likewise in the Bruker Corp. enforcement action, among the internal control failures highlighted by the government were the following:

> [Company] did not translate its training presentations into local languages, including Mandarin. And although company implemented an FCPA policy, it failed to translate that policy into Mandarin [. . .] Also, while [company] periodically distributed its Code of Conduct (containing its gifts and entertainment policies) and employee handbook to employees worldwide, it again failed to translate these documents into local languages, including Chinese.[3]

Another compliance failure highlighted in the Bruker action was that the company "relied mainly on its China-based managers to ensure that employees understood the potential FCPA implications of doing business with SOEs." Stated differently, employees know what they know and don't know what they don't know and it is not necessarily the fault of Chinese employees for not understanding the broad interpretation of "foreign official" and the common enforcement theory that deems individuals associated with alleged SOEs to be "foreign officials" on par with Presidents and Prime Ministers. Indeed, this concept is curious to many foreign national employees of multinational businesses, yet it is the organization's responsibility to ensure that its entire employee and agent base understands this concept because it presents a high degree of risk in certain countries including China.

Further relevant to effective communication is the notion that compliance policies and procedures should not leave the intended audience confused or perplexed. For instance, among the internal controls failures highlighted in the PTC enforcement action were the following:

> [The company's] Code of Ethics and Anti-Bribery policies for the provision of business entertainment were vague (i.e., stating that employees should use "good taste" and consider the "customary business standards in the community" when providing business entertainment) and not risk-based to China.[4]

To guard against the same being said about your organization, before rolling out compliance policies and procedures, compliance professionals should consider convening a focus group to better understand whether employees are confused or perplexed by certain concepts in the policies and procedures. In short, success in the field of business, just as in sports, is best accomplished through a compliance playbook that is effectively communicated to all members of the organization in a language they can actually understand and in a way that resonates with the intended audience.

## Training best practices

Implementing a compliance program and effectively communicating compliance expectations requires more than just *written* policies and procedures, but also actually *training* those in the business organization and others operating on its behalf on the policies and procedures. As stated in the FCPA Guidance:

> Compliance policies cannot work unless effectively communicated throughout a company. Accordingly, DOJ and SEC will evaluate whether a company has taken steps to ensure that relevant policies and procedures have been communicated throughout the organization, including through periodic training and certification for all directors, officers, relevant employees, and, where appropriate, agents and business partners.

However, just as all written policies and procedures were not equal, not all training methods are equal either. Thus, before a business organization plows ahead with training, compliance professionals should pause to reflect on the most appropriate way to deliver the training and highlighted next are training best practices in terms of both who to include in training and how best to convey important concepts during training.

In terms of who to include in training, although most points of contact with alleged "foreign officials" in the global marketplace that often give rise to risk do *not* involve board of director members or high-level executives, tone at the top (while perhaps an overused cliché in the compliance space) does have real meaning in terms of minimizing risk as will be further discussed in Chapter 8. Accordingly, directors and officers must be trained on the organization's compliance policies and procedures and if the organization ever becomes the subject of scrutiny it will look foolish in the eyes of law enforcement if these individuals did not receive training.

The next obvious candidates for training are employees in high-risk job functions as informed by a risk assessment. Here you can see how a risk assessment flows into other aspects of compliance because the risk assessment identified the unique points of contact the organization has with "foreign officials" in the global marketplace. Some of these points of contact are going to be similar for many business organizations, such as sales personnel, but as previously discussed most of these points of contact are going to be unique to an organization given its industry, products and services, and countries in which it operates. Third parties (such as agents, representative, distributors, joint venture partners and others) who have points of contact with "foreign officials," in terms of both sales and other interactions relevant to the organization's business, should also receive training. Here again, if an organization ever becomes the subject of scrutiny because of third party *x*, it will look foolish in the eyes of law enforcement if third party *x* never received training by the organization on its FCPA and related policies and procedures. The above candidates for training seem rather obvious, but again sometimes it takes learning of a real company, resolving a real enforcement action, with a real failure in this area to best drive home this basic compliance point.

## FAILURE

For instance, in an enforcement action against pharmaceutical company Bristol-Myers Squibb the internal control failures included:

> The . . . sales force in China received limited training and much of it was inaccessible to a large number of sales representatives who worked in remote locations. For example, when [the company] rolled out mandatory anti-bribery training . . . 67% of employees in China failed to complete the training by the due date.[5]

This real failure further highlights that a business organization needs to monitor its training program to ensure that all individuals who are supposed to complete the training *actually* do so.

Returning to the "who to train" question, it is important that compliance professionals not forget about the many boring, day-to-day aspects of the organization's business which provide points of contact with "foreign officials" and thus potential scrutiny and enforcement. Consider again a sports analogy and the importance of team-work. All sports teams have recognizable positions (such as the quarterback and running back in football, the pitcher in baseball, and the point guard in basketball). Players in these so-called "skilled positions" tend to earn the highest salaries, secure the most lucrative endorsement deals, and garner the most media attention. However, the success of a sports team is not just dependent on the "skilled positions," but more importantly execution by the whole team including the so-called "role players" (such as in football a center successfully snapping the ball to the quarterback and the ability of the offensive line to protect the quarterback; in baseball the ability of the catcher to properly position players and suggest to the pitcher the most effective pitch; and in basketball the ability to efficiently execute a pick and roll or box out your opponent to secure a rebound).

Like sports teams, business organizations also have recognizable positions such as chief executive officer and chief financial officer and these individuals tend to earn the highest salaries and garner the most media attention. As previously mentioned, these individuals have an important role to play in compliance, but compliance is more often dependent on execution by the whole team including the role players. This is largely a function of the enforcement theory that interactions with "foreign officials" in connection with various day-to-day aspects of business (such as tax, import/export and securing licenses, permits, certifications and the like) are captured by the FCPA's anti-bribery provisions. Seldom, if ever, are the top leaders of a business organization involved in these points of contacts. Rather, it is the "role players" (the relatively low to mid-level employees throughout the world) who have these points of contact with "foreign officials" and thus it is important to cascade down – perhaps even prioritize – compliance training to these high-risk job functions. In short, if a procurement manager in China, a logistics employee in Argentina, or a tax employee in India is not properly executing his or her job responsibilities consistent with company policy, compliance will fall short and the entire business organization may suffer adverse consequences.

In addition to the above candidates, a business organization should also include administrative assistants in FCPA and related training. While such individuals may not have direct contact with "foreign officials" or decision-making authority within the organization, these individuals are often familiar with channels of communication and the conduct and activity of executives and thus, if properly trained, can perhaps identify risk at an early stage.

A business organization's risk assessment will largely guide which employees and agents should be targeted for training. However, as the Bristol-Myers Squibb enforcement action instructs, the organization then needs to monitor its training program to ensure that all individuals who are supposed to complete the training actually do so and various technology resources including auditable online training platforms can help accomplish this task.

## Holistic compliance

Further to compliance being a team sport is the notion that various financial gatekeepers should play a meaningful role in minimizing risk and that compliance can best be achieved holistically throughout a business organization. For instance, the DOJ's Evaluation of Corporate Compliance Programs asks:

> Has there been clear guidance and/or training for the key gatekeepers (e.g., the persons who issue payments or review approvals) in the control processes relevant to the misconduct?

In other words, finance, audit, and other personnel with financial monitoring responsibilities should play a meaningful role in risk management and thus need to be specifically trained so that they can spot risk and red flags in their daily job functions. Finance, auditing and other personnel are obviously skilled professionals who are products of their professional training. Historically, such individuals have been trained to find supporting documentation for a corporate expense and once found move onto the next corporate expense. However, this traditional skill may be insufficient to minimize risk under the FCPA and related laws because the context of corporate expenses (such as who was the beneficiary of corporate hospitality or what underlying services did the third party actually provide) are often an issue in enforcement actions. To bridge this gap, and recognizing the important role financial gatekeepers can play in minimizing risk, business organizations should train these individuals to be intellectually curious about underlying expenses. For instance, as to a corporate dinner expense, inquiring about who attended the dinner or why a particular successful salesperson is always wining and dining customers and potential customers. Likewise as to a third party invoice requesting payment, inquiring whether there is any evidence that the third party actually provided legitimate, value-added services pursuant to a written contract or inquiring how the third party's payment request compares with other similar requests within the business organization.

Financial gatekeepers are closest to the flow of money within a business organization and therefore need to understand who "is dipping their hands into the cookie jar" so to speak because scrutiny and enforcement can arise because of access to money or other things of value such as commissions, distributor spreads, invoice approval, gifts, meals and entertainment, or petty cash. So that financial gatekeepers can play a meaningful role in minimizing risk, these individuals should at a minimum:

- Understand the broad interpretations of the anything of value, foreign official, and obtain or retain business elements of the FCPA's anti-bribery provisions and the notion that most instances of scrutiny and enforcement are far removed from "suitcase full of cash to a government official to get a government contract" type of scenarios.

- Understand the FCPA's third-party payment provisions and be able to spot and follow up on the previously identified red flags relevant to third parties. Specifically, looking for evidence that the third party actually provided legitimate value-added services before payment is made on an invoice.

- Understand who within the organization, relevant subsidiary, or business unit has the authority to authorize expenses that present risk and making sure that such authorizations are scrutinized. Among other things, because of title, prestige and in some countries gender, certain individuals tend to be subjected to less oversight and scrutiny when seeking authorization for expenses.

- Pay particular attention to various vague or ambiguous accounts. Often culpable individuals try to justify certain expenses using such accounts and the following descriptions, among many others, have been identified in enforcement actions as concealing improper payments: "additional assessments," "extra costs," "extraordinary expenses," "urgent processing," "urgent dispatch," "customs processing," "importation advances."

Financial gatekeepers clearly have an important role to play in minimizing risk under the FCPA and related laws and it is the responsibility of the business organization to provide these individuals with the tools they need to effectively play this role. In short, financial gatekeepers need "FCPA goggles" and the enforcement agencies, the SEC in particular, have high expectations that such gatekeepers will play a meaningful role in compliance including the ability to spot issues and display a high degree of intellectual curiosity regarding certain transactions and expenditures.

For instance, in an enforcement action against heating and air conditioning company York International the government stated that: "local finance personnel did not provide an independent internal control function, but rather acquiesced in questionable practices and documentation without critical review."[6] In the Eli Lilly enforcement action the government stated that the "audit department had no procedures specifically designed to assess the FCPA or bribery risks of sales and purchases."[7] Similarly, in the AGCO enforcement action the government noted that there was no oversight from the company's finance department and that "no one questioned" the various transactions giving rise to the enforcement action.[8]

In addition to the "who to include" question relevant to FCPA training and the importance of holistic compliance, before a business organization plows ahead with training, compliance professionals should also pause to reflect on the most appropriate way to deliver the training. For starters, the goal of training should not be to make each participant an expert on the FCPA's specific elements, but rather to engage participants and provide them with certain basic skills relevant to their specific job function so that they are best able to spot risk and thus report it to appropriate experts within the business organization. Towards this goal, the first few minutes of training can be critical to success and the trainer needs to properly set the tone and engage participants at their level. Consider two types of training: the first legalese, fear-based training (as depicted by the below picture) and the second team-work, spot the issues training.

As to the first type of training, consider a training session that begins with the trainer saying something along the following lines: "today I will be talking about a U.S. law that makes it a crime to bribe foreign government officials to get business." If this is how the training begins, the trainer may lose a good portion of the audience and regardless of what is said during the rest of the training session it may not be as successful as it could have been.

- *Crime?* The participant in the second row has a clean record and wouldn't hurt a fly. He coaches his son's soccer team and worships on the weekend and is thinking to himself: "I have never committed a crime and I don't intend to – what does this training session have to do with me?"

- *Government?* The job responsibilities of the participant in the first row job do not provide any points of contact with government officials and she is thinking "does this company even do business with foreign governments – what does this training session have to do with me?"

- *Business?* The logistics manager from outside the U.S. who was flown in for the training session is thinking "business, I'm not a sales and marketing guy, I just make sure our product gets into and out of the country and I occasionally help secure various licenses and permits for the company – what does this training session have to do with me?"

To avoid having the minds of participants wander like this during the first few minutes of training, it may be more effective to embrace a team-work, spot the issues type of training (as depicted by the below picture).

Consider a training session that begins with the trainer saying something along the following lines:

> Today, I will be talking about a U.S. law that applies to all of you – regardless of whether you are in the sales and marketing department, the executive office suite, the finance and audit department, or the logistics department. This law can cover a wide range of conduct the company engages in when doing business in the global marketplace. Your understanding of this law and how it may relate to your specific job function will best ensure that the company remains compliant with this law and is best able to achieve its business objectives.

Might this type of training be more engaging as it better motivates participants to spot risk in their specific job functions? Perhaps so and the take-away point here is that not all training is equal. The best way to minimize FCPA and related risk in a business organization is to provide each training participant with "FCPA goggles" so that they can then use their acquired knowledge to minimize risk in their specific job functions. Moreover, this objective is probably best accomplished not through endless and detailed power point slides, but rather case studies, role-playing exercises and question and answer sessions. While online training is often the most cost and time efficient way to reach a global work force, such training may fail to capture the beneficial aspects of live, in-person training. Nevertheless, if online training is the most practical option for a business organization, compliance professionals should recognize that not all online training is equal. Online training *can be* memorable – and thus more effective – if it engages participants through active learning such as issue-spotting exercises presented through high-quality videos, gaming aspects, and other inter-active learning exercises.[9]

Relevant to training best practices, an FCPA practitioner shared the following insight regarding his experience with business managers:

> Despite sitting through a couple of PowerPoint slides about the FCPA during a compliance training, the managers did not understand how and where bribery occurs. I'd be interviewing the manager of a company's foreign operations in a high risk country and have a stack of documents to go through with him. I'd ask him a series of questions about some fairly run-of-the-mill issues – why certain dinners occurred with some government officials, what the thousand dollars of "miscellaneous" expenses on a hotel bill were for, whether the manager ever saw any of the holiday gifts he approved a large budget for – and it would often become clear to me that the manager had no idea that I was asking him about possible bribes. It had simply never occurred to him that there could be FCPA risks associated with any of these kinds of expenses. And those kinds of blind spots existed with managers who supposedly had received FCPA training. Numerous times people have

told me that they remember the FCPA training they had, but that they never thought the Act applied to the kinds of expenses I'm asking them about.[10]

With the knowledge and skills you have acquired throughout this book, the same will not be said of your business organization in the future. Thus far you have:

- learned why spotting risk under the FCPA and related laws is an important skill for a diverse group of professionals;
- constructed your own "FCPA goggles" through an element-by-element review of the FCPA's provisions;
- practiced wearing your "FCPA goggles" through issue-spotting scenarios;
- learned various sources of compliance best practices and the common elements found in these sources;
- conducted a risk assessment of a real company based on generic corporate information; and
- learned of various risk management strategies relevant to implementing a compliance program and effectively communicating compliance expectations within a business organization.

These are all critical tasks to minimizing risk under the FCPA and related laws. However, a compliance professional's job is not yet finished, as Chapter 8 highlights various risk management strategies relevant to overseeing a compliance program.

NOTES

1 Navex Global Blog, "Compliance Training for Third Parties Needs a Game Plan," (Nov. 22, 2017).
2 Complaint, SEC v. Orthofix International (S.D. Tex. July 10, 2012).
3 In the Matter of Bruker Corporation, Release No. 73835 (Dec. 15, 2014).
4 In the Matter of PTC Inc., Release No. 77145 (Feb. 16, 2016).
5 In the Matter of Bristol-Myers Squibb Company, Release No. 76073 (Oct. 5, 2015).
6 Complaint, SEC v. York Int'l Corp., No. 1:07-cv-01750 (D.D.C., Oct. 1, 2007).
7 Complaint, SEC v. Eli Lilly and Co., No. 1:12-cv-02045 (D.D.C., Dec. 20, 2012).
8 Complaint, SEC v. AGCO Limited, No. 1:09-cv-01865 (D.D.C., Sept. 30, 2009).
9 FCPA Professor, "The Use Of Gaming To Make FCPA Training Memorable And Thus More Effective," (Oct. 27, 2015).
10 FCPA Professor, "A Practical Resource For Managers and Executives," (Dec. 8, 2010).

# 8 Overseeing a compliance program

The final chapter of this book highlights various risk management strategies relevant to: oversight responsibility and resources for a compliance program; having an internal reporting system for compliance concerns and proper protocols to investigate such concerns; and periodic assessment and continuous improvement of a compliance program once it is in place.

## Oversight responsibility and resources

Board of directors and executive officers are given wide latitude in running a business organization subject to certain fiduciary duties including an obligation to attempt in good faith to assure that an adequate corporate information and reporting system exists. Applied to the FCPA context this means that individuals entrusted to run a business organization should implement various policies and procedures highlighted throughout this book *and*, having implemented the policies and procedures, in good faith oversee compliance of the policies and procedures. Part of this oversight responsibility is so-called "tone at the top" and as the FCPA Guidance states:

> within a business organization, compliance begins with the board of directors and senior executives setting the proper tone for the rest of the company. Managers and employees take their cues from these corporate leaders.

As further stated by the government, a business organization should ensure that its directors and senior managers are knowledgeable about compliance policies and procedures and that they provide "strong, explicit and visible support" for the policies and procedures.[1] Likewise, the DOJ's Evaluation of Corporate Compliance Programs poses the following questions relevant to "tone at the top":

- How have senior leaders, through their words and actions, encouraged or discouraged the type of misconduct in question?
- What concrete actions have they taken to demonstrate leadership in the company's compliance and remediation efforts?
- How does the company monitor its senior leadership's behavior?
- How has senior leadership modeled proper behavior to subordinates?

In short, there are several things that board members and senior executives can do to best minimize risk under the FCPA and related laws. What are those things? What does the admittedly vague "tone at the top" concept actually mean? As stated by the government:

> We look not just at the written policies, but to other messages otherwise conveyed to employees, including through in-person meetings, e-mails, telephone calls, incentives/bonuses, and will make a determination regarding whether the company meaningfully stressed compliance or, when faced with a conflict between compliance and profits, encouraged employees to choose profits.

The FCPA Guidance further states:

> DOJ and SEC recognize that positive incentives can also drive compliant behavior. These incentives can take many forms such as personnel evaluations and promotions, rewards for improving and developing a company's compliance program, and rewards for ethics and compliance leadership. Some organizations, for example, have made adherence to compliance a significant metric for management's bonuses so that compliance becomes an integral part of management's everyday concern. Beyond financial incentives, some companies have highlighted compliance within their organizations by recognizing compliance professionals and internal audit staff. Others have made working in the company's compliance organization a way to advance an employee's career.

This is by no means an exhaustive list of the things board members and senior executives can do to stress the importance of compliance within a business organization and "tone at the top" may mean different things in different organizations given their size and geographical reach. Generally speaking though, "tone at the top" means (at the risk of using another cliché) that board members and senior executives are not just "talking the talk," but more importantly "walking the walking" when it comes to compliance. In other words, board members and senior executives: are subject to the same compliance policies and procedures as rank and file employees (and suffer the same consequences for violations); devote sufficient resources to compliance; and use various methods of communication at various times during the course of managing the organization to emphasize compliance and the consequences for non-compliance.

## FAILURE

Unfortunately, "tone at the top" is not present in all business organizations active in the global marketplace. For instance, in the BizJet International enforcement action the government alleged that at a board of directors meeting executives responsible for business operations discussed with the Board that the company would pay referral fees in order to gain market share in a foreign country.[2] In an enforcement action against telecommunications company Telia, senior management of the company allegedly structured certain business transactions in ways to evade (obviously not successfully) the FCPA[3] and in a related enforcement action against VimpelCom the government alleged that "rather than implement and enforce a strong anti-corruption ethic, [senior management] sought ways to give itself plausible deniability of illegality while proceeding with business transactions known to be corrupt."[4]

These enforcement actions were obviously not situations in which board members or senior executives needed to engage in a detailed inspection of the company's books and records or have sophisticated knowledge to discover the bribery schemes. Rather, the "tone at the top" failures were obvious as senior managers were intimately involved in the bribery schemes or were specifically informed that the company was engaged in bribery schemes.

Should board members or senior executives need extra motivation to fulfill their oversight responsibilities, a criminal enforcement action against Anthony Mace (the former CEO of SBM Offshore) should be a required read. The salient features of the enforcement action were:

- Before Mace become CEO, SBM Offshore, its U.S. subsidiary, and others including certain intermediaries entered into an agreement to pay bribes to foreign officials in order to obtain or retain business.
- When Mace became CEO he held oversight authority over the entire company including its Marketing and Sales Department. Further, Mace was required to personally approve payments exceeding a certain dollar amount including those made to outside sales agents.
- When Mace became CEO he was aware that paying bribes to foreign officials was a crime under the FCPA and that SBM Offshore was operating in countries with a high risk of corruption.
- Despite this, Mace deliberately avoided learning that certain payments including payments he authorized and approved were in fact bribes paid to foreign officials and in the words of the government, "Mace's deliberate avoidance was solely and entirely due to his own actions and decisions."[5]

While board members and senior executives have certain oversight responsibilities for compliance policies and procedures within a business organization, they should not be the exclusive overseers of compliance. Board members and senior executives have broad responsibilities and thus must delegate certain day-to-day business functions to those with the time and expertise to uniquely focus on specific issues. In the FCPA context, this means that board members and senior executives need to ensure that specific oversight responsibility for compliance is entrusted to competent and informed individuals who have sufficient resources to actually accomplish the task of minimizing risk. As stated in the FCPA Guidance,

> In appraising a compliance program, DOJ and SEC also consider whether a company has assigned responsibility for the oversight and implementation of a company's compliance program to one or more specific senior executives within an organization.

As further stated by the DOJ in its FCPA Corporate Compliance Policy, a factor considered in evaluating the effectiveness of a compliance program is "the quality and experience of the personnel involved in compliance, such that they can understand and identify the transactions and activities that pose a potential risk."

Like other internal control failures highlighted throughout this book, the above best practices may seem obvious, but once again sometimes it takes learning of a real company, resolving a real enforcement action, with real failures in these areas to best drive home basic compliance points.

## FAILURE

For instance, in the Johnson Controls enforcement action the government alleged:

> Managers stated that even if they had performed additional review, they did not have sufficient knowledge and understanding of [subsidiary] projects to recognize when certain vendor payments were unnecessary, whether goods ordered had actually been delivered, or whether design fees were necessary.[6]

In other words, how could the managers spot risk and then minimize the risk if they lacked sufficient knowledge of the underlying business transactions and more broadly the subsidiary's business operations? Best practices also instruct that the individual or individuals with specific oversight authority over an FCPA compliance program have meaningful autonomy from management. The Evaluation of Corporate Compliance Programs highlights the following questions to consider:

- Do compliance and other relevant control functions have direct reporting lines to anyone on the board of directors?
- How often do they meet with the board of directors?
- Are members of the senior management present for these meetings?
- Who reviewed the performance of the compliance function and what was the review process?

- Who has determined compensation/bonuses/raises/hiring/termination of compliance officers?

- Do the compliance and relevant control personnel in the field have reporting lines to headquarters? If not, how has the company ensured their independence?

In terms of the funding and resources for the compliance function, the Evaluation of Corporate Compliance Programs highlights the following questions to consider:

- How have decisions been made about the allocation of personnel and resources for the compliance and relevant control functions in light of the company's risk profile?

- Have there been times when requests for resources by the compliance and relevant control functions have been denied? If so, how have those decisions been made?

Stated differently, a business organization can conduct a thorough and comprehensive risk assessment to identify its unique risks, implement specific policies and procedures throughout its organization to minimize risk, and effectively communicate its policies and procedures including through training that motivates participants to spot risk. However, if the oversight function lacks commitment or resources (in terms of both money and personnel) to actually oversee the compliance program, particularly in foreign subsidiaries, gaps may occur and when gaps occur a business organization may face scrutiny and enforcement as the following enforcement actions demonstrate.

## FAILURE

In the Bristol-Myers Squibb enforcement action the internal control failures alleged by the government included:

> The corporate compliance officer responsible for the Asia-Pacific region . . . was based in the U.S. and rarely traveled to China. There was no dedicated

> compliance officer for China until [year], and no permanent compliance position in China until [year +2].[7]

Given the nature of the company and its unique risk profile, the Asia-Pacific region presented a high degree of risk, yet there were inadequate resources in the specific region to effectively minimize the risk. Another best practice relevant to oversight of a compliance program is centralization, or its flip-side, avoiding decentralizing in a compliance program. Granted, large business organizations have operations around the world. However to best minimize risk business organizations should implement integrated compliance policies and procedures that are then overseen by the "home office" and the government will not hesitate to fault organizations for internal control failures when deficiencies occur. For instance, in the Orthofix International enforcement action, the government stated:

> [Parent company's] reporting structure and relationship with its subsidiaries was decentralized . . . complicating parent oversight, compliance monitoring, and communication with U.S. executives. [Parent company] lacked adequate training, policies, processes, and corporate culture that would have allowed employees at its subsidiaries to raise compliance concerns to the parent level.[8]

Likewise, in the Bio-Rad enforcement action the government stated:

> [Parent company] decentralized its compliance program such that its international offices were responsible for ensuring adequate compliance with its business ethics policy and code of conduct [. . . Parent company] did not take sufficient steps to monitor its international offices.[9]

Thus far, this chapter has addressed the importance of oversight responsibility of a compliance program by board members and senior executives as well as ensuring that day-to-day responsibility is overseen by competent and informed individuals who have sufficient resources to do their jobs including through centralized systems. A business organization can act consistently with these risk management strategies yet occasional compliance failures may still occur. As stated by the DOJ:

> we recognize that companies have rogue employees who don't follow company policy so even when there is a strong company policy it may still be the

> case that somebody in the company does something that is off the reservation, that happens all the time . . . it's impossible for a big global company to make sure that all of its employees are following the law all of the time.

Nevertheless, from an oversight standpoint it is important that when such occasional compliance failures do occur, a business organization has an internal reporting system for compliance concerns and proper protocols to investigate such concerns.

## Internal reporting and investigation

A business organization should have an internal reporting system for compliance concerns by employees and third parties. To do this, organizations should maintain – either directly or indirectly through a service provider – a compliance hotline and for the hotline to be effective it should be offered in various languages so that all employees and third parties, no matter their native language or where located, feel comfortable and confident using the system. Once again, this compliance best practice may seem obvious, but sometimes it takes learning of a real company, resolving a real enforcement action, with real failures in this area to best drive home basic compliance points.

For instance, in the Bruker enforcement action among the internal controls failures highlighted by the government was the following:

> Company's toll free employee hotline, which employees were to use to report complaints anonymously, was not provided in Mandarin, limiting its efficacy.[10]

Having an internal reporting system that employees and third parties are comfortable and confident in using to report compliance concerns is a good first step; however business organizations next need to ensure that personnel who receive this information are actually acting upon it. In other words, part of having an effective system for internal reporting is having sufficient resources for investigating and documenting allegations of compliance violations. In its Evaluation of Corporate Compliance Programs, the DOJ poses the following relevant questions.

- *Effectiveness of the reporting mechanism* – In other words, how has the company collected, analyzed, and used information from its reporting mechanisms? How has the company assessed the seriousness of the allegations it received? Has the compliance function had full access to reporting and investigative information?

- *Properly scoped investigation by qualified personnel* – In other words, how has the company ensured that the investigations have been properly scoped, and were independent, objective, appropriately conducted, and properly documented?

- *Response to investigations* – In other words, has the company's investigation been used to identify root causes, system vulnerabilities, and accountability lapses, including among supervisory manager and senior executives? What has been the process for responding to investigative findings? How high up in the company do investigative findings go?

In terms of root causes, the FCPA Corporate Enforcement Policy further states that, if a business organization is the subject of scrutiny and enforcement, to receive "full credit for timely and appropriate remediation," it needs to demonstrate a "thorough analysis of causes of underlying conduct (i.e. a root cause analysis) and, where appropriate, remediation to address the root causes."

## FAILURE

The government will not hesitate to find internal controls failures based on deficient internal investigation practices and in the General Cable enforcement action the government alleged:

> Subsidiary Executive met with a high-level executive at [parent corporation] with responsibility for overseeing international operations and expressed concerns that payments to the distributor in Thailand were being used for

> corrupt purposes. Despite this conversation, the corrupt payments did not stop, nor was an investigation conducted."[11]

Moreover, when conducting an internal investigation the government may expect a business organization not only to narrowly investigate a specific issue, but also inquire more broadly to learn if the conduct under investigation is perhaps indicative of a wider issue. For instance, among the internal control failures cited by the government in the SciClone Pharmaceuticals enforcement action were the following:

> After learning of the gifts, [company] terminated the [specific third party] and conducted an internal investigation related to [third party's] conduct and practices in China. The review did not look more broadly at sales and marketing practices in China.[12]

Compliance professionals should recognize however that there may be tension between conducting a broader investigation and the government's sensible guidance to business organizations not to "aimlessly boil the ocean" as previously discussed in Chapter 1. Like other aspects of compliance, there is seldom a one-size-fits-all solution to the proper scope of an internal investigation and specific circumstances, like those mentioned in the above enforcement actions, may warrant specific responses. Regardless of the ultimate scope, the government expects a business organization to learn certain facts from an internal investigation. For instance, in the FCPA Corporate Enforcement Policy the DOJ highlights the following factors that will qualify a business organization to receive full cooperation credit:

- disclosure of all facts related to involvement in the conducted investigated by the company's officers, employees, or agents; and

- collection and preservation of relevant documents and information relating to their provenance, including overseas documents (the locations in which such documents were found, who found the documents, and where appropriate translations of relevant documents in foreign languages).

Even if a business organization decides not to voluntarily disclose a breach of its compliance policies and procedures to the government (a topic discussed shortly), the above factors remain relevant to internal investigation best practices. Stated differently, the general goal of an internal investigation is to answer the basic "who knew what and when did they know it" question and after an internal investigation a business organization should be able to answer the following questions:

- how high up in the organization did the alleged misconduct go (even if the alleged misconduct is something less than actual misconduct, but rather consciously disregarding certain information or failing to adequately supervise or ask the right questions of subordinates); and
- how pervasive was the misconduct (was it an isolated incident confined to one business unit or subsidiary or a small group of employees or was the misconduct – in the words of DOJ guidance – "due to system vulnerabilities, and accountability lapses"?).

An issue that seems to generate much attention in the compliance community is whether – to act consistent with best practices – a business organization should voluntarily disclose breaches of its compliance policies and procedures to government enforcement agencies. To be sure, government enforcement agencies have long encouraged voluntary disclosure and offered repeated assurances in non-binding policies or speeches that voluntary disclosure will result in meaningful credit.[13] These law enforcement statements are hardly surprising given that voluntary disclosure makes the job of law enforcement easier and more cost-effective from a budget and resource standpoint. However, compliance professionals and business managers need to understand that in the vast majority of situations there is *no* legal obligation to disclose. As even the DOJ has rightly acknowledged, government can't "require business organizations to voluntarily self-disclose, cooperate, or remediate."[14] As noted by a former DOJ and SEC enforcement attorney:

> Not all potential [FCPA] problems, however, are appropriate for disclosure. After investigation, allegations of misconduct may not result in a determination that illicit activity has occurred. [. . .] Prematurely attracting the government's attention may, as a practical matter, shift the burden to the company to prove the absence of a corruption problem. Enforcement officials may feel the need as a matter of basic human nature to seek some type of resolution to a case where they have invested significant time and effort. Companies need to weigh the potential benefits of cooperation against the significant costs of initiating a potentially unwarranted government investigation.[15]

Similarly, the former Chief of the DOJ's Fraud section stated:

> It often will not be in a company's best interest to disclose if, for example, the allegations prove not to be credible or if it is unclear whether the conduct even amounts to a violation of law. Under those circumstances, a disclosure could unnecessarily embroil the company in a lengthy and costly government investigation and result in other repercussions such as triggering civil litigation and harm to a company's reputation that could otherwise be avoided. It's a challenging calculus. [. . .] However, the fact that a company doesn't disclose a problem that ultimately comes to DOJ's attention is not necessarily going to damage the company's credibility with DOJ. Regulators recognize that not every allegation should be of interest to them – and, frankly, having counsel that knows when they'll be interested and when they won't is really important.[16]

As to this latter point, it is important to understand that while the decision to voluntarily disclose is a business decision of the board of directors and/or audit committee, FCPA counsel often has an inherent interest in advising the company on this issue. Simply put, if a business organization does not voluntary disclose, the engagement for all practical purposes and in all likelihood is over and the need for FCPA Inc. services diminishes. However, if the organization voluntarily discloses to law enforcement agencies, the engagement gains new steam, the "where else" question previously highlighted in Chapter 1 will probably be asked, and to answer the "where else" question a team of lawyers and other service providers will travel the globe and pre-enforcement action professional fees and expenses will mount for years. In many respects, voluntary disclosures represent a pot of gold for FCPA Inc. and the disclosure decision is often a multi-million dollar decision for a business organization. The proverbial "elephant in the room" is that the decision is also often a multi-million dollar issue for FCPA counsel advising the business organization. In highlighting the role of FCPA Inc. as gatekeepers, this section merely points out the inherent interest that is present in a typical instance of scrutiny and enforcement. However, this issue is seldom highlighted as few outside of FCPA Inc. realize how scrutiny and enforcement actually work. Another issue seldom discussed is that the enforcement agency officials who encourage voluntary disclosure are the same individuals who frequently move to FCPA Inc. after articulating this enforcement agency policy while at the government.

In short, compliance professional and business managers need to fully understand and appreciate two important points:

- voluntary disclosure of potential violations is going to set into motion a wide-ranging and expensive sequence of events that will be far more costly to the business organization than any marginal settlement amount benefit articulated in a non-binding enforcement agency policy; and

- thoroughly investigating an issue, promptly implementing remedial measures, and effectively revising and enhancing compliance policies and procedures – *all internally and without disclosing to the enforcement agencies* – is a perfectly acceptable, legitimate, and legal response to FCPA issues in all but the rarest of circumstances.

Regardless of whether a business organization discloses breaches of its compliance policies and procedures to government enforcement agencies, a business organization that conducts an internal investigation and finds compliance failures needs to actually do something tangible with the results and failure to do so may result in a separate internal control failure.

For instance, in the PTC enforcement action previously highlighted, the government stated:

> PTC investigated compliance issues at [its China subsidiary], including possible corruption involving its business partners. However, PTC failed to identify and stop the ongoing and systemic illicit payments to Chinese government officials by [subsidiary] personnel . . . and did not undertake effective remedial actions.

As this and several other enforcement actions demonstrate, implementing remedial measures in the aftermath of compliance breaches is an important component of best practices. One remedial action the government will surely expect is for a business organization to terminate or discipline culpable actors and the DOJ's Evaluation of

Corporate Compliance Programs highlights the following questions that should be addressed:

- What disciplinary actions did the company take in response to the misconduct and when did they occur?
- Were managers held accountable for misconduct that occurred under their supervision?
- Did the company's response consider disciplinary actions for supervisors' failure in oversight?
- What is the company's record (e.g. number and types of disciplinary actions) on employee discipline relating to the type(s) of conduct at issue?
- Has the company ever terminated or otherwise disciplined anyone (reduced or eliminated bonuses, issued a warning letter, etc.) for the type of misconduct at issue?

Consistent with the above guidance, the government has with increasing frequency favorably cited discipline and termination of culpable actors in enforcement actions. For instance, in an enforcement action against medical devices company Zimmer Biomet the government noted that the company engaged in remedial measures including:

> - terminating or causing the resignation of five employees who participated in the misconduct;
> - terminating one employee who failed to identify issues with the use of a [distributor] and failed to take appropriate steps to mitigate risks; and
> - disciplining two employees who failed to detect the misconduct, failed to supervise effectively those who were engaged in the misconduct, and failed to take appropriate steps to mitigate corruption and compliance risks, including by placing an official letter of reprimand in their employment files, reducing their bonuses, and requiring them to take additional anticorruption training.[17]

Likewise, in the Rolls-Royce enforcement action the government noted that the company engaged in remedial measures including:

- terminating six employees and accepting resignations from 11 other employees who were the subject of internal disciplinary investigations, where all 17 employees were implicated in the corrupt schemes [or other problematic conduct]; and
- terminating the Company's business relationships with all third-party intermediaries involved in the corrupt schemes.[18]

The many "ripple" effects of scrutiny and enforcement were previously highlighted in Chapter 1, but as relevant here the termination and discipline of culpable employees in the aftermath of scrutiny and enforcement certainly represents yet another "ripple." Indeed, the aggregate costs of this "ripple" are meaningful considering certain inevitable wrongful termination lawsuits or separation costs, lost productivity, and the time and expense of recruiting and hiring replacements.

## FAILURE

On the flip side, government enforcement agencies will probably consider compliance programs to be ineffective if a business organization fails to terminate or discipline culpable employees. For instance, in the LAN Airlines enforcement action the CEO of the company was allegedly involved in the improper conduct. However, this individual was not disciplined by the company and the government stated:

> the Company has failed to remediate adequately, including significantly by failing to discipline in any way the employees responsible for the criminal conduct . . . including misconduct by at least one high-level Company executive, and thus the ability of the compliance program to be effective in practice is compromised.[19]

In certain enforcement actions, the government has even mentioned country exits as a remedial measure. For instance, in the Ralph Lauren enforcement action based on alleged conduct in Argentina the government noted that the company "ceased retail operations in Argentina and is in the process of formally winding down all operations there."[20] Similarly, in the Bio-Rad enforcement action based in part on alleged conduct in Vietnam, the government favorably noted that the company "clos[ed] its Vietnam office after learning of improper payments by its Vietnam subsidiary."[21] Likewise, in the Key Energy enforcement action based on alleged conduct in Mexico, the government noted that the company was engaged in a "coordinated wind-down and exit of all markets outside of North America, and a commitment to exit Mexico."[22]

Query however whether such country exits should be applauded by law enforcement or represent sound policy? Is the fight against bribery and corruption advanced when ethically sound business organizations (notwithstanding the often isolated nature of the improper conduct giving rise to the enforcement action) and organizations that are generally viewed as selling the best products and services for the best prices exit foreign markets? What type of companies are going to take their place?

Policy issues aside, this section has highlighted how a business organization acting consistent with best practices should: (i) have an internal reporting system for compliance concerns that all employees and third parties are comfortable and confident using; (ii) have sufficient resources and protocols to investigate such concerns; and (iii) implement remedial measures in the aftermath of compliance breaches including by terminating and disciplining culpable actors. Before highlighting a final step relevant to overseeing a compliance program (periodic assessment and continuous improvement), consider again the sports playbook analogy that has conceptualized many risk management strategies throughout this book.

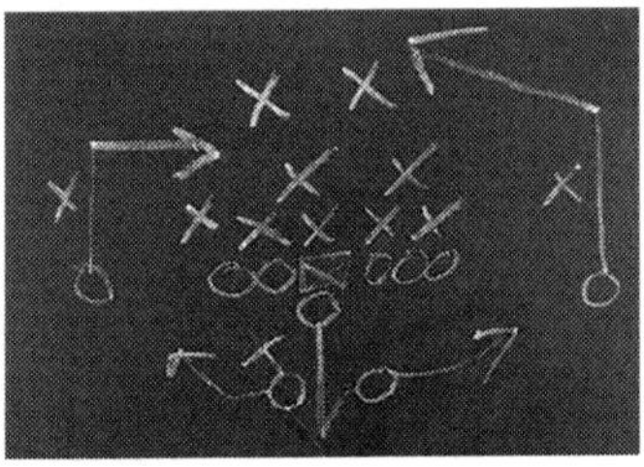

The playbook of a successful sports team is not rigid and static, but flexible and capable of evolving. Just because a certain play worked in one game, does not mean it will work in future games, and just because a certain play worked with a certain group of players, does not mean that it will work with another group of players when injuries, a trade, or retirement happen. In other words, a successful sports team is capable of evolving and coaches are constantly re-evaluating the playbook as circumstances warrant. The same should be true when it comes to the compliance playbook of a successful business organization.

## Periodic assessment and continuous improvement

A risk assessment that identifies unique points of contact a business organization has with "foreign officials" in the global marketplace, that is then used to implement specific policies and procedures, that are then effectively communicated throughout the organization, will only capture a specific point of time in the life of a business organization. However, business organizations can change and when change occurs compliance policies and procedures may need to change as well. As stated in the FCPA Guidance:

> A good compliance program should constantly evolve. A company's business changes over time, as do the environments in which it operates, the nature of its customers, the laws that govern its actions, and the standards of its industry. In addition, compliance programs that do not just exist on paper but are followed in practice will inevitably uncover compliance weaknesses and require enhancements. Consequently, DOJ and SEC evaluate whether companies regularly review and improve their compliance programs and not allow them to become stale.

Similarly, the DOJ's Evaluation of Corporate Compliance Programs poses the following questions:

- How often has the company updated its risk assessments and reviewed its compliance policies, procedures, and practices?
- What steps has the company taken to determine whether policies/procedures/practices make sense for particular business segments/subsidiaries?

There are many ways in which a business organization may evolve such as entering a new market, launching a new product or service, or personnel changes that may warrant a review of existing compliance policies and procedures. In terms of entering a new market, recall that best practices start with conducting a risk assessment that identifies points of contact with alleged "foreign officials" unique to a business organization including the countries in which it operates. Thus, when a business organization expands into a new market its risk profile and thus its compliance policies and procedures need to expand as well.

## FAILURE

If a business organization expands into new markets without an appropriate compliance game plan, the government may deem this to be an internal controls failure. For instance, in the Smith & Wesson enforcement action, the government stated:

> Despite making it a high priority to grow sales in new and high risk markets overseas, the company failed to design and implement a system of internal controls or an appropriate FCPA compliance program reasonably designed to address the increased risks of its new business model.[23]

As further stated by the government:

> This is a wake-up call for small and medium-size businesses that want to enter into high-risk markets and expand their international sales. When a company makes the strategic decision to sell its products overseas, it must ensure that the right internal controls are in place and operating.

Even if a business organization does not expand into a new market, conditions in a foreign country may change, including new laws or regulations relevant to the organization's products and services. Another way a business organization may evolve is through the launch of new products and services. Both of these developments may provide new points of contact with "foreign officials," particularly in connection with licensing, permitting or other regulatory approvals and these new developments need to be addressed through compliance policies and procedures.

Another obvious way a business organization may evolve is through personnel changes. In other words, FCPA and related risk arises when real people, subject to real business conditions, interact with real "foreign officials." When these real people leave the organization and are replaced by other real people, this change may warrant a closer look at existing policies and procedures. Thus, just because the organization's prior business manager in a foreign country was trustworthy, does not necessarily mean that the new country manager will be trustworthy notwithstanding the organization's due diligence efforts in the hiring process. Trust in new personnel develops over time and until that fully occurs the organization may want to revisit certain policies and controls relevant to new hires. Even if a business organization does not have frequent personnel change but is blessed with individuals in the same position for a long time, these real people (given the unique circumstances in their life) may nevertheless change. While a long-time, trusted employee may not present a high degree of risk compared with other areas, an organization should not automatically assume that a once compliant employee will automatically remain a compliant employee forever. Indeed, most enforcement actions are not based on the conduct of new hires but the conduct of veterans of the organization. Accordingly, long-time employees (as well as new hires) can present risk that needs to be addressed through appropriate training requirements, continued supervision, and other internal controls.

The same concepts highlighted above also apply, perhaps most importantly, to third parties that a business organization engages in the global marketplace. While compliance policies and procedures relevant to third parties were discussed in greater detail in Chapter 3, the point here is that when third parties change an organization should require the new third party to be subject to the same compliance policies and procedures as the previous third party. Similarly, even if a business organization is blessed with stable, long-standing third-party relationships, third parties (given the unique circumstances in their life or business) may change and a business organization should not automatically assume that a once compliant third party will automatically remain a compliant third party forever. In short, whether its new markets, new products or services, or new personnel (whether employees or third parties), when a business organization evolves government enforcement agencies will expect the organization's compliance program to evolve as well.

One of the most dramatic ways a business organization can evolve (in terms of markets, products and services, and personnel including third parties) is through merger and acquisition activity. Acquiring this "good stuff" is obviously what motivated the acquiring company to pursue the transaction, but along with the "good stuff" comes the "bad stuff" because legal scrutiny and liability, including in the FCPA context, may flow to the acquiring company depending on how the transaction is structured. As stated by the government:

> It is a basic principle of corporate law that a company assumes certain liabilities when merging with or acquiring another company. . . . [W]here a purchaser acquires the stock of a seller and integrates the target into its operations, successor liability may be conferred upon the purchaser for the acquired entity's pre-existing criminal and civil liabilities, including, for example, for FCPA violations of the target.[24]

It is really no different than a home purchaser being attracted to the positive features of a house (the nice yard, the finished basement, the master bedroom), but also getting the leaky roof or the shifting foundation. Given this risk of purchasing a home, most risk-averse purchasers have the home inspected prior to closing so that any deficiencies can be identified by the purchaser and dealt with prior to the transaction closing because after the transaction closes the purchaser is not only going to own the "good stuff" (the nice yard, the finished basement and the master bedroom), but also the "bad stuff," such as the leaky roof and shifting foundation.

Business organizations face a similar risk and because of the risk of acquiring a target company's scrutiny and liability, pre-acquisition due diligence is a component of best practices. As stated in the FCPA Guidance:

> A company that does not perform adequate FCPA due diligence prior to a merger or acquisition may face both legal and business risks. Perhaps most commonly, inadequate due diligence can allow a course of bribery to continue—with all the attendant harms to a business's profitability and reputation, as well as potential civil and criminal liability.

## FAILURE

Despite this guidance, several enforcement actions have alleged due diligence failures in connection with merger and acquisition activity. For instance, in the RAE Systems enforcement action the government noted that the company "did not conduct pre-acquisition corruption due diligence" of an acquired Chinese joint venture but given "the high-risk nature of the location, and the existence of numerous government customers, pre-acquisition corruption-focused due diligence was merited."[25] Likewise, in an enforcement action against beverage company Diageo the government stated:

> Diageo's history of rapid multinational expansion through mergers and acquisitions contributed to defects in its FCPA compliance programs.

The conduct at issue focused on indirect subsidiaries and a joint venture acquired in a merger and the government stated:

> at the times of these acquisitions, Diageo recognized that its new subsidiaries had weak compliance policies, procedures, and controls [but] nevertheless, Diageo failed to make sufficient improvements to these programs.

As these and many other enforcement actions demonstrate, merger and acquisition can present scrutiny and liability and therefore pre-acquisition due diligence is a component of best practices. The FCPA Guidance encourages companies engaged in merger and acquisition activity to "conduct thorough risk-based FCPA and anti-corruption due diligence on potential new business acquisitions." Likewise, the Evaluation of Corporate Compliance Programs poses the following question:

- *Due Diligence Process* – was the misconduct or the risk of misconduct identified during due diligence? Who conducted the risk review for the acquired/merged entities and how was it done? What has been the M&A due diligence process generally?

Further, and reflective of how FCPA scrutiny and enforcement can make an acquiring company skittish, a number of Opinion Procedure Releases address merger and acquisition activity and the DOJ has self-identified the following releases as being relevant to such issues.

| 84-02 | 01-01 | 03-01 | 04-02 | 08-01 | 08-02 | 14-02 |
|---|---|---|---|---|---|---|

Against this backdrop and guidance, you might be asking what does pre-acquisition due diligence really mean? Recall though the fundamentals of conducting a risk assessment which, in the context of merger or acquisition activity, seeks to understand the same "where, who, how and what" questions regarding the target company. In other words:

- In which countries does the target company do business in?
- In these countries, who are the target company's customers or potential customers?
- With an understanding of the "where" and "who" questions regarding the target company, pre-acquisition due diligence should next focus on the "how" question – in other words, how does the target company do business and/or interact with customers or potential customers? Specifically, does the target company use third parties (whether agents, representatives, distributors or joint venture partners) as part of its go-to-market-strategy or to facilitate other business tasks?
- Next is the all-important what question concerning the target company. What licenses, permits, certifications or other regulatory points of contact does the target company have with "foreign officials" in connection with its business activities? This is an important question because each point of contact the target company has with "foreign officials" will probably continue post-acquisition and become the acquiring company's point of contact.

After understanding these various mechanical aspects of the target company's business, pre-acquisition due diligence should next focus on understanding the target company's existing compliance policies and procedures including any past or pending investigations of compliance breaches. Like other aspects of compliance, it is important for an acquiring company to document its specific due diligence steps including dates conducted and personnel involved.

Engaging in the above pre-acquisition due diligence steps may not uncover every possible FCPA or related issue at the target company prior to closing. However, engaging in the above steps will put an acquiring company in the best position possible to analyze the risk of the transaction and decide whether to proceed and/or restructure the transaction based on discovered information. Moreover, should an issue undiscovered during pre-acquisition due diligence emerge post-closing, an acquiring company that engages in the above steps will be able to tell the best story possible should the issue ever become the subject of scrutiny by law enforcement.

Pre-acquisition due diligence is not the only compliance best practice in connection with merger and acquisition activity. After a transaction closes, post-acquisition integration is also a best practice. As stated in the FCPA guidance, an acquiring entity should:

- ensure that its code of conduct and compliance policies and procedures regarding the FCPA and other anti-corruption laws apply as quickly as is practicable to newly acquired businesses or merged entities;
- train the directors, officers, and employees of newly acquired businesses or merged entities, and when appropriate, train agents and business partners, on the FCPA and other relevant anti-corruption laws and the company's code of conduct and compliance policies and procedures; and
- conduct an FCPA-specific audit of all newly acquired or merged businesses as quickly as practicable.

As to this last step, in certain situations an acquiring company may encounter foreign legal impediments to engaging in optimal pre-acquisition due diligence or as a practical matter have greater access to relevant documents and personnel post-closing. Thus, while an FCPA-specific audit of the newly acquired or merged business is probably similar to the pre-acquisition due diligence steps previously highlighted, a post-closing audit may be able to uncover issues not identified during pre-acquisition due diligence.

**FAILURE**

Regarding post-acquisition integration, consider the following internal control failure highlighted in the RAE enforcement action. According to the government, as a result of due diligence conducted by the company before acquiring a joint venture, it became aware of improper commissions, kickbacks and "under table greasing to get deals". Yet, post-closing, the company implemented internal controls only "half-way" so as not to "choke the sales engine and cause a distraction for the sales guys."[26]

As highlighted above, business organizations may evolve in various ways and a component of compliance best practices is to periodically assess whether policies and procedures need to evolve as well. More broadly, this risk management strategy is consistent with a business organization's ability to oversee its compliance program and devote sufficient resources to continuous improvement.

NOTES

1 DOJ Release, "Assistant Attorney General Leslie R. Caldwell Speaks at SIFMA Compliance and Legal Society New York Regional Seminar," (Nov. 2, 2015).
2 FCPA Professor, "Where Was The BizJet Board?" (Apr. 11, 2013).
3 FCPA Professor, "Next Up – Telia As DOJ And SEC Announce Contemplated $483 Million Net FCPA Enforcement Action," (Sept. 21, 2017).
4 FCPA Professor, "VimpelCom's Uzbekistan Bribery Scheme Nets $397.5 Million FCPA Enforcement Action," (Feb. 19, 2016).
5 FCPA Professor, "Reading Assignment For All Executive Officers: The Mace Enforcement Action," (Nov. 15, 2017).
6 In the Matter of Johnson Controls, Inc., Release No. 78287 (July 11, 2016).
7 In the Matter of Bristol Myers Squibb Co., Release No. 76073 (Oct. 5, 2015).
8 In the Matter of Orthofix International N.V., Release No. 79828 (Jan. 18, 2017).
9 Bio-Rad Non-Prosecution Agreement (Nov. 3, 2014).
10 In the Matter of Bruker Corporation, Release No. 73835 (Dec. 15, 2014).
11 General Cable Non-Prosecution Agreement (Dec. 22, 2016).
12 In the Matter of SciClone Pharmaceuticals Inc., Release No. 77058 (Feb. 4, 2016).
13 FCPA Professor, "FCPA Insanity," (Apr. 11, 2016).
14 The Fraud Section's Foreign Corrupt Practices Act Enforcement Plan and Guidance (Apr. 5, 2016).
15 Timothy Peterson and Robertson Park, Inside Counsel, "Regulatory: Investigating Potential Bribery Means Looking Beyond the FCPA" (May 29, 2013).
16 Steven Tyrrell, The Metropolitan Corporate Counsel, "FCPA: Compliance And Enforcement Insights" (June 2012).
17 U.S. v. Zimmer Biomet Holdings, Inc., Superseding Information (Jan. 17, 2017).
18 U.S. v. Rolls-Royce PLC, Deferred Prosecution Agreement (Dec. 20, 2016).
19 U.S. v. Latam Airlines Group, S.A., Deferred Prosecution Agreement (July 25, 2016).
20 Ralph Lauren Corporation, Non-Prosecution Agreement (Apr. 22, 2013).
21 Bio-Rad Laboratories, Inc., Non-Prosecution Agreement (Nov. 3, 2014).
22 In the Matter of Key Energy Services, Inc., Release No. 78558 (Aug. 11, 2016).
23 SEC Release, "SEC Charges Smith & Wesson With FCPA Violations" (July 28, 2014).
24 DOJ Opinion Procedure Release No. 14-02 (Nov. 7, 2014).
25 RAE Systems Inc., Non-Prosecution Agreement (Dec. 10, 2010).
26 RAE Systems Inc., Non-Prosecution Agreement (Dec. 10, 2010).

# Conclusion

Despite the claims of some, complying with the FCPA and related laws is not as simple as "you just don't bribe." Like other forms of legal liability, *eliminating* risk is not possible. However, business organizations can most certainly minimize risk and the goal of this book was to provide a diverse group of professionals with the best available tools to accomplish this important goal. You should now understand why spotting risk under the FCPA and related laws is an important skill set and have the ability to effectively communicate the wide-ranging negative effects of scrutiny and enforcement. You should now also have a pair of "FCPA goggles" and be familiar with the wide range of circumstances in which scrutiny and enforcement may arise when doing business in the global marketplace as well as the ability to use your acquired knowledge to confidently conduct a risk assessment of a business organization. More broadly, you should now also be well versed on the many other aspects of compliance best practices highlighted throughout this book including: effective communication of policies and procedures, the importance of holistic compliance, and risk management strategies relevant to oversight responsibility and continuous improvement.

Compliance professionals and business managers often face an uphill battle when it comes to compliance with the FCPA and related laws. Remember though that the compliance function serves two goals: first and most importantly to legitimately and in good faith minimize risk; and second to allow the business organization to tell the best story possible to government enforcement agencies should non-compliance occur.

You practiced wearing your "FCPA goggles" within the context of this book and now it is time to set the book aside and wear your "goggles" in the real world. Wear them well!

# Index*



* Index compiled by Margaret McCormack.